Box 18

Frontispiece.   Bronze votive plaque dedicated to Apollo, found
on the floor of the improvised shrine

Reports of the Research Committee

of the

Society of Antiquaries of London

No. XL

The Excavation of the Shrine of Apollo at Nettleton, Wiltshire, 1956–1971

By

W. J. Wedlake, F.S.A.

with contributions by

the late D. F. Allen, F.S.A., T. F. C. Blagg, M. Canham, the late Dorothy Charlesworth, F.S.A., Elizabeth Fowler, Margaret Guido, F.S.A., B. R. Hartley, F.S.A., Hedley Hall, A. Hollowell, the late M. R. Hull, F.S.A., Richard Reece, F.S.A., E. W. Richardson, David Sherlock, F.S.A., Grace Simpson, F.S.A., Isobel F. Smith, F.S.A., Professor J. M. C. Toynbee, F.S.A., R. F. Tylccotc, F.S.A., and R. P. Wright, F.S.A.

Published by
The Society of Antiquaries of London

Distributed by
Thames and Hudson Ltd
1982

© Society of Antiquaries of London 1982
ISBN 0 500 99032 8

PRINTED IN ENGLAND BY
ADLARD AND SON LTD
BARTHOLOMEW PRESS, DORKING

CONTENTS

PART II: THE FINDS

CONTENTS

PREFACE

IT was in 1956, while I was engaged in the excavation of the Romano-British settlement at Camerton, Somerset, which is on the Fosse Way south-west of Bath (*Aquae Sulis*), that I was informed of a similar possible settlement, also on the Fosse Way but north of Bath. The Nettleton Scrubb site had been known for some years and had been partially excavated by the late Mr. W. C. Priestley, who worked on the north side of the Broadmead Brook, but my attention was drawn by Mrs. D. M. Brackenbury to wall foundations in Wick Wood on the south side of the small river, and to the possibility of excavating the site.

Having spent some 15 years excavating the Camerton settlement, I thought the opportunity to investigate a comparable settlement on the Fosse Way was not to be missed. After receiving permission to excavate from His Grace the Duke of Beaufort and Mr. Lomas Webb we began work in 1956 and continued until 1972.

It was quite early, in fact in the first year of our work at Nettleton, that we realized the significance of the site and it soon became evident that we had discovered an important religious centre. We spent the first five years excavating the large octagonal structure, overlooking the river, which has since proved to be a shrine of Apollo, a place of pilgrimage in Roman times.

During the early years of the excavation, we also gained the impression that at Nettleton we had quite a contrasting settlement to that at Camerton. I was often reminded by my friends that Camerton was only a primitive township in comparison with Nettleton with its well-planned shrine set in a delectable Cotswold valley. At Camerton, with its third- and fourth-century industrial development for the production of pewter, it was easy to visualize the hilltop site with chimneys belching forth smoke from the Somerset coal used in its furnaces and the small ribbon-like development of simple buildings alongside the Fosse Way to house the artisans engaged in the industry.

It was towards the end of the Nettleton excavation that we found that after all there was but little difference in the two settlements, especially during the third- and fourth-century occupation. The striking evidence that pewter-casting and other metal working were one of the chief pursuits at Nettleton, as they had been at Camerton at a similar period, suggests a fairly close relationship and similarity of background in such settlements along the Fosse Way.

During the past 30 years or so I have endeavoured, with the help of my friends, to obtain a general appreciation of the two Romano-British settlements, one to the south, the other to the north of the important Roman spa of *Aquae Sulis*. Our Fellow, Professor Barry Cunliffe, has fully recorded the many endeavours to elucidate the story of the Roman spa buried well below the present city (Cunliffe, 1969). This, with our two settlements and the excavations concurrently proceeding in Cirencester and Ilchester, also both on the Fosse Way, should, we hope, provide material for a general appreciation of life and its conditions, and communications, during the Roman occupation of this area of Britain. I hope the results of our labours as recorded in this Report, together with our work at Camerton published in 1958 (*Excavations at Camerton, Somerset*), will contribute to a better understanding of life in Roman

Britain and that they will be of some assistance to those who will continue to elucidate the fascinating problems of that period.

I am deeply grateful to my many friends for their patience and kindness over the years during which I was privileged to excavate the Nettleton site. First, I must thank His Grace the Duke of Beaufort for permitting us to excavate the site and for the interest that he and the Duchess took in our work on their visits to the excavations. I owe much to the late Mr. Lomas Webb and to Mrs. Webb, who during the course of the excavations were first the Duke's tenants, but later became the owners; now, however, Wick Wood has returned to the Badminton estate. Mr. and Mrs. Webb maintained an active interest and I am most grateful for their kind co-operation.

The frequent visits made by the late Sir Ian Richmond and the late Sir Mortimer Wheeler to the excavation, their valued advice, friendship and good humour are among the many pleasurable memories of the very happy atmosphere which prevailed at Nettleton. To Sir Mortimer I am also grateful for reading my original report and later, when for reasons of economy the text was cut by a third and largely rewritten, for his inestimable assistance in its presentation.

I would also wish to thank Mr F. H. Thompson for valued advice prior to the publication of this report, and also the late Mr. I. D. Margary for so kindly helping to defray the cost of additional draughtsmanship requirements. In his capacity of Secretary to the Bath and Camerton Archaeological Society I thank my friend Peter Greening. He was responsible for much of the general arrangement for the excavation, welfare of volunteers and assistance with the research and checking of this report.

The specialists' reports, so readily given by my friends, are much valued and add much to its interest. It is my pleasure to thank the following for their contributions:

The late Mr. Derek Allen, C.B., F.B.A., F.S.A.	British coins.
Mrs M. Canham.	The brooches.
The late Miss Dorothy Charlesworth, M.A., F.S.A.	The glass.
Mrs. Elizabeth Fowler, M.A.	The penannular brooches.
Mr. Hedley Hall, F.R.C.S.	The human and animal bones.
Mrs. A. Hollowell, M.A.	The goose skeleton.
Mrs. C. Margaret Guido, F.S.A.	The beads.
Dr. Richard M. Reece, F.S.A.	The Roman coins.
Mr. E. W. Richardson, F.I.M.L.T.	The painted plaster, cut human bones and cremated human remains.
Mr. D. Sherlock, F.S.A.	The spoons.
Dr. Grace Simpson, F.S.A.	The Samian ware.
Dr. Isobel F. Smith, F.S.A.	The stone axe-heads.
Professor Jocelyn M. C. Toynbee, F.B.A., F.S.A.	The statuary; altars; terra-cottas; intaglios; ivory and special bronze objects.
Mr. R. P. Wright, M.A., F.S.A.	The inscriptions.

A number of the plates which illustrate this report recall the visits of my friend, the late Maurice B. Cookson, with whom I spent so many happy hours on 'Wheeler' digs. My thanks also go to Mr. James Hancock for photographing so many of the finds, Mr. John Macdonald for other photography, Mr. Andrew Kneen for his reconstruction drawings, Mr. H. M. Hoather for pls. III, XII and XVIII, Cdr. E. H. D. Williams, R.N. Rtd., for pls. VII, VIII, XIV and XXXII, Bristol City Museum for pls. XXXIV and XXXV, the Department of the Environment for the composite pl. XI*a*, Mr. E. Masters for pl. II*b*, and for many find drawings; also to Mr. D. Browning and Lt. Cdr. M. Keighley for pottery and other drawings; Mr. N. Bridgewater for identification of soil and other samples, Mr. David Bilbie for surveying the site, Mr. Raymond Farrar, F.S.A., for advice concerning colour-coated and other wares, Dr. Michael Fulford, F.S.A., for identification of Oxfordshire wares, and Mrs. Vivien Swan, F.S.A., for identification of Savernake ware. I am grateful to Mr. Tom Blagg for much valued advice concerning the compilation of the architectural catalogue, and to Professor R. F. Tylecote, F.S.A., for identification of the crucibles. For ready advice on Roman military equipment and some of the pottery I must thank Dr. Graham Webster, F.S.A., and Mr. Brian Hartley, F.S.A., for identification of Samian ware. Finally, I am indebted to Mrs. Gilly March for her revision of my original drawings — plans, sections and finds — to bring them up to the Society's Research Report standards, and to Mr. James Thorn for the mounting of small finds for block-making. My thanks to some of the many volunteer helpers, without whose dedicated assistance I could not have accomplished so much, are recorded on page 261, note 2.

William Wedlake
January 1981

LIST OF PLATES *(at end)*

LIST OF FIGURES

ABBREVIATIONS AND BIBLIOGRAPHY

AA	*Archaeologia Aeliana*
AAC	*Acta Archaeologica* (Copenhagen)
AC	*Archaeologia Cambrensis*
Alcock, L., 1963	*Dinas Powys*
AntJ	*Antiquaries Journal*
Arch	*Archaeologia*
ArchJ	*Archaeological Journal*
Atkinson, D., 1916	*The Romano-British Site on Lowbury Hill in Berkshire*
BAR	*British Archaeological Reports*
BBCS	*Bulletin of Board of Celtic Studies*
Blagg, T. F. C., 1977	'Schools of stonemasons in Roman Britain', *BAR* 41, 51–6
Blair, P. Hunter, 1963	*Roman Britain and Early England, 55 B.C.–A.D. 871*
Blair, P. Hunter, 1977	*An Introduction to Anglo-Saxon England* (2nd edn.)
BMQ	*British Museum Quarterly*
Boehringer, E., 1959	'Pergamon', *Neue deutsche Ausgrabungen im Mittelmeergebiet und in vorderen Orient*, 121–71
Bogaers, J. E. A., 1955	*De Gallo-Romeinse Tempels te Elst*
Boon, G. C. and Williams, C., 1966	'The Dolaucothi drainage wheel', *JRS* lvi, 122–7
Brailsford, J. W., 1962	*Hod Hill, i: Antiquities from Hod Hill in the Durden Collection*
BRGK	*Bericht der Römisch-Germanischen Kommission*
BM Guide (1),(2)	*British Museum Guide to the Antiquities of Roman Britain*, 1922, 1958
Brit	*Britannia*
Brogan, O., 1953	*Roman Gaul*
Budge, E. A. W., 1907	*An Account of the Roman Antiquities Preserved in the Museum at Chesters, Northumberland*
Bushe-Fox, J. P., 1913	*Excavations on the Site of the Roman Town at Wroxeter, Shropshire, in 1912 (SARR, 1)*
Bushe-Fox, J. P., 1932	*Third Report on the Excavations of the Roman Fort at Richborough, Kent (SARR, 10)*
Bushe-Fox, J. P., 1949	*Fourth Report on the Excavations of the Roman Fort at Richborough, Kent (SARR, 16)*
CA	*Current Archaeology*
Chadwick, N. K., 1963	*Celtic Britain*
Chiesa, G. S., 1966	*Gemme del Museo Nazionale di Aquileia*
Clapham, A. W., 1922	'Roman mausolea of the "cartwheel" type', *Arch J* lxxix, 93–100
Clifford, E. M., 1961	*Bagendon: a Belgic Oppidum*
Collingwood, R. G. and Richmond, I. A., 1969	*The Archaeology of Roman Britain*
Cox, J. S., 1895	'The mining operations and metallurgy of the Romans in England and Wales', *Arch J* lii, 25–42
Cunliffe, B. W., 1964	*Winchester Excavations 1949–60*, 1
Cunliffe, B. W., 1969	*Roman Bath (SARR, 24)*
Curle, A. O., 1923	*The Treasure of Traprain*
Curle, J., 1911	*A Roman Frontier Post and its People: the Fort of Newstead in the Parish of Melrose*
CW	*Transactions of the Cumberland and Westmorland Antiquarian and Archaeological Society*
DMC	*Catalogue of Antiquities in the Museum . . . at Devizes*, Part II (1934)
Dyggve, E., 1951	*History of Salonitan Christianity*
Elkington, D., 1976	'The Mendip lead industry' and 'A list of the Romano-British pigs of lead from the Mendips', in K. Branigan and P. J. Fowler (eds.), *The Roman West Country*, pp. 183–97 and 230–4
Fishwick, D., 1969	'The imperial *numen* in Roman Britain', *JRS* lix, 76–91
Fowler, E., 1960	'The origins and development of the penannular brooch in Europe', *PPS* xxvi, 149–77
Fowler, P. J., 1971	'Hill-forts, A.D. 400–700', in Jesson, M. and Hill, D., *The Iron Age and its Hill-forts*, pp. 203-13
Frere, S. S., 1967	*Britannia: a History of Roman Britain*
GM	*Gentleman's Magazine*
Gough, J. W., 1967	*The Mines of Mendip*

Grenier, A., 1958   *Manuel d'archéologie gallo-romaine. Troisieme partie: l'architecture*

Harden, D. B., 1956   'Glass vessels in Britain and Ireland A.D. 400–1000' in Harden (ed.), 1956, pp. 132–67

Harden, D. B. (ed.), 1956   *Dark Age Britain: Studies presented to E. T. Leeds*

Haverfield, F., 1906   'Romano-British Somerset', in *VCH Somerset*, i, 207–371

Haverfield, F., 1914   *Roman Britain in 1913* (British Academy Supplemental Papers II)

Haverfield, F., 1915   *Roman Britain in 1914* (British Academy Supplemental Papers III)

Haverfield, F., 1923   *The Romanization of Roman Britain* (4th edn.)

Hawkes, C. F. C. and Hull, M. R. 1947   *Camulodunum* (*SARR*, 14)

Hawkes, S. C., 1961   'Soldiers and settlers in Britain, fourth to fifth century', *MA* v, 1–41

Hayward, L. C., 1952   'The Roman villa at Lufton, near Yeovil', *PSANHS* xcvii, 91–112

Hewitt, A. T. M., 1971   *Roman Villa, West Park, Rockbourne, nr. Fordingbridge, Hants*

Hudd, A. E., 1913   'Excavations at Caerwent, Monmouthshire, on the site of the Romano-British city of Venta Silurum in the years 1911 and 1912', *Arch* lxiv, 437–52

Hull, M. R., 1967   'The Nor'nour brooches', in D. Dudley, 'Excavations on Nor'nour in the Isles of Scilly, 1962–6', *Arch J* cxxiv, 28–64

IO   *The Intellectual Observer* (formerly *Recreative Science*)

Isings, C., 1957   *Roman Glass from Dated Finds* (*Archaeologica Traiectina*, 2)

JBAA   *Journal of the British Archaeological Association*

JGS   *Journal of Glass Studies*

JRS   *Journal of Roman Studies*

Kempe, A. J., 1829   'An account of some recent discoveries at Holwood-hill in Kent', *Arch* xxii, 336–49

Kent, J. P. C., 1957   'The pattern of bronze coinage under Constantine I', *NC*, 6th S., xvii, 16–77

Kilbride-Jones, H. E., 1935–7   'The evolution of penannular brooches with zoomorphic terminals in Great Britain and Ireland', *PRIA* xliii C, 379–455

KJ   *Kölner Jahrbuch*

Koethe, H., 1933   'Die keltischen Rund- und Vielecktempel der Kaiserzeit', *BRGK* xxiii, 10–108

La Croix, C. de, 1883   *Mémoire archéologique sur les découvertes d'Herbord, dites de Sanxay*

Larousse, 1968   *New Larousse Encyclopedia of Mythology*

Lewis, M. J. T., 1966   *Temples in Roman Britain*

Lowther, A. W. G., 1976   'Romano-British chimney-pots and finials', *Ant J* lvi, 35–48

MA   *Medieval Archaeology*

Meates, G. W., 1979   *The Roman Villa at Lullingstone, Kent.* Vol. 1: *The Site* (Kent Archaeological Society Monograph Series, 1)

MPBW   Ministry of Public Building and Works (later Department of the Environment)

Munksgaard, E., 1955   'Late-antique scrap silver found in Denmark. The Hardenberg, Hørstentorp and Simmersted hoards', *AAC* xxvi, 31–67

Nash-Williams, V. E., 1950   *The Early Christian Monuments of Wales*

NC   *Numismatic Chronicle*

Neville, R. C., 1894   'Memoir on remains of the Anglo-Roman Age, at Weycock . . . Berks. . . .,' *Arch J* vi, 114–23

O'Connor, D. M. W., 1961   *Peter in Rome*

Oxon   *Oxoniensia*

Painter, K. S., 1967–8   'The Roman site at Hinton St. Mary, Dorset', *BMQ* xxxii, 15–31

Palmer, L. S. and Ashworth, H. W. W., 1956–7   'Four Roman pigs of lead from the Mendips', *PSANHS* ci/cii, 52–87

Parker, J. H., 1850   *Glossary of Architecture* (5th edn.)

PBA   *Proceedings of the British Academy*

PBNHAFC   *Proceedings of the Bath Natural History and Antiquarian Field Club*

PCNFC   *Proceedings of the Cotteswold Naturalists' Field Club*

PDNHAS   *Proceedings of the Dorset Natural History and Archaeological Society*

PPS   *Proceedings of the Prehistoric Society*

PRIA   *Proceedings of the Royal Irish Academy*

PSAL   *Proceedings of the Society of Antiquaries of London*

PSANHS   *Proceedings of the Somersetshire Archaeological and Natural History Society*

PSAS   *Proceedings of the Society of Antiquaries of Scotland*

Porter, H. M., 1966   *The Saxon Conquest of Somerset and Devon*

Powell, T. G. E., 1959 — *The Celts*

Rahtz, P., 1951 — 'The Roman temple at Pagans Hill, Chew Stoke, N. Somerset', *PSANHS* xcvi, 112–42

Rahtz, P. 1956–7 — 'The temple well and other buildings at Pagans Hill, Chew Stoke, North Somerset', *PSANHS* ci/cii, 15–51

Reinach, S., 1922 — *Répertoire de peintures grecques et romaines*

RIB — Collingwood, R. G. and Wright, R. P., *The Roman Inscriptions of Britain*, i, 1965

RIC — Mattingly, H. *et al.*, *Roman Imperial Coinage*

Richmond, Sir Ian, 1969 — *Roman Archaeology and Art* (ed. by P. Salway)

Ritterling, E., 1913 — 'Das frührömische Lager bei Hofheim im Taunus', *Annalen des Vereins für Nassauische Alterumskunde und Geschichtsforschung*, xl

Rivet, A. L. F., 1969 — *The Roman Villa in Britain*

Rivoira, G. T., 1925 — *Roman Architecture and its Principles of Construction under the Empire*

SARR — Society of Antiquaries Research Report

Scrope, G. P., 1862 — 'On a Roman villa, discovered at North Wraxall', *WAM* vii, 59–75

Skinner, J. — BM Add. MS. 33686

Smith, D. J., 1965 — 'Three fourth-century schools of mosaic in Roman Britain', in *La Mosaique Gréco-Romaine*, pp. 95–116

SRS — Somerset Record Society

Steer, K. A., 1958 — 'Arthur's O'on: a lost shrine of Roman Britain', *Arch J* cxv, 99–110

Stevens, C. E., 1940 — 'The Frilford site — a postscript', *Oxon* v, 166–7

Swift, E. H., 1951 — *Roman Sources of Christian Art*

SxAC — *Sussex Archaeological Collections*

Talbot Rice, D., 1954 — *Byzantine Art*

TBGAS — *Transactions of the Bristol and Gloucestershire Archaeological Society*

THSFNC — *Transactions of the Hull Scientific and Field Naturalists' Club*

Toynbee, J. M. C., 1953 — 'Christianity in Roman Britain', *JBAA*, 3rd S., xvi, 1–24

Toynbee, J. M. C., 1964a — *Art in Britain under the Romans*

Toynbee, J. M. C., 1964b — *Roman Medallions*

Toynbee, J. M. C., 1964c — 'A new Roman mosaic pavement found in Dorset', *JRS* liv, 7–14

VCH — *Victoria County History*

Voss, O., 1954 — 'The Hørstentorp silver hoard and its period. A study of a Danish find of scrap silver from about 500 A.D.' *AAC* xxv, 171–219

WAM — *Wiltshire Archaeological and Natural History Magazine*

Ward-Perkins, J. P., 1947 — 'The Italian element in late Roman and early medieval architecture', *PBA* xxxiii, 163–94

Watkin, Dom A., 1947, 1952, 1956 — *The Great Chartulary of Glastonbury* (*SRS* lix, lxiii, lxiv)

Wedlake, W. J., 1958 — *Excavations at Camerton, Somerset*

Wheeler, R. E. M., 1943 — *Maiden Castle, Dorset* (*SARR*, 12)

Wheeler, R. E. M. and Wheeler, T. V., 1932 — *Report on the Excavation of the Prehistoric, Roman and Post-Roman site in Lydney Park, Gloucestershire* (*SARR*, 9)

Wheeler, T. V., 1936 — *Verulamium: a Belgic and Two Roman Cities* (*SARR*, 11)

Wilkes, J. J., 1969 — *Dalmatia*

YC — *Y Cymmrodor*

SUMMARY

THE finding of stone axe-heads, flint implements, small ditches containing pre-Roman Belgic pottery, and British coins suggests a prehistoric occupation on the small plateau overlooking the Castle Combe valley at Nettleton Scrubb. It was also the site of a small Roman enclosure, set up when the Fosse Way was constructed *c.* A.D. 47. The evidence comes from the enclosure ditches which have produced a number of Claudian coins (*c.* A.D. 41–54), brooches, Samian pottery and other wares.

Soon after A.D. 69 a small circular shrine, probably dedicated to the god Apollo, was built in the valley alongside the river, possibly superseding a Celtic religious cult already established in the valley. The construction of a large hostel alongside the Fosse Way and a spacious rectangular hall in close proximity to the shrine indicates a growing interest in the shrine. They were followed, about A.D. 230, by the erection of a large octagonal podium which encompassed the small shrine, and a precinct wall with a gateway to enclose the new centre. This arrangement continued until about A.D. 250 when the circular shrine was destroyed by fire. Subsequently, a large octagonal temple, consisting of an inner *cella* surrounded by eight chambers and an ambulatory was built on the octagonal podium which survived the fire.

After the construction of the octagonal temple a larger hostel was built and the settlement continued to develop at an astonishing rate. Additions were made to buildings to cope with the increasing interest in the cult centre. An inscribed altar, a bronze plaque, an intaglio on a finger ring and other finds testify that the shrine was probably dedicated to the god Apollo.

During the early years of the fourth century A.D. alterations were made to stabilize the shrine. Soon after A.D. 330 it ceased to be used for pagan worship and the building fell into a state of disrepair. The decline of interest in the pagan temple was probably due to the increasing adoption of the Christian religion, and evidence suggests that the building was used as a Christian church. After A.D. 370 the now ruined building was adapted for use as a homestead. But for a short period, about A.D. 370, a small north part of the former central shrine was set up and used for a brief resurgence of pagan worship.

Until about A.D. 330 it appears that visitors to the shrine had provided the means to sustain the inhabitants, but soon after this we find evidence of increasing industrial activity. Buildings were converted and used for pewter-casting and bronze- and iron-smelting operations. This is attested by the finding of stone moulds surrounding a furnace, crucibles, and wrought iron, with a quantity of iron slag.

During the latter years of the fourth century there was a further deterioration in building standards. The abundant evidence of fire, and a large number of late fourth-century coins in the fire debris, indicate that the settlement was raided on two occasions at this time. The discarded Roman currency, bad building standards, and a millefiori brooch suggest raids by Irish pirates, who came by way of the Bristol Channel. It is also possible that some of the raiders settled with the inhabitants at Nettleton. These later inhabitants buried their dead in stone-lined graves orientated east–west in wooden coffins, with no grave goods, suggesting Christian burial. At some time after the turn of the fifth century the settlement came to an abrupt end. Many human bones found in the latest level, with evidence of sword slashes, including axis and atlas vertebrae suggesting decapitation, testify that the inhabitants met with a violent death.

Apart from a farmstead built during the medieval period, when the Roman buildings were used as cattle byres or sheep pens, there was no other occupation at Nettleton apart from the presence of lime-kiln burners. In course of time the ruined settlement reverted to green pasture, which with the Broadmead Brook is such a pleasing feature of this beautiful Cotswold valley.

PART I: THE EXCAVATION

THE excavations were conducted by the Bath and Camerton Archaeological Society, with the kind permission of the owners, His Grace the Duke of Beaufort and Mr. L. Webb of West Kington. The Society extends to them its most grateful thanks for so kindly affording all facilities. The Society is also grateful to Mrs. D. M. Brackenbury for directing the writer's attention to the site.

During the course of the excavation visits were paid to the site by the President of the Bath and Camerton Archaeological Society, the late Sir Mortimer Wheeler; the late Professor Sir Ian Richmond; Professor Jocelyn Toynbee; Professor J. M. Cook; Professor Sheppard Frere; and the then Chief Inspector of Ancient Monuments, the late Mr. P. K. Baillie Reynolds. This valued interest in our work contributed to the solution of problems encountered during the course of the excavation, and is gratefully acknowledged.

Monetary grants were made towards the cost of the excavation by the following: the Society of Antiquaries; the British Academy; the Haverfield Trust; and the Carnegie United Kingdom Trust. The Bath and Camerton Archaeological Society expresses its appreciation and thanks for this valued assistance. The work proceeded with the kind co-operation of the Council for British Archaeology, and thanks are especially due to the former Secretary, Miss Beatrice de Cardi.[1]

The greater part of the work was accomplished by voluntary labour and the satisfactory results achieved compensate for the large amount of hard work involved. The writer is proud to have had the pleasure of working with such a happy band of voluntary workers who have unstintingly given their time.[2]

With the kind approval of His Grace the Duke of Beaufort the various finds, including architectural fragments, from the recent excavations have been given to the City Museum, Bristol. The material found by Mr. W. C. Priestley during his 1938–54 excavation on the north side of the Broadmead Brook is in the museum of the Wiltshire Archaeological and Natural History Society at Devizes.[3]

1. INTRODUCTION

History of the Site

The Romano-British settlement described in this paper is situated alongside the Fosse Way, which crosses the northern corner of Wiltshire; it lies north-east of Bath (*Aquae Sulis*) and about two miles north of the road junction at the Shoe Inn, where the Marshfield–Chippenham road crosses the Fosse Way (fig. 1). The site, known as Nettleton Scrubb, (or Shrub) is set in a small valley formed by steep banks of oolitic limestone capped by clay and Fullers Earth (pl. Ia, *b*). The Broadmead Brook flows through the valley to join the By Brook at Castle Combe before it joins the river Avon east of Bath.[4] Since Saxon times it has formed the parish boundary between Nettleton and West Kington.[5]

It had been known for some time that Roman remains were to be found in the Nettleton Scrubb valley. During 1911 or 1912 a lime kiln was constructed on the north side of the river and the builders came upon a piece of statuary bearing the lower part of a representation of Diana and her hound (pl. IIa; see p. 136). This fragment lay for some years in the grounds of Castle Combe Manor House, but was later retrieved and placed in the Bristol City Museum.

During 1938 and the following war years the late Mr. W. C. Priestley conducted excava-

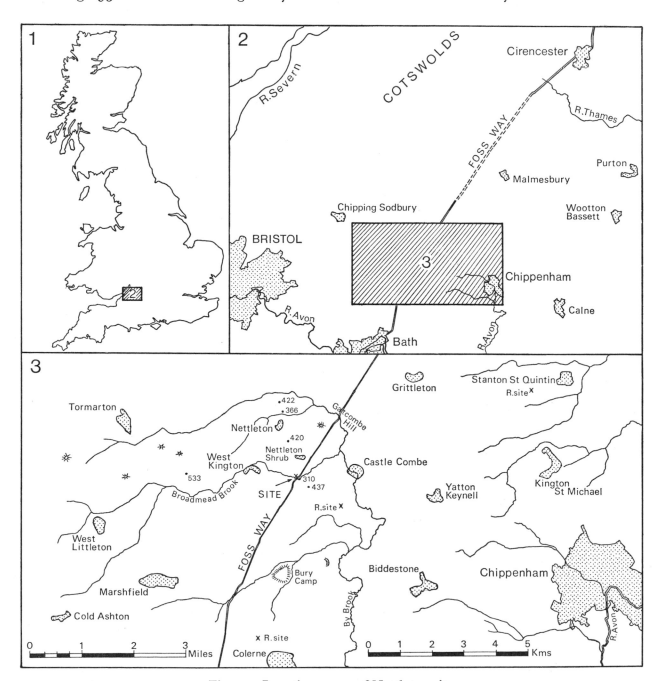

Fig. 1.   Location maps of Nettleton site

NETTLETON SCRUBB WILTS General plan of excavations 1938–1947 1956–1970

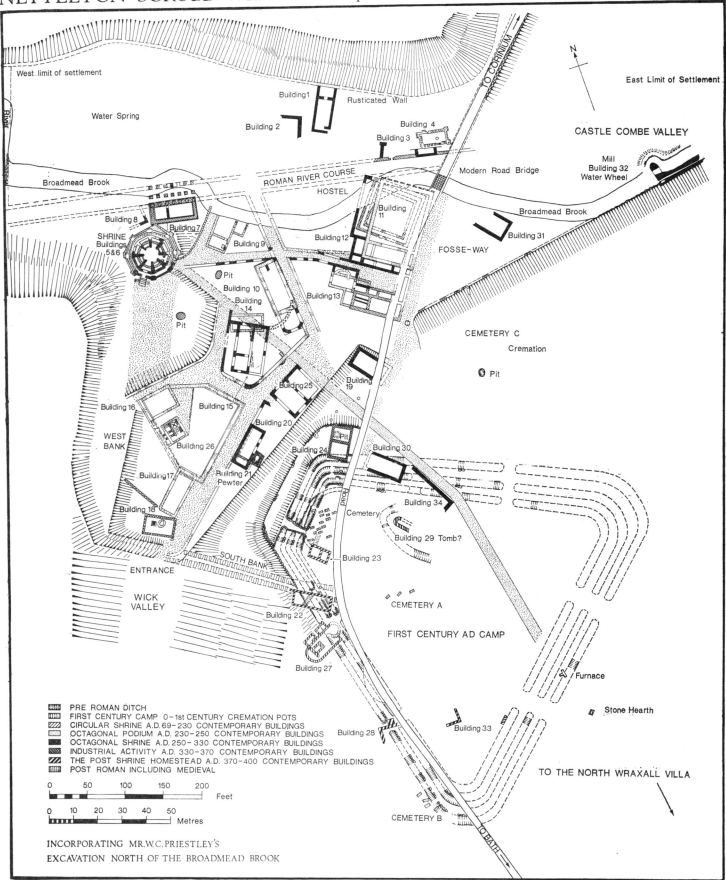

facing p. 2

Fig. 2.   Editorial note: the ditched earthwork, described as 'first-century A.D. camp', is interpreted in the report as an enclosure, possibly of a non-military nature; its plan is conjectural

tions in the meadowland on the north side of the Broadmead Brook. He removed the disused limekiln, and discovered a well-built wall, set against the rock face (pl. III*b*; see p. 56). The wall was built of large blocks of limestone with a rusticated facing and similar blocks were used in the octagonal temple wall described below (pp. 21–6).

Mr. Priestley's excavation located the site where the sculpture was found in 1911, and he recovered a further fragment, consisting of a human foot with drapery, *in situ* in the rusticated boundary wall. The wall itself was used, later in the fourth century A.D., to form the north wall of a large rectangular building (pl. III*a*). Rustication is normally an external feature, and this suggests that the relief of Diana was also originally intended to be one of a series of similar reliefs, built into the outer face of this boundary wall. Priestley's theory that the later building was a Mithraeum is unsupported, and the temple theory, based on the statuary, is also placed in doubt.

Priestley also discovered a wall near the river which he thought might be a bridge abutment. Moreover, there was an angle of walling to the west of the so-called temple, and another building to the east near the road (Fosse Way) which he identified as a medieval homestead.[6] No further excavation has been carried out on the north side of the river since Priestley's death in 1956.

The valley narrows considerably in the vicinity of the site, with steep limestone slopes on either side of the river. Limestone scree, lying on the slopes, covers the ancient quarry face, which was extensively quarried during the Roman and later periods. Excavation on the southern slope has shown that the disused Roman quarry was utilized as a dump for domestic refuse from the nearby settlement, and this has produced a number of Constantinian and later coins down to Theodosius (A.D. 378–95).

Excavation has also shown that the river has altered its course since Roman times, and the valley level has changed considerably (fig. 3). Because of the changing level of the water-table during the Romano-British occupation and the constant danger of flooding, the floor level of the riverside buildings was raised. The small river valley consequently became covered with a thick bed of alluvium, about 2 ft. in depth, and this completely buried the Roman buildings in the valley. The stream today follows a meandering course through the water-meadow formed by the post-Roman alluvium bed. Excavation has shown that the Roman buildings extend under the modern river, and that the river bed in Roman times was about 3 ft. lower than it is today (fig. 3). It has also shown that the river was canalized in the vicinity of the settlement, retaining walls were built on either side, and some of the later Roman buildings were built on the stone platforms alongside these walls.

The river was bridged alongside the large rectangular building (fig. 3), by the construction of a series of well-built square stone piers along the centre of the river bed (fig. 2). There was also some evidence to suggest that the river, at a later date, was terraced at intervals along its course through the settlement to form a series of small waterfalls. Excavation has shown that the inhabitants preferred to build on the low-lying ground alongside the river, rather than on the nearby higher ground and there must have been some compelling reason for this preference. The Broadmead Brook was the dominant feature of the settlement, and it is possible that some river cult, practised in pre-Roman times, was perpetuated in the Roman era.[7]

The excavations that form the subject of this report began in April 1956. They were confined solely to the south side of the river in the parish of West Kington. The greater part of the shrine lies in Wick Wood, but a modern 'Cotswold' dry-stone boundary wall crosses it in a southerly direction and the eastern part of the temple lies in the adjoining field, as do also the associated buildings (fig. 22).[8]

The shrine in Wick Wood was completely excavated, and the building was cleared of a large mass of discarded building debris. This material covered the surviving walls to a depth of over 6 ft. above the sealed homestead floor level, which was the last occupational level associated with the former temple.

A considerable part of the temple must have been standing in a ruinous condition when the Cotswold field boundary wall was built across the site. The radial walls of the temple survived in the wood behind this wall to a height of 6 ft. above the homestead floor level, but only the foundations were left east of the wall, and it is evident that the walls were destroyed when the boundary wall was erected (pl. XXVIIIa). During the nineteenth and early years of the twentieth century the walls of the derelict buildings were used for making the nearby dry-stone field boundary walls. Stone voussoirs and tiles may be seen built into the field walls adjoining the temple site. The Roman walls were also used in the nearby limekiln. During demolition, the stone robbers dismantled the upper parts of the walls, and any discarded material was left nearby. It was through this accumulation of discarded debris that so much of the temple walls was found *in situ*.

It was because the greater part of the shrine lay in Wick Wood that we were able to excavate fully the building and its immediate surroundings. This was not possible with the domestic buildings of the settlement, which lie in the adjoining fields. This part of the settlement was excavated primarily by following a planned grid system of cuttings, with extensions made where it was necessary to recover details of building plans and other features. While this system was not completely satisfactory, it did enable us to recover the plan of the settlement with a minimum interference to the farmland. A complete excavation of the settlement was neither possible nor desirable. We cannot hope to have wrested all the secrets from this interesting site, and there is ample scope for future archaeologists, with improved techniques, to explore the site further, which is preferable to the complete destruction of all stratigraphy in one excavation.

The recovery of plaster-coated walls standing 6 ft. above the floor level in the Nettleton shrine is unusual in Britain and the upstanding walls proved useful in the elucidation of its arrangement. There are substantial remains of other buildings in the settlement. The complete excavation one day of the Nettleton settlement, with its unique and well-preserved temple, would provide an interesting example of a Romano-British settlement occupied during the major part of the Roman occupation of Britain, and a monument comparable with similar excavated sites on the Continent, now open to the public as national monuments.

2. FOUNDATION OF THE SETTLEMENT

The Belgic Ditches

Evidence, slight but definite, indicates that the higher ground on the south side of the small valley at Nettleton Scrubb was occupied before the construction of the first-century A.D. Roman enclosure to the south of the settlement. A small ditch 3–4 ft. (0.9–1.2 m.) wide and 2 ft. 6 in. (0.7 m.) in depth, running in an east–west direction and cut in the blue clay, was found beneath the much later cross-bank on the south slope (pl. V*a*). The ditch of the first-century A.D. enclosure was also sealed by the cross-bank, and it was at this point that the ditch of the Roman enclosure cut across the filling of the pre-Roman ditch (fig. 4).

A quantity of Belgic-type pottery together with a coin of the Dobunni was recovered from this earlier ditch. A second Dobunnic coin was found in a first-century level on the east side of the valley. A second ditch of this period with a rounded termination was also found. Extensive excavation on the east slope would most likely reveal additional evidence of this pre-Roman occupation.

The Fosse Way (fig. 2)

It is evident from a glance at the Ordnance Survey map and the physical setting of the Nettleton settlement that the only possible means of entering the small valley from the north was by way of the eastern extremity alongside the 40-ft. high limestone outcrop which forms the northern limit of the settlement, and this is still the course taken by the modern road. After crossing the narrow valley and spanning the Broadmead Brook by a stone bridge, the modern road ascends the steep south side of the valley through a deep cutting into the limestone, but it takes a course westward and this necessitates a sharp bend towards the top of the hill to bring the road back on to the original course of the Fosse Way at the top of the south slope.

The usual custom of the Roman road makers was to make a straight course across small valleys and ease the gradient by making cuttings through the steeper part of the hillside. The Ordnance Survey map suggested that the Fosse Way would be found ascending the hill in the field to the east of the present road.

Exploratory cuttings were accordingly made at the foot of the south valley slope and a well-metalled road was subsequently found. Eight cuttings continuing south confirmed the course of this road and at the steepest part of the hillside the road passed through a considerable cut into the limestone to ease its gradient. It was evident that the road had been in use for a considerable period of time. Several fourth-century coins were recovered from the material covering the road surface. The natural rock is shallow, about 6 in. in depth on either side of the road, but the road surface was about 3 ft. (0.9 m.) below this, and was flanked on either side by a stone kerb, in some places two courses high.

The east wall of Building XXIV was built alongside this road. The road was traced south for 336 ft. (113 m.), when it terminated suddenly. It tended to veer too much towards the east to be the Fosse Way and is more likely to have been a service road to the Wraxall Roman villa which lies about half a mile to the south-east. It is difficult to account for the sudden termination of this road, but it may be due to the fact that the hilltop is capped with a substantial bed of Fullers Earth which lies immediately below the Inferior Oolite capping. A large hollow on the hillside south of the road termination may in fact be a quarry where this material was obtained. The several hearths and a furnace, together with slag, found nearby seem to support this theory. On the same contour in the field on the opposite, west, side of the modern road there is a well-established rabbit warren or otter set in this soft material and further west a small pond on the same contour.

It appears therefore that this road is not the Fosse Way. It seems possible that the Roman

Fosse Way ran on much the same lines as the modern road by taking a slight swerve to the west to ease the ascent of the hill. The position of Buildings XVII, XIX, XXII, XXIII and XXVII suggests that they were aligned alongside a road.

It is evident that the Nettleton settlement was planned to occupy this small valley at about the same time as the Fosse Way was constructed. If this was so, there is no reason why the Fosse Way should have taken a straight course across the valley. It is therefore more likely that the Fosse Way on entering the settlement from the north forked on the north side of the river. One branch led into the valley to serve the north side of the settlement, and crossed the river just east of the rectangular Building VII alongside the shrine, with the custodian's house (No. IX) on the east side of the road, which would bring the visitor into the precinct of the shrine. If he wished to keep outside the shrine precinct he could cross the river just east of Building IX and proceed south to where the road joined the other fork road which passed alongside the east wall of the hostel Building XII and Building XIII. The road then ascended the south valley slope by way of a cutting made through the limestone outcrop and thence passed the east end of Building XIX and continued between Buildings XXIV and XXX on much the same line as the modern road. After ascending the hill it resumed its course straight across the south Cotswolds towards Bath.

The Claudian Enclosure

A small Roman enclosure, established in the first century A.D. at Nettleton Scrubb, superseded a settlement on the same site presumably occupied by members of the Dobunni. The site is in Dobunnic territory, and coins of that tribe have been recovered from it. Set on a gentle well-drained slope (mostly on the higher ground in the field to the east of the present road), it was in close proximity to the river and commanded extensive views of the surrounding countryside, including the Castle Combe, West Kington, and Wick valleys.

On its north side the enclosure ditches were cut along the escarpment, and depended largely on the limestone rock face at the foot of the valley for security. The north-west corner was strengthened by building up a massive revetment, and this gave an impression of some strength on its north side. The ditches themselves ranged in size from about 2–5 ft. (0.6– 1.5 m.) in width and the same in depth. The ditch filling varied; in some instances it consisted entirely of yellow silt, which produced four coins of Claudius and one of Divus Augustus A.D. 14–64, with an occasional sherd of first-century pottery, but in other cuttings, especially in the upper filling, there was considerable evidence of occupation. This occupation material contained coins of Vespasian (2), Domitian (1) and Trajan (1), A.D. 69–117, and a large quantity of Samian ware, including the greater part of several large decorated and plain bowls of similar date. There was also a large quantity of coarse ware, which included Savernake Ware, fragments of beakers, and other imported wares. There was an unusual number of bronze brooches; seven were found in one small ditch cutting, with bone and other bronze objects. In several instances large flat stones were placed along the inner edge of the ditch, and in other cuttings, especially on the north side, a stone revetment to support the tail end of the inner bank was noted, probably in the form of a dry-stone wall. There was evidence for an entrance on the north side where collapsed dry-stone revetment covered the terminals of the ditches, suggesting an entrance with supporting dry-stone walls. The large amount of scattered flat stones encountered in the upper levels of the cuttings on the north side suggests that the banks and walls were destroyed when the area was converted from woodland to pasture in the nineteenth century. The old contour of the hillside is retained in the hedgerow against the present road, where the outline of a series of banks and ditches survives. The west side of the enclosure has been mutilated by the modern road, which has been cut through the limestone to a depth of several feet to ease the gradient down the hillside. The road cuts obliquely across the ditch system on its west side. The ditches on the sloping west side of the enclosure had frequent changes of level, continuing after each change on the same alignment, but at a slightly higher level as they proceeded up the south slope. A possible explanation for this stepped arrangement is that an attempt was made to keep the bottom of the ditch as level as possible. A continuous uninterrupted ditch on a slope would have created flooding problems during times of heavy rainfall. The flow of water in a continuous sloping ditch would have caused considerable damage on the lower north-west corner of the enclosure where the defences had been built up, but the shorter lengths of ditch would have obviated this. The water would also have stood in the clay-sided ditches, and added considerably to the defensive strength. Some of the ditch terminations on the west side formed part of an entrance into the enclosure.

Features also noted on the west side were small clay-lined pits about 2–3 ft. (0.6–0.9 m.) in diameter, and about the same in depth. The pits contained much burnt material, including fragments of iron and bronze slag. There were also several large stones in each pit.

In addition to the first-century A.D. finds described, there were also two polished axe-heads, and a number of flint scrapers, presumably of Neolithic or Bronze Age date found in the ditch filling (see p. 181 and fig. 74). The presence of these objects in a first-century context is of some interest. There are several prehistoric sites in the vicinity of Nettleton. The Lugbury Long Barrow is quite close to the Fosse Way, and the Marshfield Barrows were not far distant, but it is also possible that the high ground on which the first-century enclosure was constructed may also be an earlier occupied site.

The enclosure commanded extensive views of the surrounding countryside, except on its south side where the approach by way of the Fosse Way was shielded by the higher ground. Despite the presence of a few items of Roman military equipment, it can be scarcely regarded as a military site and is perhaps best interpreted as a Romano-British settlement established by the side of the Fosse Way to serve Roman forces in the area.

Time did not permit a full examination of the enclosure on its south and east sides, but sufficient work was undertaken to determine that there has been considerable later disturbance in this area. This was partly due to a bed of Fullers Earth on the south side, apparently used in connection with the industrial activity which developed within the settlement during the fourth century A.D. A furnace and much iron slag were found in this area.

The plan of the south and east side of the enclosure as shown in fig. 2 is a tentative reconstruction of its probable size and form.

3. THE CIRCULAR SHRINE AND ITS ASSOCIATED BUILDINGS
PHASE I: A.D. 69–230 (fig. 5)

The plan of the Romano-British settlement at Nettleton Scrubb was determined by its physical features (fig. 1, 3). It occupied both sides of the small river in the valley, limited on its north and west sides by steep limestone banks, which incidentally provided the material for the buildings.

Within the valley itself, similar to others in the Cotswolds, the small circular shrine of Apollo (Building V) stood on a knoll facing the river some 120 yards (108 m.) west of the Fosse Way, and was the focal point; it was reached by an approach road from the Fosse Way. It was the first stone building erected on the site, and can be dated after A.D. 69.

It was followed by the construction near the river of Building VIII, probably the priest's or the custodian's house. Only its south-east angle was recovered, but the walls, built with a white mortar, were similar to those of the shrine. The building was probably abandoned when a change in the water level made it uninhabitable. The large square building, at the junction of the south river bank and the Fosse Way (No. XI), was also erected at this time. Its position and plan suggest that it was a guest-house for visitors to the shrine. A similar building was found in association with the shrine at Lydney Park, Gloucestershire (Wheeler and Wheeler, 1932). Building XIII, opposite the guest-house on its south side, was a long narrow building with a cellar or strong-room, and this suggests that it may have been the house of the principal resident, or it could equally well have been a shop. In both buildings the distinctive white mortar had again been used.

(a) The Circular Shrine (Building V)

The first temple built at Nettleton was circular in plan, with foundations of the local limestone 3 ft. (0.9 m.) wide. The freestanding walls were 2 ft. 6 in. (0.76 m.) in width, and the overall diameter of the temple was 33 ft. (10.1 m.). A white mortar was used for the walls, whereas the later buildings in the settlement were all constructed with a brown mortar.

In his coin report (p. 117) Dr. Reece states that the Nettleton coin list begins promptly with no less than nine coins of Claudius I (A.D. 41–54). This suggests that settlement began soon after the construction of the Fosse Way in approximately A.D. 47. A coin of Claudius I found in material earlier than the circular shrine, and a coin of Vespasian found in the brown loam below the floor of the shrine are earlier than the building, and it seems likely that it was built during the last quarter of the first century A.D.

A small hoard of six coins of Nero (A.D. 54–68), Vespasian (69–79), Domitian (81–96), Hadrian (117–38), Antoninus Pius (138–61), and Marcus Aurelius (161–80), found in a small pit containing fire-ash below the floor level within the circular shrine on its south side, would seem to be a votive offering. The pit was within 3 ft. (0.9 m.) of the stone-lined votive pit found in the later octagonal shrine beneath a small aedicula. This later votive pit also contained a number of coins (see p. 44).

In its first phase the shrine consisted of a simple circular drum-like wall, but evidence from the east side of the building suggests that there may have been a series of external buttresses, as with the mausoleum at Keston, Kent (fig. 7.)[9] At Keston the buttresses were thought to be bases for freestanding exterior columns, but there is no evidence to suggest this arrangement at Nettleton. At Nettleton they are more likely to have supported rectangular pilasters as supports to the circular drum, and would be comparable with the arrangement adopted in certain Etruscan tombs, where pilasters provided a support to the burial mound (see p. 102). The evidence also suggests that there may have been internal partition walls, forming small compartments within the circular building. The white mortar footings of the

WICK WOOD WEST KINGTON NETTLETON SCRUBB WILTS

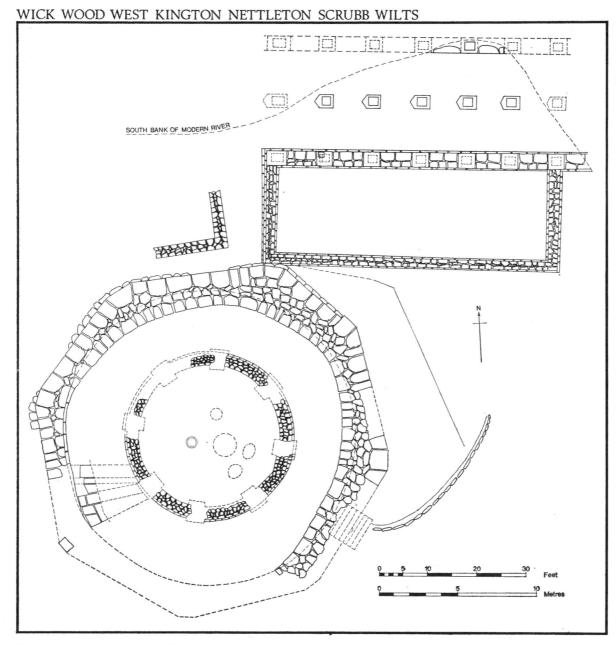

SOUTH BANK OF MODERN RIVER

Fig. 5. Plan of circular temple (Phase I), octagonal wall (Phase II), and rectangular building with riverside piers (Phase I).

partition walls can clearly be seen underlying the radial walls of the later octagonal temple (pl. V*b*). White mortar was also found in a corresponding position on the east and south sides of the building, but on the north side the evidence had been destroyed by the insertion of the later sleeper-wall foundations.

The temple had an eastern entrance and the approach to this was by way of a metalled roadway; this turned sharply to the north outside the temple and was flanked by a sloping bank with a stone kerb (fig. 2).

The floor of the temple was composed of a compact mass of small pebbles. Set firmly in approximately the centre was a curious circular slab of local limestone (fig. 5), 1 ft. 6 in. (0. 45m.) in diameter and protruding above the level of the surrounding floor by about 3 in. (7.6 cm.). Its surface was very smooth and polished as if it had been subject to constant use (pl. VIIa, b), whereas the lower part of the stone was quite rough. To suggest a function for this stone would be pure conjecture, but the central position within the shrine and the undoubted signs of use are indicative of some ritual purpose. It may be significant that the curious re-used ambulatory column, with its cup-like depression at the top, found in the small makeshift temple after the later shrine had fallen into disuse (fig. 21) was found on the higher floor level immediately above this circular stone.

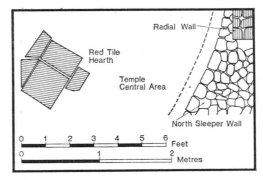

Fig. 6. Phase I: plan of red-tiled hearth below cobbled floor in central area of temple

On the hard gravel subsoil below the pebbled floor were several large circular red-burnt areas, and one area had a roughly constructed hearth formed of roof tiles (fig. 6). Roman tiles were found only in association with the first phase of the circular temple, whereas Cotswold stone slates were not found in layers associated with the circular temple. The gravel subsoil was discoloured red by burning to a depth of about 1 ft. (0.3 m.) and it was evident that fires had been made on this spot. It was not possible to determine the precise relationship of the circular hearths to the circular building because so much of the floor level had been destroyed when the later crescent-shaped foundation of the octagonal building was inserted (fig. 20). The whole floor of the circular temple was examined down to the undisturbed gravel, which overlies the limestone on the riverside slope. There was no sign of any disturbance of the subsoil below the central area of the shrine and no evidence was found of any wooden construction that might possibly have preceded it. It is probable that the hearths were made on the original floor of the circular temple and that the pebble-cobbled floor was a later repair to this much-used gravel floor. The burnt areas could be connected with some initial ceremonies that took place when the building was erected.

The main eastern approach to the building showed considerable wear, and this was particularly evident at the roughly paved area immediately outside the east entrance (fig. 23). The limestone slab extending on either side of the doorway was much worn down but not in the centre of the paved entrance (pl. VIII*a*). This suggests that the eastern portal had a double doorway; a post-hole 1 ft. (0.3 m.) in diameter at the entrance, was no doubt a door-stop (fig. 23).

The walls of the circular temple were not plastered, but a number of the stones re-used from it in the foundations of the later octagonal building had been faced with one or two coats of a white lime-wash. A large slab of limestone with a cavetto moulding was found within the central area lying on the cobbled floor (fig. 80(84)). This cornice must have been incorporated in the circular building. A number of voussoirs of a heavy elongated type suggests that the building had an arched doorway or windows (fig. 8(1)) and these, together with other smaller architectural fragments recovered, give some indication that the circular temple was not a simple plain structure, but that it had features of some architectural merit. Unlike the cornice from the outer and later octagonal wall, the cornice from the circular shrine had no provision for guttering in its upper surface, and more likely formed part of an interior shelf or cornice. A similar internal feature may be seen in the circular temple at Perigueux in the Dordogne[10] and it is also featured in illustrations of the Roman structure known as Arthur's O'on in the Carron valley north of Falkirk.[11] In both buildings the shelf or ledge is shown several feet above the ground floor, encircling the interior of the building, and it is possible that this interior cornice may have supported a wooden floor.

The circular temple was built after A.D. 69, but not later than A.D. 210. It was not possible to place the building within a narrower dating limit. Little material predating it was left *in situ*, largely because of the disturbance made when the heavy foundations of the later octagonal building were inserted. A coin of Faustina (A.D. 145–61), found lying under a large stone on the original surface just south of the circular temple wall, was apparently contemporary with the construction of the circular temple. The stone was probably put in position during the construction of the building. A coin of Plautillus (A.D. 205–10) found in the layer of white stone chippings, which was laid down when the large platform was made above the octagonal revetment wall, indicates that the circular building must have been built before A.D. 210. On balance the evidence tends to favour its construction soon after A.D. 161.

Several examples of the round buildings interpreted as temples or mausolea are known in Britain. Two such buildings were excavated during the nineteenth century. They are: (A) Keston, Kent (fig. 7, 1).[9] This was a circular building 30 ft. (9.1 m.) in diameter, 3 ft. (0.9 m.) less than the Nettleton temple. The Keston temple was excavated in 1828 and later in 1854. The foundations were 3 ft. (0.9 m.) wide, with freestanding walls 2 ft. 9 in. in width and the building was thought to have been either a tomb or a temple. Like Nettleton, it also had an eastern entrance. There was also a series of six projecting plinths which were thought to 'look indeed like the plinths of columns'. It was thought that the 'vestiges' were not later than the second century A.D. (B) Pulborough, Sussex (fig. 7, 2). Also circular in plan, this building was excavated before 1859.[12] The interior diameter was 40 ft (12.2 m.) and the walls were of unusual thickness, 11 ft. 6 in. (3.5 m.). This building was thought to be a sepulchral monument. Quantities of tufa found within its walls led the excavators to think

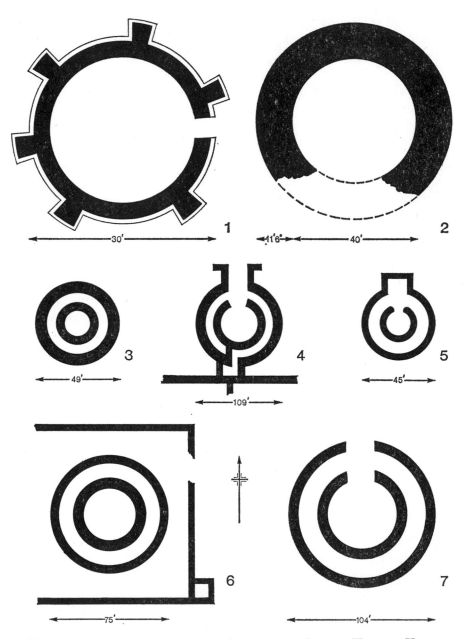

Fig. 7.   Comparative plans of circular temples: 1, Keston, Kent;
2, Pulborough, Sussex; 3, Faye-l'Abbesse, Deux Sèvres; 4, Perigueux,
Dordogne; 5, Beaument-le-Roger, Eure; 6, Craou, Mayenne; 7,
Crozon, Finistère. Note: plans at different scales

that it was used to 'arch the roof'. (C) Another building probably similar was the small structure known as Arthur's O'on, on the northern slopes of the Carron valley two miles north of Falkirk.[11] This building was demolished in 1743. It had an overall diameter of 27 ft. 3 in. (8.28 m.), with walls 3 ft. 10 in. (1.16 m.) thick. Like Nettleton, it had an eastern entrance. The roof, a cobbled dome with an aperture at the top, may not have been an original feature of the building. (D) There was also a small circular temple in association with the Lullingstone Roman villa.[13] This building was constructed during the second century A.D. The internal diameter was only 15 ft. (4.6 m.) and the building was of lighter construction than the Nettleton circular temple which was 28 ft. (8.6 m.) in internal diameter, but both buildings had entrances facing eastwards. The Lullingstone temple also produced evidence of 'ritual' fires, but not as extensive as was found within the temple at Nettleton. The Lullingstone temple was dismantled about A.D. 300, when a larger square temple with a central cult room was erected. It is of interest to note that the circular building was replaced by the larger building during the second half of the third century A.D. in much the same sequence as at Nettleton.

In France there are several known examples of circular temples, but these have a circular wall enclosing an ambulatory round the central building. There was no such wall at Nettleton (see fig. 7).

The earliest examples of the centralized (round) building are to be found in Rome, but recent discoveries at Pergamon and Istanbul show that this type was widely known at an early date and it is clear that the circular building was in fairly common use both before and during the first and second centuries A.D. It is possible that the idea may be an invention of the Hellenistic mind and its evolution traced to the simple beehive tombs at Mycenae.[14]

One of the extant examples of a round temple is now the Church of S. Maria del Sole on the Tiber in Rome. This temple, possibly of Hercules Victor, was built in 150 B.C.[15] The tomb of Caecilia Metella on the Appian Way south of Rome is another example of a round building. Constructed before 53 B.C. it is considered to be the prototype for tombs of masonry set on a high base.[16]

At Pergamon, a few miles inland from the Mediterranean coast of Turkey, a large hall known as the 'Kizil Avbi'[17] is built over a stream which crosses beneath the hall obliquely. At the east end of this hall there are two circular buildings flanking a central apsidal end of the main hall. The circular buildings, one of which is intact, had vaulted roofs with a central circular opening to the sky very similar to other examples quoted. The Nettleton circular temple was of similar construction.

But by far the most imposing surviving instance is the Pantheon in Rome founded by Agrippa in 27 B.C., and reconstructed much as we see it today by the Emperor Hadrian (A.D. 120–4). The plan of the rounded building, wherever it originated, was similar both in the east and west of the Empire.[18]

Subsequently a considerable number of later and smaller variants in the form of mausolea or temples, like the temples at Nettleton, Keston, Pulborough, and the French examples, were introduced. The classic example of the round building is the former mausoleum of Constantine's daughter, Constantia, on the Via Nomentana in Rome, built in c. A.D. 324–6 and converted into a Christian church (S. Constanza) in A.D. 1256. The circular dome is carried on a series of columns, set in pairs forming a circle, and is thought to be the first

3

instance in which this had been accomplished in a round building, and it may be called 'the swan song of Roman Imperial structures of this kind'.[19]

(b) *The Rectangular Hall (Building VII)*

An important addition to the settlement, pre-dating the building of the large octagonal podium, was the large rectangular building (VII) built within the shadow of the shrine (fig. 5). This building, 60 ft. (18.2 m.) long and 26 ft. (7.9 m.) wide had its north wall built alongside the river with a series of seven stone piers, each 3 ft. (0.9 m.) square at the base, forming a six-arched arcaded frontage alongside the river (pl. IV*a* and fig. 20). The same style may be seen in the blind arcading to the south of the circular bath at Bath (Cunliffe,

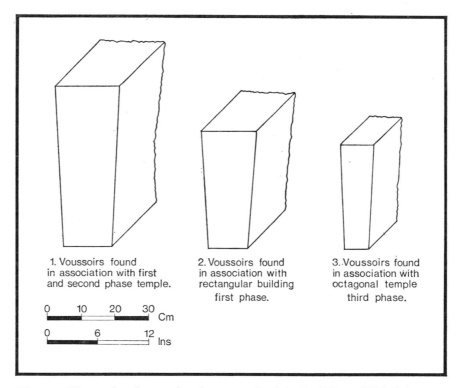

1. Voussoirs found in association with first and second phase temple.

0   10   20   30   Cm

0   6   12   Ins

2. Voussoirs found in association with rectangular building first phase.

3. Voussoirs found in association with octagonal temple third phase.

Fig. 8.   Voussoirs from circular temple (1), Building VII (2), and octagonal temple (3)

1969, fig. 36, p. 117). A number of voussoirs from the arches were recovered from a level above the hard cobbled surface, which sealed the later stone piers in the river midstream This indicates that the arcading was *in situ* after the cobbled surface had been laid down. The voussoirs were of a heavy stout type in comparison with those from the later octagonal shrine (fig. 8(2)).

The architectural features recovered from this building indicate that the structure was of some architectural merit (pl. IV*b*, *c*). The gable-ends of the building were enriched with a billet-decorated cornice carried along at roof level (fig. 81 (28, 29)). The gable-ends carried decorative finials (pl. XXXIIIa) and the roof had a covering of stone pennant tiles.

A single upright stone, set in the river bed alongside the fifth pier from the east end of the north wall, was probably used to support a wooden structure or as a tie-up or bollard for boats (fig. 3). A stone of the same diameter and 5 ft. 6 in. (1.65 m.) long, lying on the paved floor towards the east end of the building, could be a similar stone removed from the old river bed.

In the absence of any interior piers it must be assumed that the roof was one unsupported span throughout the length of the building. There was no apparent means of entry into the building, except at the south-east corner where the road surface outside and the inside corner of the hall were much worn, suggesting an entrance. There was also evidence that access to the shrine was obtained by way of a flight of steps from the north-west corner of the rectangular hall to the shrine on the higher level. The octagonal podium wall of the shrine erected about A.D. 230 was built partially over the south-west corner of the building at this point (pl. VIIIb).

A partition wall across the hall opposite the fifth pier from the east was probably constructed when the octagonal podium of the shrine was built. This created a narthex 19 ft. (5.8 m.) long at the west end of the hall, and was probably a place of rendezvous before entering or leaving the shrine. The doorway through the partition wall was about 5 ft. (1.5 m.) wide with double doors. There was a central hole for the bolt in the much-worn doorstep, and a small ridge on the west side of the doorway continued along the east edge of the doorstep. All the walls in this building were substantial and well built. The hall, after the erection of the partition wall, was 34 ft. long (10.4 m.) and towards its eastern end parts of the original floor survived, consisting of a number of well-squared blocks of the local limestone. Each line of floor blocks varied in width and they no doubt covered the whole of the east end of the building. The stones nearest the east and north walls had been taken out when the walls were taken down to foundation level. The floor survived on the south side where the wall also survived to a height of 2 ft. (0.6 m.) or more above floor level. The central part of the floor also survived and this suggests that there may have been a central aisle; but this could equally well be the point at which stone-robbing ceased, although it is curious that this central area should have been left intact. The patch of flooring on the south side of the building could also be original, but the small cobbling towards the rear part of the hall is a later addition.

A large block of rusticated limestone lying on the cobbled floor came from the octagonal podium of the shrine and it was probably used by the later squatters as a seat alongside the wall. The cobbling also belongs to the squatter phase after A.D. 370. Beneath the floor of the central part of the building was a simple drain, made by placing flat stones slantwise, to form a triangular-shaped water channel.

The north wall of the building is known to continue eastwards; it was traced to the edge of the modern river, and is thought to have continued as a retaining wall alongside the south river bank in Roman times. It is parallel with the wall found by Mr. Priestley on the north side of the present river (fig. 2).

A mass of stone tiles with burnt material, found in the south-west corner of the building with two coins of Constantine, suggests that the building ceased to be used for its primary purpose during the period A.D. 307–35, but it was later used by squatters who laid rough cobbled floors.

Purpose and Date of the Rectangular Building VII

Soon after the construction of the circular shrine it is likely that an association of 'friends' or a 'brotherhood' associated with the cult developed, and one of its prime requirements would be the provision of a *schola* or suitable building where they could meet for communal worship and for the celebration of anniversaries accompanying visits to the shrine.[20] The small circular temple had no provision for this and was not built for this purpose. But in the early years of the third century A.D. the large rectangular hall was built as an annexe to the shrine to make provision for this need and the increasing number of visitors.

The problem of the provision of a suitable building was not solved without difficulty. It was essential, to serve its purpose, that the building should be in close proximity to the shrine, but at the same time its size should not detract from or dwarf in any way the small shrine poised on the knoll overlooking the river. The only suitable site at Nettleton was the small area of land that lay on the lower level between the foot of the knoll and the river, and this was not wide enough to accommodate the proposed building. It was only by cutting back the foot of the slope to accommodate the south wall and by the construction of a heavily built wall incorporating a series of seven riverside piers on the north side that sufficient space was obtained for the building (fig. 2). Such an arrangement was the only possible solution, if the dual purpose of close proximity and the preservation of the amenities of the shrine was to be satisfied. By this device the dominant position of the small circular shrine was preserved while the much larger hall on the lower level was suitably dwarfed (pl. XI*b*).

The temple at Sanxay in the department of Vienne, France,[21] had an extension to its eastern wing which extended to the east walk of the surrounding ambulatory. This seems to have been a later extension to the temple and was probably built to serve the same purpose as the hall at Nettleton. The 'Long Building' at Lydney was built in close proximity to the shrine.[22]

The circular shrine was built before A.D. 210, and the great octagonal podium was added to it soon after A.D. 230. This was after the construction of the rectangular hall, because the foundation of the north-east angle of the podium wall rests partially on the offsets of the south-west corner of the hall, and so is structurally later (pl. VIII*b*). It therefore follows that the hall was erected before A.D. 230.

(c) *Building VIII North of the Shrine*

This building was contemporary with the circular temple and was built on the area that lay between the foot of the knoll on which the temple was built and the nearby river. Only the south-east angle of the building was recovered. The white mortared walls were not substantially built, and there is little doubt that because of the low level on which it stood it must have been subject to flooding in Roman times.

Any attempt to suggest a possible use for this building would be conjectural, but it may have been the residence of the temple priest before A.D. 248, when the octagonal temple was built. It was superseded by Building IX, which was built to the east of the temple on higher ground. The walls of Building VIII were set in a brown soil earlier than the circular shrine, but the walls were contemporary with the dark earth in which the outer octagonal wall was built. This indicates that this building was built before A.D. 230 and precedes the construction of the octagonal wall.

(d) *The First Hostel (Building XI)*

This large building occupied a prominent corner position between the river and the Fosse Way on the south side of the river, with its east wall presumably built alongside or near the Fosse Way. It was not possible to excavate the north side of the building because the river has changed its course since Roman times; but a small piece of stone foundation located on the north side of the river lines up with the west wall of this building and is possibly its north-west corner. If this is correct, the external measurement of the building from north to south would be 72 ft. (21.9 m.). The south wall had been robbed at its eastern end, but the white mortar seems to indicate a possible corner just short of the modern roadway and this wall would also be 72 ft. in length, making the building a square construction. The outer wall was well built, 3 ft. 6 in. (1.05 m.) wide, with white mortar, similar to that used in the circular shrine. A second wall, 2 ft. (0.6 m.) wide and parallel with the outer wall, formed an inner square with a narrow walk or ambulatory only 3 ft. (0.9 m.) wide between the two walls. It is possible that a number of rooms led off from the inner wall of the narrow ambulatory but, because of the disturbance made when the later Building XII was constructed on the same site, it was not possible to determine this. The size and position of the building suggest that this was a guest-house where lodging was provided for visitors to the shrine and travellers along the Fosse Way.

The plan of the later building on this site indicates that the modern road is not on the same line as the Fosse Way, which must be slightly to the east of the present road. This would allow for a suitable pull-in off the road on the east side of the building. This provision was not necessary with the later building on the site, which had a large cobbled courtyard along its south side for the reception of visitors.

A coin of Faustina I, *c.* A.D. 140, found in the wall-trench alongside the south wall of Building XI must have been lost at the time of its construction, which must be later than A.D. 140. This suggests that Building XI was erected slightly later than the nearby circular temple, which it was built to serve.

(e) *The House of the Strong-room (Building XIII)*

This building was built alongside the Fosse Way and south of the guest-house (Building XI). In its original form it was a long narrow building, built with white mortar, on an east–west axis; it was 102 ft. (31 m.) long and 13 ft. (4.0 m.) broad. The east wing of the building, long and narrow, terminated at its west end in a square room, 14 ft. (4.3 m.) by 12 ft. (3.7 m.); it was constructed in the form of a cellar or strong-room, with access and a window at its west end, and its south and east walls built against the solid rock face (pl. IXa, b). A wooden floor had been laid over this cellar and its charred remains, containing coins ranging from A.D. 370 to 385, were found on the lower cellar floor (fig. 37). The building itself was partially destroyed by burning during one of several fires which took place during the last quarter of the fourth century A.D. Adjoining the cellar to the west there was a large room 32 ft. (9.7 m.) in length and 20 ft. (6.1 m.) wide, with a window in its west wall.

Considerable alterations and additions were made to the building after the fire, and the cellar was made smaller, 6 ft. by 12 ft. (1.8 by 3.7 m.), by building a wall in an east to west direction across it (fig. 2). The north part was levelled and a cobbled surface laid to incorporate it in the courtyard. This alteration was made during or immediately following the reign of Valens (A.D. 364–78). Part of the large west window was also blocked up on its north side, and the room at the west end was extended on its north side. The north wall was dispensed with and an extension 11 ft. (3.4 m.) wide was made. But this arrangement was short-lived. In the last quarter of the fourth century A.D. the building was burnt down for the second time. Coins ranging from A.D. 370 to 385 were found in the debris of the second fire.

Other later extensions were made to the building on its south side, which was on a higher level. A large room 44 ft. (13.4 m.) long and 22 ft. (6.7 m.) wide was built on the eastern part, and adjoining this on its west side there was a further addition, 20 ft. (6.1 m.) long and 22 ft. (6.7 m.) wide (fig. 9). This room had an open stone channel running lengthwise, 11 ft. (3.4 m.) from its south wall. The width of 11 ft. between the drain and the wall would have been sufficient to house a line of three horses, but it could equally well have served as a latrine. A further extension to the building on its south-west corner was an additional room 21 ft. (6.4 m.) by 12 ft. (3.7 m.). This had a doorway at its north end, which gave access to the large room at the west end of the building.

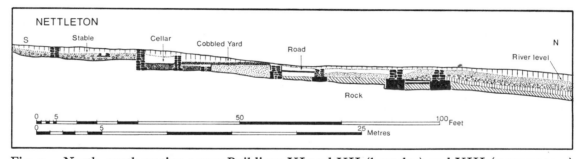

Fig. 9.   North–south section across Buildings XI and XII (hostelry) and XIII (strong-room)

Building XIII in its original form was built at the same time as or soon after the circular shrine. The white mortar used was of the same composition as that used in the walls of the latter. A coin of Postumus, A.D. 265–8, found lying on the brown mortar level, suggests that the addition was made towards the end of the third century A.D.

In its original form the building with its strong-room appears to have been the residential quarters of the overseer responsible for the general care and supervision of the settlement. Stables and other additions were evidently made to cope with the increasing traffic to the shrine, consequent on the construction of the octagonal temple after A.D. 250. Finally, the building was adapted for use in medieval times by the construction of a curious curved dry-stone wall within the western addition to the building.

4. THE CIRCULAR SHRINE. PHASE II: THE OCTAGONAL PODIUM AND ITS ASSOCIATED BUILDINGS, A.D. 230–50 (fig. 5)

The 20 years between A.D. 230 and A.D. 250 were the period of the greatest development and building activity at Nettleton. It was during this time that the quality of the work was at its best, marked by good solid masonry walls with well-prepared facing stones. The large octagonal podium, 70 ft. (21.3 m.) in diameter, with its fine rusticated facing stones was an important addition made to the circular shrine during this period (pl. X*a*, *b*). The retaining boundary walls of the settlement, built with large dressed blocks of limestone, again with a rusticated facing, were built against the north and west quarry face at the same time (pl. III*b*).

A new system of roads was laid out to conform with the accepted Roman plan though it was severely limited by the physical conditions of the site. A road running north from the original road at the Fosse Way was constructed to replace the former road to the shrine. It was flanked on either side by walls, which probably carried pillars forming a colonnade, and eventually crossed the river valley to the north. South of the present river and opposite the east entrance to the shrine a second road ran westwards from the Fosse Way to the shrine. It was flanked on its north side by a well-built wall which probably formed the frontage of a series of small compartments or shops backing on to the river, which ran parallel to this road.

An important feature of the new arrangement was the construction of a substantially built precinct wall, enclosing that part of the shrine facing the Fosse Way, designed, presumably, to control the movement of visitors to the shrine. The large rectangular building (No. X), which occupied the important corner position immediately south-west of the precinct gateway and was probably a shop, was also constructed at this time. The west boundary wall was part of an extension made to the south of the settlement in the Wick valley. This extension included a street which forked off southward along the small valley, flanked on its west side by a substantial wall which connected with the flanking precinct wall on the main street (fig. 19). This wall and road continued to the south for 112 ft. (34.1 m.), where it then turned to the west and made a gradual ascent alongside the north wall of Building XVI. The west boundary wall, built against the rock face, was utilized to form the west wall of Building XVI, just as the north boundary wall was also incorporated in Building I.

The boundary walls built against the valley rock face are unusual and are a reversal of the usual arrangement, where the wall is built against an internal man-made bank. A similar system was used in the narrow valley site at Glanum (St. Rémy-de-Provence). It is possible that there may also have been a palisade or wall built at the top of the limestone outcrop; but later extensive quarrying of the rock face makes it impossible to determine this point.

To the south of the road leading to the western entrance, the roadway at this phase continued with its accompanying west side wall for a further 112 ft. (34.1 m.), and at this point turned westward towards the high west bank. This wall was also the north wall of Building XVII and is broader than the other walls of that building. The space between the north-west corner of Building XVI was also the foot of the high bank to the west, and evidence that a wall connected these two buildings was found at three points between them. There was a considerable change of level on either side of this wall, and also a substantial revetment several feet high running north from its line. Two additional revetments on the west bank at higher levels ran parallel with the lower revetting wall (fig. 2). It is suggested that the rusticated boundary wall forming the west wall of Building XVI continued across this area as a revetment to the high bank but was destroyed when the later southern extension was made further up the valley. The wall was preserved at its western end because the later building was built against it.

The large rectangular riverside building, No. VII, erected before A.D. 230, had considerable additions made on its north side towards the end of this phase. A series of seven well-built piers, each 1 ft. 10 in. square (0.56 m.), was constructed in the river bed (fig. 5), opposite the seven piers in the riverside north wall of the rectangular building. The piers, built with squared blocks of Bath stone, rested on stone blocks 1 ft. 3 in. (0.38 m.) thick, which had cut-waters on their upstream ends. The recovery of the river piers was a difficult operation, and it was fortunate that a long dry summer drought coincided with their excavation (pl. IVa); but despite this, pumps were necessary to keep the excavation clear of water. The piers were under the south bank of the modern river, which flows at a much higher level than its Roman predecessor. At one point, where the modern river bends northwards, it was possible to recover the opposite north side of the Roman period river, and this was also faced with large limestone blocks (fig. 2).

It is possible only to surmise the purpose of the river-bed piers, but it is thought likely that the rectangular hall was extended to the north by bridging over the river. The north side was the only possible way in which the building could be extended, without blocking the eastern aspect of the shrine. It was noted that the material in the old river bed produced twigs or branches of trees, old roots, etc., such as collect against an obstruction in a river bed. The bed below the river wall also produced a surprising number of small finds (pl. IVa). These must have been accidentally dropped in the river by people standing on the open, arcaded riverside wall of the hall before the river piers were constructed (pl. XIb). The small portion of the north riverside wall recovered was on the same alignment as the riverside wall found downstream to the east by Priestley in 1938, and this suggests that the river was contained within two substantial walls within the settlement. It is possible that the flow was controlled by one or more waterfalls. This would not only add to the attraction of the settlement, but would also have ponded back water for domestic purposes.

After A.D. 305 the river piers were dismantled to a uniform level of 2 ft. 9 in. (0.84 m.). This was done to allow for the construction of a metalled floor or yard over the site of the old river bed and it is possible that the river was diverted north of its old course at this time. There must have been a considerable rise in the water table level since the floors of the riverside buildings were renewed and placed at a higher level at this period. But despite this we find considerable evidence of later flooding in the alluvial silt on the higher level (fig. 3).

The bathing establishment connected with the settlement has not been located, but opposite the shrine north of the present river there is a small spot which remains wet and soggy during the dryest summer, and it is probably the source of a strong spring of water, utilized no doubt in Roman times. The most probable site for the baths would be just east of this spring-head.

The riverside wall discovered by Priestley was thought by him to have been a bridge abutment on the line of the Fosse Way, but the recent excavations have disproved this theory (pl. XIIa). Priestley's wall was immediately opposite Buildings XI, XII and XIII on the opposite (south) side of the river, and there was no sign of a roadway on that side of the river. The Fosse Way crossed the river just east of Buildings XI and XIII, which lie partially under the modern roadway.

The square guest-house No. XI alongside the Fosse Way was about this time superseded by a larger building on the same site (Building XII). Building XIII on the opposite (south) side of the new courtyard also had considerable alterations made to its plan in this phase (pl. IX*a, b*) while Building XIV was also constructed during this period on the western slope. Another building (No. IX) was built within the temple precincts on the east side of the roadway leading north across the river and opposite the large rectangular hall. This building faced eastwards towards the entrance gateway into the temple precinct (fig. 16).

(a) *The Octagonal Podium*

The well worn doorstep at the eastern entrance to the circular shrine was a striking indication that the small shrine was in constant use during the latter part of the second century and the early years of the third century A.D. The temple in its delightful setting attracted visitors in increasing numbers, so much so that about A.D. 230 provision was made for this by improving the eastern approach and enlarging the area surrounding the circular temple.[23]

An elaborate stone octagonal podium was built out beyond the sloping knoll to the north and east so as to surround the circular building. A marking-out trench found on the slope to the east of the building would have made provision for a platform 22 ft. (6.7 m.) wide to surround the temple (fig. 5), but this ambitious plan was modified to provide a podium 18 ft. (5.5 m.) in width. This modification was probably made to avoid the blocking or over-shadowing of the adjoining rectangular building that occupied the area alongside the river at the foot of the knoll on which the shrine stood. The octagonal platform as first planned would have completely obliterated the view of the rectangular hall from the south. To carry out the modified plan, it was necessary to cut into the limestone hillside on the south and west side to make a level platform to surround the circular temple. The stone obtained from this operation was used to form a heavy revetting foundation, with an average width of 6–8 ft. (1.8–2.4 m.) on the lower part of the slope to the north and east alongside the river. The foundation trench for this massive retaining wall on the north side cut through an accumulation of occupation material, which had been dumped at the foot of the slope at some time prior to A.D. 230 (fig. 3).[24]

A coin of Plautillus (A.D. 205–10) found under the stone chippings, which were placed on the surface of the podium as a basis for the floor blocks (pl. VI*a*), suggests that the podium was built after A.D. 210, but the foundation of the north-east angle of the octagonal podium wall was set on the offset of the south-west corner of the large rectangular building, which was built before A.D. 230 (see pl. VIII*b*), so the octagonal podium is more likely to have been built after A.D. 230.

This octagonal retaining wall of the temple podium was faced with large blocks of rusticated limestone, the blocks in some of the courses on the north and east sides being 3–4 ft. (0.9–1.2 m.) in length and 1 ft. 6 in. (0.46 m.) in height (pl. X*a, b*). A close inspection of the rusticated work on the north wall suggests that the work was done with iron chisels after the wall was built (fig. 10). The wall courses towards the west side of the structure are built into

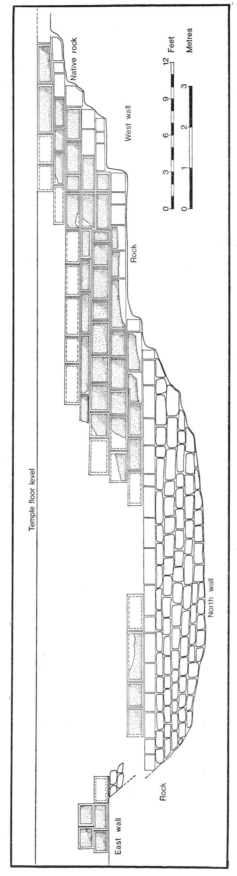

Fig. 10. Elevation of octagonal wall face to show rustication

the sloping hillside, and here the rustication appears only on the exposed faces of the stone blocks built into the bank. It was also noticed that the rustication was more emphatic and much better executed from the ground level up to the height of an average man, with the chiselled lines sloping obliquely across the face of each stone block. At a higher level the rustication is lightly chiselled and has no distinct linear pattern (fig. 10). The wall was of first-class workmanship and built to correspond with the floor level of the podium and temple floor levels (fig. 21). Each stone block had been cut precisely to the shape required and the joints were so tight that mortar was not necessary. The same type of rustication has also been found in a wall built against the limestone rock face west of the settlement and was also found by Priestley on the north side of the settlement, where it formed the north wall of the so-called later rectangular temple (Building I). The same type of rusticated work has also been found in the walls of the amphitheatre entrance at *Corinium* (Cirencester) and in the Roman city wall at *Glevum* (Gloucester). The inner face of the retaining wall at Nettleton and its core were made up of large blocks of unworked limestone. At the point of junction with the sloping limestone rock on the west side, the foundation trench for the retaining wall cut

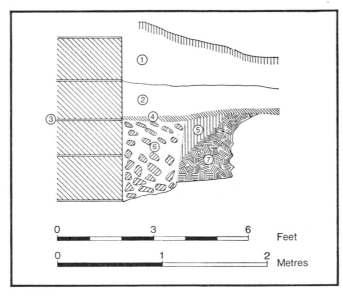

Fig. 11. Section of Phase-II octagonal podium wall, showing wall-trench (6) cutting second-century pit-filling (5, 7)

through an earlier Roman rubbish pit containing black earth, but unfortunately no dateable object was found in the pit-filling (fig. 11).

After the completion of the wall, the area surrounding the temple was levelled, and the resulting wide platform was covered with a layer of fine limestone chippings. This provided a suitable basis for the large squared slabs of limestone which formed a substantial pavement for the podium. A small area of this pavement was found *in situ* on the west side of the temple below the floor of the later ambulatory and the west wall of the later octagonal temple (pl. VI*a*). The remainder of this floor was destroyed when the crescent-shaped sleeper-wall foundations of the later octagonal temple were put in.

Externally, the octagonal retaining wall had stout pilasters at each angle and was capped at the temple floor level with a wide overhanging cavetto cornice (pl. XIV*a*),[25] which was formed to carry a lead-lined water-channel on its upper surface. Above the cornice level the wall was set back on the inner side of the stone gutter, which surrounded the building to convey the rainwater from the temple roof. The joints of this heavy stone cornice were carefully recessed to allow them to be sealed with lead, to render the guttering watertight, while the overhang of the cornice afforded protection to the rusticated wall face below. Several large blocks of the cornice were recovered, including a pilaster angle piece which clearly indicates that both the cornice and guttering were carried around the projecting angle pilasters of the octagonal wall (pl. XIV*b*, *c*).

The inner face of the octagonal wall was circular to conform with the circular temple which the new podium encompassed (pl. XV*b*). A short length was found below the floor level of the later ambulatory on the north side of the podium (pl. XV*a*, *b*) and the circular curve was clearly defined in both the base course and the first freestanding course of the wall.

We can but guess the height to which this wall was built, but it is possible that the surrounding platform was enclosed with an outer wall forming an annular passage around the circular temple and this passage was possibly enclosed with a barrel vault. This method was adopted in the construction of one of the several temples found in the group at Trier (*Colonia Treverorum*)[26] where the circular shrine was completely encompassed with an annular passage (fig. 12).

A number of well-dressed stones, including some voussoirs, found on the east side of the temple at Nettleton in material deposited after the destruction of the circular temple when the surrounding space was levelled, and voussoirs of the same type found in the filling of the wall-trench between the wall of the later building and the rock face, undoubtedly came from the circular temple (fig. 8(1)). The voussoirs were of a distinct type, large and elongated, in contrast to the lighter type found in association with the later octagonal temple.[27] They probably came from arched windows in the upper part of the circular temple. A series of windows, with heavy arches, was incorporated in the temple at Autun, Saône-et-Loire (*Augustodunum*).[28]

At Trier the outer wall, like Nettleton, was octagonal on its outer face, but inside the wall conformed with the earlier circular temple which it encompassed. The source for this type of building may be found in the cruciform chamber tomb of the Servilii on the Via Appia coming from Rome (fig. 12),[29] and the so-called tomb of Severus Alexander at Monte del Grano, *c.* A.D. 69–96, where an annular passage encircled the circular tomb-chamber.[30] There are two other instances where circular temples are enclosed with outer octagonal walls, but in each instance the wall was octagonal both inside and outside. The large temple at St. Reverien (Nièvre) (fig. 12) has an octagonal wall with no supporting buttresses at the angles.[31] The other, St. Gervais (Vendée) (fig. 12), has unusually heavy buttresses at each angle of the octagonal wall surrounding the circular shrine.[32]

An alternative arrangement of the outer wall, above the cornice level, may possibly have been a low bench-like wall on which columns were placed between the angle pilasters, thus forming a colonnade on the open platform, but apart from the provision of an open platform this arrangement would have been purely decorative.

The octagonal mausoleum at Split, Yugoslavia, erected to receive the remains of the deified emperor Diocletian in A.D. 315, had a circular interior. It was built on an octagonal podium and had a heavy cornice at floor level similar to that of the Nettleton shrine. Above the cornice the podium and the mausoleum were enclosed with an open column-supported portico.[33]

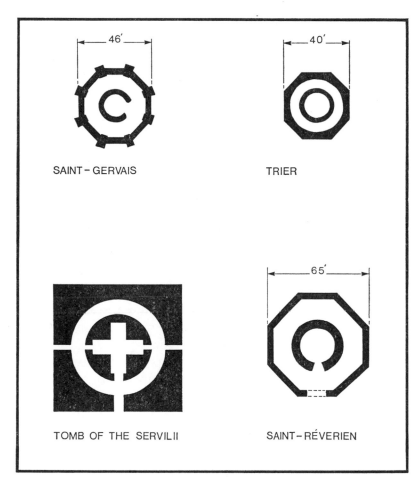

Fig. 12. Comparative plans of circular temples with octagonal external walls and plan of tomb of Servilii

At Nettleton the platform and the revetting wall provided a firm support to the shallow foundations of the circular temple and the building was firmly stabilized. Ample provision was now made to allow worshippers to process around the circular shrine. The simple metalled approach at the eastern entrance was dispensed with at this stage, to make provision for the construction of the podium on a higher level. A new eastern entrance was built by making a short flight of stone steps partially within the width of the podium wall foundation. This provided access to the podium platform and the temple from the approach road. No steps were found *in situ*, but it was noticed that there were no facing stones in the revetting wall at this point. A slope on the surviving masonry core of the wall suggests steps (fig. 13). This more dignified eastern approach to the shrine would have made an impressive addition to the circular shrine.

The roadway at the eastern entrance turned sharply to the north and was flanked by a stone kerb and bank on its western verge and on its opposite side it passed alongside the west wall of Building IX. Beyond the kerb the east end of the large hall (Building VII) abutted

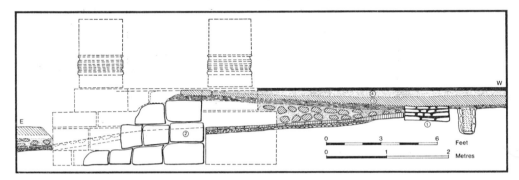

Fig. 13.   East–west section across east entrance of circular and octagonal temples (1, Phase-I circular temple wall; 2, Phase-II octagonal podium walls; 3, Phase-III octagonal temple floor, 4, Phase-IV pennant floor of octagonal temple)

on to this roadway, which, after crossing the river presumably by way of a bridge, proceeded in the direction of the so-called temple discovered by Priestley in 1939. On the east side of the octagonal podium the sloping bank between the shrine and the stone kerb was probably laid out as a garden. Set on its podium, the circular temple overshadowed the large rectangular and other buildings alongside the nearby river.

The coin evidence indicates that the octagonal podium was completed shortly after A.D. 231 and this arrangement of the shrine continued until A.D. 249 or soon after, when the circular temple was destroyed by fire. The floor of the central shrine was covered to a depth of several inches with a layer of charred burnt wood, etc. Two coins, badly burnt but legible, were found in the ash, one of Gordianus (A.D. 240) and the other of Philip the Arab (A.D. 249). Much of the burnt material from the circular temple was later used on the east, lower side of the site to raise the level of the surrounding area of the later octagonal shrine.

(b) *The Precinct Wall and Gateway to the Shrine*

The increasing use of the circular shrine after A.D. 230 not only necessitated the construction of the imposing podium, but also rendered desirable the enclosing of an area around the immediate vicinity of the shrine with a substantially built precinct wall. This wall surrounded the knoll on which the shrine was built and was 4 ft. (1.2 m.) wide. It also enclosed the ancillary buildings connected with the shrine, including the large hall (No. VII), the nearby priest's or custodian's house (No. IX) and the shop (No. X). The north end of the wall presumably joined the north wall of Building VII built alongside the south bank of the river, but unfortunately it was not possible to excavate this junction, because it lies under the present bed of the river, which flows at a higher level than in Roman times.

The precinct wall was evidently built to regulate the movement of visitors to the shrine. The roads leading from the Fosse Way converged at a point in the small valley immediately opposite the eastern entrance to the shrine and at this point, within the wall, there stood an arched gateway over the roadway into the shrine precinct. The road junction outside this gateway was much worn through constant usage, and it was no doubt a point of assembly for visitors before entering the shrine (fig. 2). The precinct wall did not completely enclose the shrine and it may well have been built like the similar wall at Lydney Park, Gloucestershire, which was thought by Sir Mortimer Wheeler to 'have been but another symptom of the wealth and popularity of the shrine, and may have been intended to give dignity to the site, and to facilitate the control of the concourse of visitors to it. It may on the other hand have had a more ominous intent, that of providing a protective barricade in the period of increasing anarchy and peril.'[34] There was no sign of the precinct wall continuing to the west of the settlement which is on much higher ground, and it is likely that this was forested in Roman times. An examination of the field to the west of the shrine failed to produce any structural or occupational evidence.

The substantial foundations found on either side of the precinct gateway, and the well-made, but much worn, roadway into the enclosure indicate a gateway of some pretension at this point. The large pieces of a former archway with some architectural detail recovered from the late fourth-century floor in the nearby Building IX are likely to have formed part of this archway (pl. XVIIIa, b). They certainly indicate a gateway of some architectural merit. It is also possible that the unusual stone finial found nearby may be one of two such finials which flanked the gateway (pl. XXXIIIa, fig. 78(54)). The roadway through the gateway was 10 ft. (3.0 m.) wide.

The precinct wall was built southward along the foot of the knoll but opposite the entrance to the small Wick valley it turned south-west and continued along the valley for 92 ft. (28.0 m.), where it then turned westward to join up with the high west bank, but it did not continue beyond this bank. The wall was later used to form the south wall of Building XVI at the western entrance.

The visitor approaching the settlement by way of the Fosse Way from the north, after passing the high limestone crag on his right, would see the large hostel first, but away to his right on the opposite, south, side of the river he would see the shrine, built on the knoll overlooking the river, probably with a background of trees. He would also see the approach road from the Fosse Way and the hostel, which led to the precinct wall gateway enclosing the shrine.

(c) *The Priest's or Custodian's House (Building IX)*

This building occupied the corner site between the street leading to the shrine and the road leading to the north of the river. It extended northwards probably to the riverside, but it was not possible to ascertain its extent because the river now flows over the north end (fig. 14).

The building was 27 ft. (8.2 m.) in width and at its south end the limestone had been cut

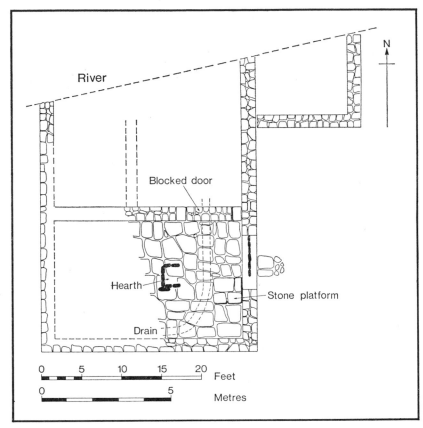

Fig. 14.   Plan of Building IX

back to make room for the building. The walls were well constructed with local limestone and the corner stones well faced and squared. The south part of the building, 17 ft. by 27 ft. (5.2 m. by 8.2 m.), was separated from its north part by a partition wall, and the entrance was through the east wall near the south-east corner. The doorway, 5 ft. (1.5 m.) wide, was probably arched as a number of voussoirs was found in and around it. There was also a doorway, 3 ft. (0.9 m.) wide, through the partition wall on its east side, with large stone jambs, and the iron socket in which the door swung still *in situ* on its west side (pl. XVII*b*, fig. 15). This doorway had been subject to constant use, so much so that the stone sill had been worn through at the centre. The doorway was later blocked up and the northern part of the building was not used in the post-temple period (pl. XVII*a*). A radiate coin of A.D. 260–90 found in the blocking wall suggests that the blocking took place in the latter years of the third century A.D.

In the southern part of the building, there was a stone floor, composed of a number of large limestone blocks (fig. 16). But this was not the original floor; the stones comprising it proved to be re-used and a number of them had architectural features on their underside (pl. XVIII*a–c*). In several cases these features had been badly damaged to make them fit into the floor. It is difficult to suggest to which building the stones had formerly belonged, but

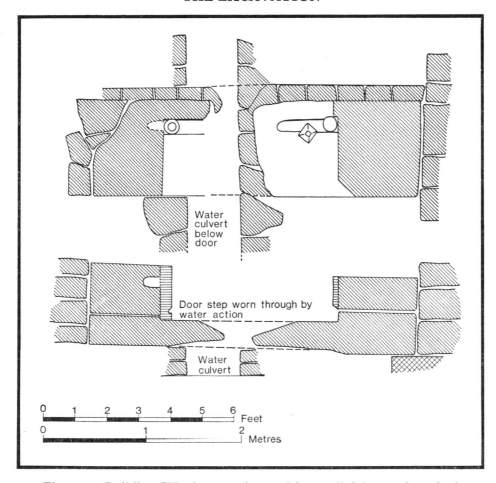

Fig. 15.   Building IX: doorstep in partition wall (plan and section)

several slabs indicate that they had formed part of an archway and they could have been taken either from the nearby eastern portal of the shrine or could equally well belong to the precinct gateway built near Building X. The stone floor was laid in the building shortly after A.D. 350. Forty-five coins were recovered from a layer containing charred wood and fire-ash immediately below it. The coins were badly corroded by fire action, but it was possible to determine that the deposit was sealed in A.D. 350. This agrees with the date given for the termination of the shrine, and represents the beginning of the 'squatter' occupation of the site. The evidence of fire is in accord with similar evidence found in other buildings within the settlement.

A curious stone platform, 4 ft. (1.2 m.) square, built on the late stone floor against the east wall of the building and partially blocking the eastern entrance, was found in the southern part of the building. The platform, like the floor, was composed of re-used architectural features (pl. XVIa).

The burnt material below the floor supports the theory that there was a disastrous fire in the settlement about A.D. 350, and this seems to have hastened the end of the use of the shrine. No attempt appears to have been made to repair it, but on the contrary parts of the building were re-used to form floors and to repair the surrounding buildings, which were later adapted for industrial purposes in the changing character and pattern of the settlement.

In its original form this building was of sound construction and the fact that it was in the precinct wall suggests that it had some initimate connection with the nearby shrine. From its position facing the precinct gateway it is likely to have been the house of the custodian of the shrine or the priest's lodging. Following the fire the building was adapted, probably to house those connected with the pewter industry on the site. This is evident from a small stone-lined hearth constructed in the north-west corner and the stone platform which

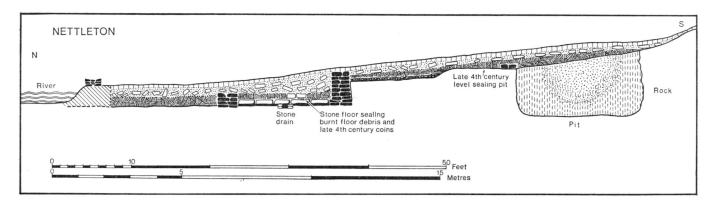

Fig. 16.   North–south section across Building IX, roadway to temple and pit

partially blocked the east doorway (pl. XVI*a*). Only the southern part of the building was used during this later occupation, and the doorway into the northern part was blocked up with stone (pl. XVII*b*). Mention should be made of a small stone drain which was laid beneath the stone floor. From the south-west corner it crossed to the east side of the room before passing under the lintel of the partition doorway into the northern part of the building. Seventeen coins were found in this drain, but they are contemporary with those found in the burnt material beneath the floor. The drain did not have separate coverstones, but was sealed by the floorstones and its sole purpose was to drain the floor area.

Part of a stone furnace was recovered in the north-west corner of the north part of the building. The flue portion was recovered, but the remaining part lies under the present river. On the east side of the building there was an annexe 13 ft. (4.0 m.) wide. This was to the north of the east entrance, but its north part is under the present river.

(d) *The Precinct Shop (Building X)*

This building occupied a central position in the settlement at the point where the north–south road joins the road leading from the Fosse Way to the shrine, and the building was placed in the angle of the two roads. It lay on a north–south axis alongside the north–south road. In its first stage it was 72 ft. (21.9 m.) long and 30 ft. (9.1 m.) wide. Its walls were substantially built, being 4 ft. (1.2 m.) wide at their foundations. Its north-east corner formed the south-west side of the temple precinct gateway. The later retaining wall which was built alongside the road leading to the shrine runs obliquely from its north-east corner in the direction of the shrine (fig. 2). The foundations of a partition wall were found at the north end running apparently lengthwise through it. The strength of the foundations suggests a two-storey building. Its position and plan may indicate that it was used as a shop with a partially open eastern frontage along the street. There would certainly be a need for such a shop where visitors could buy small votive plaques and other similar mementoes of their visit to the shrine. There would also be a need for food and drinks for the traveller. Similar provision was made at the Romano-British settlement at Camerton, near Bath, also on the Fosse Way, where two roadside buildings, similar in plan, were also probably shops, and similar provision was also made at the shrine of Nodens at Lydney, Gloucestershire.

The building in its first phase is dated between A.D. 230 and 250, and supporting evidence for this was a coin of Gallienus found on the floor of the building. An apsidal end, 27 ft. (8.2 m.) long, making the overall length 100 ft. (30 m.) was added later. Coins of Valens and Valentinian I were found in association with this extension. The greater part of this extension had been robbed of its stonework, but the firm edges of the cobbled exterior surrounding remained *in situ*. This addition to the building was apparently destroyed when a dry-stone wall was built from the original south-east corner. This wall took a curved course across the south end of the building and eventually joined the north-east corner of Building XV. The wall, several courses high and constructed with thin slabs of the local limestone, with no mortar, was one of several similar walls found during the course of the excavation where Roman walls had been incorporated in later medieval buildings.

(e) *The Second Hostelry (Building XII)*

This building was erected on the same site as the earlier hostel, No. XI, but was larger than its predecessor, and instead of facing eastwards, it faced south with a courtyard in front. The courtyard also served the nearby Building XIII (fig. 17). From this courtyard a road led westward to the main portal, which gave access to the precinct of the temple of Apollo.

Building XII consisted of a large hall which extended northwards to the riverside and a large reception hall fronting on to the courtyard on its south side. The overall size of the building was 104 ft. (33.6 m.) long north–south, and it had a 70 ft. (11.3 m.) wide southern frontage. The reception hall was 19 ft. (5.8 m.) wide and occupied the whole of the south frontage. Access to the large northern hall, 86 ft. (26.2 m.) in length, was made from the reception hall through two large doorways in the dividing wall. It was not possible to recover the northern end of this building, which lies under the present river, apart from a small fragment of masonry which survived on the north side of the present stream and which is likely to have been the north-west corner of this building. This also applies to the eastern side. The south wall and the partition wall were traced by tunnelling under the modern boundary wall to the edge of the present road, which overlies the walls at this point. A small excavation made on the opposite side of the modern road revealed the footings of a substantial wall running in a north–south direction, and this is likely to be the eastern limit of this building, abutting on to the Fosse Way.

The site would have been a convenient position for a guest-house, where visitors to the shrine could be housed and obtain refreshment. But this large guest-house soon proved to be inadequate to cope with the increasing demands and several additions were made to it.

A partition wall was built across the western end of the reception hall and it is likely that a similar wall was added across its eastern end. The purpose of adding these side chambers is not known, but they may have provided a stairway to reach a possible second storey, with small rooms in the space beneath the stairways.

An annexe was erected alongside the west wall of the building, 22 ft. (6.7 m.) wide. A similar extension made along the south frontage, 11 ft. (3.4 m.) wide, necessitated a re-alignment of the street leading to the temple, and this was altered to cause the roadway to pass along the southern frontage of the new extension. At a later date further extensions were made by adding two additional small compartments on the south-west angle of the building (fig. 2). The larger of the two additions was 16 ft. (4.9 m.) wide and 22 ft. (6.7 m.) long and the smaller room was 11 ft. (3.4 m.) long.

The walls of the original reception hall had an application of red, brown and white painted plaster. The floors of the building had been destroyed, but they are likely to have been paved with pennant slabs; there was no trace of a mosaic pavement nor has any trace of tesserae been noted at Nettleton.

It is likely that the ground floor was used for kitchens and a dining hall. In the absence of partitions on the ground floor to form cubicles for sleeping quarters, it is possible that provision was made on the second floor above the domestic arrangement.

The original hostelry was built soon after A.D. 140 with white mortar. The later building and its additions were built with brown mortar. The coins found on the floor level of this later building range from Gallienus (A.D. 260–8) to Valentinian II (c. A.D. 388), an indication that the larger guest-house was built within a few years of the large octagonal podium surrounding the circular shrine, and the several additions to the building were made in the early years following its construction.

Parts of the building must have been standing in medieval times. The southern extension was certainly used then and a dry-stone wall, constructed across the east end of the extension, had a doorway with a recessed arrangement to house the wooden door frame and there was also a medieval stone door-jamb. It is likely that this wall was built after the construction of the present roadway when the eastern part of the building was destroyed to make way for the new road.

The probable arrangement of the guest-house was a large central enclosed courtyard. On its south side was the large reception hall with two equally spaced entrances into the courtyard. Each entrance was capable of taking horse-drawn vehicles into the central open courtyard, which was surrounded on its four sides by a verandah supported by a series of stone or wooden pillars. At each corner of the courtyard steps gave access to the open verandah, which in turn gave access to a series of rooms or dormitories arranged for guests on the second floor above the domestic establishment. The cloister-like walks beneath the open verandah probably served a similar function for the kitchens and domestic arrangement on the ground floor. In fact the building was very similar to the later medieval court-yard inn. There was a similar arrangement at the shrine of Nodens at Lydney Park, Gloucestershire.

(f) Domestic Dwelling (Building XIV)

This building preceded Building XV, and was later than the first-phase roadway that

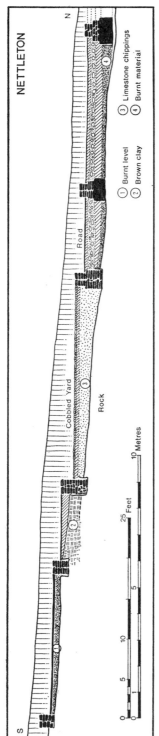

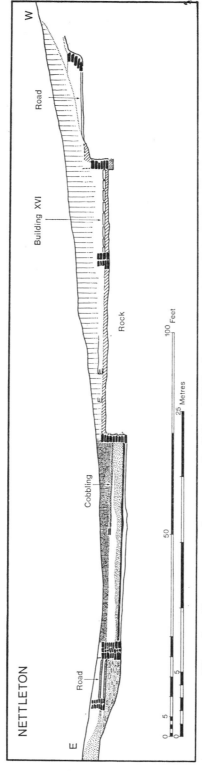

Fig. 17. North–south section across Phase-II hostel (Buildings XII and XIII)

Fig. 18. East–west section across Building XVI, the west road and the Wick valley road

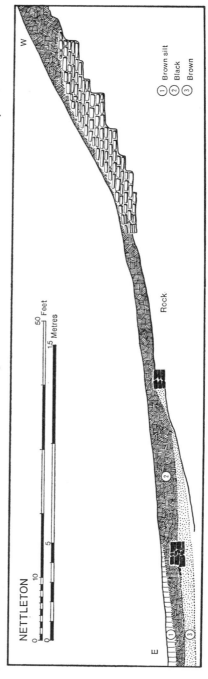

Fig. 19. East–west section across West Bank, showing drystone revetment wall and Building XVIII

crossed the small valley from the Fosse Way to the circular shrine. This roadway ceased to be used after the construction of the octagonal podium of the shrine which was after A.D. 230. The northern part of the building overlay this roadway. The building was set on a slightly different orientation to Building XV which overlies and supersedes it. It was not possible to recover the complete plan of the building, but the northern part was about 40 ft. (12.2 m.) in length, and this wing was 22 ft. (6.7 m.) wide. There was also a wall running in a southerly direction from this wing, suggesting that the building had a south-east frontage facing the main roadway that led into the settlement from the Fosse Way.

(g) *The West Lodge (Building XVI)*

This building appears to have served the same purpose and is of the same simple rectangular plan as Buildings XIX and XVIII. It was situated at the western entrance into the settlement, and its north-west wall served also as the retaining wall for the roadway which passed at a higher level alongside the building (fig. 18). The roadway was cut to make a gentle ascent from the small valley to the higher ground to the west of the settlement. The rusticated boundary wall of the settlement was utilized to form the west wall of the building. This wall, constructed with large blocks of limestone with a rusticated facing, was of the same workmanship as the boundary wall of Building I; and the same rusticated work was used in the octagonal podium of the shrine. Several of the large blocks remained *in situ* on the rock ledge which had been cut back to accommodate the wall. The building was 47 ft. (14.3 m.) in length and 27 ft. (8.2 m.) wide. The western part of the floor consisted of the natural limestone rock, but the east part was paved with large irregularly shaped slabs of limestone.

A good deal of charred material was found on the floor and the finds made from this material also showed signs of burning. It is likely that the building was burnt down in one of the two conflagrations at the settlement. A heavy iron axe-head (fig. 98(30)), found lying in the burnt material on the floor of the building, suggests that this axe was possibly used as a weapon at the time of the raid.

From the north-east corner of the building the retaining wall for the roadway continued for some distance eastward. The area surrounding the north-east and south sides of the building was cobbled to form a yard, and this had a limiting kerb of stones at its eastern limit. A quantity of iron slag together with several lumps of unworked iron recovered from the latest level in this building suggests that it was later used for the purpose of smelting iron (see p. 75). The remains of two stone-constructed furnaces were found immediately outside the south-east wall of the building.

The well-constructed walls of this building with wide offsets were later than the rusticated wall of *c.* A.D. 230, but a coin of Allectus (A.D. 293–6) found in a layer later than its walls, but prior to the major occupation material, gives some indication that it was erected during the period A.D. 230–90. The building continued in use to the late fourth century A.D.

(h) *Domestic Dwelling (Building XVII)*

Built on the west side of the roadway leading south out of the settlement this building was orientated north to south. The west flanking wall alongside the roadway was 112 ft. (31.0 m.) long, before it turned westward and continued towards the high west bank. It was not in alignment with the boundary wall, which was also the west wall of Building XVI, but evidence that there was a connecting wall across the area between the two walls has been found at three separate points. The main wall appears to have followed along the base of the high west bank and was built against and on the natural rock. It appears to have formed the southern limit to the settlement in the second building phase.

Building XVII was 62 ft. (22.7 m.) long and 29 ft. (8.8 m.) wide and the south boundary wall was used as its north wall. The south-west corner of the building was rounded, and from it a later dry-stone wall ran westward across the area at the foot of the western bank to join the bank (fig. 19). This wall, which was several feet high, completely blocked access into the settlement between the building and the west bank, and provided an additional defence on the south-west corner of the settlement (fig. 2). The dry-stone wall terminated at its east end with a large block of limestone, but it did not join the south-west corner of Building XVII by about 9 in. (22.9 cm.). The rock-face had been cut back to a line about 21 ft. (6.4 m.) west of the north-west corner of Building XVII and a revetting wall, built against the rock face, extended from its junction with the south boundary wall in a north-easterly direction.

Above the revetting wall the rock face rises in several terraced platforms and the terraces are revetted with two or more walls parallel with the revetting wall at the foot of the slope. The two parallel walls are not of the same date and differ in construction. The lower wall was well built and mortared, but the higher one was a dry-stone wall of later construction.

Building XVII was set back some 10 ft. (3.0 m.) from the west side of the road and it was probably used as a lodge before the settlement was extended up the valley to the south.

(i) *The Iron Forge or Foundry (Building XXVI)*

This small building, 26 ft. (7.9 m.) by 28 ft. (8.6 m.), occupied the space at the foot of the western slope below Building XVI which was built on the slope alongside the west road into the settlement. The south-west corner survived and was 2 ft. (0.6 m.) high and well built. It appears to have been built to house a large furnace and hearth. The furnace was built in a east–west direction with the chamber at its west end. The chamber cut in the rock was lower than the flue which was constructed also on the solid rock, but about 1 ft. 6 in. (0.46 m.) above the floor of the chamber. On the south side of the chamber there was a well-built stone channel alongside the west wall of the building, and this continued to its junction with the south wall of the building. The flue on the higher level above the chamber was a double one with two small flues divided by a narrow wall, less than 1 ft. (0.3 m.) wide. The flues had been subjected to intense heat, so much so that much of the stonework had disintegrated; both were about 2 ft. 6 in. (0.76 m.) long and beyond them to the east there was evidence of considerable burning. There was also some signs of a second furnace in the north-east corner of the building with a large area of intense red burning. In contrast to the flues there was little or no evidence of burning within the stone chamber, nor was there any in the stone channel leading off from the chamber. This suggests that the chamber served as the stoke-hole for the flues and the stone channel was the means whereby a current of air was conducted to the flues to create the necessary draught for the fire. A quantity of iron slag found within this building and the nearby Building XVI seems to indicate that this building was later used for iron smelting (see p. 75). Two curious lengths of iron were also found lying on the floor within this building (fig. 97(28)).

There was evidence that the building had fallen into disuse, but it was later roughly repaired and altered by the addition of dry-stone walls, in one of which a small statuette (pl. II*b*) was found incorporated.

This building was in close proximity to Building XVI on the western slope, and was evidently built about the same time. The related finds and stratigraphical evidence support this conclusion.

5. THE OCTAGONAL SHRINE AND ITS ASSOCIATED BUILDINGS. PHASE I: AFTER A.D. 250 (fig. 20)

It was some time after A.D. 249 that the circular shrine was destroyed by fire. But the octagonal podium, built around the circular building about A.D. 230 as a support, remained intact after the fire and this, not without some difficulty, was incorporated in the larger temple, octagonal in plan, which replaced the circular shrine on the same site. The construction of this large attractive building points to the continuing popularity of the shrine.

The replacement of the circular building must have been followed by an increasing number of visitors, and important additions to cope with this increase were made to the guest-house (Building XII) on its west side (fig. 2) (see p. 32). Alterations and additions were also made to Building XIII (fig. 2) (see p. 18) and the building on the west slope of the settlement was also replaced by a larger corridor building. It is likely that Buildings I, II and III excavated by Priestley on the north side of the river were also built about this time (figs. 2 and 34) (see pp. 57–8). Building I is certainly not earlier than this phase, but it could be later and this also applies to the small angle of wall representing Building II (fig. 2). The walls of the three buildings look from the surviving photographs to be typical of other structures of this phase. The buildings erected during this period do not display the same superior type of workmanship as in the preceding phase and the walls give the appearance of having been hastily erected.

(a) *The Octagonal Shrine. Phase I (Building VI)*

Two little used coins of Gordianus (A.D. 240) and Philip the Arab (A.D. 249) found in the burnt debris below the floor of the later shrine are an indication that the fire which destroyed the circular shrine occurred after A.D. 249 and the elaborate octagonal shrine described below replaced the circular shrine during or soon after A.D. 250. We do not know the cause of the fire, but it is known that Irish pirates were raiding and plundering across the Severn in south-west Wales about A.D. 275, and it is possible therefore that the temple was destroyed by raiders from the Bristol Channel, which is but little more than 18 miles west of Nettleton.[35]

It was not considered worthwhile to rebuild the circular building and the new shrine, built on the same site, incorporated the podium with the octagonal revetting wall of the former arrangement which had survived the fire. The new structure was so different in plan that it is evident that a fresh style of architecture had now been introduced.[36] The new building, octagonal in plan, consisted of an outer octagonal wall with a series of internal radiating walls (pl. XI*a, b*) converging from each angle of the octagonal wall towards the centre of the building, to form a series of eight chambers surrounding the central shrine. However, the two southern radial walls were constructed as elongated piers at this phase and access could

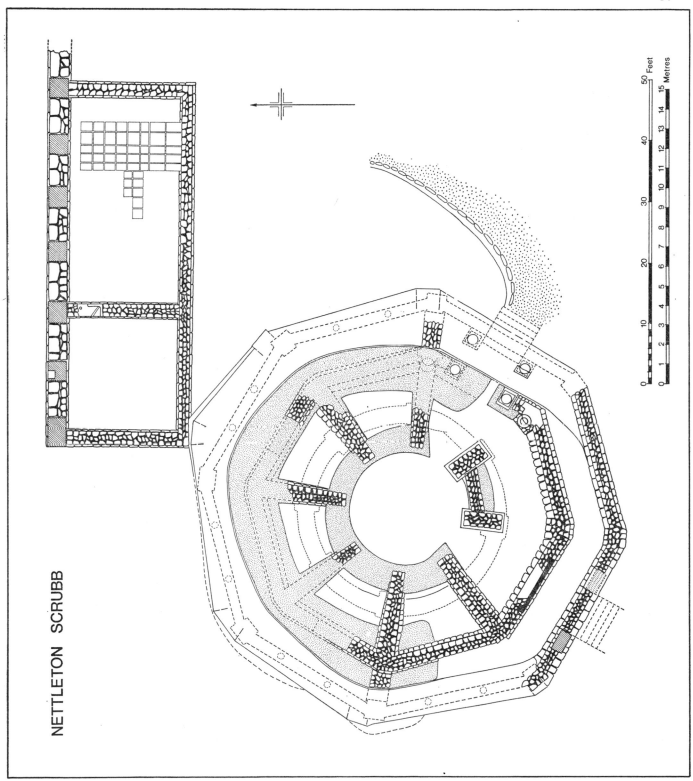

NETTLETON SCRUBB

Fig. 20. Plan of octagonal temple (Phases II and III) and riverside building (Phase II)

be made to the southern chamber through doorways on either side of the chamber (fig. 20). The radial walls were 3 ft. (0.9 m.) wide at the octagon angle, but tapered towards the centre, where they reduced to 2 ft. (0.6 m.) in width. The converging ends of the eight radial walls supported a series of eight round arches, forming a central octagonal shrine 22 ft. (6.7 m.) in diameter (pl. XIc).

In plan the building resembled an octagonal cartwheel, the radial walls representing the spokes and the central shrine the hub. The outer octagonal wall was encompassed by the surrounding stone platform or podium of the former building, and its outer wall was built up to form a covered, open-sided, colonnaded verandah. The columns and angle pilasters on the outer wall supported a pent roof which covered the area between the original outer octagonal retaining wall and the octagonal wall of the new building, to form an ambulatory or covered walk surrounding the new building (pl. XIa, b). The overall diameter of the octagonal temple, including the outer remaining wall and ambulatory, was 70 ft. (21.3 m.).

A considerable amount of preparatory work preceded the construction of the new building. Additional foundations were necessary on the northern part of the made-up platform within the perimeter of the podium wall to carry the additional weight of the new structure and a crescent-shaped foundation, 6 ft. (1.8 m.) in width, was inserted within the perimeter of the podium wall (figs. 21, 22). There was also a second horseshoe- or crescent-shaped foundation, 4 ft. (1.2 m.) wide, inserted just within the inner curve of the former circular temple foundations and the two foundations were connected or tied in to each other by a series of six radial spoke-like foundations. The heavy, deep foundations in each instance were placed on the stable limestone, and the rock slope was cut back to form a series of ledges to ensure against movement or slip of the foundations, which would threaten the stability of the new structure (fig. 21). The foundations were made with large blocks of newly quarried local limestone, and each layer was laid alternately on edge in herring-bone fashion, with a layer of consolidating brown clay between each course of stone. Foundations were not required on the south part of the platform. The rock platform, made when the podium was built, provided ample stability for the walls of the new building. The additional outer crescent-shaped foundation carried the main octagonal wall of the building and the radial foundations performed a similar function for its radial walls. The inner sleeper-wall foundation supported the converging terminals of the radial walls, carrying a series of round arches between each pair of radial walls, to form the central shrine. The arches in turn carried the weight of a central octagonal superstructure (fig. 31).

The builders of the new temple preserved the circular temple foundations and this added to the difficulties of construction (pl. XIIIa, b). A general clearance of the circular temple foundations would have obviated the need for two separate sleeper walls within the perimeter of the podium wall foundation (figs. 21, 22). The preservation of the earlier foundations, below the floor of the new building, suggests a lingering sentimental regard for the former circular shrine (pl. XIXa).

The builders also experienced considerable difficulty in incorporating the original outer octagonal podium wall in the new octagonal structure. The south and south-west walls of the outer octagonal wall, on the rock platform, were demolished and completely rebuilt, and its buttresses brought into correct alignment with the angles of the new octagonal building (pl. VIb). But the buttresses or pilasters on the surviving retaining wall were not in alignment

with those on the new plan, and in several instances the difference in alignment was as much as 2 ft. (0.6 m.). It was essential that all the outer buttresses should be correctly aligned, so that they could properly fulfil their function and take the thrust of the radial walls of the new building, which in turn carried the weight of the vaulted chambers and also took the thrust of the radial walls of the new building. These carried the weight of the vaulted chambers and also took the thrust of the vaulted central superstructure. To correct this planning error, a new wall with correctly aligned buttresses was erected on the platform within the line of the original wall cornice. This adjustment in alignment is clearly shown on the west

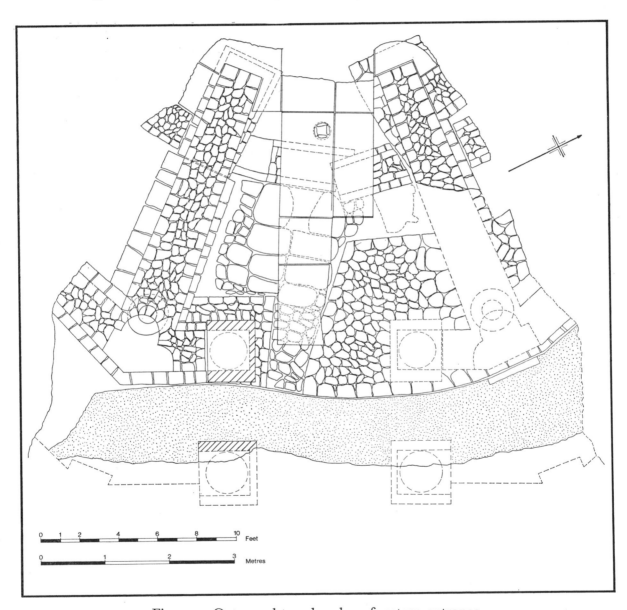

Fig. 23.   Octagonal temple: plan of eastern entrance

side of the building, where the buttress of the new alignment is placed to the south of the former buttress foundation and partially overlies it (fig. 20).

On the north-west and north-east angles of the octagonal building the radial wall foundations extended beyond the inner octagonal wall as sleeper walls below the ambulatory floor, to tie in with the outer octagonal wall, and on the north-west side this was superimposed upon the surviving stonework of the former phase-II building. This precautionary measure guarded against severe stresses or movement at this vulnerable point on either side of the building, where the hillside slope unites with the built-up podium, and the most likely point where slip or settlement was likely.

The octagonal temple was entered by way of an eastern entrance-porch or vestibule, which gave access to the central area of the temple and also by means of doors on either side of the vestibule into the surrounding ambulatory. A second entrance, by way of a flight of steps from the higher ground outside the temple to the south-west, also gave access to the ambulatory. Immediately opposite this entrance, a large window in the inner octagonal wall provided light and a view into the closed central shrine.

Entry into the central shrine was made by way of an arched portal, one of eight which formed the sides of the octagonal central shrine. Set in a prominent position on the floor of the central shrine was an altar bearing a dedicatory inscription to the god Apollo (see p. 135). The open arches gave access to chambers formed by the radial walls and windows in the outer walls provided light into the central shrine (fig. 31).

The roof of the central shrine was vaulted and carried a painted plaster design. The vault above the arches probably had a series of small semi-circular windows to provide light to the central area below. Above the vaulted roof there was probably a stone lantern, with a series of small vents or windows.

The main details of the octagonal shrine are described in more detail below.

Eastern Entrance (pl. XXIa, figs. 23, 24)

The main entrance, 7 ft. (2.1 m.) in width, lay on the east side of the temple and was approached by way of a metalled roadway, which led to a short flight of steps, built partially within the width of the podium wall. The steps led up to the stone platform on which the shrine was built, and at the top of the steps large rectangular limestone blocks on either side formed the base for the entrance portal columns (figs. 23, 24). The mortar matrix on which one of the columns stood was found on the surface of the outer wall foundation. Columns on either side of the entrance carried capitals fashioned in the plain heavy Doric (Tuscan) style (pl. XXa), one being found lying at the south side of the main entrance portal. The capitals probably supported an architrave on which was placed a small pediment.

The Vestibule

Within the entrance, the four piers of the inner and outer portals formed a small square porch which gave access to the central shrine. The piers of the outer entrance partially protruded into the width of the ambulatory walk (fig. 23). By this arrangement the entrance into the ambulatory was constricted to enable a door about 3 ft. (0.9 m.) wide to be placed on either side of the porch, so that the ambulatory might be closed.

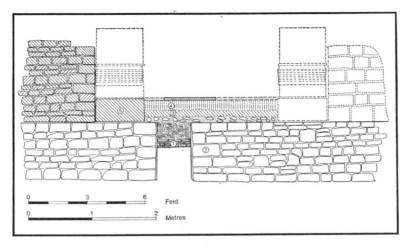

Fig. 24. North–south section across eastern entrance of octagonal temple.

Key: 1, circular temple (Phase I)   4, pennant floor (Phase IV)
2, octagonal temple (Phase III)   5, south-east entrance pier
3, *opus signinum* floor (Phase III)

The Romano-British temple at Pagans Hill, Chew Stoke, Somerset, had a similar arrangement (fig. 25).[37]

The Inner Portal

The main entrance into the Nettleton shrine from the vestibule was made by way of an inner portal, flanked on either side by columns set on large rectangular blocks of limestone. One block found *in situ* on the south side was 2 ft. 3 in. (0.69 m.) by 2 ft. (0.61 m.) and 1 ft. 3 in. (0.38 m.) thick, and the mortar impression of the column base that stood on the block, not more than 2 ft. (0.61 m.) square, could be clearly traced (pl. XXI*a*). It is likely that the three heavy column bases and the large capital, found within the central area and forming part of the late temporary shrine, are those that formerly stood at the outer and inner portals of the east entrance (pl. XXI*b*, fig. 77(4–6)). They are all of the same type and have been turned on the lathe (see pp. 188–90). The bases are 1 ft. 8 in. (0.51 m.) square and they fit the mortar impression left when the column base was removed from the block. The large circular capital, also lathe-turned, probably came from the outer portal (pl. XX*b*). It is likely that the heavy capital, found at the east entrance, came from the inner portal (pl. XX*a*). This capital has two projections which indicate that it was attached to walls in opposing directions, presumably the octagon wall, and the lintel of the ambulatory doorway. It was probably re-used from the circular temple.

The Ambulatory (fig. 26, pl. VIb)

The ambulatory or covered walk between the two octagonal walls on the platform was 6 ft. 6 in. (1.95 m.) wide and completely encompassed the new building. Entry to the

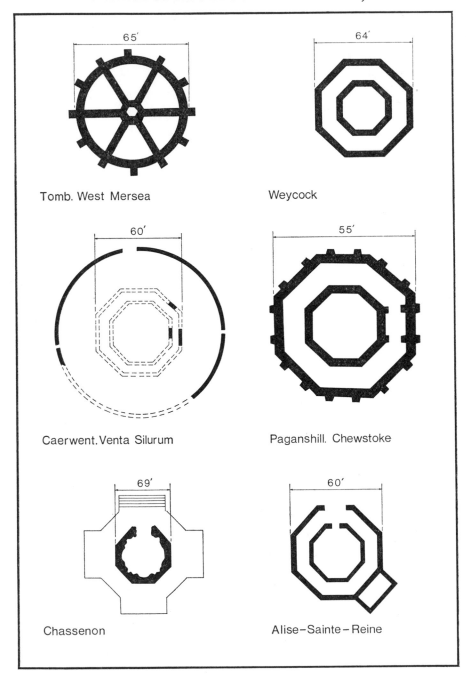

Fig. 25.   Comparative plans of octagonal temples, etc.

ambulatory could be made from the vestibule, or from outside by way of the south-west entrance, and also from the hall on the north-east side of the shrine. The floor was paved with square slabs of blue pennant limestone, but very little remained *in situ* as it was re-used by the later squatters when the temple was converted into a homestead soon after A.D. 330 (fig. 26, pl. XXIV*b*).

The ambulatory floor level was raised above the former floor level of the circular temple when the octagonal temple was built. The inner wall of the ambulatory was plastered and decorated, but only the lower part of the design survived. It had a yellow or ochre coloured background with a panelled design, with a dado 1 ft. 7 in. (0.48 m.) wide in dark red, speckled with white and blue to simulate marble. Above this was a white band ½ in. (1.27 cm.)

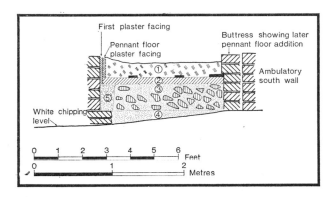

Fig. 26.   North–south section across south ambulatory of octagonal temple

Key: 1, squatter floor   3, floor make-up
     2, pennant floor   4, brown mortar

wide, next a band of Neapolitan red 4 in. (10.1 cm.) wide, followed by a white band 5 in. (12.7 cm.) wide, and after this a second band of Neapolitan red 2 in. (5 cm.) wide, completed by a 1 in. (2.5 cm.) wide egg-shell blue band. It is likely that the ochre-coloured panels carried a central design of flowers and foliage. Plaster fragments recovered from the ambulatory floor bore traces of floral and foliage decoration (pl. XLI*a*). The outer wall of the ambulatory had buttresses or pilasters at each angle of the octagon, which supported the pent roof, and it was additionally supported by two columns that stood at equal spaces between the angle buttresses and this formed an open verandah. Two of the verandah columns were found where they had fallen from the ambulatory wall-bench on the north side of the building (pl. XXIV*a*). Another was found in a similar position on the north-east angle, and fragments of others were noted on the west side. The wall-bench was capped with chamfered limestone slabs bearing a chevron and cable border design (pl. XXV*a*).

The open-sided ambulatory must have been a delightful place in summer time overlooking the nearby river (pl. XI*b*). The pent roof of the ambulatory probably had a timber frame to carry the weight of the Cotswold stone tiled roof. Many pennant stone tiles and other roof debris, including tiles with iron nails in the fixing-holes, were found alongside the outer wall where they had fallen from the pent roof.

Ambulatory Aedicula (fig. 27)

On passing from the vestibule through the doorway into the south walk of the ambulatory, there was on the right a small aedicula or shrine constructed within the width of the octagonal wall, at the angle where it is joined by the radial wall. It was in a good state of preservation and 3 ft. 1 in. (0.92 m.) in diameter with sides 4 ft. (1.2 m.) in height from the ambulatory floor level. A small part of the apsidal roof of the aedicula survived. It was built partially

Fig. 27.   Artist's view of *aedicula* above votive pit in the south-east angle of the inner ambulatory wall of the octagonal temple (from south-east)

over a small circular stone-lined pit, set within the width of the angle foundation of the octagonal wall.

The lower filling of the underlying stone pit (fig. 27) consisted of much burnt material and contained nine coins as follows:

1 Faustina II   A.D. 161–75
1 Gordianus   A.D. 240–4
2 Gallienus   A.D. 260–8

and the remainder, although not readily identifiable, not later than A.D. 270. Mixed with the burnt material were a number of small rodent bones and egg-shell, probably remnants of a rodent nest made at a later date within the pit. The upper filling of the niche consisted of building rubble and plaster. The back wall of the semi-circular niche was built over and spanned the centre of the pit below. This was probably due to a planning error in relating the pit, which was built when the temple foundations were put in, to the freestanding walls.

There is no evidence to suggest that the pit was built at an earlier date than the niche above. The aedicula was plastered and traces of a design could be seen on its back wall, but not enough to identify the design employed. The sides of the aedicula had only one rendering of plaster, and close inspection indicated that slabs of wood or marble had been placed as a decorative feature against the plaster face before it had set. The mortar impression of the adhering slabs could be clearly traced, suggesting decorative panels on either side of the aedicula. It is likely that the niche housed a small statue, or an altar, and that this stood on a wooden base overlying the votive pit. The ambulatory floor directly opposite the aedicula was discoloured red to some depth by fire action, in much the same way as were the floor levels of the former circular temple. This burning must have continued over a considerable period of time to account for the intense discoloration of the floor which had been repaired and was tightly packed. This was no doubt due to constant use by visitors who may have made their obeisance before the aedicula. It is likely that a similar aedicula occupied a matching position on the north side.

A similar aedicula was discovered at the Lullingstone Roman villa, but the pit was square and was intended to contain water. The niche was built in much the same way with an apsidal top, but it was not as large. It also had painted plaster walls, with a design representing the three river nymphs.[38]

The stone pedestal found on the right hand side of the Lydney Park temple entrance probably held a statue, and served a similar purpose.

The South-west Entrance

The south-west entrance was approached by way of a flight of stone steps, through the outer octagonal wall, into the ambulatory. The entrance was 7 ft. 6 in. (2.25 m.) wide and was flanked on either side by columns set on rectangular blocks of limestone; one of the blocks, 1 ft. 9 in. (0.53 m.) by 3 ft. 6 in. (1.07 m.), was found in situ (pl. XXIVb). This doorway was directly opposite the large window in the inner octagonal wall. The precinct area to the south of the steps leading down to the south-west entrance to the shrine was cobbled, but there was no evidence of a roadway west from the shrine.

North Entrance

There was some evidence to suggest an entrance into the northern sector through the inner octagonal temple wall. The small surviving fragment of this wall had a squared end indicating a possible doorway. The podium foundations are much wider at the point where they make contact with the south-west corner of the large rectangular Building VII. We were fortunate to recover a hard well-worn surface near the point of junction with the nearby rectangular building. The doorway placed opposite the wider retaining wall foundation, and the hard surface, suggest an entry into the hall below by way of a flight of steps from the temple.

The Windows

The one large surviving window in the octagonal wall on the south-west angle was of unusual interest (fig. 28, pl. XXVIIb). The window opening was 5 ft. (1.5 m.) wide on the outside, with splayed sides to permit the maximum light. The timber window frame was built into the wall with two upright timber supports on either side of the window set in a wooden sill. A similar timber lintel over the head of the window stabilized the four uprights

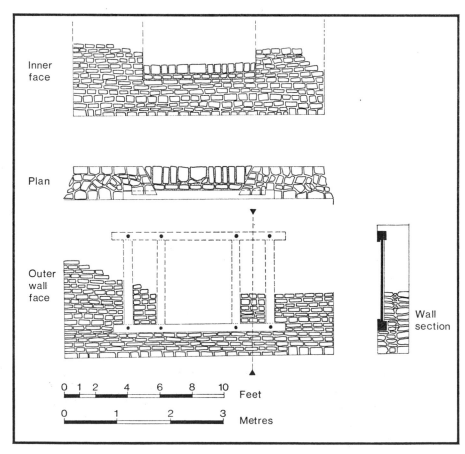

Fig. 28.   Octagonal temple: plan, elevations and section of window in
inner west wall of ambulatory

and this completed the wooden framework of the window. The window sill was 1 ft. 6 in. (0.46 m.) above the ambulatory floor (pl. XXIV*b*).

It was possible to determine the exact dimensions of the window sill, which was 6 in. (15.2 cm.) square, by the mortar impression and by the stone additions inserted by the squatter occupants when the wooden sill was still in position. The window-sill beam extended

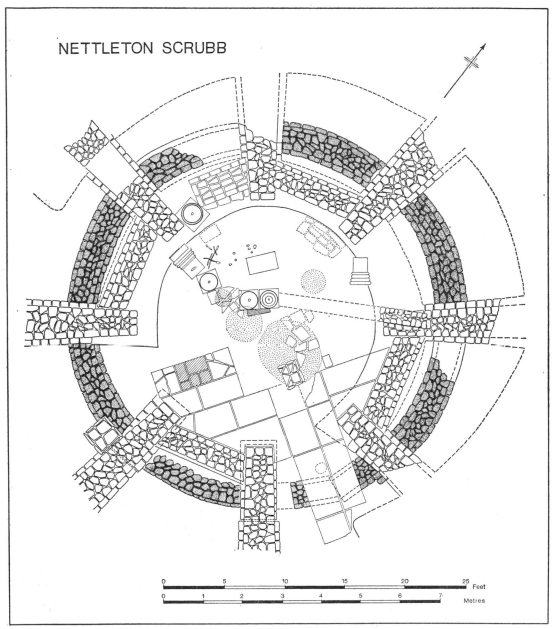

NETTLETON SCRUBB

Fig. 29. Plan of central area of octagonal temple superimposed on earlier circular temple, with detail of the improvised shrine to north and squatter farmstead to south

beyond the normal width of the window 2 ft. 6 in. (0.76 m) on either side, and it supported the additional upright window timbers. The upright timbers and the sill extensions were built into the wall in sockets, and the timbers were flush with the wall surface. The timber joints were secured by large round-headed nails. The nails, with large heads 2 in. (2.5 cm.) in diameter, were found on the floor, where they had fallen from the window frame.

A number of arch-stones found lying alongside the window are likely to have fallen from a relieving arch set above the lintel of the window frame, and there was probably a small decorative tympanum in the space between the timber lintel and the relieving arch. The timber inserts on either side of the window are unusual. The recessed space between the window and the inserted timber uprights was 2 ft. 6 in. (0.76 m.) on either side, which was half the width of the window. The recessed space on each side allowed for wooden shutters to fit flush against the wall, when they were not used to close the window. The shutters no doubt slid in grooves on the window sill. The evidence suggests that similar windows were placed in the north-east and north-west walls of the octagon.

Visiting worshippers to the shrine were not likely to have had access to the sanctuary, where the dedicatory altars of the shrine were housed. Provision was made to observe the ceremonies in the central shrine through the windows from the ambulatory, without entering the surrounding chambers or central octagonal shrine.[39]

The Southern Sector

The south sector of the building was not enclosed at this stage, but, in place of the two radial walls, two large rectangular piers, 2 ft. 6 in. (0.76 m) wide and 6 ft. (1.8 m.) in length, supported the stone arch facing on to the central area and arches spanned the space between the piers and the octagonal wall (figs. 29, 30). The archway facing the central shrine was blocked by a partition wall, forming an ante-chamber to the south of the central shrine. Entry to this south chamber was made through the arched doorways on either side of the chamber.

The Central Shrine (fig. 29)

After passing through the eastern sector from the vestibule the central shrine was reached; octagonal in form, it was 22 ft. (6.7 m.) in diameter. From the many voussoirs (in one instance several voussoirs were found still engaged together with brown mortar) we were able to determine that the arch-span was 6 ft. (1.8 m.), and an arch was reconstructed (pl. XXVIIIb). The spaces between the converging ends of the two piers and six radial walls were spanned by eight round arches, each 6 ft. (1.8 m.) in diameter (fig. 31) and they rested upon an impost or cornice set on the ends of the radial walls.

The building debris which completely covered the temple walls was composed of masses of collapsed tufa-vaulting, painted plaster, limestone, and mortar. In several instances, in the chambers and the central area the tufa lay in an integrated mass on the floor where it had fallen from the vaulted roof (pl. XXXIIa, b). This vaulting was supported by a series of limestone ribs made up from 20 or more dressed stone blocks. The ribs were probably held in position at the top of the vault by a central key-stone, and they rested on the corniced ends of the radial walls (pls. XIc, XXXIIa, b). A collapsed rib was found in the central shrine area,

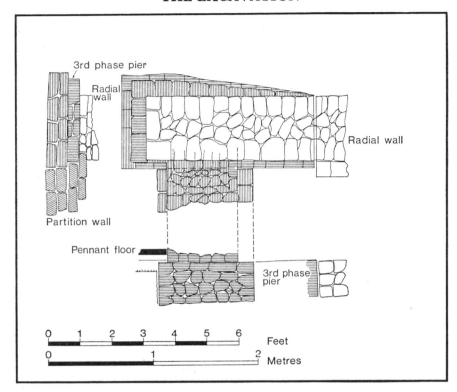

Fig. 30. Octagonal temple: plan and section of south-east radial wall
showing Phase-III and IV masonry

and this together with the fallen tufa, which gives the curve of the vault, suggests a possible interior reconstruction.

Abundant evidence of the use of tufa was found throughout the building especially in the western sector, where a piece of the collapsed vault was found intact with the painted plaster adhering to the tufa blocks. The tufa was of local Cotswold origin, and was cut and trimmed with a mason's saw to the required shape to fit into the vaulted roof (pl. XXXIIc).[40] The use of calcareous tufa in the construction of domed or vaulted roofs is well attested both in Roman and later medieval buildings in Britain. Its peculiar lightness, the ease with which it was cut when 'fresh' and its durability made it the ideal material for this purpose.

It is likely that the central vault had a series of semi-circular apertures or windows set above the arches in the central area at a sufficient height to give clearance above the roofs of the surrounding chambers. The floor of the central area at this stage was made up with *opus signinum* (pl. XXIXb). The greater part of the chief altar base, of cut limestone blocks, was found *in situ* a little south of the central position in the shrine.

The Side Chambers

Apart from the eastern chamber, which gave access from the vestibule into the central shrine, the purpose of the seven chambers is difficult to assess. The south-west sector had a large window in the ambulatory wall (see pp. 46–8). The lower courses of this wall in the

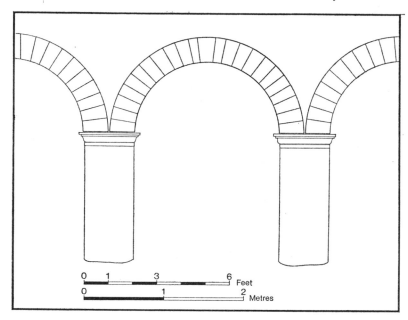

Fig. 31. Octagonal temple: reconstruction of arcade in central area

north and west chambers each had a straight, mortared joint, indicating that there had been a doorway from the chamber into the ambulatory. The ambulatory wall of the south-east and south-west chambers survived to a height of between 2 and 3 ft., which was higher than the surviving window sill in the south-west wall and there was no sign of a window or doorway in either of these chambers from the ambulatory. The ambulatory wall in the north-east and north-west chambers had been completely destroyed. It would appear that the alternate chambers did not have either doorway or window in their ambulatory walls, and the only means of access, at this stage, was by way of the arched entrance from the central shrine.

The construction of the octagonal shrine, with its radial chambers, coincides with the building of the partition wall across the interior of the nearby rectangular hall (Building VII). This suggests that the larger octagonal shrine made provision for part of the former functional purpose of the hall, and it was transferred to the shrine. A possible theory is that the chambers may have been used as supporting chapels around the central shrine.

A second theory is suggested by the plan at Lydney Park, Gloucestershire, where a number of small cells are thought to have been used by pilgrims to the temple of Nodens. The pilgrims, it is suggested, may have slept in the cells hoping that they might receive a visit in their dreams from the god whose help they had come to seek.[41] This second suggested use was the most likely purpose of the chambers in the Nettleton octagonal shrine. The chambers provided the means for a more intimate association for visiting pilgrims than had hitherto been possible in the large rectangular hall. The hall was accordingly altered to make provision for a large narthex at its west end, and this served as an assembly point for pilgrims, prior to ascending the steps which gave access to the shrine from the hall.

The collapsed vaulting suggests that the surrounding chambers, enclosed by the radial walls, each had a separate vaulted roof with an exterior covering of Cotswold stone tiles (pl. XXXIIa, b).

A feature of some interest was the method used in the radial wall construction at roof level. The west radial wall was the only one surviving to this height (7 ft. — 2.1 m.) and had a number of stone blocks placed lengthwise along the centre core of the wall with a series of stone blocks placed slantwise along either side. The central line of stones was clearly placed to act as a wedge or buffer support to the sloping stones on either side of the wall and were, with little doubt, the surviving base course of the vault which covered the side chambers.

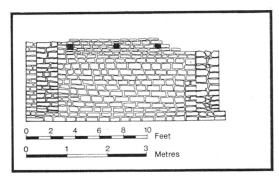

Fig. 32.   Octagonal temple: Phase-III radial
wall with put-log holes

Several large pieces of stone guttering, found within the temple, were probably used to convey rainwater from the central and radial roofs and pent roof of the surrounding ambulatory. The stone guttering was probably placed in the valleys formed by the radial chamber roofs.

Put-log or dowel holes were found in the west radial wall and in the octagonal wall to the north of the large west window. The dowel holes were 5 in. (12.7 cm.) square and they were placed 5 ft. (1.3 m.) above the offset of the wall foundation (fig. 32). They were carried through the width of the wall but they had been blocked up with small blocks of tufa, presumably when the building operation was completed. The dowel holes were possibly used to house supports for the vaulting during its construction. No other walls survived to sufficient height for other dowel holes to be identified, but they are an indication that the temple walls were carried to a sufficient height to necessitate the use of scaffolding.

Painted Plaster

The greater part of the walls within the shrine was faced with plaster painted with a variety of colours. The paintings included patterned panels of flowers and foliage and paintings portraying the human form (pl. XLIb). In two cases it was possible to photograph the design *in situ*. These were on the inner faces of the partition walls which blocked the north and west sectors from the central shrine, and are described in detail on pp. 63–4 (fig. 36, pl. XLIIa, b). Painted plaster was also found *in situ* in the south and west chambers, the eastern entrance sector, the south walk of the ambulatory and the small *aedicula* in the ambulatory. Fragments of painted plaster were found in abundance throughout the shrine in the building debris, and some with a floral design were found below the squatter level in the south walk of the ambulatory. The plaster from each part of the shrine was kept separate, and this has enabled us to give some indication of the design and colour scheme used in the building (pp. 182–8 and figs. 75, 76).

Painted plaster was found still adhering to the collapsed mass of tufa vaulting from the central area and the western sector of the shrine. A number of fragments, including the human head specimen, had a concave surface, a further indication that it came from vaulting. The plaster recovered from the central area of the shrine had a black encrustation on the painted surface, caused, no doubt, by the open fires of the later squatters. The whole of the vaulted central area and the surrounding chambers was vaulted and the plastered surface had painted designs, which included a representation of the human form, possibly that of the god Apollo (see pl. XLI*b*, *c*).

Several fragments of plaster had two applications of painted plaster, an indication that the design and colour scheme were changed. Two coats were found *in situ* on the inner face of the eastern partition wall (fig. 33).

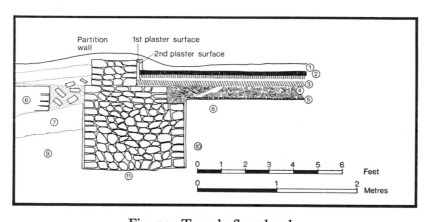

Fig. 33. Temple floor levels

Key: 1, squatter level   6, circular temple wall
      2, pennant floor   7, 8, gravel
      3, *opus signinum* floor   9, 10, limestone
      4, burnt layer   11, inner sleeper wall of octago-
      5, pebble floor   nal temple

External Appearance of the Temple

The dominating feature of the temple on its east side was its entrance. A well-made approach road led up to the steps that gave access to the platform or podium on which the octagonal temple was built. The rusticated octagonal retaining wall, capped with its projecting cornice at the podium floor level, carried a shallow rainwater gutter. A low bench-like wall surrounded the ambulatory, and at the angles supporting buttresses, augmented by two sturdy columns placed on the wall-bench between each angle of the octagon, formed an open verandah. On either side of the entrance, large columns set on stone bases were capped with heavy Doric (Tuscan) type capitals and these were probably surmounted with an architrave, which in turn carried an arched tympanum (fig. 24) set in the gable end of the vestibule roof to form a porch. We have no clue as to what type of door was used, but the doorway was 7 ft. (2.1 m.) wide, an indication that it was two-leaved.

Above the pent roof of the ambulatory the gable ends of the supporting radial chambers surrounded the central octagonal structure. From the mass of stone tiles found around the building it is probable that the vault of each chamber supported a stone tile roof, and the central octagon was probably also roofed with Cotswold tiles.[42] The summit of the central octagonal roof was no doubt surmounted with a decorative finial, similar perhaps to the fine finial found on the floor of the nearby rectangular Building VII (pl. XXXIIIb). The gable ends of the surrounding chambers probably carried matching finials similar to that found slightly east of the temple (pl. XXXIIIa). To the south-east, the building was dominated by higher ground. It is possible that the western entrance also had a porch-like roof built against the gable end of the western chamber.

The northern aspect of the temple was by far the most impressive, where the rusticated podium wall, on which the temple stood, could be seen at its maximum height of at least 9 ft. (2.7 m.). The open verandah above the wall, the gable ends of the chambers, and the octagonal central structure towering above the nearby rectangular building, with its river-side frontage, must have made an impressive sight in its beautiful rural setting (pl. XIb).

The overall diameter of the temple was 70 ft. (21.3 m.) and assuming that the building was about half its diameter in height, this would make the building 35 ft. (10.7 m.) high as seen from the east side, but from its north aspect alongside the river the height would be accentuated by at least 9 ft. (2.7 m.).

Temple Dedication

An inscribed altar found within the central shrine near the entrance to the north-east sector, where it had been used as a hearth-side seat by the later squatter occupants, bore the following inscription (pl. XXXIV):

DEO APOL/LINI CVNO/MAGLO CO/ROTICA IV/TI FIL VSLM

The accepted interpretation of this inscription is:

'To the God Apollo Cunomaglos Corotica, daughter of Iutus, willingly and deservedly fulfilled her vow' (see pp. 135–6).[43]

Professor K. Jackson notes that Cunomaglos means Hound Prince; 'hound' has an honorific force in Celtic.

The altar found within the central shrine suggested that the shrine was primarily dedicated to the god Apollo and this suggestion was further confirmed by the following finds:

(1) A small bronze plaque found on the floor of the later shrine, in the north part of the central shrine; it bears a representation of the god Apollo, with a punched inscription which reads (frontispiece and fig. 61):

D·A·POL / DECIMIVS

(2) Fine bronze ring (fig. 92(7)). The bezel retains a known representation of the god Apollo (see pp. 214–15).

(3)   A small finial fashioned in clay found in Building X (pl. XXXI*b* and fig. 58) bears a representation of a cock's head (see p. 138).

(4)   The small bronze figure of a cockerel (pl. XXXI*a*), found by Priestley on the site of Building I (see p. 143). The cockerel was an attribute of the god Apollo.

(5)   There is also the piece of statuary found in 1825, on the site of Building I (pl. II*a*). The stone relief bears the lower part of a representation of Diana, the twin sister of Apollo, with her hound (see p. 136).

The finds collectively indicate and place beyond reasonable doubt that the shrine was primarily dedicated to the god Apollo (pl. XXIII*a*). Shrines built in honour of Apollo are often found in association with the rural scene. He was the patron of flocks and herds as well of music and the arts.[44] The cult was likewise associated with, and is thought to have supplanted, the pre-Roman North British god of youth and music, Maponus, whose sanctuary has been identified at Clochmabonstane, a megalithic circle on the north shore of the Solway Firth.[45]

Nettleton was certainly not lacking in these attributes. It lies in a delightful scene of rural beauty and tranquillity, in countryside 'far from the madding crowd', and the scene is one whose natural features would provide the desired surroundings for the home of a god.[46]

It is possible that the temple of Apollo at Nettleton was a perpetuation of an earlier Celtic ritual site.[47] Celtic ritual worship was conducted in similar sites, *Nemetona*, or sacred groves, in the vicinity of rivers, lakes, or spring-heads.

(b) *The Rectangular Temple (after Priestley) (Building I)*

This building was the most important of those excavated by the late Mr. W. C. Priestley in 1943–5 on the north side of the Broadmead Brook. The only known surviving account of its excavation is contained in a copy of a letter by him to the late Mr. J. P. Bushe-Fox, and is partially reproduced on pp. 55–7).

The overall measurement of the building was 64 ft. (19.5 m.) long and 24 ft. (7.3 m.) wide, with an entrance on its south-east corner. Although Priestley does not say so in his letter, it is quite clear that the back (north) wall is earlier than the walls which are built against it, and it is equally clear that the walls are of the same type as several late buildings on the south side of the river (pl. III*a*). Priestley mentions that 'not much pottery has come out from the lower level of the shrine except several incomplete hard-baked thumb vases, having a purplish hue. Some coins have turned up (3rd or 4th century) from the same level.' The pottery, from the description given, must be New Forest ware. Priestley does not make it clear what the 'lower levels' were, but it would appear that the building was of fourth-century date, if the New Forest ware and Constantinian coins came from the same level. The small drain that ran from the rock face through the building is comparable with the late drain found in Building IX, and served the same purpose of conveying water from the rock face to the river. The cover stones for this drain look very much like re-used pennant stone tiles in the photograph (pl. XII*c*). There are also a number of broken stone tiles on the floor of the building. The wall foundations in the picture are quite shallow and rest on earth. Large lumps of uncut limestone are incorporated in the walls, and they are not substantial enough to carry a heavy superstructure (pl. III*a*). The north wall of the building rests on the native rock, and is of the same character as the wall at the rear of Building XVI, and the rusticated podium wall of the second phase shrine (pl. XIIb).

If the rusticated wall was earlier than the building it is likely that the sculpture found in this wall was also earlier. The rusticated wall was an exterior feature and Building I was built to incorporate the wall as its northern limit (see pp. 99–100).

Priestley's letter to Mr. Bushe-Fox runs as follows:

'I am enclosing some details of an excavation I have been carrying out for several seasons at Nettleton . . . which I think may interest you. . . .

'Between Bath and Cirencester the site of a Roman settlement at Whitewalls in the parish of Easton Gray is well known. This "Station" being 12 miles from Cirencester and 18 from Bath, I felt convinced that another "post" must exist somewhere in the latter section. . . . Gaining permission to dig . . . we soon struck the foundations of a medieval building, which was excavated [see p. 98] . . . Haverfield's *Roman Britain 1913* (Journal of Roman Studies) on page 49 briefly describes the discovery of some structural remains . . . of what appeared to be the site of one of the small square, Romano-British temples at Nettleton Scrubb. This I decided to follow up [fig. 34]. After removing the remains of the lime-kilns, we got down to the Roman walling mentioned by Haverfield. The N-W corner of this excavated structure shows

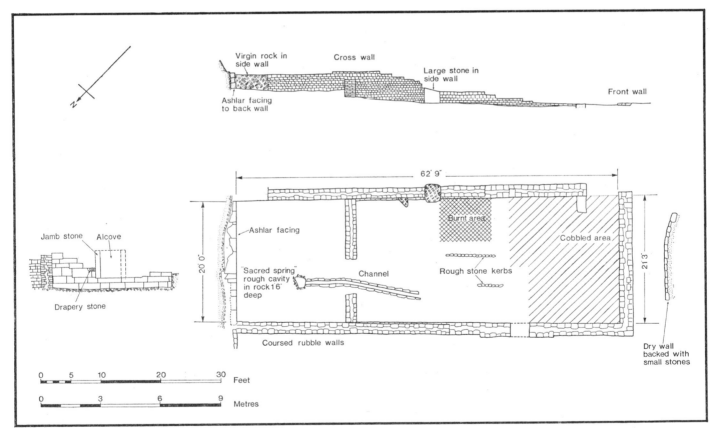

Fig. 34.   Plan and section of building excavated by W. C. Priestley 1938–47

clearly in photo [pl. IIIa] . . . this building is sunk into the ground some 6 to 8 ft. [1.8 to 2.4 m.] and its rear wall (light coloured in photo) is built of massive blocks of local stone, against the natural rock face. . . . The total internal width of the building is 20 ft. 3 in. [6.09 m.]. The side walls and part of the west wall show in shadow in photograph and are of usual Roman construction. Small and medium sized stones, well mortared, about two feet thick and left roughish internally. . . . The builders of the lime kiln, in laying down a concrete floor for the fire some 18 in. [46 cm.] thick, do not appear to have gone further than the crosswall, i.e. some 18 ft. [5.5 m.] from the massive back wall in which originally was cut the sculpture illustrated by Haverfield. If you refer to my photograph [pl. IIIa] you will gain a better impression of this back wall, while photograph [pl. IIIb] gives a "close up" of the centre of it, shewing in greater detail the remains of what appears to have been an alcove with a vertical door jamb (upper part perished) on left hand and slighter evidence of a similar jamb on right; the width of entrance then being about 3 ft. 6 in. [1.05 m.] at the front edge of the alcove we discovered two rectangular sockets some 5 in. [12.7 cm.] long by about 1½ in. [3.8 cm.] wide and 2 in. [5.1 cm.] deep, as though intended to receive the ends of the battens of a wooden shutter, which might be expected to have some sort of turn-button or fastening at the top to secure such a shutter in place, thus closing the alcove from view. Nothing was however found of any top member, the perished jamb on the left rising to only about 4 ft. [1.2 m.]. To the left of this defective jamb and about 15 in. [38.1 cm.] above its base are shown the remaining bits of sculpture *in situ* which formed part of the bottom of the subject of Haverfield's photo, consisting of "fallen drapery" and a "foot".

'The limekiln builders (1911) do not appear to have gone below this course of stones for they cut diagonally into the Roman work, and built a buttress to support the limekiln. As will be seen, a few courses of this project from the back-wall at an angle, above the sculptured parts now remaining. Traces of a similar buttress were found on the right hand side of the "alcove" though the original Roman walling is not nearly so high there. Behind this Roman rear wall is a filling of dry-stones. Owing to the natural rock in "alcove" at about 2 ft. [0.9 m.] from front edge of wall (behind where bottom of our rod stands) the jambs do *not* suggest a doorway leading inwards, or further backwards. The vertical stone, beside rod, is only one of the rough filling stones. It, together with the rubble, behind rod, having been cleared (since photograph was taken) leaves a ledge of natural rock about 1 ft. 8 in. [0.51 m.] higher than the stone with dowel holes though not parallel with "alcove" entrance. No structural remains could be detected in "alcove", apart from the small vertical stone (near right hand side at the bottom) but tooling marks shewing above this, where the natural rock had been roughly angled out presumably to receive the right hand jamb. The "alcove" is (within an inch) central in the rear wall. Leaving the back wall and taking the masonry of the building generally, its foundation and lower courses are of a very inferior order. Very rough, ill-shaped stones, and lumps of the natural limestone rock, dressing being employed here and there in the well defined lines of the walling, which may suggest wood flooring in part. Where the walling exists above the foundations to (say) 2 ft. [0.6 m.] or more, it is much better, being well mortared and the stones more carefully lined and dressed. The cross wall, which is 18 ft. 6 in. [5.55 m.] from the rear wall of the building, is not one build with the side walls and the position of "entrance" through it is not well defined. A few foundation stones remaining in the gap, suggest that the rear area was about 7 in. or 8 in. [17–20 cm.]

higher (say one step up) from area B, though remaining traces of a floor (if of *opus signinum*) are very scanty. It is only towards the central line of the building in both areas A and B that such traces exist, and then only for some 6 ft. [1.8 m.) to 7 ft. [2.1 m.] in width. From rough sketch plan, it will be seen, a gully-drain runs from the slightly higher area A, through its entrance down into area B, where it is still partly covered with red sandstone flags, about 1½ in. [3.8 cm.] in thickness. None remained *in situ* in area A, but odd ones were found nearby suggesting the drain had originally been covered with them. The width of drain is some 8 in. [20 cm.] and its depth about the same, formed of stones at the sides though its bottom appears to have been only of clay or natural rock. The flag-stone covering would appear to give approximately the original floor level.

'I mentioned a retaining wall; this runs around the lower part of the site of the shrine, and at one point, I cut a section, shown in photograph [pl. XII*d*] details of the stratification are given on back of photograph. . . . From all this and other evidence available the temple does not appear to follow conventional lines, and the only type of shrine it appears to comply with is a Mithraeum.

'Not much pottery has come out from the lower level of the shrine except several incomplete hard baked thumb vases, having a purplish hue [New Forest ware]. Some coins have turned up (3rd or 4th century) from the same level. An "Urbs Roma" was found in association with the "Nettleton Cock" [pl. XXXI*a*]. Three large "melon" beads came from the gully or drain in association with the pieces of sculptured slab, Mercury [pl. I*b*] and draped figure [pl. I*a*] and several coins.

'The "dig" has been carried on since the war, started by myself and about half a dozen helpers, usually on Sundays from Spring to Autumn.'

(c) *Building West of the Rectangular Temple (after Priestley)*

This building was also located by Priestley and he concluded that it was a 'retaining wall', presumably for the nearby rectangular Building I; but as the wall shown in Priestley's photograph has little or no foundation it is difficult to see how it could possibly function as a 'retaining wall'. Fortunately Priestley has described on the back of his photograph details of the stratification shown in the picture. The wall is clearly of the same type as several similar walls found on the opposite south side of the river and these are of late fourth-century date. Only the north-east angle of this wall was excavated and it is possible that this may be part of a building lying further to the west. The baths of the settlement have not been located and it is possible that they may have occupied this flat area alongside the river.
The notes on the photograph by Priestley (pl. XII*d*) are as follows:

'Nettleton Wilts 1940. Section cut close to the "retaining wall" to west of temple area.

A. Present turf level, just below galvanized iron sheet, then broken stone and humus mixed 2 ft. [0.6 m.] deep.
B. Stone "retaining wall" (3 courses remaining) 2 ft. [0.6 m.] wide, built on small broken stones and humus. Stratum No. 1.
2. Stratum of broken stones, mixed with brownish clay.
3. Finely broken stones and clay.

4. River silt and clay mixed.
5. Light coloured yellow river silt and gravel (clean) undisturbed.

'Wall removed (for 3 ft. [0.9 m.]) to right of 6 ft. rod to examine coarse pottery and coins sealed by wall (3rd and 4th century A.D. coins).'

It is of interest to note that the 8 ft. (2.4 m.) of deposit on the north side of the river before the natural undisturbed strata were reached agrees within a foot or so with the stratification found on the south side of the river.

(d) *Riverside Building III (after Priestley)*

This building on the north side of the river was excavated by Priestley, and apart from its plan and a photograph little is known concerning its excavation. Priestley's photograph makes it clear that the wall nearest the river is of superior workmanship to the side walls; these are 3 ft. (0.9 m.) wide, built against the riverside wall and are of later date (pl. XII*a*). This also applies to the wall of inferior workmanship to the north of the picture. The riverside wall was 26 ft. (7.9 m.) long and shows a substantial offset.

Priestley suggested that he had found 'what appears to be the Roman bridge abutment' and he mentions that a coin of Antoninus Pius was found in the filling of rough stones and quarry-brash and also part of a Samian Form 45 mortarium. He also writes that the 'long wall (the water wall) is built on the water-worn stones of an earlier ford'. It is difficult to see how the walls could possibly have been a bridge abutment. The walls are not in alignment with any known roadway on either side of the river.

We now know that the Fosse Way must lie to the east of the present roadway. This would bring it into alignment with the only possible exit to the north which is on the line of the present road, where it passes the high out-crop of limestone on its west side and there is a sharp drop into the valley of the Broadmead Brook on the east side.

It is doubtful whether a road bridge would be necessary at this point, since the river could easily have been forded, but if there was one it should be slightly east of the present road bridge. Priestley's 'bridge abutment' faces the hostelry on its south side and his medieval building is immediately north of it. It would seem more likely that the walls attached to the riverside wall are part of a riverside building that probably extended to the north and preceded the medieval building. The coin of Antoninus Pius and the Samian ware did not appear to have been recovered from a particular stratified layer, but they agree with the second-century A.D. material found on the opposite side of the river.

The substantial riverside wall was on the same alignment as the wall found on the north side of the Roman river opposite the stone piers of Building VII. This suggests that the Roman riverside wall was continuous through the settlement (fig. 2).

(e) *Domestic Dwelling (Building XV)*

This building was erected on the same site as Building XIV which preceded it, on the sloping ground to the west of Building X. It is incomplete but the plan suggests a normal corridor building 65 ft. (19.8 m.) long and 52 ft. (15.8 m.) broad, and orientated north–south.

Two complete rooms were recovered; the larger was 39 ft. (11.9 m.) in length and 24 ft. (7.3 m.) wide, and the smaller 22 ft. (6.7 m.) in length, but the partition wall was an addition and the two rooms were originally one compartment. There was an entrance at the east side of the partition wall, and the doorstep, still in position, was 5 ft. (1.5 m.) wide. There appear to have been rooms on the east and west sides of the building, but it was not possible to recover their complete plan. The east wing was 19 ft. (5.8 m.) wide, but the west side could not have been very wide. It is possible that the north wall extended beyond the corner of the building to join up with the limestone bank that had been cut back into the western slope at the rear of the building; this would enclose a small backyard between the west wall and the limestone bank which had been faced with a dry-stone revetment.

The building is of later construction than Building XIV which it overlies; the walls were sealed by a black layer in which coins of Constantine I (A.D. 320–4) and Gratian (A.D. 367–78) were found. This suggests that it had fallen into disuse about the middle of the fourth century A.D. The building partially overlay the original road which was constructed from the Fosse Way and crossed the area to provide access to the circular shrine.

(f) *The East Lodge (Building XIX)*

This building, at the junction of the north–south road through the settlement with the Fosse Way, was apparently a simple rectangular construction. The modern road passes through a limestone cutting, several feet in depth, and consequently the east end of the building was destroyed when the modern road was made. The surviving portion is 36 ft. (11.0 m.) in length and the building was 25 ft. (7.6 m.) wide, with walls of inferior workmanship. Its position at the junction of the two roads suggests that it was a lodge or guard-house. The high bank on the opposite, south side, of the settlement road was revetted with a wall to support the high steep bank on the south side of the roadway. It was built on the same orientation as Building XXX, and late fourth-century coins found in association suggest that the two buildings are contemporary (fig. 2).

(g) *Domestic Dwelling (Building XX)*

This building was placed along the east side of the road leading south from the settlement, on the narrow strip between the road and the high revetted bank. The building had well built walls, 3 ft. (0.9 m.) in width with offsets. This building is earlier than the road wall, which is built on to the south-west corner of the building on a slightly different line, 6 in. (15.2 cm.) back from the corner of the structure.

Set on a north–south orientation, the building had an overall measurement of 56 ft. (17.1 m.) and was 26 ft. (7.9 m.) wide. Its interior dimensions were 50 ft. (15.2 m.) by 20 ft. (6.1 m.). The interior walls were coated with plaster, painted with a linear pattern of red and white. The floor was made up of a mass of limestone chippings, and there was a small stone-built drainage channel running along the inside line of its west wall. There was also a stone revetment outside the east wall of the building, apparently made to ensure that the high bank to the east did not encroach on to the west wall. The interior was roughly paved with limestone slabs, including several re-used pennant roofing tiles.

A coin of Helena (A.D. 337–41) was found below this stone floor, which was covered with a thick layer of fire-ash. A quantity of broken pottery was found alongside the wall towards its west end, including New Forest ware of the hard metallic thumb-vase type. Two bronze rings were also found in this material. One was a fine signet ring, in perfect condition, with a light blue glass paste setting. It had a representation of a standing figure with one hand against a column and the other holding what appears to be a branch. The figure is thought to represent the god Apollo (see fig. 92(7) and p. 142). The second ring was a key-ring (fig. 92(9)).

The coin of Helena indicates that the building was built during the first half of the fourth century A.D. Constantinian coins and of Valentinian II found on the floor give some indication of the period of occupation.

(h) *Domestic Dwelling (Building XXV)*

This building was at the foot of the eastern slope alongside the main street running north–south through the settlement and north of Building XX also alongside this street. A fairly large building, it was 56 ft. (17.1 m.) by 48 ft. (14.6 m.). It consisted of two rooms, the southern part being 24 ft. (7.3 m.) wide and the northern part 22 ft. (6.7 m.) wide. The walls were substantially built with mortar. A cobbled roadway leading off the main street alongside its south wall led to the entrance of the building. It was not possible for the road to have been made beyond the building because its east wall was built against the high rock face.

The building had a good hard stone floor. Several coins found lying on the floor were of Constantinian date, but there were also some later coins of Gratian. This building was not extensively excavated.

(i) *Building XXX*

This building was a simple rectangular construction similar to the nearby Building XXIV and other buildings in the settlement. It was built alongside the road which leads to the south from the valley. The south wall survived to a height of about 7 ft. (2.1 m.), as the limestone had been cut into to form a platform for the building on the steep hillside. The north end of the building has been destroyed by the modern road which cuts through the limestone outcrop. The building was constructed on the site of the north ditches of the first-century A.D. enclosure. It was 25 ft. (7.6 m.) wide and the surviving side walls were 48 ft. (14.6 m.) long. The building was not completely excavated, but several late fourth-century coins (Constantius and Gratian) recovered from its floor level suggest that it was contemporary with the octagonal shrine.

(j) *Building XXXI*

This building was located alongside the Broadmead Brook a little to the south-east of the present road bridge over the river. It is orientated on the same axis as the hostel (Building XII) which is on the opposite side of the present roadway. The building appeared to be well built with five courses of well-dressed stone on its south-east corner. The building was 25 ft. (7.6 m.) wide and the side walls were traced for 44 ft. (13.4 m.). Traces of a pennant floor was also found. Unfortunately, due to its position near the riverside cattle drinking place, it was possible to make only a hurried examination, but this building merits further investigation. It was probably contemporary with the nearby hostel (Building XII).

(k) *Building XXXIV*

This building was just south of Building XXX and alongside the road which ran south from the settlement. Only the east wall, 72 ft. (21.9 m.) long and parts of its south wall, 16 ft. (4.9 m.) long, survived. The remainder of its walls had been destroyed. The building was probably contemporary with the nearby Building XXX.

6. THE OCTAGONAL SHRINE: PHASE II (BUILDING VI) (fig. 35)

During the first half of the fourth century A.D. the shrine at Nettleton was rearranged. The reason for this alteration is not clear, but the structural alterations made at the time suggest that parts of the temple had become unsafe. A large part of the building was constructed on the stone platform which had been built out from the hill-side slope alongside the river and this mass of material was held in position by the substantial outer podium wall. A slight sinkage, or movement of the stone platform, would be sufficient to threaten the stability of the eight arches on which the vaulted central structure was built. Any movement in a northerly direction would especially threaten the piers on the south-east and the radial walls on the north-east, and it is here that we find alterations made to the building.

The two piers supporting the arcade on the south-east side were dispensed with and replaced by radial walls connecting with the octagonal wall (pl. XXVIIa). The building was now better balanced, with eight radial walls instead of six. The opposing radial walls on the north-west side were also strengthened by rebuilding the southern end of the north radial wall, and the partition wall which blocked the entrance to the north-west sector was tied in to the radial wall. This is the only instance in the building where we find a partition wall built contiguous with the radial wall.

The entrances from the central shrine into the south-west, north-east and south-east chambers were blocked by the erection, on the sleeper wall, of partition walls across the arched entrance into each chamber (fig. 35). The partition walls were set back 2 ft. (0.6 m.) from the ends of the radial walls, and this formed small alcoves or recesses beneath the arches. The plastered walls within the recesses were painted with a design (fig. 36), and this provided a striking background to the central shrine (pp. 63–4). It is possible that the four recesses were provided with votive altars or that offerings were placed on the walls surrounding the central altar.

The late fourth-century temple of Nodens at Lydney Park, Gloucestershire, was planned to incorporate a series of chapels within its periphery, and their possible use is discussed in the Lydney Report (p. 43). It is therefore clear that subsidiary chapels were an accepted feature in Romano-British temples in the late fourth century A.D. The recesses formed by blocking the alternate side chambers at Nettleton may represent an attempt to conform with this practice of including side chapels, possibly as a miniature Pantheon surrounding the central shrine.[48] The new arrangement dispensed with the former open sector on the south side, and effectively blocked access from the central shrine to four of the surrounding chambers.

The partition wall blocking the entrance to the north-east sector had two renderings of painted plaster (fig. 33). The first, earlier, coat was carried down to the level of the *opus signinum* floor and indicates that the partition wall was built prior to the laying of the later pennant flag-stone floor. The second, later, painted plaster coating was flush with the

6

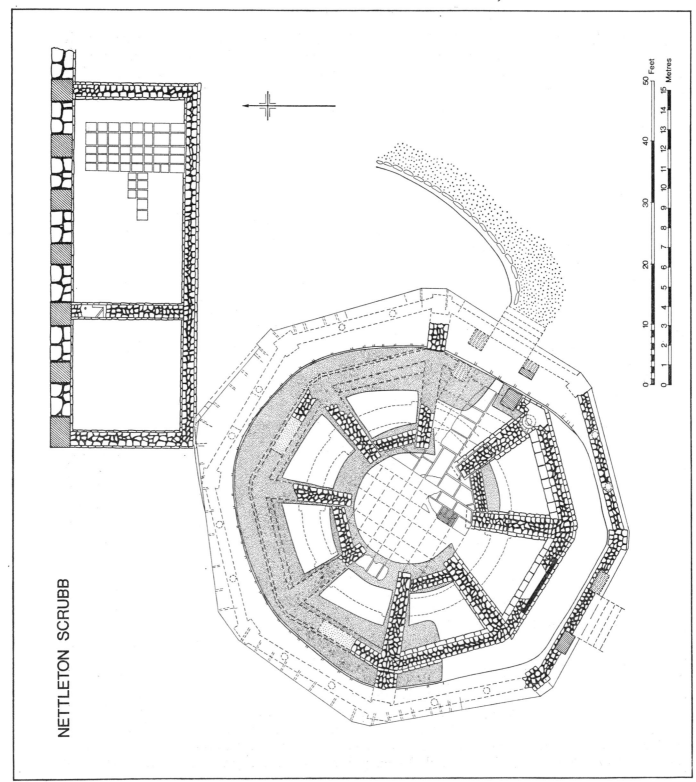

NETTLETON SCRUBB

50 Feet
40
30
20
10
0

15 Metres
14
13
12
11
10
9
8
7
6
5
4
3
2
1
0

Fig. 35. Plan of octagonal temple with sector partition walls (Phases II–IV) and rectangular riverside building (Phase II)

pennant stone floor. The *opus signinum* floor was dispensed with before A.D. 330, and the new floor of large, squared slabs of blue pennant limestone, on a slightly higher level, was laid down in the central area, the eastern hall, the vestibule, and the remaining open chambers of the shrine (pl. XXIX*b* and fig. 29).

The later wall, built across the entrance of the west sector when the improvised shrine was made, was built on the pennant stone floor (pl. XXII*a*). This is a clear indication that the open chambers were paved in this way. There was no evidence of pennant flooring within the blocked side chambers.

The Enclosed Chambers (fig. 35)

The four partition walls blocked access from the central shrine into the four chambers enclosed within the radial walls, and there was no apparent means of entry into them from the ground floor level (pl. XIX*a*). The interior walls of the blocked chambers were plastered by one rendering of plaster which sealed the joints of the partition walls with the radial walls, and it had a simple painted linear decoration, with an imitation marbled dado (pl. XLII*b*). Three of the radial walls survived to a height of 6 ft. (1.8 m.) clear of their foundations, but there was no indication of an entrance or window and the same applies to the three partition walls which blocked entry into the central shrine. The outer chamber walls were not more than 2 ft. 6 in. (0.76 m.) high. It is possible that windows were inserted at a higher level in the outer octagonal wall. To allow for clearance of the ambulatory pent roof, windows could not have been more than 3 ft. (0.9 m.) high, but they would not match with the large window in the south-west sector, which was only 1 ft. 6 in. (0.46 m.) above the ambulatory floor level.

The problem of access into the partitioned chambers at Nettleton remains unanswered. The painted plaster walls in the chambers suggest that they were intended to be seen. But it would seem that the full complement of surrounding cells was no longer required, and only the alternate chambers were retained.

The octagonal temple at Herbord, near Sanxay, Vienne, was built with only four alternate chambers surrounding the central octagonal shrine.[49] It is evident that the chambers, which had previously presumably been used by pilgrims (see pp. 104–5), were blocked to conform to the changing requirements at that time and they ceased to be a functional part of the building.

The closing of the alternate chambers had the effect of making the internal functional part of the building cruciform in plan, with an eastern entrance. It is difficult to ascertain if the resulting cruciform plan was a coincidental result of the alterations, or whether it was deliberately planned to bring it into line with the accepted plan of a Christian church.[50] In its altered form the interior functional part of the building was similar in plan to the fourth-century so-called tomb of Galla Placidia at Ravenna.

At some time following the repaving of the central shrine with pennant stone slabs, the recessed walls blocking the chambers were re-plastered and painted with a striking geometrical design (pl. XLII*a, b*). The painted plaster on the west and north partition walls survived sufficiently to enable its design to be recovered. The same design was repeated on both blocking walls, and extended to the projecting ends of the radial walls. Painted in several colours the design consisted of a pair of 'St. Andrew' crosses in an upright position (fig. 36). The crosses were painted in Neapolitan red with a large central roundel; the arms of the cross terminated at the corners with green chevrons, and the intervening triangular

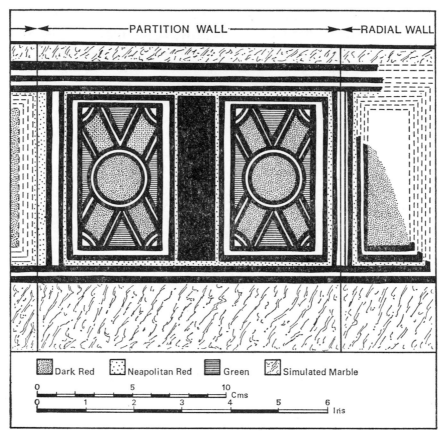

Fig. 36. Octagonal temple (Phases III–IV): painted wall-plaster on north and west partition walls in central shrine

spaces forming the background were also executed in green. Each cross was framed in a panel 2 ft. 3 in. (0.69 m.) wide, with a border of black, red, and white stripes. A band of black 6 in. (15.2 cm.) wide separated the two empanelled crosses on each partition wall. The design was enclosed at the top, sides, and bottom with a dado 1 ft. 8 in. (0.51 m.) wide, painted with a dark red background bearing splashes of white, light red, and purple to simulate marble. The projecting ends of the radial walls had a matching panelled design with a green background. The north-east, and south-east partition walls had the same or a similar design. The surviving fragments of painted plaster recovered alongside the walls suggested a similar design.

A possible explanation for the cruciform plan and the changed painted design is discussed on pp. 104–5 of this report.

7. LARGE PITS EAST OF THE SHRINE

The roadway near the eastern entrance to the shrine widens and forks to the north. Opposite this junction and 54 ft. (51.2 m.) east of the entrance to the shrine a large pit was found cut into the limestone (fig. 16). The top of this pit was only 1 ft. (0.3 m.) from the present surface. In diameter it was 16 ft. (4.9 m.) north–south, 8ft. (2.4 m.) east–west, and was 6 ft. 3 in. (1.88 m.) in depth. Its northern edge impinged on the south kerb of the roadway, and stones from the roadside kerb had fallen into the pit during the process of silting up. The pit filling consisted throughout of yellow silt, which was sterile. Apart from a few large stones around the rim there was no evidence of any superstructure around the pit. The silt filling was water-laid and was evidently the result of storm water washed down over a period of time from the cobbled surface on the higher ground to the west. This silt must have been deposited before the metalled area became covered with turf, but prior to the black layer which covered the nearby road and sealed the pit during the last decade of the fourth century A.D.

A second and larger pit to the south-west was 18 ft. (5.5 m.) in diameter north–south and 13 ft. 6 in. (4.06 m.) east–west. The filling of this pit was identical with that of the first pit, and it is clear that both pits were made at the same time and for the same purpose and became silted up during the same period of time. It was not possible to excavate fully the second pit, but testing with an iron bar indicated that it was more than 6 ft. (1.8 m.) in depth and that the silty filling was continuing at that depth. The filling of both pits indicates that they cannot be rubbish pits which are a common feature on Romano-British sites. Their position near the main eastern approach to the shrine suggests that they were made for a specific purpose in connection with the shrine.

Similar pits found outside buildings at Caerwent, Colchester and Lancing are thought to have been connected with some ritual purpose. The tholos or 'snake pit' at Epidauros placed near and within the precinct of the temple of Asclepius springs to mind. Asclepius, the god of healing, was the son of Apollo. Another site with a similar feature was the sanctuary of Apollo at Curium on the island of Cyprus where a votive pit was placed at the end of the street facing the entrance to the sanctuary of Apollo. It was at Curium that the cult of Apollo began in the eighth century B.C., and it continued to the fourth century A.D. Ritual pits are also found in many instances in association with the small Celtic temples which are found inside the rectangular enclosures or *Viereckschänze* in Bavaria. Evidence of human blood and a central pole placed in the base of the pit are features discovered in certain of the pits.

The pits at Nettleton, placed in a similar position to those at Epidauros and Curium, could have served a similar purpose, but the practice could equally well have been introduced into Britain in pre-Roman times.

An interesting feature is that both pits are on the same radius of 90 ft. (27.4 m.) from the centre point of the circular shrine. A search was made for other pits to the west on the same radius, but there were none. Any evidence on the east and north-east side of the shrine would be obliterated by Building IX and the river.

8. THE SETTLEMENT AFTER A.D. 330

Before about A.D. 330 the main roadway from the Fosse Way to the octagonal shrine, by way of the guesthouse, had been well maintained. This is evident from the good state of its cobbled surface, stone kerbs and road-side walls. Soon after A.D. 330, however, the roadway fell into disuse and debris was deposited on it by the inhabitants. A number of Constantinian and other later coins were found in this debris, and Dr. Reece has assigned a terminal date of A.D. 392 to them. This indicates in a striking fashion the decline of interest in the pagan shrine that took place at that time.

No further additions were made to the guest-house after A.D. 330 and, from this and other evidence concerning the shrine given below, it is evident that the pagan cult at Nettleton reached its zenith during the early years of the fourth century A.D. The only building activity at this time appears to have been designed to make provision for the increasing industrial activity that developed following the decline of the shrine of Apollo, and the consequent fall in the number of visitors.

The inclusion of architectural features from the octagonal temple in the later floor of the nearby rectangular building (No. VII) is an indication that the temple had ceased to be used and that interest in its maintenance had ceased. Several blocks of the heavy cornice from the temple's outer wall were incorporated in this floor to raise it above flood level at

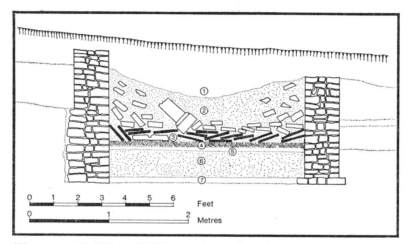

Fig. 37.   Building XIII: section of cellar fill with two fire
destruction levels

Key: 1, occupation earth (coins of Valentinian)
2, stones and mortar
3, stone tiles
4, fire ash on floor
5, second mortared floor
6, brown earth (Constantinian coins)
7, fire ash on first mortared floor

some time after A.D. 317 and this is a clear indication that the temple had fallen into a state of disrepair within a few years of that date. A number of architectural features (pl. XVIII), probably from the temple and its precincts, were also found in the southern part of the nearby Building IX (see pp. 27–30). This decline may be ascribed to the expansion of the Christian faith in Britain during and after the Constantinian period. This must have been a period of uncertainty and disruption, accentuated by a growing awareness of the danger of a sudden attack. The western coasts of Britain, and especially the Bristol Channel region, were becoming at this time particularly prone to attacks by raiders, probably from Ireland, and this kindled a sense of unease and a desire to defend what had been achieved.

The domestic part of the settlement has produced ample evidence that at least one considerable conflagration took place. During the excavation of a cellar in Building XIII in the eastern part of the domestic quarters, collapsed burnt roof-timbers, together with a mass of Cotswold stone tiles, were found lying above a thick charred layer on the cellar floor (fig. 37) which produced coins of the late Constantinian period. This building was rebuilt after the fire and a later floor was made above the cellar level. The later floor level produced coins of Constantinian date and of Valentinian, and like its forerunner the later building was also destroyed by fire. So the settlement suffered at least two devastating fires during the last two decades of the first half of the fourth century A.D. and there is clear evidence that several of the buildings were adopted for use contrary to their original purpose. The shrine is an outstanding example. It was now altered and adapted for use as a domestic homestead (fig. 43).

The seven river-bed piers which supported the northern extension of Building VII were all demolished about this time to a uniform height of 2 ft. 9 in. (0.84 m.). This was done to allow for the construction of a metalled floor over the old river-bed which, together with the stone piers, was buried below the new metalled surface. A coin of Maximianus (A.D. 295–305) was found sealed below the metalled surface (fig. 3), which itself had a thick deposit of water-laid gravel and sand on it.

The guest-house (No. XII) and Building XIII on the opposite side of the courtyard continued in use.

9. INDUSTRIAL ACTIVITY DURING THE FOURTH CENTURY A.D.

A southward extension to the settlement was made after A.D. 330 up the minor Wick valley, as far as a small limiting earth bank which was constructed across the slopes with a staggered entrance in the valley (fig. 2) (see pp. 94–5).

Building XVIII, described below, was apparently built to serve as a guard-house just within this entrance on its west side (fig. 2). An additional defensive dry-stone wall was also built to block access to the settlement by way of the space between Building XVII and the high west bank (fig. 19), made necessary by the removal of the revetting wall between Buildings XVI and XVII.

The reason that prompted the late southern extension and the consequent alterations to several buildings during this phase was largely economic. The inhabitants, deprived of their chief source of livelihood by the failing interest in the shrine, were compelled to look for alternative sources to sustain their economy. In the buildings adapted for use in connection with the increasing industrial activity in the fourth century we find that a number of hearths and furnaces were included. The additions were built with ridge-stones, tiles, etc., from the former buildings, and in one instance an inscribed stone altar (pl. XXXVc) had been profaned to build the furnace in Building XVIII (see p. 136). Building XXI was used to house a pewter-making industry (pp. 68–74), Building XIII was used for bronze-smelting (pp. 74–5) and Buildings XVI and XXVI for iron-smelting (fig. 97(28, 29)) (p. 75).

During the course of excavations conducted by the writer on the Romano-British site at Camerton, near Bath, which is also on the Fosse Way seven miles (11 km.) south of Bath, evidence of a pewter-making industry was found in the north-east corner of the settlement. The evidence included three furnaces, with portions of four stone moulds fashioned in local stone. The stone moulds were found lying around the immediate vicinity of one furnace. There was also evidence of pewter-slag and a nearby coal dump, proving that coal was used in the furnace.[51] This was the first known occasion that pewter was made in Roman Britain during the fourth century A.D.

There is a second suspected site at Lansdown, near Bath, in the Romano-British settlement excavated by the Bath Field Club in 1905–8.[52] Several stone moulds found on this site are now in the Roman Baths Museum at Bath, a number of them similar to the Camerton examples, but the smaller Lansdown moulds appear to have been made for bronze rather than for pewter.

(a) *The Pewter-casting Industry (Building XXI)*

During our work in the south-east part of the Nettleton Scrubb settlement a rectangular building with substantial walls was found (No. XX; see p. 59). It appears to have been built during the phase of building activity A.D. 230–50, and was originally a domestic dwelling. But after A.D. 340 it, like several others, ceased to be used wholly for domestic purposes and its northern part was destroyed, whilst the southern part was adapted for industrial purposes. The substantial south wall was used to form the back wall for a shed, and a lightly built wall with no mortar was constructed to the north of and parallel with the south wall to form a partially open-fronted shed, 13 ft. (4.0 m.) wide, with a lean-to roof facing on to the former northern part of Building XX which was used as an open yard. An extension 12 ft. (3.7 m.) wide was made to the east of the former building to make provision for a furnace constructed of limestone. This had been extensively used and the walls of the flue, orientated north–south, had been subjected to intense heat. The floor of the furnace-chamber at its north end was discoloured red by heat. Scattered on the floor, surrounding the furnace, portions of five different stone moulds were found (pls. XXXVIII, XXXIX). They are similar to the Camerton stone moulds, but they vary in pattern and size from both the Camerton and Lansdown examples. All but one of the moulds are broken and they appear to have been subject to rough usage since they were discarded. It is likely that they may have lain exposed around the disused furnace for some time before they became buried below the debris from the derelict buildings.

The late fourth-century soil layers in the southern part of the settlement at Nettleton are noticeably much blacker than those in other parts of the settlement. This was due to industrial activity and an increasing use of coal in the fourth century A.D. A similar occurrrence of unusually black layers in the Constantinian and later periods was also noticed in the Romano-British settlement at Camerton, Somerset.

Stone Moulds for Pewter Castings (pls. XXXVIII, XXXIX, fig. 38)

Mould No. 1 (pl. XXXVIIIa)

This mould is fashioned from a block of oolite limestone, 1 ft. 8½ in. (0.51 m.) in length, 6½ in. (16 cm.) in breadth and 3½ in. (8.8 cm.) in width. The corners of the mould are slightly rounded. On its lower side there is a slight hollow at approximately the centre of its length on either side, about 4 in. (10.1 cm.) wide and at its greatest depth $\frac{1}{3}$ in. (8 mm.). A similar hollow on mould No. 2, which is the upper or male member of the two moulds in the same position, is likely to be for strapping or binding to ensure non-slipping and a tight fitting for the opposing moulds during the pouring operation. Mould No. 1 on its upper face has a groove $1\frac{1}{2}$ in. (3.8 cm.) from the edge of the stone throughout its length. The depth of this groove is $\frac{1}{2}$ in. (13 mm.) on its outer edge and $\frac{1}{4}$ in. (6 mm.) on its inner edge. Parallel with this groove there is a flat ledge 2 in. (5.1 cm.) in width, recessed $\frac{1}{4}$ in. (6 mm.) below the surface of the mould on its outer edge. The groove on the mould is open at one end of the stone, but at the other, there is a slight blocking ridge $\frac{1}{4}$ in. (6 mm.) wide.

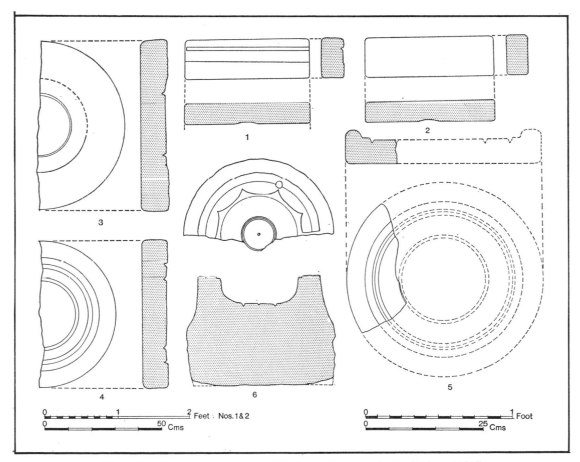

Fig. 38.   Stone pewter moulds from furnace in Building XXI

It is likely that the pouring operation was made with the two moulds standing together in an upright position, with the open end of the groove uppermost. The blocking at the lower end would prevent the molten metal from running out of the mould.

Mould No. 2 (pl. XXXVIII*b*)

This mould is of the same dimensions as No. 1, but it has a smooth face with no features.

Moulds 1 and 2 are the male and female members of a mould used to cast thin strips of metal about 1 ft. 8 in. (0.51 m.) in length and with a single V-shaped ridge. It is likely that the pewter strips formed a component of the larger dishes or other similar vessels cast at Nettleton. It is known that skillet and flagon handles were cast as separate components, and the foot rings for large dishes could be cast separately, the foot ring being annealed after the body of the dish had been cast. A strip 1 ft. 8 in. (0.51 m.) long would form a foot-ring base 6 in. (15.2 cm.) in diameter. But it is also possible that the strips were used to form the sides of panels or for some similar purpose.

Mould No. 3 (pl. XXXVIIIc)

This was about half of a circular mould, used to cast a very shallow plate about $7\frac{3}{4}$ in. (20 cm.) in diameter, with a foot ring base $5\frac{1}{4}$ in. (13 cm.) in diameter. The mould is made of oolitic limestone and is 1 ft. 2 in. (0.3 m.) in diameter. It is $2\frac{1}{4}$ in. (5.6 cm.) thick on its outer edge, and 2 in. (5.1 cm.) in the centre, and the edges are slightly rounded. There is a grooved circle 5 in. (12.7 cm.) in diameter and $\frac{1}{4}$ in. (6 mm.) in depth, but the groove is slightly more pronounced on its inner edge. Outside the circular groove there is a slightly concave circle $1\frac{1}{4}$ in. (3.1 cm.) wide. Beyond this the outer edge of the stone is quite rough and is not part of the mould.

Mould No. 4 (pl. XXXIXa)

This is about half of a circular mould, made from oolitic limestone. The mould was 12 in. (30 cm.) in diameter and its thickness in the centre was 2 in. (5.1 cm.) and $2\frac{1}{16}$ in. (5.1 cm.) on its outer edge. There are two grooved circles on this mould. The inner groove is $5\frac{1}{4}$ in. (13.3 cm.) in diameter and $\frac{1}{4}$ in. (6 mm.) in depth. The outer groove, which is 8 in. (20.3 cm.) in diameter and $\frac{1}{4}$ in. (6 mm.) in depth on its inner side, has a much sharper cut on its outer edge which is $\frac{1}{3}$ in. (8 mm.) in depth. The space between the two ridges is about 1 in. (2.5 cm.) wide and it has a slight downward slope towards the centre. There is a flat zone $\frac{1}{2}$ in. (12 mm.) wide surrounding the outer groove. The outer edge of the mould beyond this zone is quite rough. This would produce a shallow plate $9\frac{1}{4}$ in. (23.4 cm.) in diameter with two foot rings. The inner ring would be $5\frac{1}{4}$ in. (12.9 cm.) in diameter and the outer $7\frac{3}{4}$ in. (18 cm.) in diameter.

Mould No. 5 (pl. XXXIXb)

This is about a quarter of a large mould, circular, and 16 in. (41 cm.) in diameter. In the centre the mould is 2 in. (5.1 cm.) in thickness, but on its outer rim it is $2\frac{3}{4}$ in. (7 cm.) thick. The mould has two circular grooves: the inner is 7 in. (17.8 cm.) in diameter and $\frac{1}{4}$ in. (6 mm.) in depth, and the outer groove 11 in. (27.9 cm.) in diameter, $\frac{1}{4}$ in. (6 mm.) in depth on its inner side and $\frac{3}{8}$ in. (10 mm.) on its outer edge, which is much sharper than its inner edge. There is a flat zone $1\frac{3}{4}$ in. (4.4 cm.) in width and slightly raised above the level of the inner zone. Beyond the outer groove there is a flat zone $\frac{3}{4}$ in. (19 mm.) wide and $\frac{1}{8}$ in. (3 mm.) higher than the intermediate zone. On the outer rim of the mould there is a rounded curb, and this is 1 in. (2.5 cm.) higher than the central part of the mould. This mould is also made from oolitic limestone. It would cast a circular dish or tray $14\frac{1}{2}$ in. (35.6 cm.) in diameter.

Mould No. 6 (pl. XXXIXc, d)

About one-half of this mould was recovered and it is fashioned in the finer-grained white lias oolitic limestone. The white lias lends itself to much finer work than is possible on the coarser limestone. This mould differs in type from Nos. 1–5. The base of the mould, which is quite rough, is 6 in. (15.2 cm.), in diameter, but at the top it is 5 in. (12.7 cm.). The outer part is $4\frac{1}{2}$ in. (10.2 cm.) thick, but in the centre it is $3\frac{1}{8}$ in. (7.9 cm.). The lower $2\frac{1}{2}$ in (5.1 cm.) is rough, but above this the mould has been shaped with sloping sides, and around this shaped upper part there is a band of iron-staining on the stone, indicating that there was an iron clamping band around the mould $\frac{3}{4}$ in. (19 mm.) in width. There is a small central hole in the mould basin $\frac{1}{16}$ in. (1.5 mm.) in diameter and a circular groove $1\frac{1}{4}$ in. (3.1 cm.) in diameter. This groove is $\frac{3}{16}$ in. (5 mm.) in depth. The sides of the mould rise in a graceful curve outside this groove, forming a small basin, the top of which is $1\frac{1}{16}$ in. (2.6 cm.) above the base. At the top of this sloping side, which is $3\frac{1}{8}$ in. (7.9 cm.) in diameter, there is a flat ridge $\frac{1}{4}$ in. (6 mm.) wide with rounded edges and $\frac{1}{8}$ in. (3 mm.) in depth. On the surface of the ridge the mould is fashioned to give a series of eight decorative loops which form the rim. Beyond this there is a flat zone $\frac{1}{2}$ in. (13 mm.) wide, bounded by a circular groove $4\frac{1}{2}$ in. (10.2 cm.) in diameter. This groove is $\frac{1}{16}$ in. (1.5 mm.) in depth and is the outer edge of the mould. Outside this small groove there is a rough outer zone $\frac{5}{16}$ in. (8 mm.) wide. There is a circular hole $\frac{1}{4}$ in. (6 mm.) in diameter and $\frac{1}{4}$ in. (6 mm.) in depth cut into the mould on the line of the small outer groove. This is not part of the mould design, but is likely to be a locking plug hole to keep the male and female moulds in their correct position during the pouring operation. At the point where the mould is broken there is an indication of a cut across the upper surface of the mould. This is possibly a recess made to receive a flat handle for the skillet or pan, which would be cast as a separate component. The mould for a handle for this type of pan or skillet was found incorporated in a similar mould at the Camerton Romano-British settlement.[53] The Nettleton mould would produce a small circular bowl or pan $4\frac{1}{2}$ in. (10.2 cm.) in diameter, with a decorated rim $\frac{5}{8}$ in. (16 mm.) in width, a small circular bowl $3\frac{1}{8}$ in. (7.9 cm.) in diameter and a foot ring $1\frac{3}{8}$ in. (3.5 cm.) in diameter.

Other Possible Moulds

During the course of excavation in the small Wick Valley, especially in the vicinity of Buildings XVIII and XXI, a number of pieces of cut stone were found in the fourth-century levels (fig. 39). The pieces are fragmentary, which makes it difficult to determine their purpose. But they are undoubtedly parts of octagonal, square and round stone objects with either circular or oval interiors. In view of the fact that most of them were found in the near vicinity of, and in levels contemporary with, the pewter moulds, it is likely that they are parts of discarded moulds or that they were used for some purpose in connection with the pewter-casting activity in the settlement.

1. From Building XVIII

Fragment of an octagonal object with a circular interior. Its overall diameter is $7\frac{1}{2}$ in. (17.9 cm.), and the circular interior $4\frac{3}{4}$ in. (10.3 cm.). It is $2\frac{1}{2}$ in. (6.2 cm.) thick and the

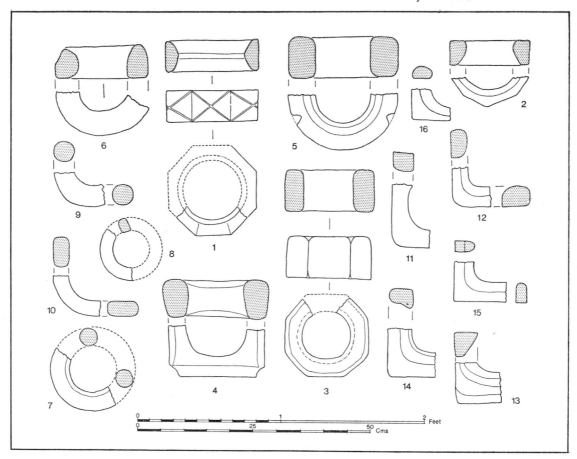

Fig. 39.   Possible pewter moulds

inner sides are rounded. On the outer side it is well finished with an incised St. Andrew cross on each angle of the octagon.

2. From a fourth-century level near Building XXI

Fragment of an octagonal stone similar to No. 1 with a circular interior. It is 6½ in. (15.3 cm.) in diameter, the circular interior 4 in. (10.16 cm.), 2 in. (5.1 cm.) thick with straight outside edges, and the inside rounded.

3. From a fourth-century level in the Wick Valley

The larger part of an octagonal stone with a circular interior. It is 7 in (17.8 cm.) in diameter and the interior 4 in (10.16 cm.). The sides are 3½ in. (7.7 cm.) thick with straight outer sides, but the corners are worn and the inside rounded.

4. From a fourth-century level near Building XXI

Part of an oblong stone with an oval interior. It is about 8 in. (20.3 cm.) in diameter, the oval interior is 5 in. (12.7 cm.) in diameter on the surviving fragment, but it is likely to have been larger on its opposite axis to complete its oval interior. It is $3\frac{1}{4}$ in. (8.2 cm.) thick. The outer edges are straight with rounded corners and the inside rounded. The upper outer edges are bevelled.

5. From a fourth-century level in the Wick Valley

A circular stone 9 in. (22.9 cm.) in diameter and an internal diameter of $4\frac{1}{2}$ in. (11.5 cm.). The inner and outer sides are straight with rounded edges and are about 3 in. (7.6 cm.) in height. There are two small notches cut on the outer edge and there were probably four in all, opposite each other.

6. From a fourth-century level north of Building XVIII

A circular ring-shaped stone about 8 in. (20.3 cm.) in diameter and 4 in. (10.1 cm.) inside. It is flat on its base with low straight walls bevelled inside and outside.

7. From Building XVIII

A circular ring 7 in. (17.8 cm.) diameter outside and $3\frac{3}{4}$ in. (8.9 cm.) inside. The circular section is $1\frac{1}{2}$ in. (2.6 cm.) in diameter.

8. From a late level near the shrine

A circular ring, flat in section. Outside diameter 5 in. (12.7 cm.), inside 3 in. (7.6 cm.), and 1 in. (2.5 cm.) thick. The sides and bottom are flat but the top is slightly rounded.

9. From a late level near Building XXI

Fragment of a circular ring similar to No. 7. The round section is $1\frac{1}{2}$ in. (3.6 cm.) thick. The ring is about 8 in. (20.3 cm.) outside diameter and $4\frac{1}{4}$ in. (10.7 cm.) inside.

10. From Building XVIII

Fragment of a probable circular stone ring about 9 in. (22.9 cm.) outside diameter and 7 in. (17.8 cm.) inside. The straight sides are $2\frac{1}{2}$ in. (6.2 cm.) high and $1\frac{1}{4}$ in. (0.1 cm.) thick.

11. From Building XVIII

Fragment of a square or oblong stone with rounded convex corners. It is about 6 in. (15.2 cm.) in diameter and the oval interior about 3 in. (7.6 cm.) across, but on its longer axis the oval would be about 4 in. (10.1 cm.) across and the outside 7 in. (17.8 cm.). The sides are about $1\frac{3}{4}$ in. (3.4 cm.) high.

12. From a late level near Building IX

Corner piece of what was probably a square stone with rounded corners and sides $2\frac{1}{4}$ in. (5.6 cm.) high, with the inner side rounded.

13. From Building XVIII

Fragment of a corner of a large square or oblong stone. The outer corner is rounded. The straight sides are 2 in. (5.1 cm.) high and the interior has a sharply sloping side. The flat base is 2 in. (5.1 cm.) wide.

14. From Building XVIII

The corner of a large square or oblong stone with straight outer sides and slightly rounded corners. The sides are 2 in. (5.1 cm.) high and the base $1\frac{1}{2}$ in. (3.8 cm.) wide. Its upper edge is rounded with a bevelled sloping inner side.

15. From a late fourth-century level in the Wick Valley

Corner of a straight-sided square or oblong stone. The corner was square. The sides $1\frac{3}{4}$ in. (4.4 cm.) high and 1 in. (2.5 cm.) thick with a flat base. Its inner side has a rounded corner.

16. From a late fourth-century level near Building XXI

Fragment of a squared outer corner similar to No. 15. Straight sides and a rounded inner edge. The sides are $1\frac{3}{4}$ in. (3.4 cm.) high.

(b) Bronze Smelting (Building XIII)

Evidence of bronze-smelting was found at Nettleton Scrubb. Three crucible fragments were recovered from a cutting on the site of Building XIII, from a late fourth-century level which, from the evidence of unusually black soil, fragments of coal, and evidence of fire, must have been a smelting floor. The three fragments have been examined by Professor R. F. Tylcote, who has identified three different types of crucible used at Nettleton:

1. An integral-lidded type.
2. A small triangular type.
3. A round or spherical type.

The present fragments are double-walled and appear to be the integral-lidded type of diameter of not more than 1–2 in. (2.5–5.1 cm.). There is no doubt that the crucibles were used for melting copper-based alloys. One piece of crucible, $\frac{3}{8}$ in. (10 mm.) thick, has fragments of green and red slag adhering to its side. Several fragments of coloured glass and bronze slag were also found on the same site, and this suggests that enamel or glass working may also have formed part of this industry, but more extensive excavation is required on the site to determine this interesting feature of the Nettleton settlement positively. The industry appears to be contemporary with the late fourth-century A.D. pewter industry on the site (see pp. 68–71).

In addition to the specimens found in Building XIII two other crucibles were noted:

A. A small fragment found in the yellow silt filling of the first-century A.D. enclosure ditch.
B. A small crucible $1\frac{1}{2}$ in. (3.8 cm.) long. It was shaped like the bowl of a clay tobacco pipe, and it had a small flat side projection, presumably for picking it up with the iron tongs from the fire. The top open end was $\frac{1}{2}$ in. (13 mm.) in diameter and the base was

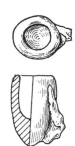

Fig. 40. Crucible from late fourth-century floor level in Building XVIII (scale ½)

the same. The sides were $\frac{3}{16}$ in. (5 mm.) thick and the bowl was $\frac{3}{4}$ in. (19 mm.) in depth. It was made from a coarse gritty clay (fig. 40).

From the late fourth-century floor level in Building XVIII.

(c) *Iron Foundry and Smelting (Buildings XVI and XXVI)*

The large amount of iron slag, together with a large lump of wrought iron (see p. 229), several iron objects found in the later floor levels associated with Buildings XVI and XXVI and the two furnaces found in Building XXVI suggest that a small iron-smelting industry was established during the latter half of the fourth century A.D. within the settlement. The iron objects found on the latest floor level indicate that iron tools and other implements were fashioned on the site (fig. 97(28, 29)) but the production was likely to have been only sufficient to supply the immediate requirements of the settlement, and was ancillary to the pewter industry established in Building XXI on the opposite side of the street.

(d) *The Cemetery Chapel (Building XXIII)*

This small but well-constructed building (fig. 41) was built towards the south-east corner of the settlement. At this point the slope becomes gentler because of the beds of oolite rock which outcrop at this point and are capped with a layer of blue-green clay.

The lower, west, part of the building was 15 ft. (4.6 m.) square, and the oolite and clay outcrop was cut back to accommodate the building. Consequently its east wall was built against the rock face, and its north and south walls were partially built likewise (pl. XXXVII*b*). Only its west wall was freestanding. The walls were 1 ft. 9 in. (0.53 m.) wide with brown mortar and the corners finished with nicely squared blocks of limestone. On the north-west corner of the building a doorstep had been cut in the limestone with a slight ridge on its outer edge; a centrally placed hole for a door stop indicated a double doorway (pl. XXXVII*a*). The walls survived to a height of about 1 ft. 6 in. (0.46 m.). The floor consisted of large blocks of limestone placed on the rock.

Along the inner side of the west wall there was a small platform built up with stones and sand, 2 ft. (0.6 m.) wide and about 4–6 in. (10.1–15.2 cm.) high. On the surface of the sandy platform there was a series of black circles containing burnt material (pl. XXXVII*c*). Three of the surviving circles were 1 ft. 4 in. (0.41 m.) in diameter, and a larger central one, 2 ft. (0.6 m.) in diameter, was surrounded by a stone kerb. The black filling of the smaller circles was 3–4 in. (7.6–10.1 cm.) deep in saucer-like depressions formed with the local clay. A

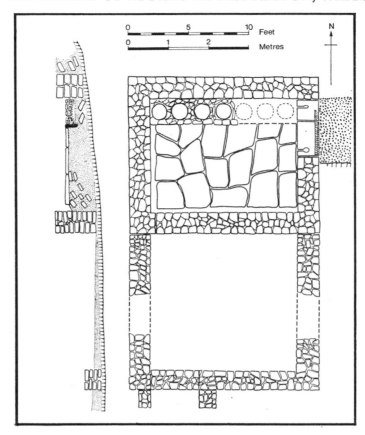

Fig. 41. Building XXIII: plan and section

small bronze pin and pottery sherds were found in the second circle from the south. The filling of the fourth and largest circle differed from the others as it was sandy. The circles towards the north-east doorway had been largely destroyed, but the remaining space alongside the west wall allowed for a further three circles, making seven in all, with the larger circle in a central position.

On the higher level to the east the building extended to include a second room as large as the lower compartment. It seems likely that the lower room was built to serve as a separate cellar and it had a second storey above on the same floor level as the eastern extension. The filling within the lower compartment consisted of a mass of building stone and mortar from the building, including a large piece of a stone door threshold, probably from the upper extension. Below this debris a thin layer of burnt material contained some fragments of coarse pottery.

The position of this building, outside the settlement, but within the area of the earlier first-century enclosure on the east side of the Wick Valley, suggests that it was not likely to have been a normal dwelling house. The building was set on an east to west axis. Access to the lower, western part of the building was by way of a cobbled pathway made on the sloping hillside, and this pathway had a stone-built revetment along its east side. The pathway provided direct access to the late fourth-century cemetery, and the building was in fact the southern limit of the cemetery.

This raises the question as to the purpose of this building. Its close proximity to the cemetery suggests some connection, and it may well be that it was a cemetery chapel. If this was so it offers an explanation for the series of black circles on the small platform within the cellar-like western part of the building. A well-established Roman pagan practice was the placing of food offerings for the dead in proximity to their graves; in fact in first-century graves a pipe-funnel arrangement was often made in the grave, and this was used to pour liquid libations down into the grave. However, this practice was later modified and food offerings were placed within the vicinity of the cemetery. Despite the introduction of Christianity in the fourth century A.D. this custom is known to have persisted. St. Ambrose is recorded as having to chastise St. Monica, the mother of St. Augustine, for persisting in the pagan custom of offering food to the dead.[54] The black circles may well be the organic remains of such offerings to the dead.

Two similar buildings, also with walls 15 ft. (4.6 m.) long in each case, have been excavated in the late Roman cemetery at Poundbury, Dorset. The two buildings are thought to be mausolea, and one has produced a quantity of painted plaster with three human figures dressed in robes, each holding a rod or staff in the right hand. The large cemetery is also thought to be of the late fourth century A.D. and probably Christian.[55]

There are, however, two other possible explanations for the black circles at Nettleton. The building lies close to the Fosse Way, and the building could have been a small shop where drink and food was served. The blackened circles could be the lower part of a bench which had a series of circular holes on the upper part that held detachable pots or pans. A small fire under the suspended pan would maintain a constant supply of hot drinks for the traveller. The construction would be similar to a Victorian kitchen boiler, or the thermopolium, a popular feature in the streets of Roman Pompeii and Ostia. It has also been suggested that the black circles might represent the decayed remains of a row of small wooden barrels, with wooden hoops, which held wine in the cellar. The close proximity of the cemetery, however, makes it an unlikely position for a shop or a wine cellar. The pathway leading directly to the adjoining cemetery suggests a connection and a cemetery chapel is more likely to have been its purpose.

(e) *Building XXVII* (fig. 42)

This building was outside the south-western limit of the settlement. Only the wall foundations were found, and therefore no part of its floor level survived. Most of the material found in and around the building was consequently of an earlier date than the building itself, which was built over the silted-up western ditches of the enclosure. It was constructed on an east–west axis, and a large apse occupied the whole of its western end (pl. XLVI*b*). The close proximity of the modern road made it difficult to determine definitely the arrangement of its east end, but it seems to have terminated within a few feet of the present road. A second apse at its east end did not extend to the full width of the building, and is likely to be a later construction.

The building was 53 ft. (16.2 m.) long and 25 ft. (7.6 m.) wide, and the walls varied in width from 1 ft. 9 in. (0.53 m.) to 2 ft. 3 in. (0.69 m.). On a lower level, there were two

7

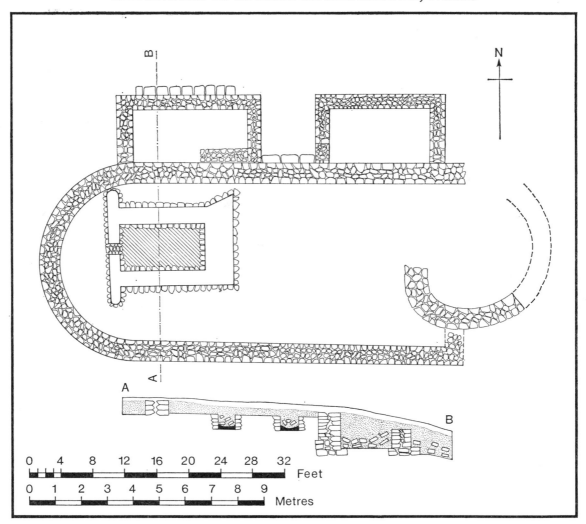

Fig. 42. Building XXVII: plan and section

annexes. The east annexe was 16 ft. 6 in. (4.96 m.) long, 8 ft. 6 in. (2.56 m.) wide, and had a doorway in its west wall against the north wall of the building. The west annexe was of the same width, but was 18 ft. long (5.5 m.), and there was an additional wall foundation built against the north wall of the main building (pl. XLVIa). Traces of an *opus signinum* floor were found in this annexe. Access to the annexe was by way of a stone step set against the north wall between the two annexes. This small space, 6 ft. 6 in. (1.95 m.) wide, was apparently used as a porch and was the main entrance into the building. A large amount of Samian ware and two bronze fibulae were found below the floor level between the two annexes.

Within the interior of the main building and towards its apsidal west end the stone-built channels of an elaborate heating system were found. The channels were not centrally placed within the building: the north channel extension abutted on to the north wall, but there was a space 4 ft. (1.2 m.) wide between the south wall and the south channel extension (pl. XLVI*b*).

The system consisted of two parallel east–west stone-lined channels, 2 ft. (0.6 m.) wide and the same in depth. The two channels were 10 ft. 6 in. (3.15 m.) long, and at their east end they connected with a cross-channel 1 ft. 9 in. (0.53 m.) wider than the side channels. At the west end the two side channels joined a second cross-channel 1 ft. 6 in. (0.46 m.) wide, and the same depth, but this cross-channel extended beyond the north and south side channels on each side for 2 ft. (0.6 m.), and they terminated with round sloping ends. At the rounded ends of the western channel there must have been a chimney for the exit of smoke from the fires. The sides of the north and south channels had considerable evidence of burning at their east ends where they connected with the wider east cross-channel. The four channels enclosed an island 10 ft. 6 in. (3.16 m.) long by 6 ft. (1.8 m.) wide. The wider east channel showed little evidence of burning but appears to have been used as a standing bay or stoke-hole for the fires which were placed in the two side channels. The resulting heat from the side channel fires circulated to the western cross-channel, but the blocking wall placed across the western cross-channel prevented a complete circulation, which would otherwise have caused a 'blow back' with the consequent risk of injury or fire in the stoke-hole.

In the absence of any evidence of the floor levels within the building it is difficult to determine if the heating system was used for heating the building or if it was utilized for some industrial purpose, but no evidence of slag or metal-working was found in or around the channels, and there was no evidence of collapsed flooring within the filling of the channels.

Apart from a coin of Magnentius (A.D. 350–3) in mint condition, found alongside the south wall of the building (see p. 143), and a small bead in the western apse foundation, no contemporary evidence was forthcoming. But the building was certainly later than the latest filling in the enclosure which dated from the first half of the second century A.D. If the coin of Magnentius is taken into consideration, together with the nearby Building XXII, it is more likely to have been a fourth-century A.D. construction.

10. THE OCTAGONAL SHRINE AFTER A.D. 360: THE IMPROVISED SHRINE OF THE PAGAN REVIVAL (fig. 43)

During the excavation of the central area of the octagonal shrine it was found that the floor levels in the northern part differed from those encountered in the southern part. The filling covering the floor levels in the north part consisted of a mass of collapsed vaulting and walls, and it was evident that this had remained untouched in that position since it had fallen over the floor and sealed the singular finds which were found only in this enclosed part of the former central area. It soon became evident from the arrangement of re-used pillars and the votive offerings found on the floor in this enclosed part of the former central shrine that the area had been utilized as an improvised shrine for the practice of pagan rites (pl. XXI*b*).

A wall, with a doorway, constructed primarily with voussoirs from the collapsed arches of the central shrine, was built across the space that had formerly provided access to the open west sector. The doorway on its west side was the only means of entry into the improvised shrine (pl. XXII*a*). This wall was built over the blue pennant floor that was laid down

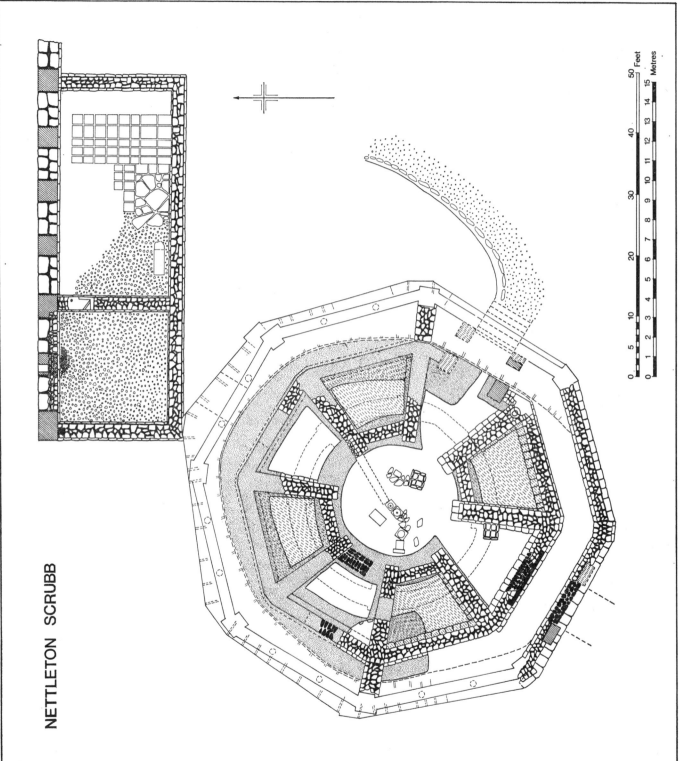

NETTLETON SCRUBB

Fig. 43. Plan of octagonal temple in final phase, with improvised shrine to north-west of central area ... to north, with plan of riverside building (Phase III)

before A.D. 330. A second wall to the south was constructed obliquely across the former central area of the shrine (fig. 29), with its east end built partially upon the remains of the north-east radial wall, and is a clear indication that the building was already by that time in a ruinous condition. This wall enclosed about one-third of the former central shrine.

Four column bases from the derelict temple were re-used to form a crude background against the oblique wall of the small enclosure (pl. XXXIIa) (see pp. 188–90). The smaller type of column used was the upper part of one of the columns that had formerly supported the ambulatory roof on the surrounding verandah. This re-used column had been roughly cut at the point where it had broken, to form a cup-like hollow or piscina in the column shaft. A coin of Valentinian (A.D. 364–78) was found lying in the bottom of this small hollow. The column lay over the same spot as the circular polished stone that was found in the cobbled floor of the circular temple at a lower level. This may be coincidental, but it is worthy of mention. It is possible that the broken column had been utilised as a makeshift altar within the small improvised shrine.

The position of the four re-used columns arranged as a background to the improvised shrine is of some interest. Three of the columns bases were of considerable weight, and it is not likely that they would have been put in the position in which they were found unless they were required for some specific purpose in connection with the hastily arranged shrine. We can but guess, but it seems possible that they were used as a substitute for the altars arranged in a similar way in the former pagan temples and they may have had painted inscriptions or have served as a base for pieces of statuary recovered from the ruinous former shrine. A large rectangular slab of dressed limestone was found immediately in front of the arrangement of re-used column bases. A large capital, also wheel-turned, was found in a jammed position across the late northern doorway into the small shrine (pl. XXIb). An attempt had evidently been made to remove this capital from the small enclosure, but its weight and bulk proved too much for the would-be removers in the restricted space of the doorway, and it was left jammed across the doorway.

The small and apparently hastily arranged shrine within the confines of the derelict building provides striking evidence of a last effort to maintain pagan worship within the shrine before the building was converted to secular use. The shrine floor was littered with objects, including a number of coins that represent the greater part of the period covered by the development of the settlement. Coins of Claudius I (A.D. 43–54), Domitian, Hadrian, Faustina II, Geta, Severus Alexander, Philip I, Postumus and Tetricus I (A.D. 270–3), were found in association with various objects described on pp. 143–50 of this report. It was noticed that most of the earlier coins were much worn suggesting that they were re-used as votive offerings at the temporary shrine. The use of this part of the building was apparently brought to an abrupt end when the surviving part of the vaulted roof collapsed, burying the remnants of the former shrine on the floor.

A possible analogy was discovered at the Romano-British settlement at Camerton on the Fosse Way south-west of Bath. A small stone statuette with a seated figure was found in a late fourth-century building (c. A.D. 380) lying alongside a column which had been re-used to form a pedestal for the stone figure.[56] Another instance was found at Maiden Castle, Dorset, where a roughly constructed late fourth-century A.D. circular stone hut superseded the nearby square Romano-Celtic temple. The finds made within this small building included the marble base of a small statuary group of Diana and a bronze pedestal for a small bronze votive figurine.[57]

There is also the series of bronze votive figurines discovered by Mrs. C. M. Bennett, at the Romano-Celtic shrine at Lamyat Beacon, Bruton, Somerset,[58] and there are doubtless other instances where the worship of pagan deities continued in the decadent fourth-century buildings. In his report on the Romano-British temple at Pagans Hill, Chew Stoke, Mr. Rahtz writes that the 'status and condition of the temple in the first half of the fourth century A.D. was uncertain'; and he also states that 'there was a revival of interest after A.D. 367 and a small sub-structure was rebuilt in the central area of the shrine'. This suggests that there was a similar revival of pagan worship at Pagans Hill.[59]

The coin of Valentinian (A.D. 364–74), found in the cup-like depression on the re-used column shaft at Nettleton, suggests that it was in use at that time. The improvised shrine reflects the conditions which prevailed at that period: the decline of the former popular shrine and the fear of piratical raids brought conditions near to poverty. Consequently it was possible to make only an improvisation within part of the former shrine for this temporary resurgence of pagan rites, which may have been inspired in some part by the construction of the shrine to the god Nodens at Lydney Park, Gloucestershire, on the opposite side of the river Severn after A.D. 364.

The pagan Julian in A.D. 362 repealed the order made by his predecessor Constantius II in A.D. 356 which commanded the closure of all temples, and the former pagan shrines appear to have had a temporary revival. It also suggests that the adoption of the Christian faith in Britain at that time was a somewhat hazardous and slow process and did not imply the total rejection of all the evidences of pagan belief. Pagan beliefs were tolerated by the Christian successors of Julian — Jovian and Valentinian I — but this was stopped by the Emperor Gratian in A.D. 382 when he deprived pagans of most of their religious rights.[60]

11. THE POST-SHRINE HOMESTEAD: ITS OCCUPANTS AND CONTEMPORARY BUILDINGS, A.D. 370–92

(a) *The Post-shrine Homestead*

Coins found within the former shrine in the latest occupational material ranged from A.D. 370 to 392. From this, and other evidence that follows, it is possible to determine that the derelict temple after A.D. 370 was adapted and used as a farm homestead until A.D. 392 or possibly later. The walls of the southern half of the building, placed upon solid rock, were still standing, and this part of the building was adapted for this secular purpose. The fallen debris covering the remains of the small improvised shrine was left intact and the wall across the central area formed the northern limit of the homestead. The former enclosed chamber on the south side of the temple, the open south-west sector, the southern part of the central area, and possibly the eastern sector, were converted for use as living quarters.

The south-west sector, with its large window (pl. XL*a*), formed the principal living room in the homestead. The southern part of the central area appears to have been used for cooking and other domestic purposes. Stone hearths, constructed with re-used pennant stone tiles, were made in the south-west sector and the central area (pl. XL*b*, *c*). The south sector was probably used as sleeping quarters (pl. XIX*b*). An entrance was made into the south walk of the former ambulatory by cutting a rough doorway through the south wall of the sector. However, the west chamber was not connected internally with the living quarters of the homestead. A separate outside entrance was made by a doorway through the north radial wall and the chamber was used as a stable or cattle byre (pl. XIX*a*). The floor of this chamber, when found, was covered with a thick layer of decomposed straw and manure. In one corner of the chamber the skeletal remains of a goose in a sitting posture were found (see report pp. 180–1). A roughly laid floor, consisting chiefly of re-used pennant roofing tiles, was laid in and around the entrance to the stable and there was no evidence of a fire hearth in this chamber. The south-west entrance into the ambulatory from outside was blocked by a roughly constructed wall (pl. XXIV*b* and fig. 44). The ambulatory, apart from a small part on the south side of the building, had fallen into disrepair and was no longer a part of the building. In its derelict state it was used by the occupants as a dumping place for their household refuse, which was thrown out of the large window into the ambulatory where it accumulated until it was level with the window-sill. To protect themselves against the prevailing south-west winds the occupants reduced the size of the large window by adding two courses of stone voussoirs from the collapsed arches of the shrine on the window sill (pl. XXVII*b*). Ash and other household rubbish was also thrown over the north outer podium wall to the lower level alongside the river. The constant dumping of rubbish buried the rusticated podium wall, and it is through the dumping of household refuse that so much of this fine wall was preserved intact. The pillars on the verandah above the retaining wall must have been still in position when the rubbish was deposited. But, later the exposed upper courses of the podium wall disintegrated, no doubt as a result of frost action, and the columns collapsed on to the surface of the former rubbish dump, where they were found (pl. XXIV*a*). These columns had later become buried by the fallen debris from the un-occupied and ruinous building.

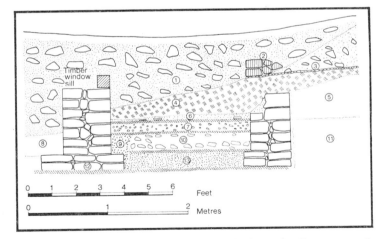

Fig. 44. Section across west ambulatory of octagonal temple. Key: 1, building debris; 2, 4, 8, squatter levels; 3, hard surface; 5, brown loam; 6, pennant floor; 7, stone chips; 9, loose rubble; 10, chips of dressed stone; 11, natural rock; 12, white stone chips; 13, brown mortar

Similar evidence has been found on several Roman sites excavated in south-west Britain in recent years. We find continuing occupation in the buildings by people who had no care for tidiness or order of any kind. They made rough hearths on the tessellated and paved floors. Some mosaic pavements were roughly repaired, not with tesserae, but with re-used stone tiles or any other suitable material which lay to hand. They did not clear their floors of the occupational debris and in due course this buried the floors. It is primarily because of the untidy methods of the later occupants of Roman buildings that the mosaic and other floors survive for us to see today. The later occupants were not interested in the mosaics of their predecessors; it is particularly noticeable that they attached more value to a floor of good solid paving stones. These were also used to block up doors and windows to make the building snug against the cold.

It is not difficult to imagine the type of people who were the last occupants of these Roman buildings. They were content to live their somewhat squalid existence just as long as the primary essentials to sustain life were forthcoming for their daily use. Their dogs, cattle, goats, and poultry shared the building with them. For a modern example of this type of life, a visit to some of the derelict Roman buildings off the Appian Way in Italy, where happy families can be seen surrounded by their domestic animals, is revealing. The Romano-British sites at Keynsham, Camerton and Lufton, near Yeovil, have all produced evidence suggesting a similar post-Roman squatter occupation, and there are a number of sites in south-west Britain with comparable evidence.

(b) *The Homestead Occupants*

A large number of human bones were recovered scattered generally throughout the building, but only in the building debris. No bones were found in articulation, and most of them were in a broken condition, but otherwise in a very good state of preservation. It is important, and emphasis must be given to the fact, that the bones occurred only in the debris which covered the building, and not one human bone was found in any other stratified layer within the temple precinct.[61] All the bones had a clean, hard and dry appearance and certainly did not look as if they had ever been buried in an earthen grave (see pp. 179–80). The general disarrangement of the bones and the material in which they were found suggests that they had been disturbed when the temple was robbed of its building stones, but it is more likely that the bodies were first disturbed by seekers after loot before the destruction of the building and that they later became mixed in the building debris. The building debris itself was an undoubted post-occupation deposit and it sealed the underlying occupational floor debris of the homestead occupants of the late fourth or fifth century A.D. (pl. XXX*a*).

A detailed cleaning, and close examination of the human bones produced very interesting additional evidence which has helped to elucidate the problem of their association with the temple. It has shown that at least 14 individuals, of both sexes, are represented.[62] Most of the bones are those of individuals under the age of 40, but the most interesting discovery has been the finding of a number of deliberate cut-marks on some of the bones, including several fragments of skull (pl. XLIII*a–d*). All the cut marks indicate that they had been made with some violence with a sword or large knife, and they were all inflicted before death had taken place. There are also seven atlas and axis vertebrae which show unmistakeable evidence of cuts or slashes, made by a crosswise blow with the weapon used (pl. XLIII*e, f*).

This is clear evidence of decapitation, which appears to have been done by a practised hand, and it indicates that the bones are those of victims of a massacre, all of whom, it is likely, met their death at or about the same time, the bodies being left or deposited within the temple. It is possible that the inhabitants of the settlement sought refuge there and the massacre may actually have taken place within the building.

After the annihilation of the occupants, the unoccupied and desolate temple soon deteriorated. The upper part of the building collapsed, and the fallen debris in due course completely buried the victims lying within the deserted building. Bronze and iron stains found on some of the bones suggest that the bodies remained intact, clothed with their personal chattels for some time within the former shrine, but the skeletal remains were later robbed of any surviving personal possessions such as rings, bracelets, etc. (see p. 179) and the skeletons became disarticulated in the process. Further disturbance and breakage of the bones took place when the building was robbed of its stone for lime-burning.

The human skeleton found by Priestley near the north-west corner of his so-called temple, Building I (see p. 256) was in a prone position, not in a grave, but in the position in which the person had died. The skeleton was in a level contemporary with the squatter occupation. The impression of the excavator 'was that of a person lying flat on her face with her hands pressed on the upper abdomen and the elbow sticking up' (pl. XLVIIIa). The skull unfortunately was smashed. A bronze bracelet, and some jet beads on a necklace were found with the skeleton. Mr Hall has identified the bones as almost certainly a female of about 18 or 19 years of age. The prone skeleton and the position in which it was found, suggests that this person was struck down while seeking a place of refuge in the small cave in the rock face behind Building I. She was evidently trying to make a getaway from the massacre which was being enacted in the nearby shrine across the river. The coin evidence from the homestead occupation level suggests that the final raid on the settlement must have been after A.D. 392.

To find an analogy for similar happenings it is not necessary to search very far. The Roman villa at North Wraxall, less than a mile south-east of Nettleton, has produced parallel evidence. The villa, a large establishment of the courtyard type, was excavated in 1859 by G. Poulett Scrope, M.P., for the owner, Lord Methuen.[63] Some of the architectural features found were very similar to those from Nettleton. Outside the west boundary of the villa several tombs containing undisturbed burials were found, obviously the normal burials of the family associated with the villa over a period of time.

The most interesting feature, however, was the contents of a well, found within a small hexagonal structure. The first 40 ft. (12.1 m.) of the well filling, which was over 68 ft. (20.7 m.) in depth, consisted of columns, capitals, bases and other carved stones, thrown into the well together with the bodies of several individuals. There is little doubt that the recovered skeletons were those of the villa dwellers who met with a similarly violent end in a raid on the villa. We have no evidence of sword cuts on the bones of the Wraxall victims, but it is possible that, had a close examination been made at the time of their discovery, similar evidence would have been found.

Both the Nettleton and Wraxall sites are within easy reach of the Bristol Channel, and it is possible that both sites were raided on the same occasion. The coin series at Wraxall ends with coins of Gratian (A.D. 367–83), nine years earlier than the latest Nettleton coin, but the story is much the same: the pirates, it may be supposed, took full advantage of the fact that Britain was left without adequate defence after the death of Maximus in A.D. 388.[64] A notable example, and equally dramatic, was at Caistor-by-Norwich, where the late Professor D. Atkinson discovered 36 victims of a massacre, who met their death by the sword. The victims were left within the building unburied and 36 skulls of the decapitated victims were found in one room. This massacre, probably made by Saxon raiders after the withdrawal of the Roman troops, is much the same story as that of Nettleton.

The theory that the Nettleton building was a mausoleum was first put forward when so many human bones were found in and around the building. This theory was based solely on the bone evidence, and no other information to support that contention was found. The important evidence, obtained by detailed examination of the bones, does not in any way lend support to the mausoleum theory. In the light of this evidence we must conclude that the sole function of the building since its inception was that of a pagan temple and that the building continued in use only for this purpose up to about A.D. 330, with a short-lived resurgence of interest after A.D. 360, followed by squatting.

Dr. Reece has identified the coins recovered from the homestead occupation level. They range from A.D. 370 to 392, and this was the last occupation level within the building. The human bones are contemporary with the latest occupation of the building, when it was converted for use as a homestead. The building appears to have been used for this purpose for at least 20 years, that is, from about the year A.D. 370 to 392. After careful consideration of the evidence, we must conclude that the bones are those of the homestead occupants, who were massacred on the site as the result of a raid on the settlement after A.D. 392. The position in which the bones were found places it beyond doubt that they cannot be earlier than the squatter occupation (pl. XLVIIIa, b).

Evidence of medieval occupation overlying the Roman buildings has been found in the settlement, and potsherds, nails, and walls of medieval date have been recovered at several points (see pp. 98–9). However, it is of interest to note that during the course of the temple excavation not a single sherd of medieval pottery was found in association with that building. It would appear that the temple site and its immediate precincts were not used in any way after the slaughter of its occupants, until at least after the medieval period.

(c) The West Lodge (Building XVIII)

This simple rectangular building (42 by 26 ft. — 12.7 by 7.8 m.) was completely excavated. It was built in the south-west corner of the settlement, and its east wall impinges on the street into the settlement, by way of the small Wick valley. Three of the four walls of the building were built against the rock and were faced only on the inside, except for the east wall alongside the street. The walls were built without mortar, from stones gathered in and around the settlement. On the south side, the building was set against the small bank which forms the southern limit of the settlement. The nearby west bank of the small valley was higher than the building, making it particularly snug and partially hidden by the south and west banks (figs. 2 and 45). The eastern part of the floor was paved with large, irregularly shaped slabs of limestone, but the western part, cut back into the natural rock, did not have a stone floor.

A stone-built furnace alongside the north wall of the building consisted of a channel 4 ft.

(1.2 m.) long, orientated north to south, with its rounded end built against the north wall. Like other furnaces in the settlement, the channel had been subjected to intense heat. In front of the channel there was a semi-circular chamber with a sloping floor, but there was little evidence of fire within the chamber (see p. 35), and no construction around its sides apart from several large stones placed along its west edge. One of these stones was a stone altar. Part of its lower end was missing, and it had been badly mutilated and discoloured red by fire (pl. XXXVc). The inscription to Silvanus on its face was badly worn (see p. 136).

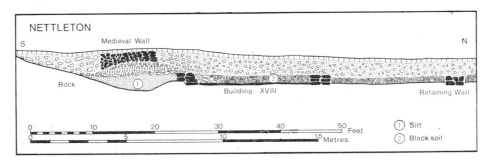

Fig. 45. North–south section through bank, Building XVIII and retaining wall

It is difficult to determine whether or not the altar had been deliberately mutilated, but it was certainly not used for its original purpose in the building, and it presumably came from the shrine.

Towards the west half of the building, centrally placed, was a well-built stone hearth (pl. XLIVc). This was open on its east side, but the remaining three sides had a stone kerb of roof ridge stones placed inwards. Since they were similar to those found on the temple site, they possibly came from the derelict shrine.

A large number of coins ranging from A.D. 333 to 402, found on the floor with other objects, appeared to have been subjected to fire. A coin of Constantine I (A.D. 317–24), found in a layer which ran under the wall foundation, was earlier than the building, and among the coins in the floor debris was an *Urbs Roma* of A.D. 330–5. This evidence indicates a mid-fourth century date for the building's construction.

An interesting feature was a heavy layer of black occupation material which had been dumped on the site of the building after destruction and robbing of the walls down to the last two or three courses of stone. The dumped material covered the walls and the floor space of the building. Some 500 coins found scattered in this soil ranged in date from A.D. 333 to 402 (see pp. 115–18). The black layer also contained a quantity of pottery sherds (see figs. 107–12) but little else was found in it, suggesting that the building was in use only for a few years prior to its destruction.

A large squared block of limestone found in position at the south-east corner of the building was probably the west side of the south gate into the settlement (fig. 2). A circular pivot-stone found lying alongside the inner face of the south wall, was probably used also at this gate (see fig. 104(12)). The stone altar to Silvanus found in this building had clearly been re-used, and this suggests that the pagan shrine had been profaned before the black layer was deposited over the walls of the building.

A large number of varied finds were recovered from the material on the floor of this building. The finds were associated with a large number of late fourth-century coins and included two bronze spoons, two decorated Kimmeridge shale spindlewhorls, a quantity of glass (fig. 65), stamped, colour-coated, and other late fourth- to early fifth-century wares. The finds also included two important items: (a) a fine millefiori bronze brooch (see p. 132) (fig. 55(76)) and (b), a *martiobarbulus* or *plumbata*, a lead-weighted harpoon used by the legionaries in the fourth century A.D. (see p. 234 and fig. 102(93)).

(d) *Building XXII (beyond the South Bank)*

This building was set at the south-west corner of the settlement in a rather surprising position immediately outside the line of the south cross-bank. The building was a long narrow one, 50 ft. (15.2 m.) by 18 ft. (5.5 m.). Its south-west and south-east corners were both rounded on the outside and built without mortar. The north wall, with large irregular floor slabs of limestone, was found under the stony make-up of the south cross-bank. Two small sherds of medieval pottery found in this make-up suggest a collapsed dry stone wall of medieval date formerly on the bank.

Several coins of the Constantinian period found on the floor level of the building suggest that it was in use at the same time as Building XVIII. Below the stone floor level of the building, a thick layer of yellow silt contained sherds of Samian and other first- and second-century pottery. This proved to be the ditch filling of the first-century enclosure which partially underlies this building.

(e) *Building XXIV (on the North Slope)*

This building was situated at the foot of the steep north slope alongside the modern road. The walls were roughly constructed without mortar and there did not appear to have been a proper floor within the building. The floor was covered with a thick layer of black occupation soil which contained a number of fragments of thin glass, an iron knife with a bronze terminal (fig. 99(40)), and over 50 coins of Constantinian and later fourth-century issues.

The building consisted of two rooms each 22 ft. (6.7 m.) square, built on different levels on the terraced slope. The south wall of each room was built against the rock face of the hillside, and most of the occupation material lay in the lower northern part.

In the northern part a large pit was found below the floor level. From its size and rough sides it would appear to have been a quarry made in the first or early second century A.D. for stone to build the first buildings or roads in the settlement. The filling of the pit included a quantity of first- to second-century Samian ware.

(f) *Other Late Fourth-century and Later Constructions*

In several instances the surviving walls of the former Roman buildings were joined up by lengths of dry-stone walling to form cattle or sheep pens, and this probably explains why no definite contemporary level of occupation has been encountered. The dry-stone walls built with thin slabs of the local limestone decreased in width as they increased in height. The following buildings had dry-stone walls incorporated or associated with them.

Building X

The wall foundation of the south-east corner of this building had been utilized to erect a rounded corner, built in a curve and last found in line with the north-east corner of Building XV. It presumably joined up with this building and blocked access to the west between the two buildings.

Building XIII

A curious length of dry-stone walling was found in the northern extension to the large room at the west end of the building. The wall, after leaving the line of the north wall makes a curve, and returns to the west wall at its junction with the north wall, thus forming a complete loop.

East to West Roadway to the Fosse Way

A similar rounded corner was also made on the corner foundation of the north-west road walls. The roadway between the precinct gateway and the Fosse Way must have still been in use when this dry-stone wall was built.

South Roadway into the Settlement

A dry-stone wall was found built obliquely against each face of the west wall alongside this road. The wall had a rounded corner on its west face.

Revetting Wall on Bank above the Eastern Exit from the Settlement

The high bank south of the eastern exit was revetted with a dry-stone wall several courses high, also probably of late date.

The evidence of post-Roman occupation in the settlement is of interest and poses questions as to the possible period of time of this occupation. What happened on the site during Saxon times? There is no evidence of a sterile period following the late fourth-century occupation in the stratification, apart from flood alluvium that has accumulated in the Wick valley along the course of the south road out of the settlement, and this indicates that this road was not used in post-Roman times.

Most of the late Roman pottery and the medieval sherds were found in the area between the precinct wall and the present roadway, but there was no well-defined stratification. Both late Roman and medieval sherds were found mixed and quite near the surface. The late Roman pottery consisted mostly of coarse heavy cavetto rims, heavy rims with thumb and jabbed decoration and some stamped decoration (pl. XLVb-d). There is no proof as to the correct dating of these various dry-stone walls. The medieval sherds may have come from the medieval building (Building IV) discovered by Mr. Priestley on the opposite north side of the river.

12. THE CEMETERIES

(a) *Cemetery A (associated with the Cemetery Chapel, Building XXIII)*

During the examination of the area within the south-east corner of the settlement adjacent to the Fosse Way, alongside the modern road, a cemetery was located on the limestone outcrop which forms a small shelf above the Wick valley. The area was part of the small Claudian enclosure which formed the nucleus of the settlement (pp. 6–7). The small nearby Building XXIII, erected prior to A.D. 330, standing when most of the burials were made, was probably used as a cemetery chapel (see pp. 75–7).

Fifteen burials were located, but others were destroyed when the present roadway cutting was made, and there are additional burials in the adjoining field on the east side of the present road. The graves had been cut through earlier occupation levels on the site, which has produced Samian and other wares of the first and second centuries A.D. (fig. 46). A brown mortar spread sealed this material and was contemporary with the construction of Building XXIII. Above this mortar spread, a layer of black occupation soil produced a mid third-century A.D. coin, and this material was also cut through when the graves were made. The graves varied in depth from a few inches to just under 3 ft. (0.9 m.), but this was largely due to the erosion of the hillside, and it is likely that the graves were originally all about the same depth.

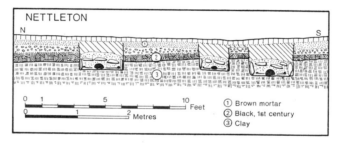

Fig. 46. Section through late fourth-century graves

All the burials were orientated east to west, with feet to the east. A number of iron nails found along the sides and ends of the grave suggest wooden coffins. Most of the burials had several flat limestone slabs, which on first sight appeared to have been placed on edge along the sides of the grave, but careful excavation proved that the stones were not in the position in which they were placed when the burial took place (pl. XLIVa, b). The stones, when found, partially covered the leg and arm bones at the side of the grave. This could be accounted for by slip, but the coffin nails were found on the outer side of the upright stone slabs. This suggests that the stones were originally placed over the wooden coffin; but when the coffin collapsed the stones slipped down and came to rest along either side of the skeleton. If the stone slabs were placed, at the time of burial, along the sides of the grave the iron nails would be found between the skeleton and the stones.

Not all the graves located were fully excavated, but in those examined there were no associated grave goods, apart from a coin of Constantine II (A.D. 337–41) which was in mint condition and lost at the time of burial.

A bronze fibula of first- to second-century type found with burial No. 2 (fig. 51(30)) did not appear to be associated with the burial, but was probably thrown out from the earlier stratified material when the grave was dug and thrown in when the grave was filled. A number of similar brooches have been found in the nearby ditches of the first-century A.D. enclosure.

Building XXIII formed the southern limit of the cemetery and no burials were made south of the building. A small ditch with a stone revetment on its outer side found on the northern limit of the cemetery was probably the boundary of the cemetery and no graves were found outside this ditch (fig. 2).

Details of the graves excavated are as follows:

Grave 1. Skeleton fully extended, with hands resting on the pelvis. Iron nails and flat stones along sides of the grave. This grave overlay a small ditch with a yellow silt filling which produced sherds of first- and second-century date. A coin (Constantine II, A.D. 337–41) was found in the grave-filling. Skeleton of a male. Adult and elderly. Height about 5 ft. 4 in. (1.62 m.).

Grave 2 (pl. XLIV*a, b*). Skeleton fully extended, arms straight. Grave 2 ft. (0.6 m.) deep. Iron nails and stones as in No. 1. A coin of Domitian was in the undisturbed material at the side of the grave. The skeleton rested on the undisturbed clay. A bronze fibula (No. 52) was found in the grave-filling. Skeleton of an adult female, not very old. About 5 ft. 3 in. (1.59 m.) in height. Advanced osteoarthritis in both hip joints.

Grave 3. Adult burial, not fully excavated. Depth of grave 2 ft. 9 in. (0.84 m.). Iron nails and flat stones associated. Skeleton probably of a male adult from its size and maturity. Osteoarthritis in M.P. joint.

Grave 4. Adult burial not fully excavated. Depth of grave 2 ft. 9 in. (0.84 m.). Iron nails and flat stones associated.

Grave 5. Grave of a young person. Skeleton fully extended. Depth of grave 2 ft. 10 in. (0.86 m.). Iron nails and flat stones associated. Skeleton of a child aged seven years. Estimated height 4 ft. 7 in. (1.40 m.). Sex not determined. Left-handed.

Grave 6. Only the head end of this grave was excavated. The grave was 2 ft. 9 in. (0.84 m.) deep, and iron nails and flat stones were associated. This skeleton was probably that of a young adult male.

Grave 7. Only the foot end of this grave was excavated. Flat stones and iron nails associated. Skeleton of an adult aged about 17 years.

Grave 8. Grave of an infant. This grave was made at the north end of the cobbled approach to Building XXIII. Coffin nails and flat stones associated.

Grave 9. The foot end of this grave was destroyed when the present road cutting was made. Flat stones and iron nails associated.

Grave 10. Not fully excavated. Flat stones associated.

Grave 11. This grave was not fully excavated, but it was close to the small ditch which formed the limit of the cemetery.

Grave 12. This grave was located but not excavated.

Grave 13. Not fully excavated, but the grave was cut through a black layer which produced a mid third-century coin.

Grave 14. Grave located, but not excavated.

Grave 15. Grave located, but not excavated.

The burials appear to be contemporary with, or later than, the adjoining Building XXIII which was presumably built to serve as a cemetery chapel (see pp. 75–7). The cobbled walk from its north entrance gave direct access to the cemetery. The fact that the burials were placed in an area which had formerly formed part of the first-century A.D. enclosure is of some interest. The position of the cemetery within the area of the early settlement suggests that the Roman rule which did not permit human burial within the confines of a settlement was not complied with and no longer had any force.

The orientation of the graves with the absence of grave goods points to Christian burial. The coin of Constantine II, found in grave 1 was in mint condition, and suggests that burials were being made in the cemetery during the second half of the fourth century A.D. and they could well have been later.

(b) *Buildings XXIX and XXXIII: ?Tombs*

Two small buildings, XXIX and XXXIII, are thought to have been tombs connected with the cemetery. They were both alongside the Fosse Way and in the area of the cemetery. Neither of the buildings was completely excavated but the following information concerning them was revealed.

Building XXIX

This building was a small apsidal-ended construction. No mortar was used in its walls, which were built with thin slabs of limestone. These walls were very shallow, and consequently little remained of the building, which was placed on a east to west axis with an apse at its west end. The south wall was traced for 18 ft. (5.5 m.) and also the outline of the apse, but because of the sharp slope the north wall was destroyed. A small ditch located in two places on its north and west sides may be related to the building. Time did not permit a full investigation, but the narrow building, not more than 12 ft. (3.7 m.) wide, and its orientation suggest that it was probably a tomb structure in the cemetery alongside the Fosse Way. Fourth-century coins were found in association with this building and it was certainly not earlier than the fourth century A.D.

Building XXXIII

Building XXXIII was also a small construction alongside the Fosse Way. Only its south and east walls had survived. The east wall was traced for 13 ft. 6 in. (4.06 m.) and its south wall for 16 ft. (4.9 m.). The walls were sunk below the outside level of the building and were faced only on the inside. There was no trace of a stone floor, but considerable evidence of burning on its clay floor. The building was orientated east to west. No coins or sherds were found in association but the small building suggests that it was a tomb.

(c) *Cemetery B (south of Building XXVIII)*

This second cemetery of the settlement appears to be quite distinct and separate from the small cemetery A which was nearer the settlement. The second cemetery was discovered when trenches were made alongside the modern road to trace the western ditches of the first-century enclosure on the sloping ground south of Building XXVIII. The first grave was found towards the southern end of the field, towards the summit of the hill. The sloping ground south of Building XXVIII consists primarily of alternate layers of clay and lime-stone, capped on the higher ground by a thick layer of what appears to be Fullers Earth, and it is in this material, easily excavated and ideal for grave-digging, that the burials had been made.

Three burials were discovered. No further search was made for other graves but it is likely that this was the primary cemetery connected with the settlement. Its situation along-side the Fosse Way and the position towards the summit of the hill lead to this conclusion. It would appear to be earlier than cemetery A, but later than cemetery C.

Grave 1. Adult and a normal burial. About 30 years of age.

Grave 2. This grave was not fully excavated. Skeleton probably of a male adult.

Grave 3. This grave was fully excavated. The burial was a normal one with the arms extended. Several iron nails were found in the grave which suggests a wooden coffin. Skeleton of a male. Height 5 ft. 5½ in. (1.66 m.). Estimated age from teeth 30 years. Healed fracture of the left humerus and left clavicle.

The writer thanks Mr. Hedley Hall, F.R.C.S., for the report on the human and animal bones on pp. 178–9 of this report.

(d) *Cemetery C (First to Second Century A.D., East of the Fosse Way)*

A series of exploratory cuttings was made on the sharp slope down to the river on the north-east side of the settlement with the intention of finding the southern limits of the valley settlement. The stone-revetted bank in the western part of the settlement was found to continue eastward on the opposite side of the present road and to join up with the steep south bank of the river at the north-east end. This stone-revetted bank is towards the bottom of the steep slope, and the first-century enclosure was made at the top of this slope to the south.

It was in the steep sloping space between the revetment and the defensive ditches of the enclosure that two interments were found. One was an inhumation of a young person in a grave orientated in a north–south direction. The burial was made in a shallow grave in the clay. A coin of Vespasian was found in the grave. A few feet away to the south-east a second burial in the form of a cremation was found buried in a pot in the clay. The pot, of early type, 6½ in. (16 cm.) high and body 5¼ in. (13 cm.) in diameter, was decorated with a lattice design (fig. 105(26)).

It is likely that there are other burials and cremations in this area. The early type of crema-tion pot, the coin of Vespasian, and the orientation of the burial suggest that the cemetery of the first- to second-century inhabitants was on this slope below the enclosure overlooking the river in the valley (see p. 177).

Six large grey ware urns were found on the west slope (see p. 243, and figs. 2 and 105(34, 35)). In each case the rim and neck were missing. The urns contained a quantity of charcoal and burnt bone. It seems likely that the constricted top part of the urn was pur-posely smashed in order to facilitate putting the cremated remains into the urn. In several other instances, in the same area, charcoal with burnt bone was found deposited in small circular pits. This seems to be a continuation of the cemetry around the western slope.

8

13. THE WICK VALLEY CROSS-BANK

This bank at the western limit of the settlement crosses the small Wick valley from its west side to the opposing east side and terminates where it joins the modern road just south of the sharp bend in the road. The bank survives today as a low mound, and is best seen in the evening light, or after a drifting snowfall when the bank is left bare of snow.

A series of small cuttings made in the field west of the cross-bank has produced negative results with the exception of the area south-west of the cross-bank near the modern road where Buildings XXII and XXVII and the west side of the first-century A.D. enclosure have been found. The upper layer of the valley cross-bank consisted of a spread of thin blocks of oolite limestone collapsed from a former dry-stone wall built on the bank in medieval or later times. A few sherds of medieval pottery were found among the loose stones, and it was clear that the wall had formed the boundary between two areas of cultivation. The plough lines on the south-west side of the bank can be clearly seen on the sloping field, but they do not extend to the north of the cross-bank. It is likely that the dry-stone wall was contemporary with the medieval homestead on the north side of the river.

Several cuttings have been made through the cross-bank: (a) on the western valley slope; (b) in the valley near the point where the street leaves the settlement; (c) two cuttings near the modern road on the eastern slope.

Cutting (a) (fig. 47) made on the west slope of the valley indicated a small earthen bank which had a rock-cut ditch outside the bank. A thick layer of black earth overlay the bank on the inner north side. This produced a quantity of Roman sherds of late type. It also included some New Forest ware and coins of fourth-century date.

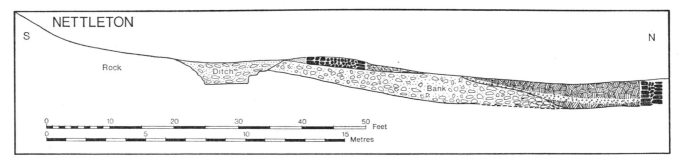

Fig. 47.   Section across west bank showing superimposed medieval wall

Cutting (b) (fig. 45) made across the bank near the entrance produced similar evidence, but in this cutting the inside revetting wall of the bank had been utilized to serve as the south wall of Building XVIII (see pp. 86–8). A large number of coins ranging from A.D. 333 to 398 were found in the burnt debris overlying the bank and the south wall of Building XVIII.

Cuttings (c) made across the bank on the east side of the valley (fig. 4) have produced additional information. The bank at this point has been made over the silted-up ditches and stone revetment of the south-west corner of the first-century A.D. enclosure and the small pre-Roman ditch. The late fourth-century Building XXII was built over the silted-up ditches and the dry-stone medieval wall was in turn built over the surviving floorstones of Building XXII. Building XXII was contemporary with Building XVIII and has produced coins of corresponding date. A coin of Constantine (A.D. 317–24) found in a layer of earlier date than Building XVIII but later than the earth bank suggests that the western bank at this point was made prior to A.D. 317. The structural evidence clearly indicates that the west part of the bank is of earlier construction than that part which is on the higher east side of the valley.

There appears to have been a small bank extending from the west side of the valley to the opposite east side, but it only extended as far as the rockface revetment which formed the corner of the fourth-century settlement and was also the western limit of the first-century A.D. enclosure. The rock revetment was probably faced with a stone wall when the bank was constructed prior to A.D. 317. The rock revetment was the eastern limit of the later settlement, and the cross-bank did not extend beyond the revetment.

The later medieval field boundary bank was surmounted with a dry-stone wall across the small valley and it continued beyond the rock-faced revetment southward above the valley to join the present road. The medieval doorway found in the adapted Building XII alongside the present road suggests that the latter was constructed during medieval times to ease the gradient and replaced the steep, more direct, line which the Fosse Way took up the hillside.

In the absence of additional dating material, it is suggested that the west part of the cross-bank was made when raids on the settlement were threatened, as happened with so many other Romano-British settlements which were strengthened by defensive earthern ramparts during the third century A.D.[65] This bank formed the southern limit of the settlement until about A.D. 360–70, when the defences were slighted following an attack upon the settlement. There is no evidence to suggest that a stone wall was added, apart from a stone revetment at the base of its inner face, and no attempt was made to strengthen the bank. Buildings XXII and XXVII were well beyond the confines of the Roman bank on the east side of the valley, and were built in the late fourth century A.D. when the bank had ceased to have any functional purpose.

14. THE WATER-WHEEL HOUSING (BUILDING XXXII) (figs. 48, 49 and pl. XLVII)

As a result of a tropical storm which swept across north Somerset (Avon) and the south Cotswolds on the evening of July 10th, 1968, there was considerable flooding of the river valleys. This resulted in much destruction and the normal course of the river was changed. Though the Nettleton Scrubb valley was not badly affected, the flood water deposited material in some places in the Broadmead Brook whilst in others the river banks were denuded. The river east of the present road bridge crosses the narrow valley to its south side (fig. 2). It then flows alongside the outcrop of oolitic limestone at the foot of the hillside and this formed the southern boundary of the settlement. It was alongside this river bank that a large block of dressed limestone was exposed after the storm. The block was lying on its side where it had fallen from a ledge immediately above. The block was 5 ft. 2 in. (1.56 m.) in length and at its widest part was 2 ft. 6 in. (0.76 m.) (fig. 49). On its dressed face it had a smaller slot 2 in. (5.1 cm.) in depth and 1½ in. (3.8 cm.) wide cut into the stone (pl. XLVII*b*). Further investigation revealed a similar stone block *in situ* built into the river bank and this had an identically cut slot. This proved to be the splayed intake of a water channel 1 ft. 6 in. (0.46 m.) wide (pl. XLVII*a*).

Two large blocks controlled the water supply into the channel, which was 1 ft. 2 in. (0.35 m.) in width. The two cut slots were made slantwise to house a blocking slab of stone or timber which could be raised or lowered to open or close the culvert as desired. The effective part of this stone channel was well constructed with large cut blocks of limestone that varied in length from 3 ft. 9 in. (1.14 m.). This part of the channel was 8 ft. 10 in. (2.66 m.) long. The floor of the channel immediately east of the slots sloped downwards in a gentle curve and was evidently made to conform to the curve of a circular water-wheel that was housed in the narrow channel. The stone blocks forming the lower part of the channel were cut in one piece to act as both bottom and sides and to prevent any leakage here (pl. XLVII*b*).

The sides of the channel were preserved to a height of 1 ft. 8 in. (0.51 m.). The channel continued beyond the well-built part, but it was constructed with smaller blocks of limestone and increased in width to 2 ft. (0.6 m.). It was traced for 17 ft. 10 in. (5.36 m.) and it was continuing east to join the river downstream.

The channel was filled with fallen blocks of stone which included some pieces of blue pennant roof tile. On the south side of the well-built part, against the high bank, there was a small level platform 2 ft. 10 in. (0.76 m.) in width with a dry-stone wall 2 ft. (0.6 m.) high. The platform east to west was 5 ft. 7 in. (1.69 m.) wide and there were the footings of a small

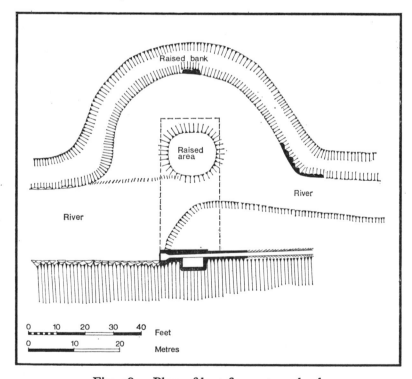

Fig. 48.   Plan of leat for water-wheel

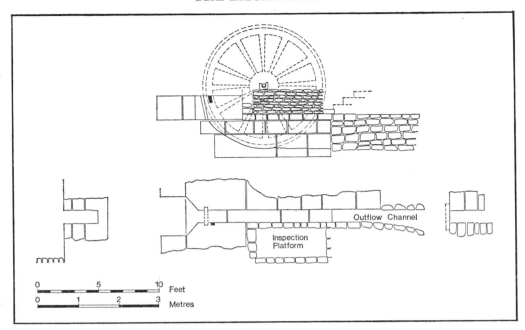

Fig. 49. Plan, elevation and sections of leat and housing of water-wheel

wall at its west side, but on its east side a stone step *in situ* appeared to be the bottom step of a flight of stairs which gave access to the higher ground above the river. The platform seems to have served as an inspection chamber for the water-wheel in its housing, and was reached by way of a flight of steps on its east side. The step was 9 ft. 10 in. (2.95 m.) from the culvert stop at the mouth of the water channel (fig. 48). Apart perhaps from the blue pennant stones in the channel no dateable objects were found in association with the wheel-housing.

To the north of the wheel-housing on the opposite (north) side of the river there is a circular raised bank with a stone revetment still visible in places (fig. 48). In the centre of the area enclosed by this bank there is a slightly raised area and during rainy periods the swollen river flows around this circular mound.

The floor level of the culvert at its mouth was 2 ft. 4 in. (0.71 m.) above the level of the present river. The high level at which the culvert is placed indicates that there must have been a considerable damming of the river to the west of the culvert to bring the water to a level sufficient to feed and drive the water-wheel. The diameter of the wheel as indicated by the sloping curved floor of the culvert was 8 ft. 6 in. (2.56 m.). The central point would be 2 ft. (0.6 m.) above the level of the inspection platform, a suitable level for this purpose.

A search in the Wiltshire County Records of tithe maps, early Ordnance Survey maps and other records for West Kington, Nettleton, and Castle Combe valley, did not produce any indication of a mill at this point in the valley. The former upstream mill at West Kington is shown, as also is the former mill downstream west of Castle Combe village, and remains of both these mills may still be seen. Mr. Lomas Webb, whose family have resided for many years at West Kington, had no knowledge of a mill at Nettleton Scrubb, but he was aware of the other two mills.

The use of such large blocks of stone in the wheel-housing suggests Roman work and the position at the eastern extremity of the Roman settlement is one to be expected. The large blocks suggest that it was built at or about the same time as the octagonal podium of the temple, i.e. before A.D. 230. The Nettleton water-wheel was apparently used to provide power for a mill and depended on the force of water going through the narrow channel to provide the motive force to drive the wheel. The addition of buckets would not be necessary in this case. The Dolaucothi drainage wheel used in the Roman goldmine to raise water from a lower level of the 80 ft. (24.3 m.) deep mine was used manually for this purpose.[66] In this case the wheel was about 11 ft. 8 in. (3.51 m.) in diameter. Other water-wheels of Roman date found in Spain are as much as 20 ft. (6.1 m.) in diameter. The wooden water-wheel now in the British Museum which was used in the Roman Rio Tinto mines in southern Spain was one of 30 such wheels used for raising water from lower levels. The wooden wheels were assembled primarily with wooden plugs, but iron nails were also used. Little or no evidence has been found to date Roman water-wheels more closely.

15. THE MEDIEVAL PERIOD

(a) *Building IV*

During the course of W. C. Priestley's excavation on the north side of the river he found the walls of a building which, from its plan and the objects discovered within and around it, he was able to ascribe to the medieval period (Building IV). The building, 36 ft. (11.0 m.) long and 18 ft. (5.5 m.) wide, had corner buttresses and there was also a centrally placed circular hearth, 5 ft. (1.5 m.) in diameter, constructed with re-used stone roofing tiles (presumably Roman).

Priestley states that 'much late Roman coarse pottery was mixed with the filling when the site was levelled up', and he also mentions 'pieces of medieval pottery (thirteenth and fourteenth century), portions of a large green-glazed jug, enough to show the shape, an iron knife, and a medieval horse-trapping buckle'.

Apart from the plan (fig. 2) this is all we know of the building. It is unfortunate that Priestley does not mention whether the walls were mortared or dry. During the recent excavations on the south side of the river, a number of sherds of medieval date were also found in the highest levels, but were often mixed with late Romano-British pottery; there did not appear to be any level that could definitely be stated to be purely of medieval date. It is certain, however, that the ruinous walls of several of the former Romano-British buildings were incorporated in buildings or sheds erected on the site during the post-Roman period.

(b) *Building XII*

A short length of dry-stone walling was built across the area between the two south walls towards its south-east corner (fig. 2). There was a doorway at the south end of this wall and the dry-stone wall had been built against the face of the Roman wall to form a recess that had evidently held a wooden door post. A large stone door jamb of medieval type was found lying in this doorway. The wall was probably built to serve as an entrance into the late enclosed area of this building from the roadway, which, by that time, had been diverted from the original line of the Fosse Way to the course that it takes today. The original southeast corner of Building XII lies under the modern roadway.

(c) *Medieval Pottery*

The medieval pottery, which amounted to some seventy sherds, came mostly from the small Wick valley. It ranges in date from the eleventh century and both plain and glazed wares were noted. It included Selsey Common and Ham Green ware. The sherds do not call for any special mention, but they do indicate a continuous occupation of the valley, which was confined within the area bounded by the west bank or dry-stone wall which crossed the small Wick valley on its west side.

16. DISCUSSION AND CONCLUSIONS

It may well be that the choice of the Nettleton Scrubb valley for settlement by the Romans was due to the fact that it was the first suitable site with a sizeable river north of Bath (*Aquae Sulis*) on the course of the Fosse Way. The circular Roman shrine built on the south river bank, immediately opposite the spring on the north side of the river, suggests that the site was selected for the Roman shrine because the spring already had some ritual significance in pre-Roman times. Evidence of pre-Roman occupation was found at the Pagans Hill and Lydney Park shrines. It also occurs at Nettleton: coins of the Dobunni tribe and Belgic pottery found in ditches underlying the ditches of the first-century enclosure testify to a pre-Roman occupation of the site.

The ditches which form the first-century enclosure and the area enclosed by them have produced a quantity of first- and second-century pottery, including Samian and St. Remy wares, in association with coins of Claudius I, Nero, Vespasian and Domitian and an unusual number of fibulae. The Roman coin series at Nettleton begins with at least nine coins of Claudius I, which is unusual. There is also a high proportion of Claudian and Neronian wares, consistent with a definitely early date for the founding of the settlement (see pp. 155–71). This suggests that the enclosure was constructed about the same time as the Fosse Way, *c.* A.D. 47. Its function is uncertain, though it is unlikely to have been military and more in the nature of a small native settlement, which ultimately expanded because of religious associations.

The association of Cunomaglos (Hound Prince) with the god Apollo inscribed on the shrine altar (see pp. 135–6) suggests that Cunomaglos was associated with a tribal god of the natives who had settled at Nettleton and that this cult later became Romanized by its assimilation with the classical Apollo.

The Enclosure of the Settlement

The fine rusticated wall discovered by Priestley, which formed the north wall of the rectangular Building I on the north side of the valley, was earlier than its other walls. Rustication is an external feature and it is evident that the building was added to this wall, built against the rock face in the small valley.

Apart from the first-century enclosure on the small plateau on the south side of the valley, the Nettleton settlement lies primarily in the Broadmead and Wick valleys, both formed by extensive limestone outcrops. Unfortunately the limestone has, since Roman times, been extensively quarried for the lime-burning operations in the nearby kilns.

The question of defence or enclosure at Nettleton was resolved by cutting the limestone outcrops back to a vertical face, and the fine rusticated wall was built against the rock face. This method was adopted on the north side of the valley for about 160 yards (146 m.) and also on the south side of the valley from its south-east corner, where the water-wheel was housed. It continued west along the side of the valley for about 256 yards (234 m.) from the water-wheel. Buildings XX and XXV were built against this wall. The same method was used at the foot of the west bank in the Wick valley, where it formed the west wall of the later Building XVI, but its length on this side is uncertain. The constricted, narrow settlement at *Glanum* (St. Rémy-de-Provence), set in a valley between hills, has similar walls built against the cut-back rock face.

To complete the enclosure of the settlement, free-standing walls would be necessary at three points in the valley: (a) across the valley at its narrowest point (downstream) from the water-wheel in the south-east corner of the settlement, to the high limestone rock face where the present road (the Fosse Way) leaves the valley going north (the valley at this point is about 80 yards (73 m.) wide); (b) across the small but steep-sided Wick valley at the south-west end of the settlement, a distance of approximately 37 yards (34 m.); (c) across the Broadmead Brook valley (upstream west of the shrine) from the point where the river takes a sharp turn to the south and crosses the valley to its steep south side, a distance of approximately 37 yards (34 m.). The footings of a substantial wall have been traced in the river bed at this point. The present river bend suggests that it ran alongside the outer face of this wall and served as a moat across the valley. The river crosses the valley, in a similar manner to its north side, at the eastern limit of the settlement and probably served a similar purpose.

Excavation has failed to trace any wall across the small plateau west of the shrine, between the two valleys. It is possible that this area was wooded to the west of the shrine and a strong fence would have sufficed.

The northern entry into the valley is made by way of a rock-cut roadway, with the high limestone outcrop on its west side. This is, and was, the only means of entry into the valley from the north. It is likely that an imposing gateway gave access to the valley settlement at this point in Roman times and a similar gateway gave access to the settlement from the south. It is possible that banks or ditches were made on the higher ground on the outside of the wall-faced limestone outcrops, but because of the later quarrying of the limestone this cannot now be proved.

The rusticated wall facing found by Priestley and that at the foot of the west bank are identical with the rusticated facing of the octagonal podium to the circular shrine. The podium wall was constructed between the years A.D. 230 and 250. This was a period of general development within the settlement and it is likely that the limestone outcrops were given their rusticated facing at about the same time.

The Circular Shrine, the Rectangular Building and the Octagonal Podium

The large rectangular hall built alongside the river as an annexe to the central shrine before A.D. 230, followed by the construction of the elaborate octagonal podium which encompassed the small shrine, testify that these important additions were made to cope with an increasing activity at the shrine. It also enhanced its general appearance and transformed it from a small parochial shrine on the slope to an imposing construction set on a large surrounding platform.

Two comparable sites, excavated in Britain in recent years and both within easy reach of the Bristol Channel, are: (a) the Romano-British shrine at Lydney Park, Gloucestershire, on the opposite side of the river Severn;[67] (b) the Romano-British octagonal shrine at Pagans Hill, Chew Stoke, Somerset.[68]

The two shrines are later than Nettleton, and have a different physical setting. Both were set on the spur of a small, but commanding promontory, whereas the Nettleton settlement lies in a small river valley. Despite this difference, certain similarities suggest that they followed a basic traditional intent.

The Romano-Gaulish settlement excavated in 1883 at Herbord, near Sanxay, Vienne,[69] set in a small valley along both sides of the small river Voune, had similar features incorporated in its plan. The octagonal shrine was its dominant feature. But none of the three shrines mentioned has produced evidence to suggest that an earlier Roman shrine occupied the same site. The octagonal shrine at Nettleton, built soon after A.D. 250, superseded the circular shrine on the same site.

The Lydney Park shrine was not built before A.D. 364 and the smaller shrine at Pagans Hill was a late third- or early fourth-century construction. The earlier date for the Nettleton circular shrine may be due to its close proximity to the Fosse Way, a first-century A.D. arterial highway, but it more likely superseded an earlier cult venerated in pre-Roman times. The later shrines at Lydney and Pagans Hill probably owe their origin to developments in connection with mining operations for lead on the Mendip Hills and iron in the Forest of Dean.

The Rectangular Hall (Building VII)

This building was erected in close proximity to the circular shrine to cope with the increasing activity and to accommodate some innovations in connection with the regular observances at the shrine. Similar buildings at Lydney Park and Pagans Hill form part of the common plan of subsidiary buildings constructed around the shrine, and although Pagans Hill was on a smaller scale, both conform to much the same basic plan.

At Sanxay, where much more space was available, a rectangular appendage was made to one of the side chambers surrounding the central shrine. The earlier hall at Nettleton, built within the temple precinct as an addition to the circular shrine, and the similar hall at Sanxay, were built to conform to an additional requirement that had not previously formed part of the recognized plan. It is suggested that the large hall was a recognized feature of the uniform plan when the later Lydney and Pagans Hill shrines were built, but at Nettleton it was a new feature, incorporated not without some difficulty in the small space between the shrine and the river before A.D. 230. It was probably a place of assembly for family gatherings, when commemorative feasts were held on the anniversaries of past worshippers at the shrine (see p. 16).

Some 20 years later, about A.D. 250, the circular shrine was destroyed by fire. It was replaced on the same site by the larger octagonal shrine, with eight chambers surrounding a central shrine. At about the same time the interior of the rectangular hall was altered by the building of a partition wall across its western end, with a doorway. (The well-worn doorstep was an indication of its constant use.) This restricted the hall to about two-thirds of its original size and created a large narthex at its west end, where it adjoined the octagonal podium. Access to the shrine was made by way of a flight of steps from the narthex which was probably used as a place of rendezvous. The octagonal shrine, with its side chambers, provided a more intimate setting for worshippers to the shrine and the internal arrangement of the hall was altered accordingly.

The Octagonal Shrine (Building VI, c. A.D. 250)

The development of the 'cartwheel' type of Roman building formed the subject of a study by the late Sir Alfred Clapham, published in 1922.[70] The building was primarily an octagonal, polygonal, or circular structure with an internal arrangement of radial walls, generally eight, that converged on its centre to form a central chamber. The central chamber was generally used as a place of sepulture, or the central cella of a shrine, and its area was adjusted to the purpose for which it was required. The central chamber was in turn surrounded by a series of chambers, formed by the converging radial walls. The Nettleton shrine, erected c. A.D. 250, is one of two such buildings known in Britain. The other was the circular mausoleum, excavated in 1896–7, at West Mersea, Essex, and this formed the basis for Clapham's study (fig. 25). Another possible example in Britain is the partially excavated building at Caerwent, Monmouthshire (fig. 25).[71]

As far as can be ascertained, the Nettleton shrine is the only known octagonal temple in Britain that had a series of internal radial walls. Unfortunately the West Mersea mausoleum is not dated, but its small central chamber contained cremated human remains, which suggests a first- or second-century A.D. date for its construction. The Pagans Hill shrine, built during the late third or early fourth century A.D.[72] did not have radial walls, nor did the temple at Weycock, Berks. (fig. 25),[73] but in each instance the central shrine was surrounded by an octagonal ambulatory. The shrines at Alesia (Côte-d'Or) (fig. 25),[74] Goh-Ilis (Morbihan)[75] and Chassenon (Charente) (fig. 25)[76] also conform to this same plan.

The 'cartwheel' building, with radial walls, appears therefore to be of earlier date than the simple Pagans Hill type of shrine. The later closing of the alternate radial chambers at Nettleton suggests that they ceased to have any practical use and in similar buildings of later date the radial wall chambers were omitted. This enabled the later builders to enlarge the central shrine, and the ambulatory, without increasing the overall diameter of the shrine. The overall diameter of the Nettleton octagonal shrine was 70 ft. (21.3 m.), and that of Pagans Hill was 50 ft. (15.2 m.). The central shrine at Nettleton was 4 ft. (1.2 m.) less than that at Pagans Hill and the ambulatory at Nettleton was 2 ft. 6 in. (0.76 m.) less than that at Pagans Hill. This was also the case at Weycock, but, on the other hand, the earlier sepulchral radial-walled mausoleum at West Mersea reduced the diameter of the central chamber to only 5 ft. (1.5 m.). The vaulted roof of the central chamber at Nettleton was held in position by eight stone groins, which rested on the ends of the radial walls, and the intervening spaces between the groins was filled with light-weight tufa blocks. A quantity of tufa was also found at Pagans Hill and Lullingstone.[77] Apart from the Roman villa at Lufton, Yeovil, Somerset,[78] which had an octagonal bath, there is little evidence of the use of tufa in other octagonal buildings in Roman Britain. Both Pagans Hill and Lufton also had external buttresses. The combination of the use of tufa and buttresses suggests that the central part of the building had a stone vault, and that the vault limited the size of the central area of the building.

Other buildings incorporated in the second- to third-century development of the settlement include a water-wheel, presumably for grinding corn, with a substantially constructed housing. The bathing establishment has not been located, but it was most likely placed opposite the shrine on the north side of the river and the water supply was probably obtained from a spring which emerges at this point.

On the whole, the Nettleton settlement falls into line with other Roman establishments in Britain where substantial buildings erected before the early years of the third century A.D. were permitted to fall into a ruinous condition, and in some instances used as rubbish dumps. At Nettleton, this was primarily due perhaps to a dramatic change in the water-table level. The riverside buildings were inundated by flood and abandoned. They were replaced by buildings of inferior workmanship which did not compare with the earlier work. The new buildings were erected on the higher ground away from the river. Similar evidence of this change in the water level has been found in the Roman baths at Bath, where the floors were raised to a higher level, and also on the Somerset moor levels where Roman remains in several instances have been discovered below a considerable depth of alluvium.

The Hostelry or Guest-house (Buildings XI and XII) (fig. 2)

The Nettleton shrine was set in a delectable Cotswold valley and was, and still is, an attractive place to visit. Visitors to the shrine were catered for by the provision of at least one shop (Building X) where they might obtain suitable votives to offer at the shrine, and doubtless other amenities were also provided. Soon after A.D. 140 a hostel to accommodate guests was constructed alongside the Fosse Way. However, shortly after A.D. 250 the increasing use of the shrine necessitated its replacement by a larger building, with an interior courtyard on the same site. The several later additions made to this second hostel, which included stabling for horses, testify to its increasing use from the latter part of the third century A.D. up to the early years of the fourth century. Additional accommodation was provided soon after A.D. 250 when extensive additions were made on the north side of the large rectangular hall (Building VII) within the precincts of the shrine. This important extension entailed the erection of a series of square stone piers in the river bed, opposite the riverside piers of the rectangular building. By this means the riverside building was extended across the river, on a series of arches or wooden beams, and it was doubtless related to buildings on the north side of the river.

In one way or another the traveller was well provided for at the Nettleton shrine. Similar amenities were available in the well-planned Lydney shrine, and also on a smaller scale at the Pagans Hill shrine. The Romano-Gaulish shrine at Sanxay followed a similar pattern, where the shrine faced east, with an elaborate colonnaded approach which formed a covered way to the shrine. The roadway that led from the guest-house at Nettleton to the shrine was flanked on either side by lightly constructed walls, which suggests that it also had a colonnaded approach to the shrine. The column found in Building XIII (fig. 78(15)) may have come from this colonnade.

Nettleton has provided evidence to suggest that several deities were honoured there. Three objects, the inscribed altar, the bronze plaque and the bronze ring intaglio, suggest that Apollo was its principal deity and the association with Diana suggests that the shrine was a centre of healing, where visiting pilgrims could obtain refreshments and consolation to help sustain them on their journey. Other pagan cults represented at Nettleton are those of Silvanus, Mercury, Rosmerta and an unidentified deity, probably a local goddess. Devotees were apparently given the choice of seeking solace from the favourite deity, but the reference to the *Numen Augusti* on the Silvanus altar reminded them of their overriding duty, of paying obeisance to the official Imperial cult. There is little doubt that more excavation would reveal further additions to this miniature pantheon at Nettleton.

Additional amenities at Sanxay included a bathing establishment, a theatre, and two smaller temples. Similar provision was probably made at Nettleton, but the later quarrying operations have unfortunately obliterated the evidence. A likely site for the theatre would be on the north side of the river, where the high limestone outcrop would have provided an excellent site for the auditorium. A second, and more likely, site for a small theatre was the west bank of the settlement. Despite the later quarrying of the bank there is some evidence to support this suggestion. The roadway which ascends the west slope on the north side of Building XVI did not go beyond the upper terrace and it was evidently made to give access to the terrace. A cobbled area on the north side of the shrine joined this road. At the foot of the west bank wall a level area extended to the wall alongside the road leading up the Wick valley. This wall, 4 ft. (1.2 m.) wide, was much too substantial to form a skirting wall alongside the road, and it is more likely that it was part of a substantial building, which may well have been the backstage wall of a small theatre facing the auditorium on the west valley slope. Unfortunately the bank was quarried for limestone in the fourth century A.D. and it was later used as a dump for rubbish. This rubbish has produced a large number of late fourth-century coins and a quantity of late contemporary pottery. The rubbish dump extended beyond the bank and completely covered the walls of Building XVIII and the roadside wall, a clear indication that the buildings were destroyed prior to the disposal of the rubbish. Similar evidence was found by Dr. Kathleen Kenyon during the excavation of the theatre at *Verulamium* where large numbers of late fourth-century coins were recovered from a rubbish dump which completely covered its remains. The late Sir Ian Richmond has suggested that this dumping of rubbish in the disused theatre represented the renouncing, in a spectacular fashion, of the heathenry practised in the theatre, and this was replaced by the nearby pagan temple, which was converted and used as a Christian church.[79]

During the last decade of the first half of the fourth century A.D. the four alternate side chambers surrounding the central shrine at Nettleton were blocked by partition walls. Externally the appearance of the former shrine remained unaltered, but the internal effect of this alteration converted it from an octagonal shrine, into the cruciform plan of a Christian church with a central crossing surrounded by four open transeptal chambers. In its altered form the internal arrangement was similar to several continental examples and was not unlike the oratory of St. Lawrence the Martyr, popularly known as the tomb of Galla Placidia, sister of the Christian emperor Honorius, at Ravenna.

The plastered walls which sealed the chambers at Nettleton bore a painted design, and this replaced an earlier painted design which was contemporary with the *opus signinum* floor in the central area of the shrine (see fig. 33). The later painted plaster coating was contemporary with the pennant stone floor in the central area. There was no pennant flooring in the sealed chambers. The later design on the partition walls was executed in red, black, white and green. It consisted of two empanelled X crosses, with a large central roundel at the cross junction of each X. It is possible that this design, which replaced an earlier design, may be of some ritual significance in connection with the rearrangement of the building. The outline of the central roundel of the design was scribed on the plaster with a compass prior to being painted red, but the detail of the design was not well preserved. The central roundel seems to have no purpose unless it was to give prominence to some symbol, which might well have been a Chi-Rho.

The mosaic discovered in 1963 at Hinton St. Mary, Dorset, has as its central motif a representation of what is generally accepted to be a portrait of Christ with the Christian Chi-Rho monogram. Attention has been focused on this central feature of this important mosaic, but little or no mention has been made of its background which is an X-type cross, a truncated elaboration of the painted design at Nettleton.[80] Dr. D. J. Smith suggests that the Hinton St. Mary mosaic and other fourth-century mosaics in Britain were laid after A.D. 315–25, but before A.D. 340–50.[81] His date thus covers the period when the Nettleton shrine declined and ceased to be used for pagan worship.

Professor J. C. Toynbee, writing in 1953, has stated that: 'In 312, Constantine's conversion to Christianity and the so-called "Edict of Milan" gave peace to the Christian Church . . . It is clear that by then the Christian population of Britain was already organized on normal Catholic lines with bishops in seats of government at the leading urban centres. For only two years later, in A.D. 314 . . . three British bishops were summoned to the Catholic council of the western episcopate at Arles . . .' It is clear however that 'during the first half of the fourth century pagan worship had lost its former fervour'.[82] The paucity of Christian remains in Britain of fourth-century date is not indeed surprising, but the relative evidence obtained from Nettleton and other excavated sites in recent years certainly indicates that Christianity was more firmly established in Roman Britain in the fourth century A.D. than had previously been inferred.[83]

The blocking of the side chambers during the first half of the fourth century A.D. with walls which carried a painted plaster cruciform design is in accord with Professor Toynbee's remarks. It is possible that the former shrine was converted for use as a Christian church after A.D. 330. The changed internal plan and the cruciform design may be a symbolic expression of this change.

The recent discoveries at Hinton St. Mary of the Christian mosaic, the possible (and probably much later) church plan at Cadbury Castle, the late fourth-century Christian tombs found by Mr. Green at Poundbury, Dorset, and the re-examination of the Christian church at Silchester by the late Sir Ian Richmond discount the theory that the Christian religion did not reach the countryside, and it was only practised in the larger towns in the fourth century A.D. Although Roman Nettleton was in a rural setting, it was alongside a main arterial highway and in easy contact with *Corinium* and other centres of population. It would therefore be well informed of any changes which would affect the way of life of its inhabitants. *Corinium*, it may be recalled, has at least produced a well-known cryptogram.

Industrial Activity, A.D. 330–90

After A.D. 330 there was a marked deterioration in building standards and the use of mortar for building purposes ceased. The neat, squared floors of pennant stone were roughly repaired and little respect was paid to the former shrine; its altars were profaned and taken down. One was used as a hearthside seat within the former shrine and another was incorporated in a furnace which was used in the later industrial activity in Building XVIII. The former period of prosperity had ended and the changed conditions were strikingly apparent throughout the settlement.

Following the decline of the shrine towards the end of the first half of the fourth century, there was marked industrial activity and this completely changed the character of the settlement. Care for the comfort of visitors to the shrine was replaced by the stoking of furnaces, pewter-casting, bronze- and iron-smelting, and life for the inhabitants was drastically changed. The approach road to the shrine was littered with debris. The floors of buildings formerly used to provide creature comforts for visitors were also littered with evidence of this change.

The establishment of smelting and pewter-casting operations was dependent on the necessary technical knowledge and skill to carry out this task. It is possible, in the first instance, that this knowledge was acquired from the imperially controlled lead-mining centre at Charterhouse-on-Mendip. Pewter-casting was practised during the middle of the third century A.D. at the Romano-British settlement at Camerton, Somerset (Avon), and it continued well into the fourth century A.D.[84] Similar activity was noted at Lansdown, Bath.[85]

It is of interest to note that the pigs of Mendip lead recovered in Britain and elsewhere bear the insignia of first- and second-century Emperors.[86] Haverfield, writing on the Mendip lead mines,[87] notes that inscribed pigs continued to be produced until *c.* A.D. 169, and that the cessation might have been caused partly by a failure of accessible ores and partly by a change in the system. But he found it hard to accept that lead working did not continue in some form until, say, the middle of the fourth century. If he had known of the evidence for pewter-working in Roman Britain, his views would have been strengthened.

The undisputed evidence of pewter-casting in the fourth century A.D., illustrated by the finding of stone moulds and the associated furnaces at Camerton, Nettleton and possibly Landsown, suggests that the discontinuance of making lead pigs for export purposes was due to the large percentage of lead used for making pewter ware in Britain. The export of lead ore, in the form of lead pigs, was replaced by the export of pewter plates, bowls, skillets, pans and other similar vessels made in Britain. The three known pewter-casting sites were within easy reach of the Bristol Channel for the purpose of export.

The two chief centres in which Roman pewter objects have been found in Britain are the Cambridge region and Somerset, especially in the Somerset Levels. Very little Roman pewter has been found north of the river Severn and the Fosse Way beyond Cirencester, but both of these regions have extensive peat-bearing plains, which are conducive to the preservation of pewter and other objects, and many of the pewter finds made in these areas have been preserved by this means. Apart from this density of finds, the Somerset region has other claims to be the centre of pewter-casting in Roman times. The country around Bath in the south Cotswolds and north of the Mendip Hills was particularly suited for the production of pewter. The coal outcrops in the north Somerset coalfield were known and worked in Roman times, and the nearby lead mines on Mendip meant that only tin, the smaller constituent of pewter, had to be brought some distance, from Cornwall. The three known sites, Camerton, Nettleton and possibly Lansdown in this area, suggest that a pewter industry developed during the Constantinian period for the production, in some quantity, of pewter plates, dishes, paterae, skillets and other pewter utensils.

The production of so many domestic utensils in pewter must have had a considerable effect on the pottery industry. Each settlement seems to have specialized in its own particular type of plates, dishes and othe utensils, and there is little doubt that some pottery forms were replaced by unbreakable replicas in pewter. It is particularly noticeable that there are few equivalents in fourth-century Roman pottery of the shallow saucer-like forms that are comparatively common in earlier first- and second-century contexts. The common pie-dish, with straight sides, is the nearest approach to the saucer that we get in fourth-century common wares. Can it be that they were not required, because they had been replaced by pewter equivalents? If this pewter was made in quantity, we may well ask why we do not find more specimens during the course of excavations on Romano-British sites. The answer to this probably lies in the value of the metal. Most Roman pewter in Britain has been found in wells, peat-beds and other places where it has been accidentally lost or purposely hidden. In several instances complete vessels have also been found in a rolled or bent-up condition. One such example occurred at Nettleton and another at Camerton, and in each case it was found alongside a wall where it had fallen. Pewter, it is suggested, in view of its metal value, would be high on the list of the looters' haul from raided settlements. Pewter dishes, etc., were either rolled or broken up for ease of transport, in much the same way as certain caches of silver and bronze found in late contexts in Britain and in Denmark where they were taken by raiding pirates (see p. 236).[88] A small amount of pewter was found in the folds of the 'packets' of silver found at Traprain, Scotland, and this was suspected loot from southern Britain.

Little is known concerning the method employed by the Romans to make the pewter alloy, which consisted of an admixture of lead and tin. The pewter moulds at Camerton and Nettleton were found in association with the same type of furnace, which consisted of a stone-built channel below ground level, some 4–8 ft. (1.2–2.4 m.) in length and about 1 ft. 6 in. (0.46 m.) in depth. The top of the stone channel was flush with the surface and was apparently open at floor level. The sloping sides of the channel were about 2 ft. (0.6 m.) wide at the top, but only 1 ft. (0.3 m.) at the bottom, and the channel floor was paved with limestone blocks. At its open end the channel connected with a semi-circular chamber, which was enclosed with a stone kerb and the chamber floor sloped gently down from the kerb to the open mouth of the stone-built flue channel. Apart from the kerb there was no other construction surrounding the chamber and there was little or no evidence of fire in the chamber itself, but the adjoining stone channel had been subject to intense heat. The heat had discoloured and pulverized the stones in the channel, which terminated with a sloping, rounded end against the wall of the building. This presumably connected with a chimney to dispose of the fumes.

The furnace seems to have been of similar construction to the hearth furnaces used for lead smelting until about 1720 in the Wirksworth district of Derbyshire.[89] We learn from this that 'The form of rude furnace that was used throughout the Wirksworth district till about 1720 (when the cupola began to succeed it) was probably identical with the means resorted to by the Romans. The Derbyshire hearth furnace consisted of large stones placed in the ground so as to form an oblong cavity, varying from 1 to 2 ft. [0.3–0.6 m.] in width and depth and from 6 to 14 ft. [1.8–4.3 m.] in length. Into this cavity the fuel and ore were put in alternate layers, the heat being raised by a large pair of bellows which were sometimes worked by a water-wheel. The fuel used was generally a mixture of wood and coal . . . This crude form of smelting left much metal in the slag and the refuse heaps of the Roman miners of Derbyshire have yielded from time to time most excellent lead when re-smelted.'

This operation was repeated at the former Roman lead-mining centre at Charterhouse-on-Mendip, Somerset, when an extensive and systematic re-excavation and re-smelting of the Roman spoil heaps was made for commercial purposes in 1867.[90] Unfortunately, little or no record was made of 'the stone buildings and rough smelting furnaces' found during the course of this re-examination. A description, with sketches, of the furnaces found in 1867 would prove useful today. The constructional detail of the Camerton and Nettleton furnaces is very similar to that of the Derbyshire examples. It explains why there was little evidence of fire in the stone chambers. The abundant evidence of fire in the stone channels suggests that the fire was confined in or above the stone channel only. The fuel and ores were laid in alternate layers above the stone channel and the molten metal resulting from the fire mixed in the bottom of the stone channel. The chamber was used for stoking the fire and also to control the necessary draught for smelting the ores by means of a large stone slab placed upright in a groove at the mouth of the channel. This would be opened or closed to obtain the required draught in accordance with the prevailing wind. One of the two furnaces found in Building XXVI was situated on the west bank slope and its stoke-hole, cut into the solid rock, had no evidence of fire. In this instance, the flue channel was placed on a higher level than the chamber, with its double opening to the fire channel, and its solid rock floor was considerably worn down by constant stoking and the intense heat. It was abundantly clear in this instance that the chamber, placed at a lower level than the channel, was intended for the stoker to stand in while tending the fire. The fire channel in this case was at about knee level. It is likely that the furnace served a dual purpose (a) for mixing and blending the metals and (b) for the final pouring of the alloy into the moulds.

The Late Fourth-century and Post-Roman Period

A striking feature of the Nettleton excavation has been the unusually large number of coins that cover the period from A.D. 330 to 402 (see Dr. Reece's report, pp. 115–18). A large proportion of these coins has been found in material that had been dumped on at least four separate sites within the settlement. Some 400 coins covering the period A.D. 330–402 were found scattered over the ruinous walls and floor of Building XVIII. This building was destroyed down to its lowest three or four stone courses before the material containing the coins, pottery and other finds were dumped over them (see pp. 87–8). Coins of the same period have also been recovered from material overlying the approach road to the shrine, in the quarry to the west of the shrine, and in the mass of dumped refuse which covered the west bank. It has been demonstrated that this material was dumped following the decline of the shrine after A.D. 330. In his coin report, Dr. Reece suggests that despite the fact that so many of the coins have been found scattered, especially those from Building XVIII, they may form one, or perhaps two dispersed coin hoards which were found and dispersed probably by raiders. Group 'A' was associated with Building XVIII, and was probably deposited before A.D. 364–7. The second group 'B', deposited before A.D. 380–5, was found dispersed in the debris that covered the walls of Building XVIII. The coins were evidently not current at the time of their dispersal and consequently of little value to looters.

After A.D. 370 two raids were made within a short space of time on the settlement and the abundant evidence of burning has been demonstrated in several buildings, especially Building XIII (fig. 37). Buildings assigned to this period were constructed with small undressed stones without mortar. In several instances the walls were superimposed on the earlier mortared walls and the outer corners were rounded. It was at this time that a large part of the former shrine was adapted for use as a homestead. The roughly constructed fire hearths made from discarded stone roof tiles; the partial blocking of the south-west window with re-used voussoirs; the conversion of the west sector into a stable; the large accumulation of household rubbish on the floors and the disused ambulatory used as a rubbish dump all testify to the squalid way of life of the later occupants of the settlement.

The coin dispersal coincided with a rearrangement of the settlement. Some roads and buildings were dispensed with and the sites levelled with the debris containing the dispersed coins, but the coins do not date this re-arrangement and it may well be that the levelling operations were made at a later date for the purpose of agriculture. The evidence of squalor and the changed building standards suggest a change in the direction and control.

Hunter-Blair has drawn attention to instances in Britain where successful attacks, presumably by Irish pirates who came by way of the Bristol Channel, on Romano-British settlements were followed up by their assimilation into the community.[91] It is possible that this happened at Nettleton; the deterioration in building standards suggests such a change. There is no apparent reason why this occupation should not have continued well beyond the date of the latest currency (A.D. 402) into the fifth and sixth centuries A.D. The small bronze brooch decorated with millefiori technique (see p. 132) was recovered from the burnt floor of Building XVIII in association with late fourth-century coins. This brooch had the appearance of wear over a long period of time. Its projecting corner knobs had been broken off in antiquity and the broken ends had become quite smooth with later use. Professor Toynbee writes that the brooch was probably made c. A.D. 150–250.[92]

The interments made within the confines of the first-century enclosure, on its north side, suggest that this fourth-century cemetery was sited by inhabitants who no longer regarded, and did not observe, the Roman rule that forbade human burial within the recognized boundary of a settlement. The orientation of the stone-lined graves, and the complete lack of grave goods suggests Christian burial (see pp. 90–2). It also implies that they were not pagan Saxon burials, otherwise finds similar to those found at the transitional cemetery at Camerton, Somerset, some 20 miles south on the Fosse Way, would be expected.[93]

Associated with the millefiori brooch and the coins in Group 'A' in the burnt debris on the floor of Building XVIII, a *plumbata* (*martiobarbulus*) was found. This was a lead-weighted feathered javelin head which formed part of the kit carried by the Roman legionaries. Three of these weapons have been recently recovered in a late fourth- or fifth-century context at

Wroxeter. Another specimen, in the museum at Shrewsbury, was found with a *francisca* or Saxon throwing axe in the baths at Wroxeter in the nineteenth century.[94] The *plumbatae* are unlikely to have reached Wroxeter before A.D. 400 which suggests that they were used against undesirable occupants in the ruinous Roman town. The Nettleton example was also found in a late fourth- to fifth-century context and poses an interesting problem. If the weapon was used exclusively by the Roman legionary, were they used by them in an attempt to clear the Nettleton settlement of undesirable occupants who had taken possession of the settlement, as a result of a raid made during a period when the discipline of Roman rule had become somewhat lax due to difficulties in other parts of Britain?

Sir Mortimer Wheeler writes in the Lydney Park excavation report that: 'the poverty of post-Roman relics upon the site is eloquent of a population which, behind its refurbished second-hand earthworks, eked out a sort of second-hand existence entirely lacking in cultural initiative'.[95] Apart from a miserable south cross-bank, Nettleton has no visible surviving earthworks, but Sir Mortimer's remarks apply equally well to the Nettleton settlement at the end of the fourth century A.D. It is this poverty of post-Roman relics that leaves us with so little positive evidence concerning the post-Roman occupation. The lack of coin evidence in the settlement after A.D. 402 does not necessarily imply that occupation ceased. A quantity of pottery sherds, primarily late fourth-century wares, e.g. stamped, rosette, and colour-coated wares, recovered from the same material as that in which the scattered coin hoards were found, also contained a number of sherds of coarse dark stone-coloured ware, made with an admixture of dark clay, crushed fossil shell and stone grit. This pottery had an angular shaped cavetto rim, with a wide band of fine combing around the upper part of the pot. Sherds of this distinctive pottery have also been found by Dr. Peter Fowler at the Romano-British settlement at Overton Down, Wilts, in association with late fourth-century coins. Dr. Fowler has suggested that late Roman pottery conventionally dated to the fourth century A.D. could continue in use into the fifth and sixth centuries A.D. and suggests that more serious consideration should be given to the so-called 'squatters' and their continuing occupation into the fifth and sixth centuries A.D.[96] Dr. Wade-Martins has also recovered similar pottery at North Elmham, Norfolk, in association with Saxon pottery.[97] Miss Charlesworth has dated some of the glass from Building XVIII to the late fourth and early fifth centuries A.D. (pp. 150–3), and Mrs. Guido has suggested that some of the beads are likely to be of Saxon date (pp. 153–4). The large coin dispersal and the associated late pottery suggests a continuing occupation after the Roman withdrawal by people who had no use for Roman currency and had different living standards.

It is suggested that after the Roman withdrawal the remaining inhabitants, with the probable addition of some Irish Christian settlers, continued to occupy the settlement after A.D. 402. The duration of this occupation is uncertain, but we know that the occupants were ultimately the victims of an attack which differed from the previous raids. The earlier raids were made to obtain as much loot as possible by creating a state of chaos by setting fire to the buildings. There was no evidence of fire in this final assault which was intended to obliterate the settlement by the massacre of its occupants. The scattered human bones found with evidence of sword slashes and decapitation in the former shrine testify that they were the victims of a determined and vicious attack. The evidence suggests that this form of attack was repeated at the nearby Wraxall villa (see pp. 85–6) and there is similar evidence from Brislington and Kingsweston, sites which were within easy reach of the Bristol Channel, suggesting that they too came to a violent and abrupt end.

The richest group of Roman villas in Britain was centred around the towns of Ilchester and Bath, including the south Cotswold country, and we know that most of them survived beyond A.D. 367.[98] It is also significant that a large number of visitors centred on the great spa at Bath (*Aquae Sulis*). This suggests that a visit to the temple of Minerva and the spa was a necessity for those who could visit such places in Roman Britain. The popularity of the spa at Bath would urge others to emulate and provide similar counter-attractions in this comparatively populous area. The rural shrines at Pagans Hill, Henley Wood, Lamyatt Beacon and Nettleton would cater for this in much the same way as the spas at Cheltenham, Glastonbury and Hotwells, Bristol, competed with Bath in the eighteenth and nineteenth centuries.

Nettleton was therefore a rural wayside shrine, dedicated primarily to the god Apollo, and possibly a minor spa which, however, attracted considerable attention from the early second century until about A.D. 330, but after that date its popularity waned. It then continued as a simple rural community which became involved in the growing industrial activity of pewter-casting, iron-smelting and bronze-casting. After A.D. 330 it seems to have partially assimilated the Christian religion, but about A.D. 360 there was a temporary pagan revival. Currency apparently ceased to reach the settlement after the end of the fourth century A.D. which accords with similar Roman sites in south-west Britain. The minting of coins apparently ceased in Britain and few coins were entering the island from the continent.[99] But the evidence suggests a continuing occupation after the end of the fourth century A.D.

As stated, the millefiori brooch probably came to the settlement by way of Ireland in the late fourth century or later. The nearby Roman villa at Wraxall has produced a Germanic fourth-century belt buckle.[100] Graham Webster writes that: 'It would not therefore be unreasonable to suppose that rural life continued for example in the Cotswolds based on the villas after A.D. 400'. The evidence, not supported by coins, is admittedly slight, but the poor building standards with disjointed, curved, or circular dry-stone walls together with the slight, but definite, pottery evidence suggests a continuing occupation. The meagre evidence of pottery from the site at this time may be accounted for by its replacement by pewter, and as stated the small number of pewter finds recorded at Nettleton may perhaps be accounted for by its value as loot from the settlement.

It is therefore not unreasonable, after due consideration of the evidence, to suggest that the final assault on the Nettleton settlement, which resulted in the obliteration of the settlement and the massacre of its inhabitants, was one of a number of exploratory raids, that preceded the conquest of the Cotswolds by the invading Saxons. Isolated settlements, such as Nettleton and the nearby Wraxall villa, occupied by a 'squatter' community, would be particularly vulnerable to such exploratory surprise raids, which would most likely have preceded the conquest of Badon, Dyrham, Cirencester and Bath in A.D. 556 which followed the conquest of the Severn valley and the Bristol region by the Saxons after A.D. 550.[101]

PART II: THE FINDS

1. THE BRITISH COINS

by the late Derek F. Allen, C.B., F.B.A., F.S.A.

1. This coin is a typical example of a Dobunnic uninscribed silver coin of the type Evans F7, or Mack 380–1; and falls within Class E of the Allen classification of Dobunnic coins. Such coins are found in all parts of the Dobunnic area and the north-west fringe of Wiltshire, bordering Gloucestershire, is within the normal distribution. The date of striking was probably about the end of the first quarter of the first century A.D.; it must have been between the date of the earliest finds at Bagendon, *c.* A.D. 10, and the burial of the Nunney hoard, dated by the Roman coins in it to *c.* A.D. 43. As the Nunney hoard shows, such a coin could well have been in circulation at the time of the Roman conquest in this area or even a little later. The obverse has what is meant for a beardless face, probably of a goddess, with two dolphins in front, but it has been reduced to a barely intelligible formula. Like all Dobunnic coins, the reverse has a horse with a triple tail.

   The coin was found in a first- to second-century A.D. level on the east side of the shrine in association with a penannular brooch (fig. 55(79)).

2. The second British coin, also a Dobunnic silver coin, falls into Allen Class C, that is, an uninscribed coin fairly early in the sequence, but not at the beginning. It therefore falls just within the first century A.D. though one cannot be precise. It was used and worn in antiquity and probably was not buried until quite a bit later.

   The coin was found in the filling of the first-century A.D. enclosure ditch in association with coins of Claudius I and Vespasian.

2. THE ROMAN COINS

by Richard M. Reece, B.Sc., D.Phil., F.S.A.

References

Augustus to A.D. 330:
RIC (see Abbreviations and Bibliography, p. xvi).

A.D. 330–402:
HK = *The Bronze Coinage of the House of Constantine A.D. 324–346* (Carson, Hill and Kent, 1960, Part I)
CK = *Bronze Roman Imperial Coinage of the Later Empire A.D. 346–498* (Carson, Hill and Kent, 1960, Part II)

Consolidated Coin List

2 British	See separate report, above
1 Divus Augustus	Copy as *RIC*, 6
2 Tiberius	Copy as *RIC*, 11, 11 ff. (1)

14	Claudius I	64, copy as 64, 66, copies as 66 (9), illeg. (2)
4	Nero	176, copy as 304 in the manner of Claudius I, 321, silver, illeg.
7	Vespasian	486, 497, illeg. (5)
6	Domitian	As 242A, 351 (2), 354b (2), illeg.
2	first century	Otherwise illeg.
4	Trajan	245, illeg. (3)
12	Hadrian	578, as 678 but cos III in the exergue, illeg. (10)
5	Antoninus Pius	As 924 but a Dupondius, illeg. (4)
4	Faustina I	(Ant. Pius) 1103B, 1124, 1184, illeg.
6	Marcus Aurelius	(Ant. Pius) 1234c, as Caesar but otherwise illeg., (M. Aurelius) 1003, 1227, as Augustus but otherwise illeg. (2)
4	Faustina II	(M. Aurelius) 1688, 1711, illeg. (2)
4	Lucilla	Illeg. (4)
2	Commodus	512, 545
5	Septimius Severus	93, as 140, illeg. (3)
2	first or second century	Otherwise illeg. (2)
1	Geta	148
2	Caracalla	100, 179
1	Plautilla	(Caracalla) 367
2	Elagabalus	88, 125
1	Julia Mamaea	(Severus Alexander) 360
4	Severus Alexander	As 5, 93, 178, 212
1	third century	Illeg. denarius
3	Gordian III	As Caesar 1, as Augustus 300b, illeg.
2	Philip I	162b, illeg.
1	Volusian	167
3	Valerian I	99, 106, illeg.
1	Mariniana	3
24	Gallienus	Joint reign 179, illeg.; sole reign 157 (2), 160, 163, 171a (2), 179, 180 (3), 181, 193 (2), 230 (2), 245, 297, 300, illeg. (4)
2	Salonina	Sole reign 5, illeg.
34	Claudius II	18 (2), 34 (2), 41, 48, 53, 54, 57, 66, 75, as 105 but B in field, 106, 107, 109, 113, 171, as 179, 261 (5), 266 (6), illeg. (5)
1	Aurelian	62
1	Tacitus	63
1	Probus	31
7	Postumus	54, 67, 76, 83, 170, 376, illeg.
16	Victorinus	61, 71 (2), 114 (5), 118 (6), illeg. (2)
58	Tetricus I	48, 56 (2), 70, 77, 80 (3), 82, 86 (2), 87 (4), 88 (4), 90 (2), 100 (4), 101 (6), 102 (3), 121 (3), 122 (3), 130, 132, 133, 136 (6), 146, illeg. (8)
10	Tetricus II	224, 247, 248, 254, 255, 260, 270, 272 (2), 274
22	Radiates	Regular but otherwise illeg. (22)
89	Barbarous Radiates	As Tetricus I 188 (1), as Tetricus I 90 (1), as Claudius II 261 (1); reverses with Altar (2), Fides (2), Fortuna, Invictus (3), Laetitia, Pax (11), Pietas (3), Salus (9), Spes (10), Victoria, Virtus (4), network of lines, confused figures, illeg. (37)
11	Carausius	255, 347, 878 (2), 893, 1019, 1037, as 1060 or blundered VIRTVS, illeg. (3)

8	Allectus	28, 33, 55, 75, 105, 125, illeg. (2)
1	Diocletian	*RIC* 5 as 35
2	Maximianus I	*RIC* 6 Tr 143, Tic 31b
2	Licinius I	*RIC* 6 Tr 844b, 845b
1	Maximinus II	*RIC* 6 Tr 845a
1	Constantius I (Divus)	*RIC* 6 Tr 789
6	Crispus	*RIC* 7 Tr 372, 440, 453; Lug 133, 215; Thess 113
6	Constantine I	*RIC* 6 Lon 79, 119, as 121a; Tr 772a, 898; Rome 112a
20		*RIC* 7 Lon 10 (2), 289 (2); Tr 76 (3), 213 (2), 291, 305 (2), 341 (3); mm. illeg. as Lon 158 (2), 240
30		HK 1, as 12, 48, as 48 (3), 48a, 55, 60 (5), 92, as 98, as 106, 114 (3), 169, 197, 231, 362 (2), 398 (2), 542, 656, 934, 957
29	Constantinopolis	52, as 52 (11), 59 (3), 66, 71, 77 (3), 86 (2), 191, 201, 206, 356, 390, 557, 746
27	Urbs Roma	51 (2), as 51 (9), 58 (4), 65 (3), 70 (2), 76, 85, 184, 190, 205 (2), 355
3	Delmatius	97 (2), 223
7	Constantine II	*RIC* 7 Lon 190, 236; Tr 300, 353, 412, 433; mm. illeg. as Lon 291
43		HK 49 (2), as 49 (2), 56, 63 (2), 68 (2), 88 (6), as 88 (6), 93 (2), 107 (2), 125, 172, 181 (2), 187 (2), 203 (2), 232, 253, 374, 379, 389, 411, 416, 419, as 580, reverse smooth (1)
11	Theodora	As 105 (6), 113 (3), 120 (2)
19	Helena	35, as 104 (8), 112 (2), 119 (4), 128 (4)
106	Constans	84, as 90, copy as 90, as 102 (3), 103, 110, as 110, 127, (4) 131, 133 (8), 134, 136, 138 (3), as 138 (2), 140 (13), 142 (2), 144, 148 (8), 149 (7), 150 (7), 153, 155 (3), 156, 158 (5), 159 (2), 160 (7), 168, 227, 236, 251 (3), 261, 262, 267, 274, 401, 413, as 445, 450 (2), 454, 456, 633, 638, illeg. (1)
26		CK 28, 33 (8), as 33 (5), 35 (5), as 36, as 41 (2), 43, 140, 155 (2)
61	Constantius II	HK as 50 (3), 64, 69 (3), 74, 89, as 89 (3), 94 (2), as 100, 108 (3), 109, 126 (3), 130, copy as 130, 132 (4), as 137, copy as 137, 139, 141, 145 (3), 146, 147 (2), 151 (2), 157a, 164, 230, 234, 242, 252, 256, 264, 269, 354 (2), 400 (3), 434, 444 (2), 446, 455, 578, 792, as 958
52		CK as 25 (8), copies as 25 (10), 32 (2), 34 (3), 40, as 42, 72, as 72, large copy as 72, as 77, 202, 249, 252, 256 (7), as 256 (7), 262 (2), 452 but only 13 mm. diameter, 677, 936, 1218
1	House of Constantine	As *RIC* 7 Lon 291
119		As HK 48 (10), copies as 48 (7), copies as 5L (6), copies as 52 (13), as 53, copy of 65, as 87 (19), copies as 87 (13), as 99, as 121, copies as 132 (2), copies as 133 (2), as 137 (23), copy as 137, as 158, copy of 181, copy of 184 (2), copy of 185, copy of 186, copy of 220, copy of 239, as 355, copy as 355, copy of 356, hybrids obv./rev. 51/52 (2), 51/104, 52/51 (3), 52/57, 52/184
108		CK as 25, copies as 25 (84), copies as 25 overstruck on coins as HK 48 (3), 110, 137, 180, 376; as CK 32 (5), as 34, as 40 (2), copy as 72, as 77, as 182, as 256 (3), copy as 457
28		illeg. (28)
1	Constantius Gallus	CK 454

30	Magnentius	3, as 8 (5), copies as 8 (11), 10, 12, 15, good copy as 19, copy as 19 overstruck on HK 145, as 49, 50, 55, 56, copy as 56, 58, 214, copy as 217
1	Julian	Reverse VOTIS/XXX/MVLT/XXXX in copper. Possibly the core of a plated siliqua
1	Jovian	473
120	Valentinian I	As 96 (12), as 275 (20), as 279, 281, 284, 285, 287, as 296, 300, 307 (4), 317 (3), as 317, 321, 324, 330 (2), 338 (5), 342, 477, 479 (2), 481 (4), as 481, as 498, 501 (4), 502, 503c as 504 but VIB (2), 508, 512 (3), as 512, 514, as 514 (4), 518 (2), 520, 521 (3), 525 (4), 527 (3), 712, 718, 724 (2), 986 (2), 998, 1011 (2), 1014 (2), 1015, 1032 (2), 1035 (2), 1349, 1350, 1390, 1420, 1425 (2), 1426, 1435
164	Valens	Silver *RIC* Thess. p. 175, no. 126; copper CK 82, as 82, 97, as 97 (42), 104, 276, 277, 278, 280, as 280 (2), as 282 (7), 285, 288, 289, 291, 295, as 301, as 303, 306, 309, 319 (4), 322 (4), 332 (2), 336, 340 (3), 344, 480 (2), as 480, 483 (4), 485, 486, 492 (5), 495, 497, 501, 502 (4), 510 (2), 513 (3), 516 (4), 519, 520, 523 (5), 526 (6), 528 (14), 542, 710, 725 (3), as 725, 968, 970, 974, 983, 985, 987, 1012 (2), 1031, 1036 (3), 1427 (3), 1428
92	Gratian	98, as 98 (6), 297, as 297 (4), as 299, 304, 310, 320, 322, 331, 335, 337 (2), 339 (4), 341, 353, 360, 367, 371 (5), 377, 503, as 503 (13), 505 (4), 511 (2), 517 (3), 523a (5), 528, 529 (19), 531, 533, 536, 726 (2), 1037, 1421, 1423 (2)
130	House of Valentinian	As 79, as 96 (68), as 275 (39), as 275 but no obverse, as 279, as 280, as 317 (2), as 481, as 498, as 514, as 967, as 1418, illeg. (13)
23	Valentinian II	142, as 162 (6), 165 (2), 389 (6), 562 (5), 799, 1105, 1107
6	Magnus Maximus	As 156, 387 (3), 560 (2)
1	Flavius Victor	1004
24	Theodosius I	163, as 163 (4), 391 (2), 547, 551, 565, (5) 787, 790, 797 (4), 800, 1106 (3)
31	Arcadius	164, as 164 (10), 392 (5), 566 (8), 569, 783, 801 (2), 1107 (2), 2570
9	Honorius	As 174 (3), 396 (2), 570, as 570, 806, 1111
116	House of Theodosius	As 162 (61), copies as 162 (2), as 389 (2), as 562 (3), as 796 (26), copy as 796, excellent copy with a bearded portrait DN TEO SIVS PFVG and reverse of Victory walking left VICTO/ / / /VGG and a blundered mint-mark 11RM, reverses illeg. (20)
167	Uncertain	Third or fourth century (76), fourth century (56), corroded broken and burnt (1 silver and 34 copper)

Groups of Coins

From the coins found in Building XVIII two groups of coins have been listed separately as they seem to belong to hoards or deposits; listed in this way they will not bias the individual site finds.

Both groups belong to the middle and end of the fourth century, but although the first was found as a group and noted as such, the second group only became apparent during the identification of the coins, when it was noticed that a large number of coins from a single deposit were remarkably similar in date, degree of wear, patina, and occasional corrosion. The first group may well be complete, but the second group is almost certainly too small since no coin was included unless it had all the necessary characteristics. One point that makes the second hoard almost certain is the lack of wear on these coins of Valentinian I and his co-rulers. In a site which went on to the end of the fourth century such good condition is most surprising, and can only be accounted for by the coins having been lost together or hoarded.

Group A

1	Victorinus	*RIC* 114
2	Constantine I	*RIC* 7 Tr 435, HK 62
5	Constantine II	HK 63 (2), 88 (2), 203
5	Urbs Roma	HK 51, as 51, copy as 51, 70 (2)
7	Constantinopolis	HK 52, as 52, copies as 52 (3), 71, copy as 185
3	Theodora	HK as 105, 120, 129
6	Constans	HK 131, 150, 251; CK 33, 35, 888
5	Constantius II	HK 57, 108; CK 32, 40, 252 but mm. SLG
1	Magnentius	Copy as CK 8
19	House of Constantine	HK as 48 (2), copies as 48 (5), as 87 (2), copies as 87 (2), copies as 137 (3); CK copies as 25 (2), illeg. (3)

Group B

All the coins belong to Valentinian I, Valens, and Gratian and have been listed according to CK numbers, in mints.

3	Trier	82, 86, 115
38	Lyons	275, 288, 293 (2), 294, 303, 304, 307 (2), 309, 310, 316, 317 (2), 319 (2), 322, 330, 332 (3), 333, 334, 336, 338 (3), 340, 343 (2), 348, 353, 356, 364, 371 (3), as 317
62	Arles	477, 480, 481 (2), 483 (3), 484, 486, (2) 487, 488, 490, 492, 498, 499, 501 (3), 502, 503, 505, 510 (2), 512, 513, 514, 515, 516 (2), 517, 518, 520 (2), 523, 523a, 526, 527 (2), 528 (7), 529 (11), 532, 538, as 479, as 503 (2)
2	Rome	711, 731
12	Aquileia	996, 997, 1012 (2), 1014, 1015, 1017, 1021, 1028, 1033, 1035, as 965
5	Siscia	1294, 1390, 1409, 1414, 1417
9	Uncertain	As 97 (8), as 275 (1)

These references can be summarized by Emperor and by date as follows:

Emperor	Uncertain date	364–7	367–75	375–8	378–83	Total
Valentinian I	3	12	27	—	—	42
Valens	8	12	37	1	—	58
Gratian	2	—	23	3	3	31
Totals	13	24	87	4	3	131

Group A ends with a copy of a coin of Magnentius (died 353) and copies of the House of Constantine of *c.* 353–5. The next issue which might have been included is the prolific issue of the years after 364. It seems likely therefore that Group A was deposited, or at least formed, before about 364–7.

Group B probably ends with coins of 378–83, though it is just possible that these are intrusive. This will affect the date of the deposit very little, however, for the group could have been formed and buried any time up to *c.* 388 when the issues of the House of Theodosius came into Britain in large numbers. Accepting the coins of 378–83 suggests a date for deposition around 380–5.

One point which can usefully be made on the composition of Group B is to note that there are 24 coins minted in the first three years of the period (364–7) and only 87 coins for the next nine years. This becomes surprising when it is accepted that coins of these first three years are usually uncommon in Britain. At the other end of the period, the continuity of mint marks at Arles means that some of the coins given to 367–75 should probably belong to the last three years 375–8. Since the composition of the hoard is uncertain it is probably wiser not to push analysis any further.

General Comments

It seems quite certain that the coin list of Nettleton spans the whole period of Roman rule in Britain. To be more specific, there are enough coins of Claudius I, and copies of this same date, to use the coins as evidence of some sort of occupation around the middle of the first century A.D. At the end of the fourth century there are enough coins of the House of Theodosius and, more surprisingly, copies of such coins to be reasonably sure that some substantial occupation continued up to, and beyond, the year 400.

Between these two limits the coin evidence is less compelling. The large number of first- and second-century coins which are heavily worn and illegible cannot be used to prove occupation from Claudius I to Septimius Severus, their dates and periods of issue, for they could all have entered the site in the early third century when much worn bronze coinage was being used, and hoarded. This point must be settled from the strictly archaeological record for the coins can only buttress an existing argument and not initiate a new one.

The numbers of coins of the first half of the third century, most of which after *c.* A.D. 230 are distinctly uncommon as site finds, strongly suggest a revival, or intensification of activity. This seems to have continued unbroken through the third and fourth centuries with a peak in the 360s and 370s. The pitfalls of further analysis of the finds from the fourth century are shown in the composition of Group A, for all these coins which span a period from 270 to 355 could have been brought to the site in that last year, in which they were probably buried, so that they say nothing about occupation during the years in which they were struck. This is not to suggest that all the coins struck between 320 and 360 entered the site after 360; the important point to note is the uncertainty of when the coins were imported.

Final comment must be reserved for the copies of regular coins which were found in the excavations. The copies of the Minerva As of Claudius I are well enough known not to need explanation. They occur commonly on sites in the Lowland Zone of Britain which were inhabited soon after the conquest of A.D. 43. Much rarer, and therefore more interesting, are the copies of coins struck under Tiberius in his own name and for the Divus Augustus. Both these copies are perfectly recognizable first as regards their prototypes and, second, as copies. This means that they are not the one-off products of a British metal worker with an eye to quick forgery, but the careful work of someone who appreciated what he was copying, and had experience of the task. All these comments apply equally to the copy of a coin of Nero, and this coin by itself suggests that wherever the copying took place it continued after the year 64 when Nero's bronze coinage first became available for imitation.

The next wave of copying noted is that of the bararous radiates now generally agreed to belong to the years 270 to *c.* 285. These copies are usually uninspired and often muddled. One is listed as having a reverse showing 'confused figures', but rather than jump to the conclusion that it was produced in the fifth century, I suggest that one should consider what a poor die-cutter could do with such reverses of Claudius II as *Fides Exerc*, showing Fides holding two military ensigns.

Copying seems to have been endemic throughout the fourth century from adequate copies of the Altar (*Beata Tranquillitas*) reverse of *c.* 320, through the Wolf and Twins of *c.* 335, to the copies of the Fallen Horseman of *c.* 353–360. The final surprise comes after 388 when four copies of the small Victory coinages occur. One of these is highly accomplished and may be an import from the continent, but the others seem to show that Somerset forgers continued to the bitter end.

3. THE BROOCHES (figs. 50–56, 113)

Note

This report is the work of a number of people: brooches described by Mrs. M. Canham are distinguished by (C) after the number; the late M. R. Hull, F.S.A., identified the brooches from the Priestley excavations (now in Devizes Museum) from drawings provided by Priestley; Professor J. M. C. Toynbee, F.S.A., has reported separately on no. 76; the remainder have been dealt with by the author, being the large quantities derived from the ditch of the first-century enclosure in the later stages of the excavation.

General

An interesting feature concerning the brooches was the unusually large number recovered from the ditch-filling of the first-century enclosure. Only a small portion of the ditches was excavated, but in one small cutting eight brooches, Nos. 12, 27, 38, 43, 46, 54, 61 and 68, were recovered from the upper part of the filling. Altogether 30 brooches were recovered from the small cuttings across the ditches, in most instances from the upper part of the filling in association with a thin black, burnt streak which overlay the yellow silt in the ditch.

The Fosse Way ditch at Camerton, Somerset, excavated by the writer, which is now thought to form part of a similar Claudian enclosure, also produced a large number of brooches, and they too were associated with a similar burnt layer which overlay the yellow silt in the ditch; the evidence is suggestive of unsettled conditions, possibly armed attacks during the first two decades of the Roman occupation.

Note by Mrs. Canham

The brooches from Nettleton Scrubb form an interesting group of a variety of types. Several of them are of widespread distribution throughout Britain, e.g. the 'Hod Hill' and 'Head Stud' types, but one or two are more specifically characteristic of the south-west, e.g. No. 48. Some are of comparatively rare occurrence, e.g. No. 79, while others, although they can be assigned with some confidence to well-known types, have no exact parallel, e.g. No. 18.

The enamelled brooches are particularly fine. A number of the Nettleton brooches can be fairly closely paralleled with types from Camerton, and it is interesting that both sites have produced the unusual blue enamelled brooch in the form of an axe, No. 71.

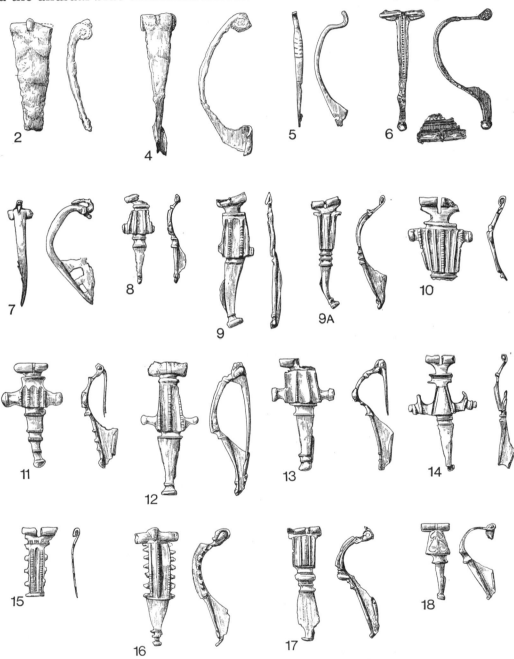

Fig. 50.   Brooches (scale $\frac{2}{3}$)

In date the majority of the Nettleton brooches would seem to belong to the first or second centuries A.D. but some of the enamelled brooches may be of third-century date.

I am grateful to the late Mr. M. R. Hull, M.A., F.S.A., for his notes on Nos. 18, 48, 55 and 65.

Bow Brooches of Iron

1(C). Corroded iron brooch with humped bow of D-shaped section. From the first-century enclosure in an earlier level than No. 95. Not drawn.

2. Bow only of a plain iron brooch with simple hinge socket for the pin which is missing and the foot end also missing. The bow is ⅝ in. (15 mm.) wide. From the first-century enclosure ditch.

3. Simple bow type iron brooch. From the first-century enclosure ditch under Building XXVII. Not drawn.

4. Iron bow brooch, pin is missing, simple swivel type hinge. Unprovenanced.

4(A). Bow of small iron brooch in poor condition with split end. Pin missing. From a first-century level. Not drawn.

Bow Brooches of Bronze

5(C). Incomplete brooch with flat tapering bow, bearing traces of horizontal incised ornament. From the fourth-century squatter level. The 'Nauheim' form of one-piece La Tène III brooch. Camulodunum (Hawkes and Hull, 1947) Type VII, and at Camulodunum only proved for the period Claudius–Nero (cf. Hull, 1967, 31, fig. 11, No. 1).

6(C). An 'Aucissa' brooch now in three pieces. The letters 'AVC' are visible on the head. The bow is decorated with longitudinal mouldings and central beading, and the foot is knobbed. From an earlier level than No. 8. Camulodunum Type XVII, Hofheim (Ritterling, 1913) A. In Britain most examples are from sites occupied under Claudius and Nero.

7. Bronze brooch with simple round shaped bow. The catchplate is large and has two perforations both rectangular in shape. The bow continues beyond the spring casing and is bent back to form a loop over the head of the brooch. The spring and pin are missing but the spring was held in position by the disc terminals at each end of the spring housing. From a first- to second-century level.

8(C). A rather small example of a 'Hod Hill' brooch. The bow has longitudinal mouldings and two projecting knobs, and is separated from the flat tapering leg by central mouldings. Foot has weak knob. Shrine: later level than No. 6. Camulodunum Type XVIII B. Current in Britain during the period Claudius–Nero.

9(C). Another brooch of 'Hod Hill' type bearing traces of tinning or silvering: now in a crushed state. Bow has knurled longitudinal mouldings and two projecting knobs. Found in a fourth-century level. Camulodunum Type XVIII B, Claudius–Nero.

9(A). Brooch with longitudinal mouldings, similar to No. 9, but there are no projecting knobs. From the first-century enclosure ditch on the north side.

10. The upper part of a brooch of the same type as Nos. 8 and 9. It has a simple swivel hinge but the pin is missing. The upper part of the bow has six longitudinal ridges. From the yellow silt above the first-century A.D. ditches.

11. Bronze tinned bow brooch of the same type as Nos. 12–14. The pin is of the simple swivel type with a fairly wide catchment plate for the pin. The bow is decorated with three fluted mouldings and has wide sturdy projecting side knobs. The lower part is decorated with five cross ribs which divide this part of the brooch. The ribs become narrower as they reach the

rounded knob which forms the foot. From the first- to second-century ditch-filling south of Building XXVII.

12. 'Hod Hill' type similar to Nos. 8 and 9 with pronounced side knobs. The upper part of the bow has two fluted mouldings with a central rouletted rib. The pin is hinged and the bow terminates in a nicely formed foot. From the ditch-filling of the first-century enclosure.

13. 'Hod Hill' type and similar to Nos. 8 and 9 with pronounced side projections. The brooch is tinned and the upper part of the bow has three fluted mouldings. The ridges between the mouldings are decorated with a rouletted device and the bow terminates in a well-pronounced foot. The pin is hinged. From the filling of the first-century ditch. For a similar brooch see Wheeler, 1943, fig. 85(29).

14. Same type as No. 8, but slightly larger. The longitudinal mouldings do not have the transverse decoration as with No. 8. The projecting side wings are wider in this brooch and curved projections on the upper edge of the wings give the brooch the impression of a bird in flight. The foot end has been broken off. There are traces of tinning on the brooch. From the floor level of Building XVIII and in association with fourth-century coins.

15(C). Upper part of tinned or silvered brooch. The flat strip bow has three small projections on each side, and longitudinal and transverse panels of decoration. Hinged. Found in association with a coin of Theodosius, A.D. 388. The projecting knobs and style of decoration would seem to relate this brooch to the 'Hod Hill' or 'Aucissa' series (cf. Bush-Fox, 1949, pl. XXVI).

16. This brooch is similar to No. 15. It has a series of six small projecting knobs on either side of the bow which is fitted on either side with a pronounced raised central rib, which is decorated. The pin, which is missing, was held on a small swivel. From the filling of the first-century enclosure ditch, west side.

17. This brooch is similar to no. 12, but it has no side wings. The upper part of the bow is fitted with a raised central ridge, and the lower part widens in an unusual manner. The flat surface is decorated with a series of pin-point lines. The pin socket is iron-stained suggesting that the missing pin was iron. From the lower filling of the first-century A.D. ditch, west side.

18(C). Tinned or silvered brooch, the flat bow decorated with a punched pattern in the form of two hearts. Wide central moulding and slender tapering leg. Mr. Hull suggests this brooch should be related to the 'Hod Hill' type but has no parallel for it in his corpus. Claudius–Nero. Found on the west side of the shrine: from a level earlier than the circular shrine.

19. This brooch is of the same type as No. 20, but it is larger and has only one central globular feature. The bow is tinned. From the first-century enclosure.

20. Small brooch with a swivel type hinge, similar to No. 19. The bow is decorated with several traverse ribs placed between two globular features. The bow is tinned. From the first-century enclosure ditch associated with St. Remy ware.

21. Small bow type brooch with a fluted cross wing, $\frac{1}{4}$ in. (6 mm.) wide on either side. The top part of the bow has two raised ridges which continue below the cross wing, but the lower part is plain and the front of the bow is tinned. The pin is held by a simple swivel hinge and the catch-plate is plain. From the upper filling of the first-century ditch south of Building XXVII.

22(C). Brooch with tapering flat strip bow; the edges of the bow are slightly bevelled. At the head the bow broadens and curls over to the back; hinged pin missing. From a level prior to A.D. 260. This is Mr. Hull's 'Maiden Castle' type, which appears at a number of early sites, e.g. Maiden Castle and Hod Hill. Date A.D. 25–75, though possibly in use longer.

23(C). A rather heavy brooch, now fragmentary and worn, the flat bow bearing longitudinal notched ridges. Hinged. From the shrine, fourth-century A.D. squatter level. Though difficult to parallel exactly this brooch is similar to types found at Hod Hill (Brailsford, 1962, fig. 7, C40, C41, C42).

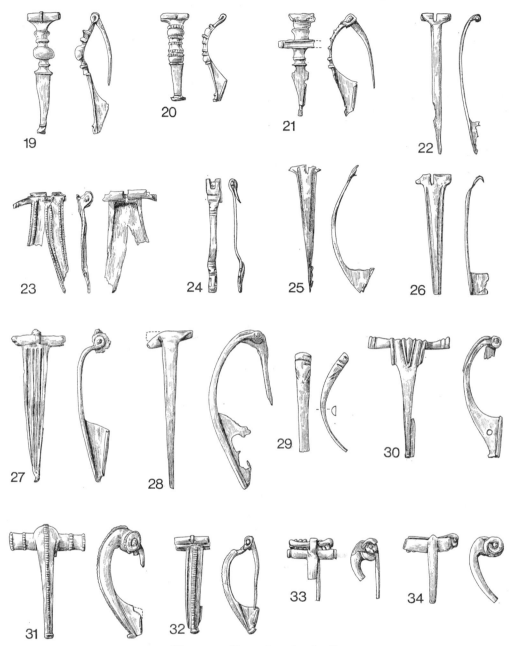

Fig. 51.   Brooches (scale ⅔)

24(C).   A very simple brooch with flat strip bow bearing horizontal incised lines. Catch-plate is small and formed by folding over the lower part of the bow. The hinge arrangement is formed by folding over the top of the bow to leave a flat 'tag' at the back. From the fourth-century A.D. squatter level. For a similar arrangement cf. Wheeler and Wheeler, 1936, fig. 44(31).

25.   This brooch is similar to nos. 22 and 26, but the bow is more pronounced. Found in association with first- and second-century Samian ware. Wedlake, 1958, fig. 53, no. 42, is the same type.

26.   Similar to Nos. 22 and 25, slightly smaller, but with the same simple decoration along each side of the bow. Found on the floor of Building XVIII associated with fourth-century A.D. coins. For a similar brooch see Wheeler, 1943, fig. 84(18).

27.   The bow of this brooch has a series of five longitudinal ribs decorated with a rouletted pattern. The pin has a simple swivel hinge. From the ditch filling of the first-century A.D. enclosure.

28.   Plain brooch with simple swivel-hinged pin. The catch-plate is broken, but was perforated similar to No. 94 and Nos. 22, 25, 26, and 27. From the first-century enclosure ditch.

29.   Bow only of a brooch with transverse decoration at the top of the bow and other incised lines form a triangle below. From the first-century enclosure ditch.

30.   This brooch is similar to No. 35, but it has a simple swivel-type hinge. The brooch is the same length as No. 35, but the side wings are broader. The bow is decorated with six pronounced ridges which come over the head of the brooch and they converge in pairs on the bow. The pin is missing, but iron staining of the swivel plate suggests an iron pin. The catch-plate has a small circular perforation. Found in the filling of grave No. 2 in cemetery 'A'. Wedlake, 1958, fig. 50, No. 10, is the same type.

31.   The bow has a central notched raised rib throughout its length, terminating with a plain catch-plate. The heavy side wings have two similar raised ridges which are also notched. The side wings give the impression of a hidden coiled spring, but the pin is held in a simple swivel. From the top filling of the first-century A.D. enclosure ditch.

32.   Brooch with hinged swivel for the pin. The bow is decorated with a high raised ridge with a series of transverse markings throughout its length; No. 46 also has this high ridge. At the top of the brooch there are narrow side wings. From the yellow silt layer above the first-century enclosure ditch.

33(C). Upper part of brooch with plain bow of D-shaped section, and side wings which are almost flat. The eight turns of the spring are held to the head by a lug cast on the head through which passes the chord of the spring, and by a second lug, which is an extension of the first lug, and through which passes the axial bar of the spring. There are no disc terminals on the side wings. From the shrine on the west side of the ambulatory, fourth-century demolition level. Typologically this brooch falls between the Camulodunum Type III brooch where the chord is secured by a hook, and the 'Polden Hill' type which has the lugs and also perforated disc terminals on the side wings to receive the axial bar, as in No. 35. This brooch lacks the crest normally on the head of brooches of this type, but cf. Atkinson, 1916, pl. X(49).

34(C). Of similar type to No. 33. East side of shrine unstratified.

35(C). A well-preserved brooch with tapering channelled bow. The side wings are grooved, and have disc terminals to receive the axial bar. The spring has ten turns and the chord passes through a lug on the head of the bow. Found in association with first- and second-century A.D. pottery sherds. In general type similar to the Camerton brooches (Wedlake, 1958, fig. 50, Nos. 5–8) and Nor'nour (Hull, 1967, fig. 25(262)).

36.   Brooch with long slender bow which is decorated. Incised lines form an elongated diamond on the front of the bow. The catch-plate is broken, but it had two triangular perforations. The cross bar has two zones of notched decoration on either side and is hollow at the rear to house the spring of 18 coils, which was held in place by a cross pin. The end of the spring wire is held by a central lug at the rear of the bow which is placed high on the cross bar. From a second-century A.D. level below Building XXVII.

36(A). A well-preserved brooch and similar to No. 36. The tapering plain bow is surmounted at the head by a projecting hook which keeps the loop of the 13-coiled spring in the recess at the rear of the cross arm. The front of the cross arm is decorated on either side with four incised

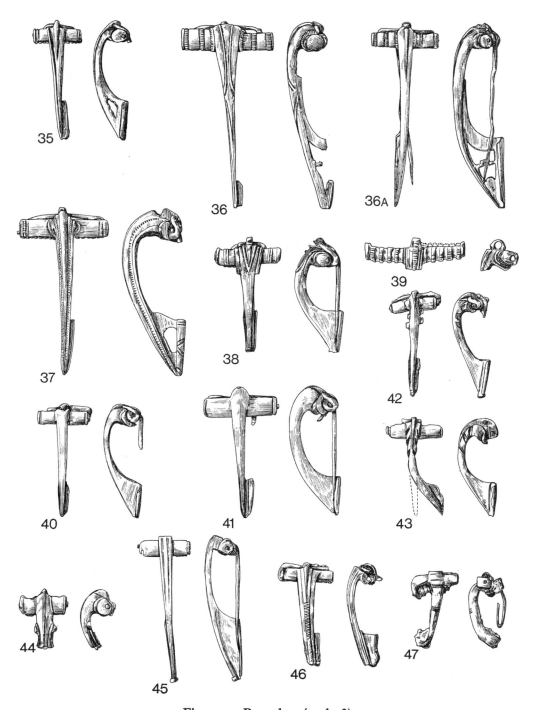

Fig. 52. Brooches (scale $\frac{2}{3}$)

lines and there is a small notched raised flute on either side of the bow at its junction with the cross arm. The wide catch-plate has two perforations divided by a cross bar. From a first-century level within the early enclosure and in association with penannular brooch No. 84(A).

37. This brooch is also similar to No. 36, with a wide cross arm and a sturdy bow. The bow has a high central ridge with a notched ridged decoration on either side. The catch-plate has an egg-shaped perforation and the cross arm is decorated on either side. The spring of 14 coils is held in place by a central lug which is extended to the head of the cross arm to hold the end of the wire spring. From a first- to second-century A.D. level below Building XXVII.

38. This brooch, in a good state of preservation, is similar to the Camerton brooches, fig. 50, Nos. 5–8 and No. 35 is similar. The side wings are grooved to receive the spring of eight coils and the chord is held in place by a lug on the head of the brooch. From the upper filling of the first-century enclosure ditch. For a similar brooch see Hull, 1967, fig. 25(262) (Nor'nour).

39(C). Head and side wings of a brooch. Side wings are long, semi-circular and decorated with notched moulding. Pierced disc terminals. Head of bow is grooved and the lug is cast solid with the head. Found in a pre-A.D. 250 level. Cf. Wedlake, 1958, fig. 50, No. 5, for similarly decorated side-wings.

40. This brooch is similar to No. 45. The bow is plain and the catch-plate. The spring of ten coils is held in position by a central lug which has two perforations; one holds the back loop of the wire spring and the other the wire which supports the spring. From the filling of the first-century enclosure ditch.

41. This brooch has a plain bow and the coiled spring is housed within the hollow cross arm. The spring is held in place by a cross wire pin. The coiled spring has been broken in antiquity and the pin has been replaced by twisting the end over the cross wire. This brooch is similar to No. 34. From the first-century enclosure ditch filling.

42. The bow of this brooch has three small projections on either side. The coiled spring is held in place by a lug and the catch-plate is plain. From a first- to second-century A.D. level.

43. This is a small brooch with wings on each side to hold the spring which is missing. There is some decoration on the upper part of the bow, but the catch-plate is plain. From the upper filling of the first-century A.D. enclosure ditch.

44(C). Upper portion of brooch with humped bow, high central rib, and projecting mouldings on each side of the bow just below the head. Spring arrangement as in No. 35. Axial bar is of iron. Unstratified. For a similar brooch with mouldings just below the head, cf. *PSANHS*, xcvi (1950), fig. 1B.

45. Bow brooch with narrow side wings. The bow has three raised ridges, but the hollow side wings are plain, and the catch-plate is also plain. The spring is held in place by a central pin which originally had six coils, but it was broken in antiquity and has been renewed by looping it over the cross pin. Found alongside the south wall of Building XXVII.

46. The bow of this brooch is decorated with a raised ridge and a series of transverse lines. The side wings house the coiled spring, but the pin is broken. Similar to Nos. 32 and 92. From the top filling of the first-century enclosure ditch.

47. Small brooch with plain bow, but for two incised transverse rings on the centre part of the bow. The head of the brooch is much corroded, but it had side wings which housed a coiled spring. Similar to No. 34. In general date Nos. 33–47 should not be later than the second half of the first century A.D.

48(C). Large brooch with head loop and triangular head plate, the lower edge of which is rolled back to form a cylindrical cover for the iron hinged pin. The bow is decorated with longitudinal and transverse beaded mouldings, the leg is straight and flat and the foot splayed. The underside of the bow is hollowed out in the centre. Found in association with first- to

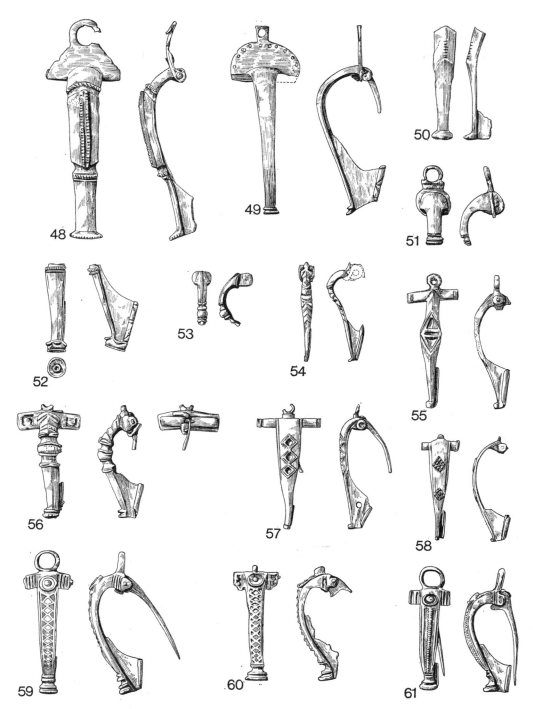

Fig. 53. Brooches (scale ⅔)

second-century A.D. pottery. Mr. Hull has no exact parallel for this brooch. In general size and appearance it resembles a brooch from Caerwent (*Arch* lxxx (1938), 239, fig. 2, No. 1) which Mr. Hull has classed in his 'Ugly South-West Type'. This type includes a brooch in Reading Museum (*VCH Berks* (1906), p. 225, fig. 11), one from Holt (*YC* xli (1930), fig. 54(8)) and from Cold Kitchen Hill (*WAM* xliii, pl. IIa), but all these lack the triangular head plate. At Camerton, Wedlake, 1958, fig. 52(23), would appear to be in the same tradition.

49. Brooch of unusual type. The bow is round and plain with a double raised ridge terminating the foot end. The catch-plate is wide and well made with a linear decoration on the catch. The broken pin is held on a simple swivel hinge. At the head of the brooch there is a raised fan-shaped plate with a square projection at the top which has a circular perforation. The outer edge of the fan-shaped plate is decorated with a series of small incised circles. From the first-century A.D. enclosure ditch, below Building XXVII. A similar brooch from Radstock, Somerset, is in the Taunton County Museum.

50(C). Lower part of a brooch. Bow has notched crest, the leg is straight and flat, and the foot splayed. Underside of the bow is hollowed out in the centre. Probably of the same general type as No. 48. From a level earlier than A.D. 250. Nos. 48 and 50 are possibly of second-century date.

51(C). Upper part of brooch with trumpet head and fixed head-loop. Plain mouldings at summit of bow on the front only; underside of bow is flat, and pin sprung between two lugs (Collingwood Riii type). From the shrine in a level associated with a coin of Faustina, A.D. 141–50. Cf. Bushe-Fox, 1913, fig. 10(8) (Wroxeter), *YC* xxxiii (1923), fig. 56(1) (this example from Segontium is hinged).

52(C). Lower part of brooch with ornate foot and incised pattern on fold of catch-plate. Possibly from the same type as No. 51. From a level associated with a Constantinopolis coin.

53(C). Upper part of a brooch with weak trumpet head meeting flat, oval head plate. Bow has central longitudinal ridge and transverse mouldings at the summit on the foot only. From the shrine in a fourth-century squatter occupation. Of Collingwood Riii type and similar to Wedlake, 1958, fig. 50(13), but it perhaps lies closer to a brooch from Winchester (Cunliffe, 1964, fig. 24, No. 3) where the variants of this type are fully discussed by Mr. Hull. See also Hull, 1967 (Nor'nour).

54 Trumpet-headed brooch similar to No. 53. The pin was hinged on a projecting flat plate. The upper part of the bow is waisted and has a central longitudinal ridge, with a series of well-formed mouldings below. The lower part of the brooch is decorated with a series of incised lines. From the top filling of the first-century A.D. enclosure ditch.

55(C). A T-shaped brooch with head loop which has not been fully drilled out. The bow has triangular panels, the upper of which still contains fragments of yellow enamel. The side wings are cylindrical and the hinged pin is missing. The catch-plate is set to one side of the longitudinal axis. Found in association with a coin of Carausius, A.D. 286–93. This brooch is similar to the Collingwood Group N type of brooch. A considerable number of brooches with cast head loop have triangular or lozenge-shaped recesses for enamel on the upper part of the bow (Collingwood and Richmond, 1969, fig. 103(28) (Caerleon), *VCH Oxford* I (1939), pl. XVIB (Woodeaton)). Mr. Hull lists the following sites where similar brooches have been found: Chew Stoke and Charterhouse-on-Mendip (in the Bristol Museum), Chewton Meads, Mendip (in Taunton Museum), Silchester (in Reading Museum), Cold Kitchen Hill, and near Marlborough (both in Devizes Museum), Cirencester (in Cirencester Museum) and Nor'nour (Hull, 1967—five examples). Mr. Hull suggests that the type was made at Nor'nour.

56. Solid well-made brooch similar to No. 44. It has a series of decorative mouldings on the

central part of the bow. The side wings are flat on the front and have a square panel on either side enclosing what appears to be a bull's head in each panel. This feature was much better defined before it was cleaned. The side panels are framed with a silver or tin finish and the lower part of the bow is decorated with a waved pattern executed in either silver or tin, and a large part of the brooch also appears to have been tinned or silvered. The pin has been renewed in antiquity and is held in place by a broken bronze bar, but the twisted end of the original pin remains in the socket. There is a broken loop at the head of the brooch. This brooch seems to have been much prized before it was finally lost and was probably a heirloom. From the first-century enclosure ditch filling.

57.   Similar to No. 60, but it has no head stud. The bow is decorated with three diamond-shaped projections which appear to have held within them small circles of enamel or stones. The head loop is broken and the pin is hinged. The catch-plate has a small circular hole. From a level associated with Building XVI. A brooch from Camerton is similar (Wedlake, 1958, fig. 55(15A); cf. Hull, 1967, fig. 11(7A) (Nor'nour)).

58.   This brooch has narrow side wings and a hinged pin. The bow is decorated with two diamond-shaped zones which are raised slightly above the surface and each diamond is made up with small squares. There is a slight knob at the head of the brooch. No. 57 is similar. Unstratified (cf. Hull, 1967, fig. 11(7A) (Nor'nour)).

59.   This 'Lamberton Moor' type brooch has a head stud which was inlaid with enamel. It has a prominent well-formed loop at the head of the brooch. The foot is decorated with a series of rounded mouldings and the bow has a series of lozenge-shaped panels. Rouletted strips decorate the side wings. Found in association with a coin of Nero (cf. Hull, 1967, fig. 17 (103–5) (Nor'nour)).

60(C).   A 'head stud' brooch with traces of blue enamel in the lozenge-shaped panels on the bow. This example is hinged and has no head loop; from shrine in association with a coin of Claudius II, after A.D. 270. A well-known type found on many sites throughout Britain. For the crest above the head stud, cf. Traprain Law (*PSAS* lv (1921), 187, fig. 21(2)), and Stanwix (*AJ* xi (1931), 38, fig. 2). Usually dated to the Antonine period.

61.   This brooch is similar to Nos. 59 and 60. There is a circular boss or stud at the head of the brooch and also a bronze loop. The bow is decorated with two raised longitudinal ridges with a series of transverse lines between the two ridges. The foot is shaped like a horse's hoof and the two narrow side wings are decorated with incised lines. The pin is hung on a simple swivel-type hinge. From the upper filling of the first-century A.D. enclosure ditch.

62(C).   Brooch with trumpet head and head loop. The bow bears a disc with three (once four) projecting lugs and concentric rings of enamel. The leg tapers to a knobbed foot. Found in association with Nos. 67 and 99 (cf. Hull, 1967, fig. 17(111) (Nor'nour)).

63(C).   A larger, less well-preserved brooch of the same type as No. 22. Found in association with Nos. 71 and 73 and a coin of Tetricus I, A.D. 270–3 (cf. Hull, 1967, fig. 17(111) (Nor'nour)). This type of brooch and its distribution has been discussed by Miss K. M. Richardson, F.S.A. (*AJ* xl (1960), 200ff.).

63(A).   Brooch with simple swivel for the pin which is missing. The brooch is not bowed, but flat, apart from the top where it is shouldered for its hinge. The brooch is tinned and its lower part is wide and flat; it tapers towards the top. Above this it becomes circular with a small rounded projection on either side. There is a small circular perforation that appears to have held an iron rivet for an attachment to the circular face which is not tinned. The lower part has a single incised line throughout its length which probably held a coloured enamel. There are two ridges above the circular centre. The catch-plate is plain. From the area of the first-century A.D. enclosure.

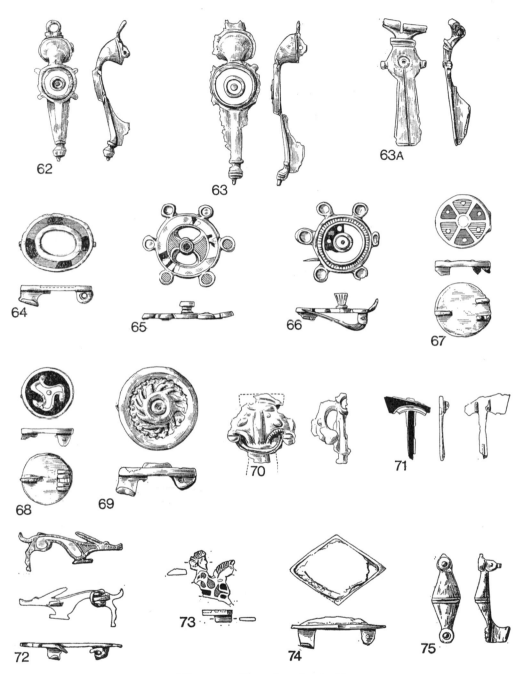

Fig. 54. Brooches (scale ⅔)

Plate Brooches

64(C). Oval brooch, the outer ring containing strips of green and blue enamel in the central position. Found in association with a coin of Faustina, A.D. 141–50. Cf. Richborough (Bushe-Fox, 1949, pl. XXIX (48)); South Ferriby (*THSFNC* iii, pt. IV (1906), pl. XXX(8)); Rushall Down (*DMC* pl. LXVI(9)); Nor'nour (Hull, 1967, fig. 22(196)).

64(B). This brooch is described on p. 148 (fig. 63(5)).

65(C). Enamelled circular brooch with six circular lugs and central boss. Most of the enamel has now gone, but there are traces of blue in the circular band, red and black in the lugs, red in the pelta-shaped panels, and orange and black on the central boss. From a fourth-century A.D. level north of the shrine. Mr. Hull assigns this brooch to a series basically shaped like wheels, with spokes and hub, and projections added. As British parallels he cites a brooch from Nor'nour (Hull, 1967, fig. 22(205)); the Lansdown brooch (*PSAL* xxii (1907–9), pl. opp. 35), and two in Corbridge Museum. No brooch is pierced exactly like this one.

66. Circular brooch similar to No. 65 and about the same size. It has six circular bosses or lugs which have held enamel on the outer edge and a central boss that has traces of blue and red enamel. The solid central part of the brooch has a blue enamelled background with small circular inserts of red and light green enamel. This central part is surrounded by an inner and outer raised circle enclosing a circular rouletted band. The raised central boss is decorated with a series of incised lines. The pin is held on a simple swivel hinge. Found in association with the stone cobbling in Building XII. Cf. Nor'nour (Hull, 1967, fig. 25(251)).

67(C). Circular brooch with alternative segments of green and black enamel, and a small stud of bronze in each of the segments. Found in association with Nos. 62 and 99. Cf. Bushe Fox, 1913, fig. 9(2).

68. Small circular brooch with a blue enamelled background. A triskele in the centre has a yellow-green enamelled infilling and a central bronze knob. No. 67 is a similar type of brooch. Found in association with a coin of Vespasian, in the upper filling of the enclosure ditch. Cf. Nor'nour (Hull, 1967, fig. 25(257)).

69. Circular brooch decorated with a flared Catherine wheel which stands in relief from the cupped surface of the brooch. The centre is raised with a central bronze box enclosed with blue enamel. A raised outer rim encloses a circle of small circular dots raised above the background. From the first-century A.D. enclosure ditch.

70. Brooch of an unusual type with a circular plate with a raised ridge as its background plate The broad miniature bow of the tinned brooch springs from the top of the back-plate and has a raised central ridge which joins the back-plate towards the bottom. The truncated bow flares out on each side and terminates on either side with a small circular ball which has an incised circular ring around the centre. There is also a raised pear-shaped boss on the centre of the central ridge and a similar boss on each of the flared wings of the brooch. There is a notched device on each side of the brooch. The pin and spring are missing. From the top filling of the first-century A.D. ditch on its west side. For a similar brooch see Bushe Fox 1913, fig. 9(3). It belongs to the same group of brooches as two from Camerton (Haverfield, 1906, 293, fig. 60, and Wedlake, 1958, fig. 51(20)) (now in Bristol City Museum).

71(C). Blue enamelled brooch in the form of an axe, with traces of red enamel in the band at the base of the blade. On the back there are the remains of two lugs for the pin attachment. Found in association with Nos. 63 and 73 and a coin of Tetricus I, A.D. 270–3 (cf. Wedlake, 1958, fig. 54(55)).

72(C). Enamelled brooch in the form of a running dog. The front panel contains red enamel, and there are traces of green in the rear panel. Pin sprung. From the shrine in a fourth-century A.D. level. Cf. Stanwix (*AJ* xi (1931), 38, fig. 2); London, Guildhall Museum No. 3419;

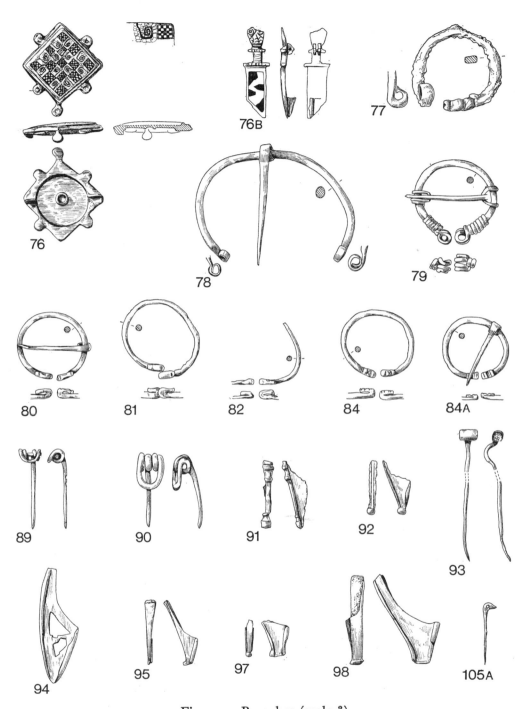

Fig. 55.   Brooches (scale $\frac{2}{3}$)

South Ferriby (*THSFNC* iii, pt. IV (1906), pl. XXV(13)); nr. Birdoswald (*CW* N.S. xix (1919), pl. II(15)).

73(C).   Brooch in the form of a running horseman, with panels of blue and red enamel. Found with Nos. 71 and 63 with a coin of Tetricus, A.D. 270–3. Cf. Woodeaton, Oxon. (*Oxon* xiv (1949), fig. 3(6)) — two examples; Cold Kitchen Hill, Wilts. (*WAM* xliii (1925–7), pl. IID); nr. Woodyates, Dorset (*BM Guide* fig. 11(41)); Nor'nour (Hull, 1967, fig. 18(132)); Brettenham, Norfolk (in the Ashmolean Museum); Hundley, Suffolk (in the University Museum of Archaeology and Ethnology, Cambridge); Corbridge (*AA* 3rd s., vii (1911), fig. 27 opp. 186).

74.   Lozenge-shaped brooch with remains of decayed enamel. From an early level in association with first- and second-century A.D. pottery. Cf. Wedlake, 1958, fig. 54(54) (Camerton); Atkinson, 1916, pl. IX(33) (Lowbury Hill).

75.   Small lozenge-shaped brooch with a raised central rib and rounded terminals at each end which have held small globules of blue glass which were set in a greenish-coloured cement or paste. The missing pin was held by a simple swivel type hinge. Found in association with first- to second-century pottery including Samian ware. Cf. Hull, 1967, fig. 23(212–14) and fig. 25(250) (Nor'nour).

76.   This brooch, from the floor of Building XVIII, consists of a square surface of millefiori decoration backed and framed with bronze, with five projecting bronze knobs, one at one corner and one at the centre of each side. It is 1 in. (2.5 cm.) square, and to judge from the grooves on the back for the now vanished pin, it was worn diamond wise, with the corner knob at the top. The brooch appears to have been of some antiquity when it was lost and it is evident that it was in use over a long period after two of the four projecting knobs had been broken off. The broken end of the projecting knob is worn quite smooth and testifies to much use. The brooch was lost when a fire destroyed Building XVIII and it was found with burnt material associated with a large number of coins ranging from A.D. 360 to 402. The coins, the brooch and the many other finds were all encrusted with black ash from the fire. The brooch pin was held in a simple swivel hinge. Millefiori decoration was produced by cutting a thin section through a series of minute, continuous, coloured glass rods, so arranged as to constitute patterns. Here the pattern consists of 25 small squares, five each way, forming a chequer-design. Each square has a white ground. Squares outlined in red and covered with minute blue chequer pattern, with a red dot at the centre, alternate with squares carrying a blue spiral but lacking a red outline. There are 13 of the former, and 12 of the latter. One square had the appearance of having been repaired in antiquity. The alternate squares have a white background with a device rendered in blue glass the shape of which is similar to that of a shepherd's crook. For other examples of millefiori chequer pattern from Roman Britain see Curle, 1911, 329, pl. 89(25), belt mount: red and white squares; Bushe-Fox, 1949, 117, pl. XXIX (47) (disc brooch, blue and white squares). For diamond-shaped brooches from the Rhineland, see *BRGK* xxix (1939), Taf. 12, One of these, a broken specimen from Zugmantel (*ibid.*, Taf. 12, No. 3, III, 2, and p. 97, No. 3), has a millefiori chequer pattern in blue, white, black and yellow. For red, white and blue millefiori chequer patterns on a bronze disc in the Berlin Antiquarium and on a bronze hexagonal pyxis in the Römisch-Germanischen Museum in Cologne, see *KJ* ix (1967–8), 28–30, Taf. 4 (I owe these references to Mr. David Brown of the Ashmolean Museum, Oxford). There is a very similar brooch to the Nettleton brooch in the Vatican Museum. The date of manufacture of the Nettleton brooch was probably *c.* A.D. 150 and 250, as is suggested by comparative material abroad, although it was found in association with late fourth-century coins in Building XVIII.

76(A).   Back-plate of an oval-shaped brooch. Face missing. From the shrine.

76(B). Small brooch in the form of a handled dagger. The blade is decorated with white and blue enamel. The white enamel is in the form of a wavy broad line down the blade. The lower part of the handle has a series of ridges above the hilt. The top part is flat and decorated with incised circles, lines and semi-circles. The pin is missing but it was held on a simple swivel hinge. Found in the area of the first-century enclosure. An exact parallel, for this brooch, apart from the colour of the enamel, was found at Nor'nour (Hull, 1967, fig. 24(236)).

Penannular Brooches (the classification used is Fowler, 1960)

77(C). Iron penannular brooch of rectangular section. Only one terminal now survives and this is curled upwards and backwards at right-angles to the plane of the ring. Type C. Unstratified.

78(C). A large, and now distorted, brooch. The ring is circular in section, but becomes flattened just behind the terminals. These are coiled backwards at right angles to the plane of the ring, and the end of the pin is wrapped round the ring. Type C. Found in association with a coin of Constantine I, A.D. 350–60.

79(C). Penannular brooch with ring of circular section. The terminals are drawn out into wire coils, and the surplus wire is twisted round the ends of the ring. Found in association with No. 81 and a British Dobunnic coin (see p. 112). Parallel found on military sites — Wroxeter, London and Hod Hill. Type C1. Possibly first-century A.D.

Nos. 80–83 are all of Type D, on which the terminals are bent back at right angles to the plane of the ring, but because of their worn condition it is not really possible to assign them to a sub-group of the type.

80(C). The ring is circular in section, the pin straight with its end wrapped over the ring. The terminals are notched with transverse lines, and on one there is a definite attempt to portray an animal's head. Type ?D1. Found in association with a coin of Theodosius, A.D. 388.

81(C). Similar to No. 80. The terminals are very corroded but they do show some indication of having been moulded. Type D. From the shrine in a fourth-century A.D. level in association with No. 72.

82(C). As No. 80, fragmentary and corroded. Type D. Found in association with a coin of Claudius I, A.D. 41–54.

83(C). As No. 82. From a first- to second-century level (not illustrated).

84. Small penannular brooch but the pin is missing. The terminals are bent back and notched with incised lines. Similar to Nos. 80 and 81. Type D3. Unprovenanced. Found on military sites and at Camerton, Somerset.

84(A). This brooch is of a type similar to No. 84. The terminals are bent back and decorated with incised lines and falls into Type D3. This brooch was found in association with No. 36(A) in the interior of the first-century A.D. enclosure.

85. Badly corroded iron brooch. From Building XVIII (not drawn).

86. Badly corroded iron brooch. From the West Bank (not drawn).

87. Bronze brooch with rounded ends. Unprovenanced (not drawn).

88. Bronze brooch with simple bent-over terminal (not drawn). From the top filling of the first-century enclosure ditch.

Notes on Fragmentary and Corroded Brooches

89(C). Springs and pins of bronze brooches. Unprovenanced.

90(C).

91(C). Lower part of bronze brooch with transverse mouldings, possible 'Hod Hill' type. Found with a coin of Theodosius, A.D. 388.

92(C). Lower part of a bronze brooch with thin reeded leg and knobbed foot. From a fourth-century level.

93(C). Bronze pin probably not a brooch. Found in association with a coin of Claudius I, A.D. 41–54.

94(C). Bronze catch-plate with ornamental piercing. First-century A.D. Unstratified.

95(C). Lower part of a bronze brooch. From the first-century enclosure.

96(C). Badly corroded disc brooch with traces of decayed enamel. Not drawn.

97(C). Foot and catchplate of bronze brooch. Found in association with a coin of Victorinus, A.D. 270–90.

98(C). Crushed lower part of bronze brooch. From a pre-A.D. 250 level.

99(C). Bronze disc with iron core possibly not a brooch. Not drawn.

100. The back plate of an oval shaped brooch. Similar to No. 64. From Building XVIII.

101–105 are fragments of similar types previously described. These, apart from 105(A), are not illustrated. A number of brooch pins, springs and other fragments were also recovered.

Brooches from the Priestley Excavation (fig. 56)

106. A Polden Hill type brooch of the early slender type; pin strung; the chord presumably passed through the eyelet on the head; crossbar comparatively small, quite plain; small oval appendages on each side of the head; catch-plate with stepped piercing and small terminal knob. One from Bagendon (Clifford, 1961, No. 26, fig. 31(5)) should be pre-Roman, but there are plenty of examples, e.g. from Cirencester, from first-century Roman sites.

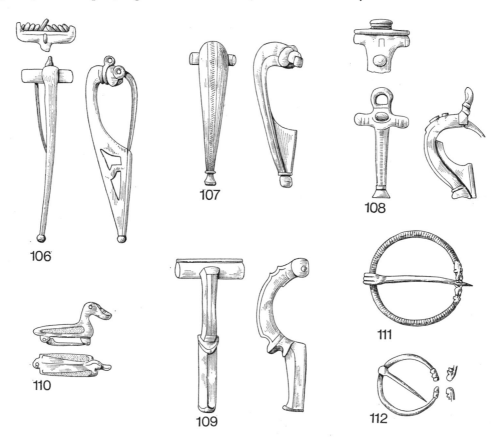

Fig. 56.   Brooches from the Priestley excavation (scale $\frac{2}{3}$)

107. Another Polden Hill type brooch, but of the much heavier and more developed type; arms of crossbar absurdly small. Oval appendages on the head, bow very heavy, with two incised lines down the middle, with a row of punch marks between; solid catch-plate with double knob. One could quote many examples, especially from Wroxeter. Since this is an advanced development of the type it probably runs into the second century. Some examples have the rearward hook, which is an early feature, and should be first-century, but we cannot see from the drawing anything about the construction behind the head.

108. Lamberton Moor type. The head-loop appears to have been fixed; drawing of arms inadequate; bow plain, not enamelled; of standard type, with cup at toe for a stone and stud on head with remains of a crest above it. The ridge of the bow is notched. Similar brooches have been found at many places, including Traprain Law. The dating has still to be studied, but is certainly partly first- and partly second-century. In this case the fixed head loop may indicate the latter date.

109. Late P-shaped brooch. Larger and heavier than most. The number of turns of spring unknown; bow deeper than wide, and why, in the profile, the outer line should be double is not explained. The general design is close to one from South Shields (Newcastle University Museum) and one from Corbridge (*AA* 3rd s., vii (1910), No. 24).

110. Enamelled duck. The body is flat, with head and neck in the round and hinged pin beneath. If the drawing is accurate the type is similar to, but not the same as, a standard type which is known from Colchester (three), Thistleton, West Deeping, Lincoln, Chevenage, St. Albans (two) and York (two in one grave).

111. Penannular brooch of the late zoomorphic type. This is not large, being about the same size as No. 4334 from Aldborough (Yorks.), which it further resembles in having the ring closely cross-grooved and the pin much bent, with ribbed hinge. The animal's head of the terminals has ears, eyes and pointed snout, with a line along the head; the Aldborough brooch lacks the snout, or it is ill-defined, and the ears are rendered differently. One might also compare this brooch to one from Traprain Law (Kilbride-Jones, 1935-7, fig. 4(9)) — see also his fig. 28(91 and 92) from South Shields and I think we may also draw in his fig. 28(93), from Birdoswald). All belong to his 'Northern Developed Type', which he attributes to the third and fourth centuries. 'E' of Elizabeth Fowler's type series. Similar brooch found at the Witcombe villa, Glos. (Clifford, 1954, fig. 14(1)).

112. Penannular brooch with terminals laid back on the ring. Ring round and smooth, with straight pin; terminals segmented by three cross-grooves. This seems to agree completely with both D1 and D6 in Mrs. Fowler's classification and she ascribes both to the first to third centuries.

4. THE INSCRIBED ALTARS; STATUARY; TERRACOTTAS; INTAGLIOS; AND SPECIAL BRONZE OBJECTS

by Professor J. M. C. Toynbee, F.B.A., F.S.A.

1. The Inscribed Apollo Altar (pl. XXXIV)

The altar is of limestone, with plain back and sides and a rectangular focus, and it now measures 18 by 23 by 11 in. (45.7 by 58.4 by 27.9 cm.). The base is lost. It was found in 1958, turned upside down and re-used as a seat beside a hearth in the late occupation of the octagonal temple. The inscription which is cut in good, clear, well-spaced lettering reads:

DEO APOL/LINI CVNO/MAGLO CO/ROTICA IV/TI FIL VSLM

('To the god Apollo Cunomaglos Corotica, son (or daughter) of Iutus, gladly and duly fulfilled his (or her) vow'.)

Cunomaglus is a Celtic name hitherto unrecorded, although the form Maglocunus, with the two halves of the name in reverse order, was already known (Nash-Williams, 1950, 197, No. 353). Believed to mean 'Hound-Prince', this name appears as an epithet of Apollo, or, rather, as a conflation of Apollo with some Celtic god, for the first time here. Taken in conjunction with the bronze plaque (fig. 61, p. 143) and the bronze finger ring (fig. 92(7), p. 142) the altar suggests that it may have been to Apollo, as divine patron of the whole religious settlement at Nettleton, that the octagonal temple was dedicated (see also p. 104 and *JRS* lii (1962), 191, No. 4).

2. *The Silvanus Altar* (pl. XXXVc)

The upper part of a whitish oolite stone altar 13 by 16 by 11 in. (33.0 by 40.6 by 27.9 cm.), with plain sides. The top of the capital has a six-sided focus and bolsters; its mouldings are preserved on either side, but on the front are mosly worn away. On the die the text is weathered and nothing survives beyond the middle of line three.[102] It was found re-used as part of the furnace chamber in Building XVIII.

It reads:

(Primary text)	O . . . . M.N
(Secondary text)	SILVA[NO] ET
	NVMINI[A]VGN
	[A]VR PV[. . . . .

As a parallel to this dedication to Silvanus and the *Numen Augusti nostri* see the statue base of A.D. 155, set up at Somerdale, Keynsham, Bristol, to the *Numina Divorum Augustorum* and to Silvanus.[103] The inclusion of the *Numen Augusti* suggests that the inhabitants were interested that due regard should be paid to the official imperial cult (see p. 104).[104]

3. *Relief of Diana (?) and Hound (Bristol Museum)* (pl. IIa) (see pp. 1–3)

This fragment of a votive, or perhaps architectural, relief is 22 in. (56 cm.) high, 25 in. (63 cm.) wide, and 17 in. (44 cm.) thick at its greatest extent.[105] The material is oolite limestone. The carving shows the virtually complete figures of a hound on the left and part of the body and legs of a heavily draped female figure on the right; while to the left of the group is a broad, vertical frame or pilaster projecting slightly in front of the figures' background.

The surviving portion of the relief is worked on two superimposed blocks, with a straight horizontal join between them running just above the legs of the hound. Both the vertical and drooping folds of the women's tunic and cloak are very sensitively sculptured and reveal the form of the right leg beneath them. Most attractive is the rendering of the hound, whose powerfully built body and sinewy legs are seen from the front and who seems to be thought of as seated on its haunches at a slightly higher level than that on which the female figure stands. The dog wears a heavy collar and its snout is raised vertically, turned towards the spectator as it gazes into the now vanished face of its human companion, while one long ear droops down over the left shoulder.

There can be little doubt that the female figure on the right is a goddess; and a goddess with a stalwart hunting dog as adjunct can hardly be other than Diana. It is, of course, true that in the art of the Roman provinces Diana is much more frequently depicted in hunting-costume — short, high-girt tunic and boots. But in numerous coin and medallion reverse designs, minted in the capital during the second century A.D., she wears a long tunic reaching to the feet.[106]

The style and technique of the Nettleton relief suggest that the carver was not a native of Briton, but an immigrant artist, possibly from Gaul, who could have known something of the art types of Mediterranean lands.

4. *Relief of Mercury and Rosmerta (?) (Devizes Museum)* (pl. II*b*)

From the Priestley excavation.

This fragmentary and somewhat crudely carved votive relief shows two frontal figures standing in a curved niche. In its present state the piece is 11.5 in. (29.5 cm.) high and 8.5 in. (22 cm.) wide at its greatest extent. The material is oolite limestone.[107] The figure on the left is female, headless, but otherwise complete, wearing a long tunic and a cloak. Her right arm lies horizontally along her waist-line, and she holds in both hands a round object, perhaps a small basket or a large fruit or cake. Her feet are concealed behind a curved feature, resembling a low wall; and at the 'wall's' termination on the right there stands, between her and her companion, a tall, cylindrical altar-like object topped by a feature projecting upwards, possibly intended to represent flames. Of the male figure on the right the body below the waist and the legs is lost. His face and hair are badly worn and his right arm is broken away. In his left hand he grasps the shaft of what seems likely to be meant for a *caduceus*, identifying him as Mercury; and it may be that the projecting feature above the altar is not flames, but the remnant of a purse held in the god's now vanished right hand.

There can, then, be little doubt that we have here a votive relief of Mercury and his consort, probably Rosmerta. Such groups of Mercury, with one or two female companions, have come to light on other sites in Roman Britain — at Gloucester, Cirencester, and Bath for example.[108]

5. *The Carved Limestone Fragment* (pl. II*c*, fig. 80(73))

From a late fourth-century A.D. level in Building IX.

The fragment, measuring 6 by 7 by 3 in. (15.2 by 17.8 by 7.6 cm.) at its greatest extent, represents part of a male human figure, from shoulders to waist, carved in high relief against a background which was once carved evenly behind, as can be seen from the surviving portion of the original surface on the spectator's left, but is now much broken and battered at the rear. The figure's bare right arm, hanging down close to his side, is preserved to just below the elbow. The left arm, also bare and in a similar position, survives as far as the elbow only. The person portrayed wears a sleeveless tunic, V-shaped at the neck and gathered into close-set, regular pleats above a thick waist-belt. Against the left side of the subject's chest leans a vertical staff, once, no doubt, grasped in his vanished left hand, topped by what appears to be the twin blades of a double-axe. A double-axe is, of course, the standard attribute of Jupiter Dolichenus, but here there is no trace of the cuirass with which that god is normally equipped. Nor would there seem to have been room on the lower part of the relief for the bull on whose back he is usually shown as standing. It may be that we are dealing here with an otherwise unknown local deity whose attribute was a double-axe. The same object does indeed, appear in the hand of one of the four unknown Celtic deities on the great column capital at *Corinium* (Cirencester).[109]

Alternatively, what looks like the blades of a double-axe could conceivably be the lower portions of the two intertwined snakes of a *caduceus*. In that case the god would be Mercury, with the upper part of his body draped, instead of being naked, as is usual, after the manner of the Mercury relief from Embleton in Buckinghamshire.[110] On that relief the pleats of the skirt of Mercury's tunic are also very closely set and regular. Both there and on the Nettleton fragment the treatment of the drapery is characteristic of native work.

6. *The Limestone Votive Relief* (pl. IId, fig. 57)

From the late fourth-century level in Building XXVI.

Apart from a portion of the top, this stone is virtually complete, and it is flat and worked smooth at bottom, back, and sides. It now measures $7\frac{1}{4}$ by $4\frac{3}{4}$ by $2\frac{1}{2}$ in. (18.5 by 12 by 6.2 cm.). The piece is clearly votive in purpose. Carved in high relief is the neat little figure of a goddess standing in a kind of niche, with a horizontal projecting ledge below, on which her feet rest, and a vertical projecting ledge on either side of her. To judge from what is left of the lateral ledges at the top, the niche would appear to have had a flat rather than a curved roof. The goddess, whose head is unfortunately lost, wears a calf-length sleeved tunic, girded at the waist by a broad belt, identical in type with the waist-belt of No. 5. Between the neck and waist there are two V-shaped folds, either of the tunic or of a cloak which comes down to a point on the chest, passes over the shoulders, and hangs down the back. Round the neck is what may be either a rolled collar or the upper hem of the tunic. A hem is indicated at the bottom of the tunic; and the folds of the garment converge diagonally and symmetrically on a vertical crease between the legs. Shoes with pointed toes are worn. In her left hand the goddess holds a basket or casket, the surface of which is somewhat worn. What, if anything, she held in her right hand has gone. The strictly frontal pose and the patterning of the drapery are the hall-marks of native, Romano-British workmanship. It is possible that Nos. 4 and 5 were carved by the same hand.

7. *The Terracotta Figurine* (pl. XXXIb, fig. 58)

The figurine, which takes the form of the head and neck of a cock, is $3\frac{1}{2}$ in. (9 cm.) long and $1\frac{1}{2}$ in. (3.8 cm.) in diameter at the base. The comb, eyes, beak, and crop of the bird are all recognizable, but stylized; and the neck feathers are indicated by lightly incised strokes. The circular surface at the base of the neck is flat and even and would appear to have been the termination of the figurine as it emerged from the mould. Here it would presumably have been attached to some object of the same material as an ornament, possibly as the finial or acroterion on a small terra-cotta shrine.

The piece comes from a late fourth-century level near Building XXVI.

8. *The Terracotta Fragments* (pl. XLVa, fig. 59)

(i), (ii). These two fragments, each of which forms part of a shallow cup, with a frilled or notched rim and sides that taper downwards from it, join at their bases, so as to produce

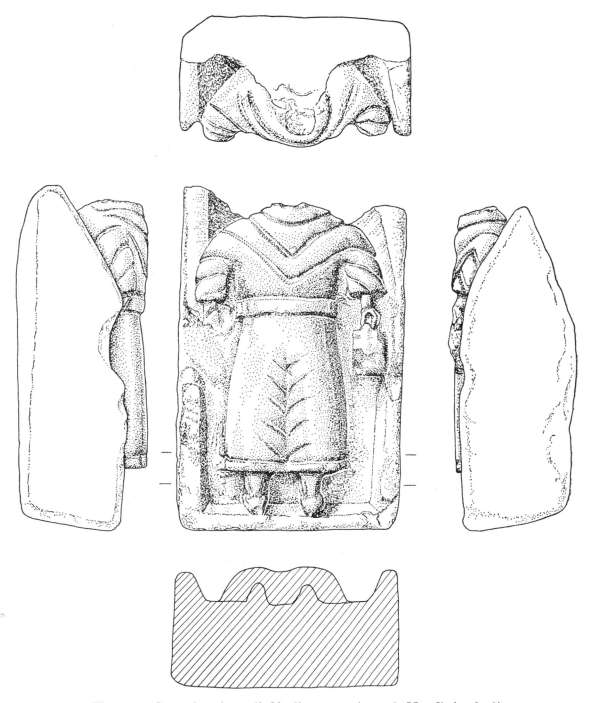

Fig. 57.   Carved votive relief in limestone (p. 138, No. 6) (scale ½)

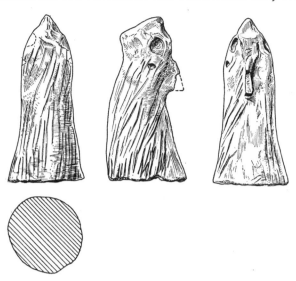

Fig. 58.   Terracotta figurine of cock (scale ½)

a reel-shaped vase (fig. 59 (374)). They are of light red clay. The purpose of the double cupping is not self evident; but presumably one half, that with the shallower cup, functioned as a stand, while the other half held something, possibly offerings or a small lamp. One cup does in fact, show traces of burning. In the Chesters Museum there are two terracotta vases from Coventina's Well, inscribed with dedications to the Nymph by one Saturninus Gabinius and much more elaborately decorated, which have frilled or notched splayed-out rims. But these appear to be cupped only at the top and are not waisted in to make a reel.[111] The larger Nettleton piece is 2¼ in. (5.6 cm.) high and was originally about 4 in. (10.1 cm.) in diameter at the rim: the smaller piece is 2 in. (5.0 cm.) high and perhaps 3⅓ in. (8.4 cm.) originally in diameter.

The two fragments were found together with Nos. (iii) and (iv) west of the hostelry in a fourth-century A.D. level.

(iii), (iv). Both of these fragments, made of red clay of a slightly deeper tone than that of fragments (i) and (ii), are on a curve and would seem to have formed parts of two similar but separate, objects (fig. 59 (371–2)).

The larger piece measures 3 in. (7.6 cm.) horizontally and is 2 in. (5.0 cm.) deep, 1¼ in. (3.1 cm.) thick on one horizontal surface, and 1 in. (2.5 cm.) thick on the other. On the outer side, along each curved edge, there is a series of large coarsely cut notches; and between the two rows of notches, also on the outer side, is a series of incised, crescent-shaped stabs. A series of similar, but smaller stabs ornament each flat horizontal surface. The smaller fragment has larger and even coarser notches along one curved edge on the outer side and a series of incised crescent-shaped stabs on the flat horizontal surface above the notches. On the outer side, below the notches, is a series of similar stabs which are, however, smaller than those above the notches and curve in the opposite direction. The flat, horizontal surface below these stabs is unadorned.

The curved shape of these two fragments, their notched decoration, and their substantial

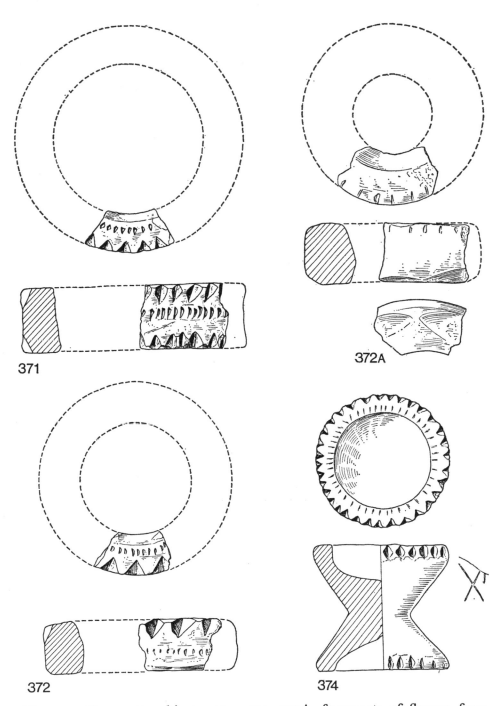

Fig. 59.   Terracotta objects: 371, 372, 372A, fragments of flanges from
? chimneys; 374, restored drawing of ? lamp (scale ⅓)

character suggest that they probably each formed part of one of the horizontal, flange-like rings, that separated the tiers of windows on two different objects, variously described as lamp or incense-burner chimneys, chimney pots or finials.[112] Found with Nos. (i) and (ii) west of the hostelry. (Another fragment from the vicinity of the temple has been found since Professor Toynbee contributed this report. This piece is the same size as (iv), but it has only a series of incised stab marks around its upper outer edge (372A).)

9. Intaglios (fig. 92(7))

1. This bronze ring, found in a burnt layer in Building XXI with Constantinian coins, has an oval hoop, connected with the oval bezel by two triangular elements, each incised with a pair of volutes. The hoop measures $1\frac{1}{8}$ in. (2.8 cm.) at its greatest extent. The bezel has a concave indentation on each of its long sides. On the bezel is a pale blue glass paste engraved with the figure of Apollo, who stands, cross-legged, after the manner of the sculptural Apollo Sauroctonos type, with a pillar at his right side. With his right hand he steadies his lyre, which rests on the top of the pillar; and in his left hand he holds a lustral branch in his capacity as purifier and healer. This ring, together with the inscribed altar and the bronze plaque, makes the third of a trio of Apollonian objects from the Nettleton site. The delicate workmanship of the intaglio suggests that it was either imported into Britain from the Continent or engraved in Britain by a foreign artist. Apollo is rarely found on gems from Roman Britain. Other possible instances are *Arch.* lxxxviii (1940), 224, No. 8, and fig. 15, No. 8 (Wroxeter), and *AA*, 4 s., xxxix (1961), 32, gem No. 13, and pl. V, No. 4 (South Shields). For gems from the Mediterranean area depicting Apollo with pillar, lyre, and branch, see, for example, Chiesa, 1966, pl. III, Nos. 50–55, 58, 59, 61, 65. (I owe these references to Dr. M. Henig, F.S.A.)

2. For description of Intaglio 2 see p. 148 (fig. 63(6)).

3. A plain, thin, oval silver frame from a late fourth-century level in Building XXVI, measuring $\frac{1}{2}$ in. (12 mm.) at its greatest extent and once mounted on the bezel of a ring, surrounds an intaglio engraved on the convex surface of a carnelian (fig. 60). The design shows the delicately worked head and shoulder of a horse, the head being turned back over the shoulder towards the spectator's left. An abundant mane flows down the neck. The

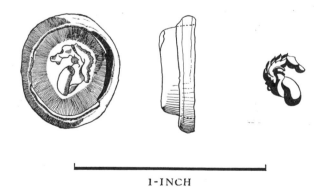

1-INCH

Fig. 60.   Horse's head intaglio ($\frac{2}{1}$)

fineness of the workmanship suggests that this piece was imported into Roman Britain from the Continent or from the Mediterranean world. For a gem cut with the same motif, but cruder in execution, see Chiesa, 1966, pl. LIV, No. 1077.

10. *Bronze Cockerel (Devizes Museum) (pl. XXXIa)*

From the Priestley excavation.

This perfectly preserved solid cast bronze cockerel, $2\frac{1}{2}$ in. (6.2 cm.) high and $2\frac{3}{4}$ in. (7.2 cm.) long from the beak to the outer curve of the tail-feathers, served as a candlestick and carries on its back a plain bronze candle-holder slightly wider at the top than at the base. Like the very similar, but less well preserved, candlestick cockerel found at East Lulworth in Dorset,[113] it is obviously of local Romano-British workmanship,[114] lively in its modelling and with comb and feathers rendered by attractively ornamental hatching. The outlines of the large, almond-shaped eyes are boldly incised and each eye has a small round central hole to represent the pupil. Both in its modelling and in its feather patterning the Nettleton bird outshines the Dorset piece and the latter's eyes are less expressive and less clearly defined. Candlesticks of such elaboration, taking the form of birds or animals, are perhaps, more likely to have been used in shrines and temples than in domestic contexts. The much larger pewter stag with a candle-holder on its back, now in the Roman Baths Museum, Bath, certainly came to light in a religious milieu, near the temple of *Sulis Minerva*.[115]

11. *Bronze Coin of the Emperor Magnentius (A.D. 350–3), 1 in. (2.5 cm.) in diameter*

The obverse depicts Magnentius bare headed, wearing a cuirass and cloak and facing three-quarters right. The legend reads: D(*ominus*) N(*oster*) MAGNENTIVS P(*ius*) F(*elix*) AVG(*ustus*). On the reverse is a large Chi-Rho monogram flanked by Alpha and Omega, with the legend SALVS DD (= *Dominorum*) BB (= *Nostrorum*) AVG(*ustorum*) ET CAES (*arum*). In the exergue is the mint mark AMB.AM = Ambianum (Amiens); B officina II (second workshop of the mint). Found in Building XXVII.

5. BRONZE, IVORY AND IRON OBJECTS RECOVERED FROM THE FLOOR OF THE LATER IMPROVISED SHRINE

1. *The Bronze Plaque (frontispiece and fig. 61)*

This thin bronze plaque is $4\frac{1}{4}$ in. (10.7 cm.) high and 3 in. (7.6 cm.) wide at its greatest extent. On the front it is worked in repousse and behind it shows traces of the iron backing to which it was soldered.

The subject of the relief is the bust of Apollo under an *aedicula* which is composed of an arch adorned with cable pattern and supported on two balusters with capitals, bases, and shafts that swell outwards at the centre. Above the arch the plaque forms a triangle with blunted apex and serrated edges. In the space between the arch and the bust is pricked out an inscription:

D·Λ·POL
DECIMIVS
D(eo) Apol(lini) Decimius

Fig. 61.   Bronze plaque of Apollo (scale ¼)

The plaque is thus identified as votive in character, dedicated by one Decimius to Apollo, whose large head and relatively small bust occupy the rest of the area between the balusters. The god is strictly frontal, with full, round cheeks, a broad nose, a small mouth, a dimpled chin, and large eyes, which are now hollow but were once, no doubt, filled with enamel or glass-paste. His thickly waved hair forms a toque-like frame to his face; and behind his head is a nimbus, the outline of which, at the neck, merges on either side with the outer edge of what seems to be a cloak, lightly incised with diagonal lines to represent folds and fastened in front below the chin by a round brooch that is actually the head of a rivet, part of whose stem is visible behind. The shoulders covered by the cloak are unnaturally small and narrow in proportion to the head. This may be due to lack of skill or it could have been deliberate, to enhance the impact of the disc-like nimbed countenance. There can be little doubt that we are dealing here with native, or at least with northern provincial, work, comparable in technique and style with the locally worked silver and bronze votive plaques from Bewcastle (Mars Cocidius) and Woodeaton (Mars, Cupid) (Toynbee, 1964, 330–1, pl. 77a) which are the native counterparts of the probably imported silver plaques with figures of Mars, Vulcan, Minerva, Apollo, and the Three Mothers, found at Barkway in Hertfordshire, at Stony Stratford in Buckinghamshire, in London, and at Burgh Castle on the Saxon Shore (*ibid.*,

328–30, pl. 76). As seems to have been the case with all of these, the Nettleton Apollo plaque must have been mounted on a metal sheet before being offered in the temple. See also pp. 53–4 (*JRS* lii (1962), 191, No. 3).

2. *The Bronze Disc* (pl. XXIIIa, fig. 63(1))

This thin disc, 2⅜ in. (6 cm.) in diameter, is almost perfectly flat, what would appear to be the upper surface being only very slightly concave, if, indeed, this concavity did exist in the original state. At the centre of this surface are five small incised dots, one in the middle and the other four grouped around it. Both surfaces are slightly pitted, the under surface more so than the upper one; and on the under surface, ¼ in. (6 mm.) from the edge and concentric with it, are the traces of a lightly incised circle which seems to be unfinished in several places.

The disc must have been mounted on, or let into, something; but what that something was it is difficult to guess. It can hardly have been the *umbo* of a shield, since that would probably be convex. Could it have been a piece of harness ornament, attached at the crossing point of leather straps?

3. *The Ivory Object* (pl. XXIIIb, fig. 62)

This oblong object, found in the small central area of the octagonal temple, is carved from a single piece of ivory, 3 in. (7.6 cm.) high, originally *c.* 2 in. (5.1 cm.) wide, and *c.* 1 in.

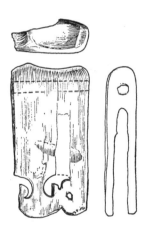

Fig. 62.   Ivory ? belt-fitting (scale ½)

(2.5 cm.) thick at its greatest extent. It appears to have preserved most of both its ends, the 'bottom' end being straight with slightly rounded edges, the other, the 'top' end being cut in an undulating line, part of the larger, central curve and the whole of the right-hand lateral curve having been broken off. On one side these two ends are linked by the polished outer surface of the object, the extant left-hand edge of that surface being also slightly rounded. Cut out of that surface on the extant left side is a vertical oblong slot, 1¼ in. (3.1 cm.) long and ⅜ in. (10 mm.) wide and terminating near the undulating end of the piece in a cut-out notch curving inwards; part of a corresponding notch is left in the right hand of the surface; but the two notches are not quite symmetrically curved. The right-hand portion of the surface has been broken off along the left-hand edge of its vertical slot. Below the left-hand lateral curve of the undulating end there is pierced a small round hole: there would presumably have been a corresponding hole below the right-hand lateral curve.

The thickness of the piece is somewhat greater at the undulating end than at the rounded end. Part of the surface of that thickness on the surviving side has been lost, but enough remains to show that what we may call the 'back' surface, parallel to the open work 'front' surface already described, sloped upwards towards its centre at a slight acute angle and was presumably met at the centre, gable wise, by a corresponding slope coming from the other side. On the preserved side of this surface, at the end corresponding to the undulating end of the other surface, there is a notched edge that may represent part of an open work pattern, with a horizontal slot near the top corresponding exactly with the little hole in the other surface. Towards the rounded edge at the 'bottom' the piece of ivory seems to have been originally solid, but was pierced by a horizontal slot that runs from a fairly large hole bored through the thickness of the piece and presumably ended in a corresponding hole in the thickness of the lost side. On the other hand, most of the 'upper' portion of the piece towards the undulating end appears to have been hollowed out, as though to take some object. Whether the large V-shaped notch in the 'upper' end of the extant thickness of the piece is deliberate or accidental cannot easily be gauged.

But the major problem, as yet unsolved, is the purpose of the piece. What was its interior meant to hold? What passed through the holes and their corresponding slots: wires, string, or metal pins? And what was the function of such wires, strings or pins? Mr. J. W. Brailsford has suggested to me that the object might be the ornamental chape of a sword-sheath, as with the Richborough example (Bushe-Fox, 1932, 79–80 and pl. XI (22)), with other references. But in that case would not the bottom end have been pointed or curved? And how would the holes and slots have worked?

(Professor Toynbee is prepared to agree with my suggestion that the horizontal hole is at the top of the object and not the bottom. Since no satisfactory suggestion has been made for its use, is it not possible that it was held by a waist girdle which was threaded through the horizontal hole at the top? The hollowed part could have secured a leather pouch or wallet, carried on the side at hip level. The small holes were probably used to secure the wallet by means of string or bone or metal pins. The wallet or pouch was possibly used by the hunter for his arrows. Alternatively it could have been worn in a frontal position purely for a decorative purpose in much the same way as the Scot wears his sporran today. W.J.W.)

4. *The Bronze Knife* (pl. XXIIIa, fig. 63(2))

The length of the knife, from the tip of the blade to the end of the handle as it now is, is $7\frac{3}{4}$ in. (19.7 cm.). The blade is very thin and has now cracked across at a point $1\frac{1}{2}$ in. (3.8 cm.) from the tip, where two small holes had been pierced through the metal. Along the curved edge of the blade, on its upper surface, are four small round indentations of varying size, as though for the perforation, which was never carried out, of other holes. What the purpose of these holes and indentations was remains obscure. There is much pitting on the under surface of the blade. The hollow, cylindrical bronze handle was open on the underside and contains an alloy, pewter or lead, shank, the crumpled end of which projects for 1 in. (2.5 cm.) beyond the end of its bronze container, and this was probably a knob at the end. The alloy

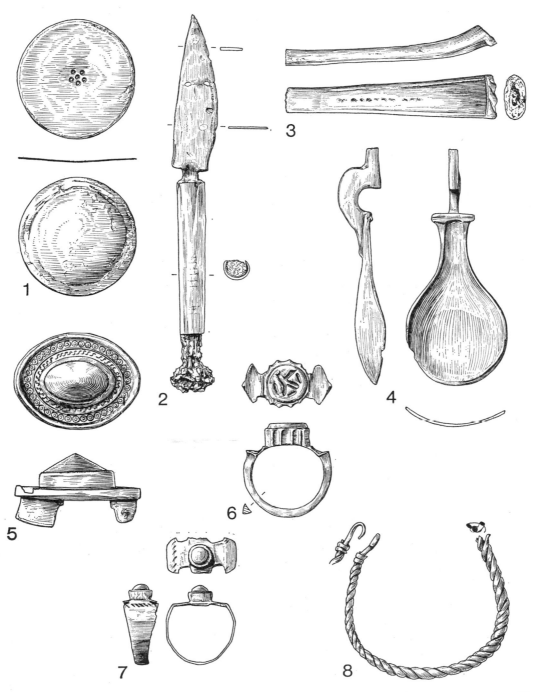

Fig. 63. Bronze objects from floor of later improvised shrine (scale $\frac{1}{1}$, except 1 and 2, $\frac{1}{2}$)

shank and knob make the knife unusually heavy; the bronze blade could not have been used for cutting and the very pointed tip suggests that it was used for piercing or penetration. It is possible that it had some ritual or sacrificial purpose.

5. *The Bronze Handle* (pl. XXIIIa, fig. 63(3))

This object, 2¼ in. (5.6 cm.) long and slightly curved, would appear to be part of a small bronze handle. It is wider at one end than at the other and is broken at each end. On the upper surface, at the broader end, there is a narrow raised fillet.

6. *Part of a Bronze Spoon* (pl. XXIIIa, fig. 63(4))

This bronze fragment, 2½ in. (6.2 cm.) long, consists of the undecorated, shovel-shaped bowl of a spoon end and of its curved, indented handle attachments. The bowl is very shallow and the spoon could well have served a ritual rather than a domestic purpose.

7. *The Brooch* (pl. XXIIIa, fig. 63(5))

A conical-shaped, oval, dark brown piece of opaque glass is mounted in a bronze frame. The overall length is 1¼ in. (3.1 cm.), the overall width at its greatest extent is 1 in. (2.5 cm.). The upper surface of the bronze frame carries two decorated borders, the inner one with a 'wave-crest' design, the outer one with a series of contiguous circles. There is a raised ridge between the two borders and another at the outer edge of the outer border. Parts of the fastening of the pin survive at the back.

For an almost identical brooch, but with its pin complete, see *DMC*, 121–2, pl. 39a, No. 5 (from Cold Kitchen Hill). Cf. also *BM Guide*, 20, No. 36, and fig. 11(23).

8. *The Intaglio* (fig. 63(6))

This bronze ring has an oval hoop connected with the bezel by two oval concave elements. The hoop measures ⅞ in. (22 mm.) at its greatest extent. The bezel has four oblong indentations on two of its opposite sides. Mounted on the bezel is a dark green glass paste engraved with what appears to be the crude figure of a man striding towards the right with his arms outstretched in front of him. There is a horizontal line beneath his feet and a vertical one behind him. This intaglio is almost certainly native work.

For similar motifs on imitation gems from Romano-British sites, see M. Henig in *Arepo: an Oxford Classical Journal*, ii (1969), 9–13, with references.

9. *Miscellaneous Bronze Objects* (pl. XXIIIa)

   (i) The pin of a brooch with curled head, 1½ in. (3.8 cm.) long.
   (ii) A finger ring, plain and narrow, ¾ in. (19 mm.) in diameter.
   (iii) (fig. 63(7)). A finger ring varying in width from ⅞ in. (22 mm.) on the side opposite the bezel to ⅜ in. (10 mm.) on the flattened side that carries the bezel. The latter bears a plain grey stone or glass paste set in a raised bronze rim. The diameter of the ring is ⅝ in. (16 mm.).
   (iv) (fig. 63(8)). A small twisted bracelet, 1¾ in. (4.4 cm.) in diameter and presumably worn by a very small child. One end is broken off, while attached to the other end is the hook of the fastener.

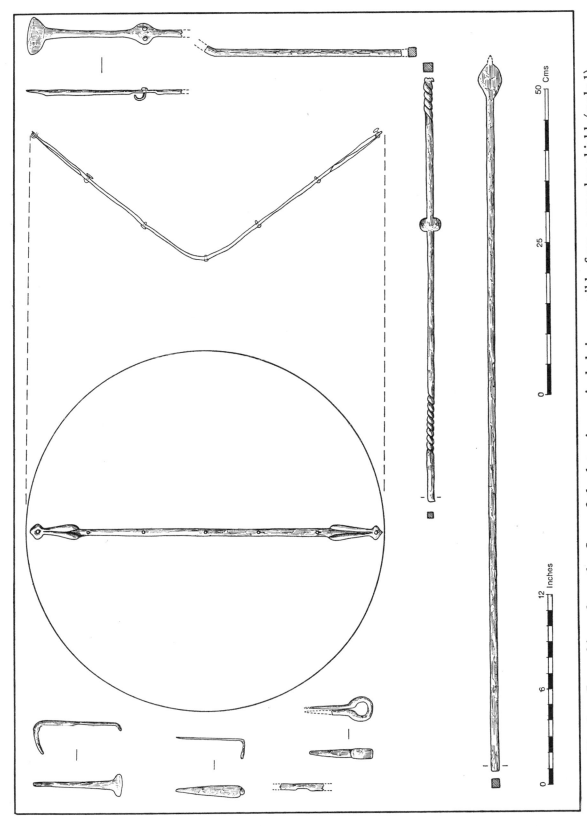

Fig. 64. Iron objects from the floor of the later improvised shrine, possibly from a wooden shield (scale ⅙)

10. Iron Objects (pl. XXII*b*, fig. 64)

(a)   Plain iron rod 3 ft. 6½ in. (1.06 m.) in length, broken at one end, where it is square in section with ½ in. (12 mm.) sides. At the other end it has a flattened terminal 2 in. (5 cm.) long and 1¼ in. (3.1 cm.) wide, terminating in a rounded end which may have been pointed.

(b)   A second rod, broken at each end, has the same diameter as (a) and is 2 ft. 2¼ in. (0.67 m.) in length. At one end it has a zone of twisted spiral decoration 2½ in. (6.2 cm.) long, and at the other a similar zone 3½ in. (8.9 cm.) in length. At one point the rod has been flattened out to form a flange on either side with a hole to house nails, presumably for fixing to a wooden object. It is possible that this rod forms part of (a).

(c)   An iron rod 10 in. (25.4 cm.) long but broken at one end. The bar is ½ in. (12 mm.) wide. At the unbroken end it is flattened out 1½ in. (3.8 cm.) wide in a similar manner to (b) to take two nails, one remaining *in situ*. The nail is clinched at the end, presumably to secure a wooden backing to the rod. It was probably part of (a) and (b).

(d)   A small piece of iron 2½ in. (6.2 cm.) long, broken at each end and of the same diameter as (a), (b) and (c). It is recessed in the centre and was probably part of (a) and (b).

(e)   A flat iron bar 1 ft. 10 in. (0.56 m.) in length. The flat bar is ⅜ in. (10 mm.) wide, is slightly rounded on its upper surface and has five equally spaced nail holes, which are recessed or countersunk to ensure a flush fitting. The two ends are worked into flat diamond-shaped terminals 3 in. (7.6 cm.) long and 1 in. (2.5 cm.) wide at the maximum width; each has a central perforation which is larger than the nail holes in the cross bar. The bar was bent sharply back on either side of the central nail hole. Several of the nails remain *in situ* and one is riveted, ¾ in. (19 mm.) long. It is likely that the bar formed the iron support for a wooden shield, and the sharp bend at the centre point suggests that it was convex in shape. It is also likely that the other associated iron objects (a) to (d) are components of a wooden shield approximately 1 ft. 10 in. (0.56 m.) in diameter.

(f)   Iron rod 5½ in. (14 cm.) long and flattened at one end 1½ in. (3.8 cm.) wide. The opposite end was pointed and bent back for 2 in. (5.1 cm.).

(g)   A small flat iron rod 4½ in. (11.4 cm.) long with a blunt point at one end. It is ¾ in. (19 mm.) wide and is bent back for 1½ in. (3.8 cm.) at the unpointed end.

(h)   An iron split pin 4 in. (10.1 cm.) long. The eyelet is 1½ in. (3.8 cm.) wide.

6. THE GLASS (fig. 65)

by the late Dorothy Charlesworth, F.S.A.

The glass is, as usual from an inhabited site, very fragmentary and many pieces cannot be identified with any certainty. They range in date over the whole period of the Roman occupation and include many pieces of fine quality ware, but there is more glass of the second half of the fourth century than of the earlier periods. The glass from Building XVIII which is all of this later period is predominantly colourless and, unlike the normally lightly weathered glass from Roman Britain, it has a flaking, black weathering which recalls that on medieval glass. This weathering is not found on the glass, even of the same date, from other parts of the site and must be due to some special local condition in the building (see note).

Some fragments from Building XVIII and elsewhere can be dated to the last quarter of the fourth century and the early years of the fifth century. It is not always certain whether these fragments are late Roman or post-Roman, since the shapes of the vessels and the

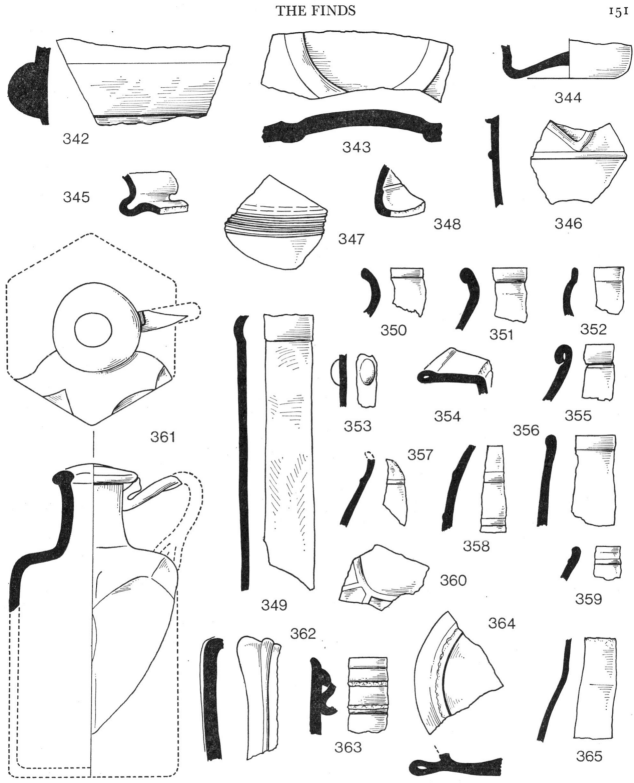

Fig. 65.   Glass (scale ½)

techniques are the same or similar. There is no break in the history of glass-making at this time in the middle and lower Rhine area from which most of the British finds are thought to come. There is some difference in the metal, the late Roman being thin and colourless with small bubbles and striations or a strong yellowish green, whereas the post-Roman is yellowish to colourless and often thicker than the late Roman. No. 19 is a late Roman type and No. 20 has a style of decoration more familiar in this country on post-Roman glass.

1. Fragment of a pillar-moulded bowl in blue-green glass. Isings form 3. A common first-century type which probably ceased to be made c. A.D. 100. From a level contemporary with the circular shrine (fig. 65(342)).

2. Part of the base of a square bottle with a moulded base marking of two concentric circles. Two fragments with moulded base markings, one with three concentric circles and one with a quarter circle at the corner, are the only distinctive pieces. Fragments of over 30 bottles were found, but no complete example; c. A.D. 70–130. For discussion of the type see JGS viii (1966), 26ff. From the shrine, earlier than the octagonal temple (fig. 65(343)).

3. Fragments of a hexagonal bottle in green glass, c. A.D. 70–130, from a first- to second-century level near Building X (fig. 65(361)).

4. Part of the base of a flagon in amber-coloured glass, made in the Seine/Rhine area c. A.D. 70–150. Isings form 52. AA, ser. 4, xxxvii (1959), 52, fig. 8. Four other fragments may also be from flagons, two in blue-green glass and two in yellowish green. From a first- to second-century A.D. level (fig. 65(345)).

5. Fragment of good colourless glass with a group of four cut lines round it, probably from a beaker or cylindrical bottle of second- to third-century date (fig. 65(347)).

6. Fragment of colourless glass from the carination of a beaker, probably of the same type as that found at Crundale or Hardknott in a second-century context. AA, ser. 4, xxxvii (1959), pl. 2.2, fig. 7(6), from a third- to fourth-century level (fig. 65(348)).

7. Fragment with a cut line from a beaker similar to 6, also in colourless glass, from a third- to fourth-century level (fig. 65(357)).

8. Thicker metal than 6 but probably the same type of vessel.

9. Good colourless fragment with a polished surface and ground horizontal rib, slight flaking iridescence. First- to second-century. Building debris of circular shrine (fig. 65(358)).

10. Rounded, slightly thickened rim of good colourless glass from a straight-sided beaker. Rhenish, second- to third-century; for complete example see AA, ser. 4, xxxvii (1959), pl. 1.4. From a level prior to A.D. 250 (fig. 65(360)).

11. Two fragments of colourless glass, much rubbed, with some strain cracking, decorated with a diamond pattern, either trailed or moulded; probably from a flagon, late second- or third-century. Isings form 120c (cf. AA, ser. 4, xxxvii (1959), fig. 8(10)). Contemporary with circular shrine (fig. 65(360)).

12. Part of the handle of a small jug, broken vertically as well as horizontally, in green glass. Second century. From level contemporary with circular shrine (fig. 65(362)).

13. Part of the infolded rim, neck and handle of a bottle in poor quality greenish glass with a yellowish streak in the rim. Second- to third-century. From a second- to third-century level (fig. 65(363)).

14. Part of the base of a vessel in blue-green glass, foot-ring formed with pincers. First- to third-century. From a level prior to A.D. 250 (fig. 65(364)).

15. Knocked off, unworked rim of a funnel-shaped beaker in thin colourless glass. Isings form 106. Unstratified (fig. 65(364)).

16. Rim and side fragments of a beaker in greenish glass with bubbles and striations, rim knocked off,

unworked with a faint cut line below. Isings form 106. From the west bank in a fourth-century level (fig. 65(349)).

There are fragments of several beakers similar to 15 and 16 in colourless or greenish glass, poor metal with bubbles and striations, typical of the later fourth century. A complete example was found at Winthill with the bowl with a hunting scene (*JGS* ii (1960), 52, figs. 8 and 9); note a variant in a burial at Glaston (*Ant J* xxx (1950), 72–3).

17. Rounded rim fragment of funnel-shaped beaker in green glass. From shrine (fig. 65(351)).
18. Another in yellowish green glass with bubbles and striations. From a fourth-century level (fig. 65(350)).
19. Base in typical late fourth-century metal, colourless with pinhead bubbles, concave with pontil mark.
20. Base of fourth-century beaker, greenish, some pinhead bubbles and striations. Similar base fragments among glass from Building XVIII. Unstratified (fig. 65(344)).
21. Fragment of green glass with a blob of emerald green applied to it. Fourth century. Rhenish. From a fourth-century or later level (fig. 65(352)).
22. Fragment of a folded foot, probably from a beaker of late fourth-century or early fifth-century type. Isings form 109 (cf. *JRS* lii (1962), pl. xxiv, 1, for one in the group from Burgh Castle). From the floor level of Building XVIII (fig. 65(354)).
23. Base in colourless glass with pinhead bubbles, faint opaque white marvered trail round centre, pontil mark. Late fourth- or early fifth-century.
24. Fragment of colourless glass with some bubbles, decorated with a trail running horizontally round vessel and a zigzag trail below it. This decoration, the unmarvered trail in high relief, is typical of fifth- to seventh-century glass. This piece is unusual as normally vessels of that period are in coloured glass. From a late fourth-century level or later (fig. 65(346)).

The trailing on 23 and 24 separates them from the fourth-century material and makes it probable that they are fifth-century or later. 23 would seem to belong to the same group of fragments as those found at such sites as Mote of Mark (Harden, 1956, 149–51) and Dinas Powys (Alcock, 1963, 178–85).

Window Glass

Many fragments of window glass both of the rather thick matt/glossy first- to second-century variety and of the thinner blown panes of third- to fourth-century date were found.

7. THE BEADS

with notes contributed by C. M. Guido, F.S.A.

Some 29 beads were found in varying levels. The beads are nearly all Roman rather than native and are fairly typical of their period.

1. Melon type, light blue.
2. Melon type, bright blue.
3. Melon type, light blue.
    Beads of this type have been found at Alchester, Jewry Wall, Leicester, and other sites.
4. Translucent bottle green, segmented. A type fairly common on Roman sites, e.g. Brislington, Somerset, Carrawburgh (*Procolitia*), Ham Hill, Catterick, etc.

5. Necklace. The seven small blue and green beads are common on Roman necklaces, and the three red and white striped ones are almost certainly on a blue background and are comparable to examples from Ospringe, *Verulamium*, Great Chesters, etc.

6. Small light blue bead of common Roman type.

7. As 6 but light green.

8. Shiny translucent bottle green. Hexagonal. This is certainly Roman. *c.* A.D. 370–400.

9. Hexagonal, opaque. Roman *c.* A.D. 370–400.

10. Flattened example of an hexagonal bead, bottle green. Same type as Nos. 8 and 9.

11. Biconical opaque black (four similar). The form is common in Roman contexts but opaque glass is not usual.

12. Opaque, bottle green. Roman.

13. Long oval opaque terracotta coloured (three beads). Very thin and looks painted but is probably comparable to a bead from Bagendon (Glos.). First-century A.D. An annular bead of this glass has been found at Croft Ambrey Fort (Hereford). Probably first-century A.D.

14. Light green typically Roman type of which there are many examples, *e.g.* from Chesters, Scarborough, Park Street Roman villa, *Verulamium*.

15, 16. Similar to No. 14. Light green.

17. Small blue glass bead. Badly made and more probably Saxon than Roman.

18. Blue with white streaks. Could be Saxon on typological grounds.

19. Very light blue. Translucent. This annular bead is quite normal in Roman contexts (cf. Bath, the Romano-British cemetery at Portland and elsewhere).

20. Wooden bead. 1 in. (2.5 cm.) long, ¼ in. (6 mm.) diameter.

Nos. 4, 5, 6 and 12 all came from material deposited to the north of the circular shrine before the octagonal podium wall was built. No. 13 was associated with the circular temple, but Nos. 1, 11 and 16, also found within the temple area, can be dated after A.D. 330. No. 3 was in material earlier than A.D. 284. Nos. 7, 9, 10, 14, 15, 18–20 came from post-Constantinian levels. Nos. 8 and 17 came from post-Roman levels and No. 2 was unstratified.

8. THE SAMIAN POTTERY

by Dr. Grace Simpson, F.S.A.

This report was brought up to date in 1977. Part of my original report was subsequently rewritten, without my knowledge, and I wish to thank Mr. Wedlake for making many attempts to obtain it, so that I might see how it had been changed. I have kept the running numbers which had replaced the site numbers. Sherds which I have not seen are Nos. 12, 32, 59, 159–61, 170 and 189.

Mr. C. W. Priestley's collection, now in Devizes Museum, is illustrated on fig. 72, nos. 1–24 in the text following Mr. Wedlake's sherds. The sherds excavated by Mr. Wedlake are in Bristol Museum.

Notes on most of the potters' stamps were contributed by Mr. B. R. Hartley, F.S.A., as follows: they are distinguished by an S before the number in the text: S4, 8, 12, 25, 32, 48, 59, 63, 64, 76, 82, 84, 89, 92, 108, 116, 118, 120, 132–4, 144, 146, 151, 166–8, 189. A list of the name-stamps is given on p. 176 below. I have read some of the names differently: Nos. 34, 81, 82(i) and 166.

The Earliest Sherds

These are Nos. 1–3, 5, 14, 26, 30, 35, 64, 123(ii), and 172. They represent the Claudian occupation, although several were found in later levels where they had been redeposited during later building phases. Much of the later sigillata was found in the filling of the early enclosure ditch, Nos. 8–77, and has nothing to do with that phase: it was rubbish used to fill the ditch and level the area. The sherds are arranged as follows:

1–77	From the first-century enclosure ditch.
78–83	Pit-filling below the floor of Building XIX.
84	From the enclosure ditch below Building XXIV.
85–93	From the foot of the west bank.
94–98	From the area of Buildings XVI and XXVI.
99–110	Buildings XI and XII: the guest-houses or hostels.
111–114	Building XIII.
115–121	Building IX
122	Building X.
123–130	The circular shrine.
131–152	The octagonal podium of the circular shrine.
153–158	Levels associated with the octagonal shrine.
159–189	Levels surrounding this shrine.

Abbreviations (additional to list on pp. xvi–xviii)

E.D. = enclosure ditch; L.D.F. = lower ditch filling; U.D.F. = upper ditch filling.

C.G. = Central Gaulish; E.G. = East Gaulish; S.G. = South Gaulish.

Atkinson, *Pompeii* – D. Atkinson, 'A hoard of Samian ware from Pompeii', *JRS* iv (1914), 27–64.

D. or Dech. – J. Déchelette, *Vases céramiques órnes de la Gaule romaine*, 1904.

Hermet = F. Hermet, *La Graufesenque*, 1934.

Karnitsch, 1959 = P. Karnitsch, *Die Reliefsigillata von Ovilava*, 1959.

Knorr, *Aislingen* = R. Knorr, *Die Terra-Sigillata-Gefässe von Aislingen*, Dillingen, 1913; reprinted in G. Ulbert, *Die römischen Donau-Kastelle Aislingen und Burghöfe*, Limesforschungen, Band I, 1959.

Knorr, 1907 = R. Knorr, *Die verzierten Terra-Sigillata Gefässe von Rottweil*, 1907.

Knorr, 1912 = R. Knorr, *Südgallische Terra-Sigillata Gefässe von Rottweil*, 1912.

Knorr, 1919 = R. Knorr, *Töpfer und Fabriken verzieter Terra-Sigillata des ersten Jahrhunderts*, 1919.

Knorr, 1952 = R. Knorr, *Terra-Sigillata Gefässe des ersten Jahrhunderts mit Töpfernamen*, 1952.

Oswald = F. Oswald, *Index of Figure-Types on Terra Sigillata*, 1936–7.

Oswald, *Stamps* = F. Oswald, *Index of Potters' Stamps on Terra Sigillata*, 1931.

Oswald and Pryce = F. Oswald and T. Davies Pryce, *An Introduction to the Study of Terra Sigillata*, 1920; re-issued 1966.

Ricken and Fischer = F. Ricken, *Die Bilderschüsseln der römischen Töpfer von Rheinzabern*, Tafelband, 1942; Charlotte Fischer, textband mit Typenbildern, 1963.

Rogers = G. B. Rogers, *Poteries Sigillées de la Gaule Centrale*, I, *Les motifs non figurés*, XXVIIIe supplément à *Gallia*, 1974.

Stanfield and Simpson = J. A. Stanfield and Grace Simpson, *Central Gaulish Potters*, 1958.

Terrisse = J.-R. Terrisse, *Les céramiques sigillées gallo-romaines des Martres-de-Veyre (Puy-de-Dôme)*, XIXe supplément à *Gallia*, 1968.

Nos. 1–77. *From the First-century Enclosure Ditch*

Fig. 66

1. Dr.30. S.G. The ovolo is incomplete and not attributable. The hare is O.2049. Claudian–Neronian. L.D.F.

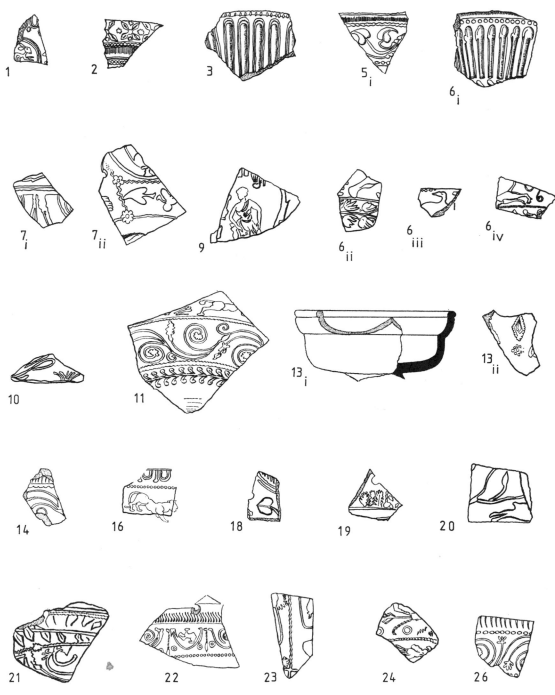

Fig. 66.   Samian ware (scale ½)

2. Dr.29. S.G. The frieze consists of four small leaves arranged in a cruciform pattern with central rosette and rosettes between the leaves, like Knorr, 1952, Taf. 8, B, from La Graufesenque. Related designs are illustrated by Knorr on the same plate. Claudian–Neronian. L.D.F.

3. Dr.29 S.G. Rounded profile. Large gadroons in series, irregularly impressed. A common decoration in the Claudian period. Claudian. L.D.F.

S4. Dr.15/17 or 18. S.G. Stamped OFPASSE. One of the late stamps of Pass(i)enus of La Graufesenque, noted at Caerhun, *Segontium* and twice at the Nijmegen fortress, *c*. A.D. 60–75. L.D.F. (Note by B.R.H.)

5. (i) Dr.29. S.G. Frieze with small, opposed, very pointed curved leaves, and a scroll-binding of three lobes. Claudian–Neronian. L.D.F.
   (ii) Dr.33 S.G. Rim only. L.D.F.

6. (i–iv) From the yellow silt. E.D.
   (i) Dr.29. S.G. Short hooded gadroons below large beads, with traces of a basal wreath. Too blurred for attribution. *c*. A.D. 55–75
   (ii) Dr.37. S.G. Basal wreath, like Knorr, 1907, Taf. xvi, 10, and Karnitsch, 1959, Taf. 3, 9. *c*. A.D. 80–100.
   (iii) S.G. Bird looking backwards, D.1009 = O.2247, used by many Flavian potters.
   (iv) Dr.37. C.G. Les Martres de Veyre style with very fine beaded border. Dog, possibly O.1979. Fragmentary basal wreath. *c*. A.D. 100–120.

7. (i-ii) From enclosure, north side.
   (i) Dr.37. S.G. Festoons and spirals damaged when the bowl was removed from the mould. A.D. 80–100.
   (ii) Dr.37. C.G. Les Martres de Veyre. Style of Igocatus with his two-handled vase Rogers T9. The opposed leaves Rogers H170 were also used by Drusus I (Potter X-3), see Stanfield and Simpson, 13, fig. 4, 11. *c*. A.D. 100–20.

S8. Dr.31R. C.G. Stamped CELSIANI.OF, a common stamp at Lezoux, and found elsewhere occasionally on Walters 79 and 80. *c*. A.D. 160–200. U.D.F. (Note by B.R.H.) Site E: cutting XV, D.

9. Dr.37. C.G. Vulcan without tongs, as on a bowl in the early Cinnamus style signed by Cerialis below the decoration, see Simpson and Rogers, *Gallia*, xxvii (1969), 6, pl. 2(13), and pl. 3(21) in a large winding scroll, as here. *c*. A.D. 135–70. U.D.F.

10. Dr.37. S.G. Floral ornament at left, and grass-tuft, indicate manufacture *c*. A.D. 80–100. E.D. Found with 15 and 77.

11. Dr.37. S.G. Fragmentary upper zone with dog to right and floral ornament. A winding scroll below, and basal wreath, which both appear on a Dr.29 from Rottweil, Knorr, 1919, Taf. 73, A. *c*. A.D. 70–85. E.D.

12. Not illustrated. [Not seen by G.S.] Dr.37. S.G. Panels with a triple-bordered festoon with a spiral and pedant, cf. Karnitsch, 1959, Taf. 8, 6; and tendrils like Knorr, 1919, Taf. 80, E. A leaf, similar but larger than the one used on the tendrils, is below the decoration. *c*. A.D. 75–95. E.D. (Note by B.R.H.)

13. (i) Dr.27. S.G. Lacking footring. Flavian. E.D.
    (ii) Dr.37. C.G. Two details which are characteristic of the Quintilianus group. Stanfield and Simpson, 145, fig. 17, 7 and 21, Rogers C281 and U28. *c*. A.D. 120–45. E.D.

14. Dr.29. S.G. Fragmentary scroll from the frieze, fine work. Compare No. 26. Claudian–Neronian. E.D.

15. A mixed South and Central Gaulish group (not illustrated) ending in the Hadrianic or early Antonine period. E.D. Found with 10 and 77.

16. Dr.37. C.G. The small ovolo of Sacer, Stanfield and Simpson, fig. 22(1); Rogers B14. The panther is O.1519, the smaller size. *c*. A.D. 125–45. U.D.F.

12

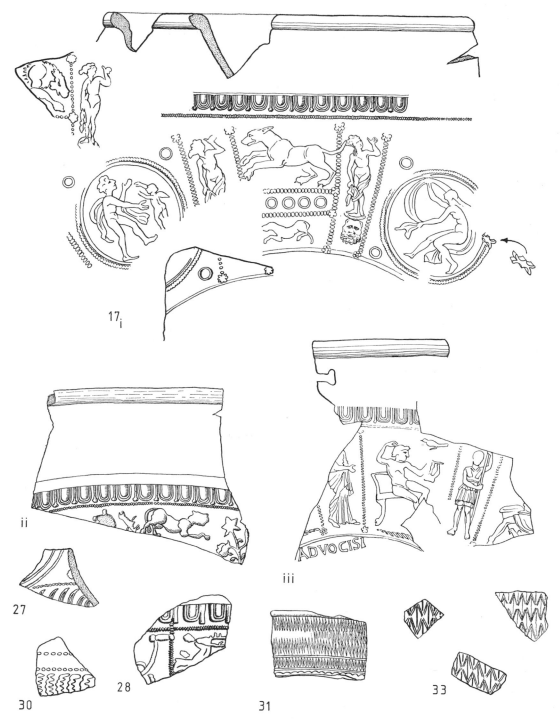

Fig. 67.   Samian ware (scale ½)

Fig. 67
17. Three bowls (i–iii) in U.D.F.
   (i) Dr.37. C.G. Irregularly-stamped ovolo, as drawn, of the 'Donnaucus-Sacer style', see Stanfield and Simpson, pl. 84, also pl. 50. From the left, lion, probably O.1379, Venus on a bearded mask of which the eye-balls are clearly visible, O.304; large beaded medallion with man with a cloak D.398 = O.689 and an uncertain type; large animal to left (new type); panther D.805 = O.1570; a similar beaded medallion with dancer (close to O.361A). Large rivet still in position. c. A.D. 125–45.
   (ii) Dr.37. C.G. Larger panther D.799 = O.1518, and part of the tree Rogers N7, used by Sacer, see Stanfield and Simpson, pl. 82, 5. Style of Sacer. c. A.D. 125–45.
   (iii) Dr.37. C.G., stamped ADVOCISI below the decoration. The border below the ovolo is only partially impressed. The ovolo is Stanfield and Simpson, fig. 33, 2. In many fragments, with rivet-holes. Draped woman O.926A; damaged Apollo D.52 = O.83; bird (type uncertain); warrior O.159A; Bacchus D.534 = O.571. Mr. Hartley has noted a similar bowl from Wilderspool, except that O.926 is replaced by D.523 = O.905. c. A.D. 150–80.

Fig. 66
18. Joins 39.
19. Dr.30. S.G. Irregular leaves to left of a vertical border. A late example. Flavian. E.D.
20. Dr.37. C.G. A deer below a scroll design. Hadrianic or Antonine. U.D.F.
21. Dr.29. S.G. Damaged during manufacture. The lowest zone has a spurred and stipuled leaf in a festoon. c. A.D. 65–85. E.D.
22. Dr.29. S.G. The unusual festoon is also found on a bowl stamped ALBIM from La Graufesenque, now in Rodez Museum. c. A.D. 45–60. (Note by B.R.H.) Found with a Central Gaulish sherd, probably Antonine. E.D.
23. Dr.30. S.G. A fragment, found with a Dr.18 which is Neronian or early Flavian. E.D.
24. Dr.37. S.G. Two wreaths: the upper one is like Knorr, 1919, Taf. 55, E. c. A.D. 65–75. E.D.
S25. Dr.33. C.G. Stamped RVFVS F, probably a Lezoux potter. His work is very uncommon and has been noted only five times in Britain. Antonine. U.D.F. (Note by B.R.H.)
26. Dr.29. S.G. The frieze has a scroll which is close to, but not identical with, the frieze on a Dr.29 from Mainz, Knorr, 1919, Taf. 8, B. c. A.D. 45–60. Found with a Dr.27 not later than early Flavian. E.D.

Fig. 67
27. Dr.37. S.G. A basal wreath of large S-shaped gadroons, cf. Atkinson, *Pompeii*, pl. xiv, 74. c. A.D. 85–100. E.D.
28. Dr.37. C.G. The Cinnamus group ovolo 3B, Simpson and Rogers, *Gallia*, xxvii (1969) 4, fig. 1, and 6, fig. 2, 9. An incomplete stag, and the feathers in the field which are common on this style, Rogers J178. c. A.D. 135–60. Area of E.D.
29. Not illustrated. Dr.31R, burnt. C.G. Middle to late Antonine, found with a Dr.18/31R, burnt. C.G. Early to middle Antonine. E.D., north-west corner.
30. Dr.29, slightly burnt. S.G. Rounded profile. Immediately below the central moulding there is a closely impressed wreath, cf. Knorr, 1952, Taf. 2, stamped by the bowl-maker Albus. c. A.D. 40–60. E.D.
31. Dr.29, rim only. S.G. A late and deeply rouletted rim in two zones. c. A.D. 75–85. E.D.
S32. Not illustrated. [Not seen by G.S.] Dr.27. S.G. Stamped SULP]ICI, by Sulpicius of La Graufesenque. Although this particular stamp is only known otherwise from Corbridge, there is plenty of dating evidence for this potter's work. c. A.D. 80–100. (Note by B.R.H.) Found with Flavian–Hadrianic sherds. E.D.

33. East Gaulish. Four fragments from a vase with 'cut-glass' decoration, cf. Oswald and Pryce, pl. lxxvii, 4, from Rheinzabern. Antonine. U.D.F.

S34. Stamp read by G.S. as CAV[the AV being ligatured but wrongly shown on fig. 73. Trajanic or earlier. U.D.F.

Fig. 68

35. Dr.29. C.G. Micaceous Lezoux ware with soft orange-coloured slip, see H. Vertet, *Revue Archéologique*², ii (1967), 255–86; for the largest series of illustrations, see Joseph Martin, *Bull. Hist. et Scient. de l'Auvergne*, lxii (1942), 181–210, especially 201, nos. 27, 28, 30; 203, nos. 61 and 62. Probably Claudian. E.D.

36. Dr.29. S.G. A straight wreath below the central moulding and attached to its lower border is a curved stalk ending in a small heart-shaped leaf, as on the frieze of Knorr, 1952, Taf. 83, stamped SEVER, which also has similar grass-stalks below the animals .The dog is not identifiable. Found with a Dr.18. c. A.D. 75–85. E.D.

37. Dr.37. C.G. The style of Cinnamus, see Stanfield and Simpson, pl.159, 26. The Pan mask, O.1214, and the dolphins over a basket, Rogers Q 58. c. A.D. 150–80. U.D.F.

38. Dr.29. S.G. Too fragmentary for identification. c. A.D. 65–75. E.D.

39. Dr.29. S.G. Joins 18 above. Rivet-hole. Bird, probably O.2249, within a small medallion, like Knorr, *Aislingen*, Taf. viii, 6, which also has a large scroll design. c. A.D. 50–70. E.D., north side.

40. Dr.37. C.G. See no. 101 below. The bear D.820 = O.1627 and Sacer's bundle of leaves, Rogers L19, were both used by Attianus, see Stanfield and Simpson, pl. 85, 9, and pl. 86, 12. c. A.D. 120–45. E.D., north side.

41. Not illustrated. Dr.37. S.G. A chevron basal wreath. Not the same as No. 137 below. Found with No. 42. Flavian. E.D.

42. Dr.37. C.G. Panther to left, looking right. Hadrianic or Antonine. E.D.

43. Dr.29. S.G. A narrow frieze divided into panels. The floral ornament is not the same as the one on No. 24 above. Earlier than some of the potters listed by Knorr, 1919, Textbild 12, 7. c. A.D. 65–75. E.D., north side.

44. Dr.30. S.G. Large single-bordered ovolo, and an unusual method of filling a panel. Probably Neronian. E.D., north side.

45. (i) Dr.29. S.G. A scroll design on the soffit.
(ii) Dr.37. S.G. A basal band of ovals, like Atkinson, *Pompeii*, pl. vii, 40; pl. x, 53.
(iii) Dr.37. S.G. Diana and the hind, type uncertain; found with two other late first-century fragments. Flavian. First-century enclosure.

46. Not illustrated. Dr.37. C.G. In poor condition. Wavy line border. Probably Hadrianic. First-century enclosure, north side.

47. Dr.37. C.G. Sphinx D.497 = O.857, and below, a bear, type uncertain. Early Antonine. First-century enclosure, north side.

S48. Dr.18/31. C.G. Stamped [AB]ALLAN[F] by Aballanius, probably of Lezoux. His work is relatively common in the Rhineland and that, as well as his frequent production of Dr.27, suggests a period c. A.D. 125–50. First-century enclosure. (Note by B.R.H.)

S49. Dr.37. C.G. Censorinus of Lezoux, with part of his curved name-stamp [CENSORI]NI in the single-bordered festoon, see Stanfield and Simpson, pl. 101, 1, 2, 4, 7, 9, also 17. His ovolo 1, see S and S, 191, fig. 29, 1; Rogers B206. Cup in the right hand of the man with a wineskin D.360 = O.626. c. A.D. 150–80. First-century enclosure.

50. Dr.29. S.G. Frieze of vertical wavy lines, cf. Knorr, *Aislingen*, Taf. x, 12, 15. c. A.D. 60–80. Found with a Flavian Dr.18. First-century enclosure.

51. Not illustrated. Dr.31. C.G. One sherd burnt. Antonine. First-century enclosure.

Fig. 68. Samian ware (scale ½)

52. Dr.37. C.G. Rivet hole for repair. Possibly the left shoulder of Hercules gripping a snake in left hand D.464 = O.783 used by Criciro. The trifid terminal is different from his, cf. Rogers G67. Hadrianic or early Antonine. First-century enclosure, north side.

53. Dr.29. S.G. Good quality rim, and a rosette in the decoration. First-century enclosure.

54. Not illustrated. Dr.31R. C.G. Late Antonine. First-century enclosure, north side.

55. Dr.37. C.G. Large scroll design. Antonine. First-century enclosure, north side.

56. Dr.37. C.G. Two sherds. Damaged ovolo, probably one used by Criciro, see Stanfield and Simpson, pl. 118, 17, Rogers B101. Early Antonine. First-century enclosure.

57. Dr.37. C.G. style of Potter X-2. See No. 164. Trajanic. First-century enclosure.

58. Dr.29. S.G. Two sherds join. Leaftips in series above, not illustrated; and a saltire on the soffit includes the ornament Knorr, 1919, Taf. 65, 39. Found with a Hadrianic Dr.27 and a slightly later Dr.35. First-century enclosure.

S59. Not illustrated. [Not seen by G.S.] Dr.18/31. C.G. Stamped [RO]PVS.FE, from Les Martres de Veyre. There are examples from the second fire of Roman London, and from military sites abandoned *c.* A.D. 125. *c.* A.D. 100–25. First-century enclosure. (Note by B.R.H.)

60. Dr.37. C.G. Ovolo 3 and bird O.2315 of Cinnamus. Antonine. First-century enclosure.

61. Not illustrated. Dr.37. C.G. Astragalus border. Antonine. First-century enclosure.

62. Dr.37. C.G. An example of a new ovolo for Cinnamus, see Rogers B5 on a Dr.37 with the large stamp CINNAMIOF in the Musée des Antiquités Nationales, Saint-Germain-en-Laye. Victory D.474 = O.809. Antonine. Interior of first-century enclosure.

S63. Not illustrated. Dr.31. C.G. Stamped [DRA]VCIM, a stamp known at Lezoux, and elsewhere, on Forms 31R, 79 and 80. *c.* A.D. 150–90. First-century enclosure, north side. (Note by B.R.H.)

S64. Dr.27. S.G. With grooved footring and stamped DAMONVS. This potter worked at La Graufesenque, see Hermet, 1934, pl. 111, 47. This is not one of his earliest stamps and it may be dated *c.* A.D. 40–55. Enclosure material below Building XXVII. (Note by B.R.H.)

Fig. 69

65. Dr.29. S.G. Two basal wreaths. The upper one is a Germanus leaf, and the lower leaf in series is like Knorr, *Aislingen*, Taf. xii, 5. *c.* A.D. 60–75.

66. Dr.37. S.G. An unusual design. The boxer O.1174A is a rare La Graufesenque type. *c.* A.D. 80–100. First-century enclosure, north side.

67. Not illustrated. Dr.27. S.G. Flavian. First-century north enclosure.

68. Dr.37. C.G. Two sherds join. Style of Potter X-5, very like Baillie-Reynolds, Caerhun, *AC* (1931), 290, fig. 8, S125, identified by G. B. Rogers, see his M10, the vine scroll, and the column Rogers P10, damaged at the top, as here. Hadrianic. North-east side of first-century enclosure.

69. Dr.37. C.G. Les Martres de Veyre, Trajanic. North side of first-century enclosure.

70 and 71. Dr.37. C.G. The opposed dolphins, used by 'Ranto' and Advocisus, see Stanfield and Simpson, pls. 27, 325; 114, 28 (not in Oswald), and a seahorse. Trajanic to early Hadrianic. North-east side of first-century enclosure.

S72. Illegible stamp on a Dr.18/31 or 31 base. C.G. Hadrianic or Antonine. North side of first-century enclosure.

73. Dr.37. C.G. Candelabrum, cf. No. 105. Antonine.

74. Dr.30. S.G. Probably pre-Flavian. From a level below the south cross-bank.

75. Dr.37. C.G. Possibly Vulcan, without tongs, D.39 = O.66. Early Antonine. From a level below the south cross-bank.

S76. Dr.33. C.G. Stamped SEVERVS.F, a new stamp, which belongs to the Hadrianic to Antonine

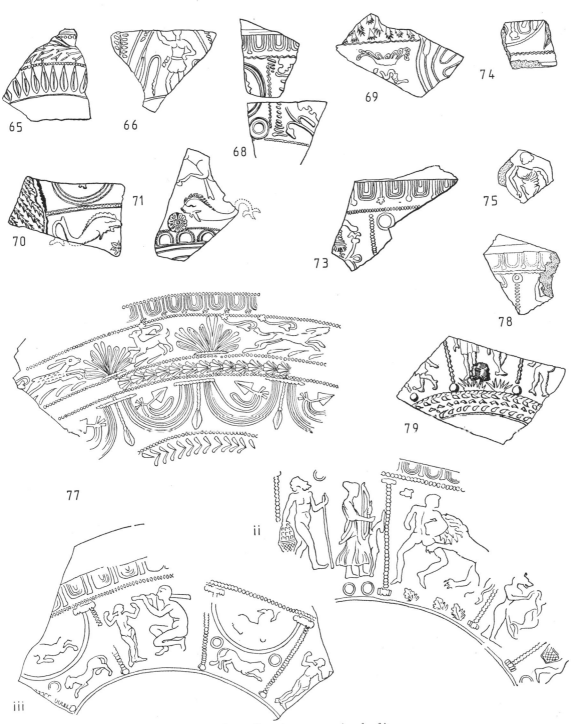

Fig. 69. Samian ware (scale ½)

Severus of Lezoux, rather than the late Antonine potter. From a level below the south cross-bank. (Note by B.R.H.)

77. Three bowls. From top filling of ditch on the north side of the enclosure, with Nos. 10 and 15.

 (i) Dr.37. S.G. Large bowl in many fragments. Ovolo with three-pronged tongue. Spotted hare to right, not in Oswald; dog to left looking right O.1573A; plant ornament and dog to right with head up like Knorr, 1919, Taf. 57 G, by Mercato. The lower zone has festoons with alternating spurred and stipuled leaves. Flavian.

 (ii) Dr.37. C.G. Many fragments in the style of Mapillo, kindly identified by Dr. G. B. Rogers from his forthcoming publication on the Plicque Collection. The ovolo was also used by Potter X-6, see Stanfield and Simpson, ovolo 1 = Rogers B35; also the tree, see S and S, pl. 75, 15. The figure-types are new for Mapillo, except for the Diana. Most interesting is the Anubis, a new type, not quite complete on this bowl. The others are: man with basket O.595; Diana with hind O.103D; Hercules and lion O.796. The leaf tips below the lion are a characteristic of Mapillo's style. The special astragalus on the border terminals, and the small rings, are on the signed fragment from Rouen. The dog's head above the shoulder of Hercules was used by Rentus, see G. B. Rogers, *Gallia*, xxiv (1966), 237, and fig. 2. *c.* A.D. 125–50.

 (iii) Dr.37. C.G. Style of the Cinnamus group. Ovolo 3, but it is not clear enough to identify whether 3A or 3B = Rogers B143 or B144. The figure-types are: O.1704 in festoon; panthers, to left O.1570, and to right O.1518; Venus O.281; crouching man, a rare type, but used by Cinnamus, D.358 = O.605. *c.* A.D. 140–70.

Nos. 78–83. *From the Pit Filling Below the Floor of Building XIX*

78. Dr.37. C.G. The ovolo is Rogers B103, used by Advocisus and Divixtus. Antonine.
79. Dr. 37. S.G. Repaired with a lead rivet. Panel decoration and a basal wreath. The grass tufts indicate a period *c.* A.D. 80–100.

Fig. 70

80. Dr.37. C.G. Tail of a dolphin in a plain double festoon, and coarse, roped borders. Antonine.
S81. Dr.33. Stamp read by G.S. as]A . . . vvs. The stamp has not been noted before and the reading is uncertain. Probably Antonine. (Note by B.R.H.)
S82. (i) Dr.31. C.G. Stamped D[. . . .]MA (much eroded). A longer name than Decimus, suggested by Mr. Hartley, seems to be needed here. Antonine.
 (ii) Dr.31. C.G. Stamped CI[NTVSMIM]. Cintusmus of Lezoux, *c.* A.D. 150–80. (Notes by B.R.H.)
83. Dr.30. S.G. Small double-bordered ovolo. Neronian–Flavian.
S84. Dr.31. C.G. Stamped REVBRRIOF. This stamp occurs at Lezoux in groups of middle Antonine products. *c.* A.D. 150–75. From the enclosure ditch below Building XXIV. (Note by B.R.H.)

Nos. 85–98. *From the Foot of the West Bank*

S85. Curle 23. C.G. A rosette stamp in the base. This particular stamp is fairly common at Lezoux in Antonine groups of sherds.
S86. Not illustrated. Dr.18/31. Stamped BAL[. . . Graffito on the underside.
87. Dr.37. C.G. Ovolo, very like Butrio 3, Rogers B82, and top of a tripod or possibly Rogers Q10, see No. 95 below. Hadrianic to early Antonine.
S88. Dr.31. C.G. Stamped [IVS]TIMA. Iustus of Lezoux. *c.* A.D. 160–200.
S89. Probably Dr.33. C.G. Stamped TIT[. . . Second-century. (Note by B.R.H.)
90. Dr.37. S.G. Stag looking backwards D.859 = O.1738. *c.* A.D. 80–100.

Fig. 70.   Samian ware (scale ½)

91. Dr.37. C.G. Two sherds in the style of Cinnamus of Lezoux. Figure uncertain. His ovolo 4; Rogers B145. Antonine.

S92. Walters 79. C.G. Stamped [IVL.N]VMIDI by Iulius Numidus, probably of Lezoux. This stamp is always on mid to late Antonine forms, and it has recently been recorded from the Brougham cemtery where the contents are all later than A.D. 160. *c.* A.D. 160–200. (Note by B.R.H.)

93. Déch. 68. C.G. A black slip vase fragment, with red interior, see Grace Simpson, *Ant J* xxxvii (1957), 29–42; liii (1973), 42–51. Coarse rouletting above the decoration, and the little column is Rogers P2, see Stanfield and Simpson, pl. 96, 3; and S. N. Miller, *The Roman Fort at Balmuildy, on the Antonine Wall* (1922), pl. xxxii, 3. The acanthus, Rogers K11 or 12, and the bird O.2252, were both used by Attianus.

Nos. 94–98. *From the Area of Buildings XVI and XXVI*

94. Not illustrated. Dr.37. C.G. A damaged ovolo and beaded boder. Antonine. From the early level south of Building XVI.

95. Dr.37. C.G. The lower part of the very rare detail Rogers Q10, not very clear on this sherd. See also Stanfield and Simpson, pl. 70, 18, from Birdoswald, see the detail in the right-hand panel, where the foot of the lowest cup or cauldron should be turned up, as on this sherd. Dr. Rogers notes that the Birdoswald Dr.30 is like a bowl signed by Butrio in Roanne Museum. The ram's horn on the right is probably Rogers G368, and the trifid terminal on the left is not clear enough for attribution. Hadrianic to early Antonine. From the early level in the area south of Building XVI.

96. Dr.37. C.G. Close to the style of Sacer and Attianus, but the rosette, with probably eight tiny depressions, is not recorded on their work. But it was used by Caletus, see Rogers C103, also Stanfield and Simpson, pl. 128,4. *c.* A.D. 125–45. From a level prior to Building XVI.

97. Not illustrated. Dr.37. C.G. The ovolo Rogers B206. Antonine. Found with a fragment from a large Central Gaulish vine-scroll. From an early level below Building XXVI.

98. Vase fragment. C.G. With 'cut-glass' decoration, see No. 33 above. Antonine. Found with an East Gaulish Dr.38, late second- or early third-century. Below the floor level of Building XXVI.

Nos. 99–110. *Buildings XI and XII: the Guest-houses*

99. Not illustrated. Walters 81. C.G. Small size, see Oswald and Pryce, pl. lxi, 7. Antonine. From a pre-hostel level.

100. Probably Dr.29. S.G. Lion to right and a fragmentary basal wreath. Flavian. From a level earlier than Building XI.

101. Not illustrated. Dr.37. C.G. Very similar in fabric to No. 40 and probably from the same vessel. For the scheme of decoration cf. Stanfield and Simpson, pls. 46, 542; 49, 579 and 590. *c.* A.D. 110–30. From a pre-hostel level.

102. Dr.37. E.G. The style of Perpetuus, see Ricken and Fischer, Taf. 236, for the large circle O.147. Probably early third century. Level contemporary with Building XI.

103. Dr.37. E.G. Ricken and Fischer ovolo E33 in the style of Pervincus of Rheinzabern. Probably early third-century. Associated with the first hostel.

104. Dr.37. C.G. Free-style with large leaf-tips in the field, cf. Stanfield and Simpson, pl. 163, for the Cinnamus group. *c.* A.D. 140–80. Found in association with the first hostel.

105. Dr.30 C.G. Candelabrum, small size, Rogers Q42 used by Cinnamus, Stanfield and Simpson, pl. 158, 16. *c.* A.D. 140–80. Associated with the first hostel.

106. Not illustrated. Dr.29. S.G. Plain gadroons below the central moulding. Matt gloss. Flavian. From the road leading to the shrine.

107. Not illustrated. Dr.37 rim. C.G. Ovolo 5 of Cinnamus: Rogers B182. *c.* A.D. 140–80. Early level east of the shrine.

S108. Dr.33. C.G. Stamped CARVS[SA:] by Carussa of Lezoux, where there are several examples of this stamp. It also occurs at five sites which were re-occupied after A.D. 160, after long gaps in their occupation. *c.* A.D. 155–90. Below the floor of Building XII. (Note by B.R.H.)

109. Dr.30. S.G. Part of a saltire containing the large flower used by several potters, Knorr, 1919, textbild 10. *c.* A.D. 65–85. From a level earlier than Buildings XII and XIII.

110. Dr.29. S.G. A chevron wreath in the frieze. Coarse red fabric. Flavian. From a level below Building XII.

Nos. 111–114. *Building XIII*

111. Dr.30. E.G. A plain triple medallion containing a right leg, possibly from Ricken and Fischer, M111, a cupid. The dog is probably *ibid.*, T139. Late second to early third century. From a level contemporary with Building XIII.

112 and 113. Dr.37. C.G. The style of 'G. I. Vibius', now Geminus, Stanfield and Simpson, pls. 65 and 66. Hadrianic. From the lower filling of the cellar in Building XIII.

114. Dr.37. C.G. The style of Martialis of Lezoux, with the same caryatid as here, and the small trefoil Rogers G113, used by Martialis, at the border junctions, see Stanfield and Simpson, pl. 96, 2. The caryatid is D.655=O.1207. The large ram's horn is Rogers G345, used by Drusus II, *ibid.*, pl. 89,13, and the same caryatid was used by him, *ibid.*, pl. 88,4. *c.* A.D. 125–50. From the lower filling of the cellar in Building XIII.

Nos. 115–121. *Building IX*

115. Not illustrated. Dr.18/31. C.G. Probably early second-century. From a level prior to Building IX.

S116. Not illustrated. Form uncertain. C.G. Stamped MARCIM retrograde. The stamps of Marcus of Lezoux are frequently found in forts re-occupied about A.D. 160. *c.* A.D. 165–200. From a level earlier than Building IX. (Note by B.R.H.)

117. Dr.29. S.G. The large flower is also known on two bowls from Aislingen, which are reproduced in Knorr, 1952, Taf. 10, F and G. The cogwheel medallion is larger than *ibid.*, Taf. 10, G. *c.* A.D. 55–75. From a first-century level below Building IX.

S118. Form uncertain. C.G. Stamped PATERNI. The earlier potter of this name. This stamp appears at Xanten, where Central Gaulish ware later than A.D. 150 is very rare indeed. *c.* A.D. 130–60. From a level earlier than Building IX. (Note by B.R.H.)

119. Fragment of black slip ware, Lezoux, see No. 93 above. Hadrianic or Antonine. From a level earlier than Building IX.

S120. Dr.31. C.G. Stamped [RE]BVRRI.OFF. Reburrus of Lezoux was an early Antonine potter. From a level below Building IX. (Note by B.R.H.)

121. Dr.37. C.G. The ovolo Rogers B7, as defined by him in *Les Motifs non figurés*, 22, for Potter X-13, which is a part of the Donnaucus group of Stanfield and Simpson, and similar to the style of pl. 46(547). *c.* A.D. 100–20. From a level below Building IX.

Building X

S122. An illegible Central Gaulish name-stamp. Probably Antonine. From a level below Building X.

Nos. 123–130. *The Circular Shrine*

123. (i) Dr.29. S.G. Fragments of the same flower which is on No. 117 above, in a different medallion. *c.* A.D. 55–75. From the brown loam below the floor of the circular shrine.

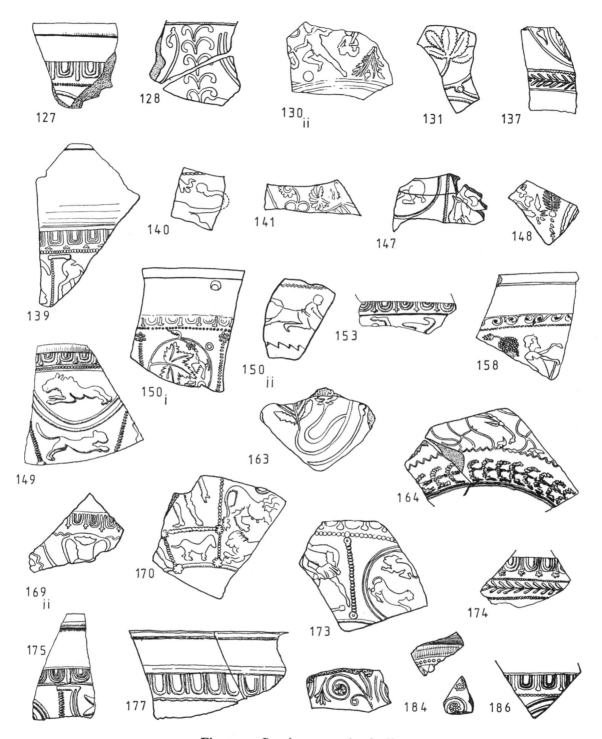

Fig. 71. Samian ware (scale ½)

(ii) Dr.29. S.G. Fragments from a frieze which shows the large floral ornament, Hermet, pl. 12, 57. *c.* A.D. 40–55. From the brown loam below the floor of the circular shrine.

124. Not illustrated. C.G. Fragmentary ovolo. Probably Hadrianic. From a level contemporary with the circular shrine.

S125. Dr.18/31 or 31. C.G. Stamped]TX.F. Probably Antonine. From a level contemporary with the circular shrine.

126. Dr.37. Three small sherds. Not attributable. Contemporary with the circular shrine.

Fig. 71

127. Dr.37. C.G. The ovolo 5 of the Cinnamus group, Rogers B182. Antonine. From a level associated with the circular shrine.

128. Dr.37. C.G. Potter X-6 style, with ram's horns in series Rogers G367, see Stanfield and Simpson, pl. 75, 19; also his plain-ended festoons, *ibid.*, pl. 74, 10. Very good quality gloss, but now too much damaged for identification of the ovolo. *c.* A.D. 125–50. From a level contemporary with the circular shrine.

129. Not illustrated. Dr.35. C.G. Antonine. From a level contemporary with the circular shrine.

130. (i) Not illustrated. Dr.37. C.G. Borders of diagonal beads. The fish below the border is probably O.2418. Antonine.

(ii) Dr.37. C.G. Potter X-6, see No. 128 above. A double ridge below the decoration, partly damaged. A triton D.20, smaller than O.25, and the warrior O.216. The large floral ornament on the right is Rogers H113, known on a mould made by Libertus I, see Rogers, 112. For its use by Potter X-6 see Stanfield and Simpson, pl. 74, 10, and for its later use by Cinnamus, see *ibid.*, pl. 159, 26. *c.* A.D. 125–50. From a level contemporary with the circular shrine.

Nos. 131–152. *The Octagonal Podium of the Circular Shrine*

With the exception of No. 151, all come from levels earlier than the podium.

131. Dr.37. C.G. Burnt. A large vine-scroll from Lezoux. *c.* A.D. 140–70.

S132. Walters 79. C.G. Stamped TITVRON[ISOF] by Tituro of Lezoux. Common in late Antonine contexts, and several burnt examples have been found in the Wroxeter Forum. *c.* A.D. 155–90. (Note by B.R.H.)

133. Dr.18/31 or 31. C.G. Stamped SACIRO.FI by a Sacero of Lezoux. The early stamps read SACIRV, and this later stamp almost certainly belongs to the potter who is represented at Corbridge and Newstead in the Antonine period. *c.* A.D. 140–70. (Note by B.R.H., and see No. 146 below.)

S134. Dr.31. C.G. MA[LLVRVI] by Malluro of Lezoux. *c.* A.D. 150–80. (Note by B.R.H.)

S135. Not illustrated. Dr.33. C.G. Stamped]VMA. Hadrianic–Antonine.

136. Not illustrated. Dr.38. C.G. Antonine.

137. Dr.37. S.G. With a chevron basal wreath. Flavian.

138. Not illustrated. Dr.37. C.G. The ovolo is close to the 'Donnaucus–Sacer style', see No. 17(i) above. *c.* A.D. 110–40.

139. Dr.37. C.G. The style of Docilis, his ovolo 2, Rogers B208, and his long astragalus. Gladiator to right, Stanfield and Simpson, pl. 92, 12. The bear on another sherd which is probably from the same vessel is not identifiable, but cf. *ibid.*, pl. 93, 20.

140. Dr.37. C.G. The lion D766 = O.1450 used by several Lezoux potters, see Stanfield and Simpson, 290, and pl. 82, 1, by Sacer. *c.* A.D. 125–45.

141. Dr.37. S.G. A scroll design. *c.* A.D. 80–100.

S142. Not illustrated. Ludowici form Tg. C.G. A platter, in five joining fragments, with a rounded foot like a Dr.37, see Oswald and Pryce, pls. lx, 1; lxviii, 7. Stamped SIICVNDINIM within a narrow ring of fine rouletting. In the foot-ring there are two grooved circles. Beautiful quality gloss, much damaged by the local soil conditions. These vessels are rare: one was found at Castell Collen in 1955 stamped DECMAN, and another, found at Lullingstone Villa, is stamped SABINMA. Mr. Hartley adds that the stamp on No. 142 matches an example from Lezoux in a late Antonine context, and that this potter also made Walters 79 and 80. *c.* A.D. 160–95.

143. Not illustrated. Dr.35. C.G. Probably from Les Martres de Veyre. Early second-century.

S144. Dr.27. S.G. With an illiterate stamp of the kind commonest in the Flavian period. (Note by B.R.H.)

145. Not illustrated. Dr.33. C.G. Stamped]M. Probably Antonine.

S146. Dr.33. C.G. Stamped SACIR[. . . This is probably by the same potter as No. 133 above, but it is the only known example from this die, and therefore the reading cannot be completed. Antonine. (Note by B.R.H.)

147. Dr.37. C.G. Hare to left, and Apollo in his chair to right. *c.* A.D. 130–80.

148. Dr.37. C.G. The style of Paternus II, see Stanfield and Simpson, pl. 104, 2 and 3. His leaf, *ibid.*, fig. 30, 8, Rogers J119, *c.* A.D. 150–90.

149. Dr.37. C.G. The style of Advocisus, *ibid.*, pls. 112–14, and his small ovolo *ibid.*, fig. 33, 2; Rogers B102. Antonine.

150. (i) Dr.37. C.G. Several sherds in the 'Donnaucus style', Rogers Potter X-13 and his vine spiral M10. This spiral appears on Stanfield and Simpson, pl. 49, 578. *c.* A.D. 110–40.

  (ii) Dr.37. C.G. A mounted Amazon, smaller than O.241, and different in various details. A wavy-line border above and a damaged basal wreath below. Trajanic or Hadrianic.

S151. Dr.33. Probably C.G. Stamped MIN[VLI.M] see Oswald, *Stamps*, 206. Dr. Oswald listed three examples, from Leicester, Great Chesterford and London. Mr. Hartley has only seen the Great Chesterford example, on a Dr.31, apparently from the same die as this broken stamp. Dr. Oswald did not attempt to date his examples; but Mr. Hartley suggests that Minulus was a Central Gaulish potter, working about the middle of the second century. From a level contemporary with the podium.

S152. A small fragment, reading, in very good lettering, SID[VS.FECIT]. The complete reading is obtained from Oswald, *Stamps*, 420, which records that both of the letters S are reversed. Dr. Oswald considered that Sidus was an East Gaulish potter, and Mr. Hartley suggests that he worked in Central Gaul, and I also thought that the fabric is Central Gaulish. No other examples have since been added to the two (from Caerwent and London) recorded by Oswald (Dr.31, cf. *BBCS* v (1930–1), 180, No. 96; and London Museum no. A.28490).

Nos. 153–158. *From Levels Associated with the Octagonal Shrine*

153. Dr.37. S.G. An ovolo with a three-pronged tongue. Flavian.

S154. Dr.31. E.G. Dull orange slip. Half of the platter is extant. Stamped SOLLOFIIC by Sollo of Rheinzabern, Oswald, *Stamps*, 305–6, where this stamp is recorded from Rheinzabern, Rome, Speier and Aquincum. Late second- to early third-century.

S155. Not illustrated. Dr.31R. E.G. Almost complete, large and late form, repaired by rivet-holes. Stamped MA[. . . Cf. Ludowici type Sb, Oswald and Pryce, pl. xlvii, 3. Rheinzabern. Probably early third-century. Loose rubble below squatter level.

S156. Dr.33. C.G. Stamped [C]AMPAN[IM]. Campanus worked at Lezoux, see Oswald, *Stamps*, 56, 365, where he noted a Walters 79 from the Pudding Pan Rock. *c.* A.D. 160–90.

157. Not illustrated. Dr.37. C.G. The tiny ovolo of the 'Ioenalis group', see Stanfield and Simpson, fig. 10, 1; Rogers B51, which has a rosette with a central dot on the tongue. Glossy red slip, and pale yellow body without mica. Trajanic.

158. Dr.37. C.G. Style of the 'Donnaucus group', Stanfield and Simpson, pl. 46, 545, which comes from Papcastle in Cumbria, and not from Carlisle as stated on that plate. Trajanic.

Nos. 159–189. *From Levels Surrounding the Shrine*

159. Not illustrated. S.G. A late Dr.15/17 variant. [Not seen by G.S.] From the pre-podium level north of the shrine.

160. Not illustrated. Two fragments of Dr.37. C.G. [Not seen by G.S.] Early level east of Building IX.

161. Not illustrated. Dr.18/31. C.G. [Not seen by G.S.] From an early level east of Building IX.

S162. Dr.33. C.G. Stamped ALBVCIANI, Oswald, *Stamps*, 11. Albucianus of Lezoux, a contemporary of Campanus, No. 156 above. He made Walters 79, also Dr.33 from the Pudding Pan Rock. *c.* A.D. 160–90. East of the shrine.

163. Dr.37. C.G. Two leaves in the style of Aventinus II, see Stanfield and Simpson, pl. 156, 10. *c.* A.D. 140–70. East of the shrine.

164. Dr.37. C.G. Style of Potter X-2, *ibid.*, 9, 109. *c.* A.D. 100–20. Early level east of the shrine. Probably the same bowl as No. 57.

165. Not illustrated. C.G. Various sherds from Dr.18/31, 31 and 33. Antonine. Early level east of the shrine.

S166. Dr.31. C.G. Stamped MACRIAM with a reversed C, read by Mr. Hartley as MVSICI.[M], by Musicus of Lezoux, the same stamp as was found at Alchester in a pit group of A.D. 150–60, and another in Gauting, Bavaria, a heavily burnt sherd, probably from the destruction of A.D. 162. *c.* A.D. 150–70. Found with Antonine sherds of Dr.31, 33, 36, 38 and Curle 23. East of the shrine. (Note by B.R.H.)

S167. Dr.31. C.G. Stamped [AL]BVCI. Not one of the early stamps of Albucius of Lezoux, because it is often found on Dr.31R and Walters 80. *c.* A.D. 155–70. East of the shrine. (Note by B.R.H.)

S168. Dr.31. C.G. Stamped [TI]BERI.M. Tiberius was an early to mid Antonine potter at Lezoux. This is likely to be one of his latest stamps, judging by the forms involved. *c.* A.D. 150–80. East of the shrine. (Note by B.R.H.)

169. (i) Not illustrated. Dr.37. C.G. Style of Butrio, with the mask D.715 = O.1223 which is on the Dr.30 from Jort by Butrio, Stanfield and Simpson, pl. 57, 651, on the tier of little cups, *ibid.*, fig. 13, 7; Rogers Q77. *c.* A.D. 120–45.

    (ii) Dr.37. C.G. Style of Igocatus (Potter X-4), *ibid.*, pl. 19, 239, with the same ovolo 2; Rogers B37, and the same two-handled cup, Rogers T9. *c.* A.D. 100–20. From an early level east of the shrine.

170. Dr.37. C.G. [Not seen by G.S.] The figure-types are uncertain. Close to the 'Donnaucus group' and the 'Donnaucus–Sacer group'. *c.* A.D. 110–40. From the brown loam north-east of the shrine.

171. Walters 79. C.G. See Oswald and Pryce, pl. 58, 2 and 5. These are both Pudding Pan types. *c.* A.D. 160–90. From a level below the roadway east of the shrine.

172. Dr.24/25. S.G. Rim only. Claudian–Neronian. From a level below the roadway just within the precinct gate.

173. Dr.37. C.G. Style of Cinnamus, and his ovolo 2; Rogers B231. *c.* A.D. 140–80. From the south-west corner of Building VII.

174. Dr.37. S.G. Ovolo of the potter of the large rosette of La Graufesenque. *c.* A.D. 70–85. Found with a Dr.31, C.G., late Antonine. From a level east of the shrine.

175. Dr.37. C.G. Style of Pugnus, his ovolo 4; Rogers B143, and the large flower in his special double festoon, exactly like Stanfield and Simpson, pl. 155, 26; Rogers C2. *c.* A.D. 140–80. A late level north of the shrine.

S176. Dr.31. C.G. Stamped]NI. A late fabric with a few large specks of mica in it. Found with a Dr.31R, stamped]NM, also late Antonine, and a large Dr.36. From a late level east of the shrine, in association with five sherds from a large imitation Dr.31 which has red colour-coating and an illegible name-stamp or cipher-stamp.

177. Dr.37. S.G. Montans ware, showing the ovolo used by several late potters, see Grace Simpson, *Brit* vii (1976), 244–73, for a study of late Montans decorated styles. *c.* A.D. 110–45. From an early level (6 ft. 9 in. deep) east of the shrine.

178. Not illustrated, which is unfortunate, as my rubbing of the small sherd shows part of the rare Central Gaulish figure-type D.573 = O.1159, the *biga* or two-horse chariot to left. There is nothing to help with attribution to a potter. Hadrianic or Antonine. An early level east of the precinct wall.

179. Not illustrated. Dr.37. C.G. From the same bowl as No. 164 above. East of the precinct wall.

180. Not illustrated. Six sherds including a piece of Rheinzabern ware. Late second- or early third-century. From east of the shrine.

181. Dr.18/31. C.G. Stamped [AL]BVCI. This seems to be the same as No. 167 above. From the area between the shrine and the hostel.

182. Not illustrated. Dr.45 with broken lion-spout. C.G. Much used, the grit has almost gone. Late second-century. From a level alongside the river.

183. Not illustrated. Dr.35/36 with a barbotine leaf on the rim. C.G. Antonine. From dumped material west of the shrine.

184. Dr.29. S.G. Fragments, in poor condition, of a winding scroll design. Flavian. From dumped material west of the shrine.

185. Not illustrated. C.G. A very thick basal fragment. Late Antonine. From the small ditch alongside the Wick Valley road.

186. Dr.37. C.G. Antonine. From a level alongside the river.

S187. Dr.31 base. C.G. Stamped SA[. . . Late Antonine, with four other sherds from Dr.31. From a level alongside the river.

188. Not illustrated. Dr.37. C.G. Two sherds in the style of Paternus II, with his six-petalled rosette Rogers C126, see Stanfield and Simpson, fig. 30, 3, on one sherd, and a male figure with a cloak on his left arm, and astragalus borders, on the other sherd. Unstratified.

S189. Not illustrated. [Not seen by G.S.] Dr.33. C.G. Stamped PRISCIN[I.M.], by Priscinus of Lezoux. This stamp was sometimes used on Dr.37 bowls. (Note by B.R.H.) Late Hadrianic to early Antonine. Unstratified.

The C. W. Priestley Collection in Devizes Museum

Fig. 72

1. Dr. 37. C.G. Fourteen fragments. Vine-scroll design. The ovolo is probably Rogers B144, but it is not clear. The leaf may be Rogers H11, used by Carantinus. Small plain circles in spaces. Antonine.

2. Dr.37. S.G. Scroll design with an irregularly impressed ovolo. Very poor quality. Probably *c.* A.D. 90–110.

S3. Dr.37. C.G. Part of the cursive signature of Drusus II, DR[. . . below the decoration. This sherd is more glossy than the other, but the fabric seems to be the same. Small six-beaded rosette on the border junctions. Cupid to right D.236 = O.401; dancer D.210 = O.368: both are on Stanfield and Simpson, pl. 88, 1; and the small warrior is D.614 = O.1059; small cupid D.255 = O.426. Uncertain figure to the right of D.236. The legs of O.1059 are wrongly restored in Stanfield and Simpson, pl. 89, 10. Hadrianic.

Fig. 72. Samian ware from Priestley collection (scale ½)

4. Not illustrated. Dr.37. C.G. Two sherds in the style of Potter X-3, Drusus I, of Les Martres de Veyre. Two small dolphins are repeated in place of an ovolo, see Stanfield and Simpson, fig. 4, detail 4, Oswald 2407A. Part of the sphinx to right, as on *ibid.*, pl. 16, 204, D.498 = O.855.

5. Dr.37. C.G. Les Martres de Veyre. Fan-shaped plant Rogers J17, cf. Stanfield and Simpson, pl. 37, 432, and for examples from Les Martres, see Terrisse, pl. xvii–xix. Trajanic.

6. Dr.29. S.G. Four fragments. At least two bowls are represented. The hooded straight gadroons illustrated here have been damaged during manufacture, like No. 6(i) above, found by Mr. Wedlake. Nero–Vespasian. *c.* A.D. 55–75.

7. Dr.37. C.G. Seventeen small sherds. Cinnamus group, ovolo 2 = Rogers B231. Leaping stag D.852 = O.1720 and resting stag D.847 = O.1704 are on Stanfield and Simpson, pl. 158, 21 and pl. 163, 66. Panthers O.1508 and D.797 = O.1520/1; pygmy O.696A; cornstook Rogers N15. *c.* A.D. 140–70.

8. Dr.37. C.G. Three sherds join. Criciro style. The large caryatid and the erotic group in a medallion are like Stanfield and Simpson, pl. 117, 7. Wavy border below the ovolo like *ibid.*, pl. 118, 17. Vertical borders are beaded. *c.* A.D. 140–60.

9. Dr.37. C.G. Wavy border below the ovolo. Lezoux. Hadrianic or Antonine.

10. Dr.37. C.G. Small ovolo Rogers B185 used by Criciro and Attianus, cf. No. 8.

11. Dr.37. C.G. Very fine borders. The cupid is probably D.265 = O.450. Trajanic.

12. Dr.37. S.G. The tongue of the ovolo is three-pronged to right. Flavian.

13. Dr.37. S.G. Glossy slip. Poor impression, probably from a worn mould. Bird looking backward within a small festoon. Flavian.

14. Not illustrated. Dr.30. S.G. Two small sherds. Flavian.

15. Imitation Dr.30. When R. E. M. Wheeler illustrated the lower part of the decoration on an imitation Dr.30 from Brecon (*YC* xxxvii (1926), 231 and fig. 102), he also illustrated six sherds in a similar style in the Stourhead Collection in Devizes Museum, and one piece from a mould (*ibid.*, fig. 103). Mrs. E. M. Cunnington described another instance of this remarkable pottery, imitating a Dr.37, found at Bear Farm, Heddington (*WAM* xlix (1940), 219–20). She had previously found a similar fragment at the Roman villa near Oliver's Camp, near Devizes.

Nos. 16–23 are not illustrated

16. Dr.38. Two sherds join. Much worn, and flange missing. Antonine.

17. Imitation Dr.38, with flange. Rim missing. Red colour wash.

18. Dr.46 rim. Thin-walled. Glossy. Probably Lezoux. Hadrianic.

S19. Potter's stamp reading AL.BI.N.I.M. with serifs, on a Dr.33 found on November 5th, 1939. Lezoux. Oswald, *Index*, p. 10.

S20–23. Four fragmentary potters' stamps: SA[on a Dr.18/31 base; VI . .? on a Dr.27 base; BITV[, Bitvrix of Lezoux, Oswald, p. 360, on a Dr.18/31 base, Antonine; and DAGO, as at Newstead (period I), dated by Bernard Hofmann, *Catalogue des estampilles sur vaisselle sigillée* (Touring Club de France), No. 22, 1972, from A.D. 80–130 at Les Martres de Veyre, see his pl. iii.

24. Coarse ware mortarium rim. Orange-brown fabric, slightly more orange in the centre of the micaceous body. Traces of a thin colour-wash of reddish brown. The stamp is bordered by deep rectangular depressions. Mrs. Katharine Hartley, F.S.A., kindly informs me that this is an unique stamp by an illiterate potter.

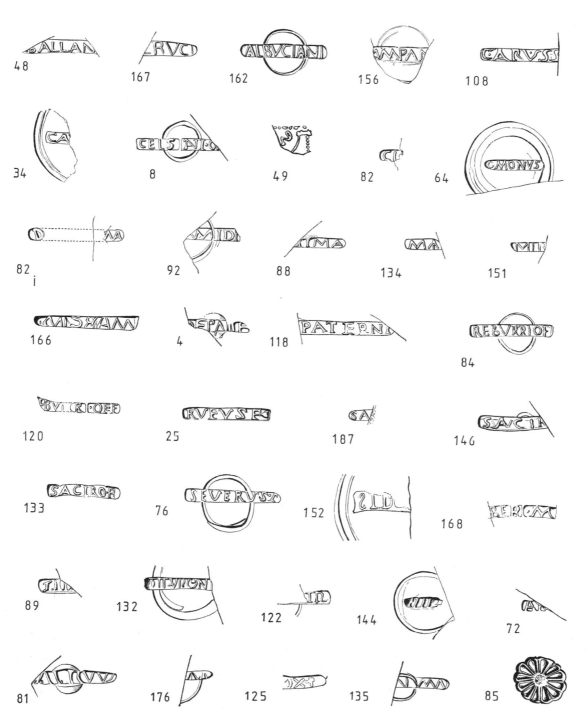

Fig. 73. Samian potters' stamps (scale ½)

The Potters' Stamps in Alphabetical Order

Fig. 73 (names marked with an asterisk are not illustrated).

[A]BALLAN[F]	S48	SACIR	S146
[AL]BVCI	S167	SACIRO.FI	S133
ALBVCIANI	S162	*SIICVNDINIM	S142
*BAL[	S86	SEVERVS.F	S76
[C]AMPAN[IM]	S156	SID[VS.FECIT]	S152
C.ARVSS[A]	S108	*SOLLOFIIC	S154
CAV[	S34	*[SVLP]ICI	S32
CELSIANI.OF	S8	[TI]BERI.M	S168
[CENSORI]NI	S49	TITI[	S89
CI[NTVSMIM]	S82(ii)	TITVRON[ISOF]	S132
DAMONVS	S64	Illegible	S122
D[.....]MA	S82(i)	Illiterate	S144
*[DRA]VCIM	S63	A[	S72
[IVL.N]VMIDI	S92	[..]A...VVS	S81
[IVS]TIMA	S88	[....]NI	S176
MA[LLVRVI]	S134	[....]TX.F	S125
*MARCIM	S116	[....]VMA	S135
MIN[VLI.M]	S151	Rosette	S85
MACRIAM	S166		
[O]FPASSE	S4		
PATERNI	S118	*Priestley Collection*	
*PRISCIN[IM]	S189	DR[	No. 3
REBVRRIOF	S84	*A.L.BI.N.I.M	No. 19
REBVRRI.OFF	S120	*SA[	No. 20
*[RO]PVS.FE	S59	*VI[	No. 21
RVFVSF	S25	*BITV[	No. 22
SA[	S187	*DAGO	No. 23

9. INSCRIPTIONS

by R. P. Wright, F.S.A.

The inscriptions from Nettleton Scrubb on stone, bronze, lead, and pottery were submitted to Mr. R. P. Wright for identification and publication in *JRS*.

1. Part of a limestone altar with plain sides and a rectangular focus, 18 by 23 by 11 in. (45.7 by 58.4 by 27.9 cm.); the base has been cut off. For the inscription, interpretation, and description see p. 135 and *JRS* lii (1962), 191.

2. The upper part of a whitish oolitic stone altar, 13 by 16 by 11 in. (33 by 40.6 by 27.9 cm.), with plain sides. The top of the capital has a six-sided focus and bolsters; its mouldings are preserved on either side but on the front are mostly worn away. On the die the text is weathered and nothing survives beyond the middle of line three. For the inscription and its interpretation see p.136 and *JRS* lix (1969), 235.

3. Bronze votive plaque. Inscribed:

D·A·POL
DECIMIVS

D(eo) Apol(lini)/Decimius

See also p. 144 (fig. 61), and *JRS* lii (1962), 191.

4. Lead roundel, $1\frac{5}{8}$ in. (3.8 cm.) diameter by $\frac{5}{32}$ in. (4 mm.) in thickness. Obv.: primary text incised nearly in the centre: V; secondary text: LII, with superscript bar squeezed in to precede the primary V. '5;52'. It is less satisfactory to interpret it as '57' in the wrong order. This was not a weight. Found in third- to fourth-century material in the shrine of Apollo. See also p. 235 and fig. 92(4) (*JRS* lvii (1967), 206).

5. Irregular roundel, max. diam. $1\frac{3}{8}$ in. (3.5 cm.), $\frac{3}{10}$ in. (8 mm.) thick cut from grey coarse pottery. Obv.: central hole; rev.: M above central hole. From a third- to fourth-century level (*JRS* lix (1969), 235).

6. Part of the base of a Samian bowl, form Drag 18/31, stamped . . . .] E. A graffito reads: PΛIIT[. . . . *Paet*[. . . . (*JRS* lix (1969), 243).

7. Pottery fragment from the wall of a grey vessel found in Building XVIII. A graffito reads: A BE[. . . . (fig. 110(435)) (*JRS* lix (1969), 244).

10. HUMAN REMAINS FROM CREMATION BURIALS

by E. W. Richardson, F.I.M.L.T.

(i) A cavetto-rim pot, with the usual band of lattice decoration, found in an upright position alongside the street that leads west from the Wick valley, contained human cremated bones. The pot was 10 in. (25.4 cm.) in height and the rim diameter was $7\frac{1}{2}$ in. (19.1 cm.) (fig. 105(66)). The accompanying yellow silty layer, beneath stones which had become displaced from the street wall, produced sherds of first- to second-century date.

The bones, in a very fragmentary condition, were washed, dried, and weighed. The total weight was 1450 g., representing about half the weight of a normal adult skeleton following cremation (normal range 2260–3170 g.). The appearance of the sutures in the skull fragments suggested that the person cremated was a young adult, but there was insufficient evidence for sex determination.

The right patella, which was well preserved, showed an interesting malformation. Approximately one-third of the lateral side was missing, though the damaged area showed evidence of regeneration of the articular surface with some cateophyte formation. Whether this was a congenital defect, the result of a pathological process, is not certain. I think it is more likely to be a healed injury.

(ii) This second cremation burial was found in a pot (fig. 105(26)) on the slope below the first-century A.D. enclosure, south-east of the revetment wall of the settlement. An extended inhumation was also found nearby. The pot was in an upright position in a small pit made in the hillside clay.

The weight of cremated bone was 576 g. All the fragments showed evidence of burning. No complete bones were present and no teeth were found among the fragments but sufficient of the left astragalus and skull fragments with well-defined sutures survived to indicate that the person was an adult. There was insufficient evidence for determining the sex, and no indication of the cause of death.

The pot, associated sherds and a coin of Vespasian (A.D. 69–79) found in association suggest a first- to second-century date for this cremated burial (see p. 93).

11. REPORT ON THE HUMAN AND ANIMAL BONES

by Hedley Hall, F.R.C.S.

1. Amongst the animals the sheep were the most numerous with a high percentage of immature bones, and a curiously high proportion of forelimb bones. Next in number were the oxen, with a low percentage of immature bones, presumably because they were used primarily as draught animals rather than for food production. Pig bones were few, one quarter being immature. The eight horse bones represent at least two animals.

The picture is that of a farmstead in which sheep and oxen were kept in comparatively large numbers, and pigs, horses and chickens in small numbers. There was no evidence of disease in any of the bones, human or animal, only signs of trauma or degenerative changes (see following table).

2. *Human Bones*

The six baby skeletons were all less than one year old. Two were found singly; the remaining four were found in two pairs. The skeletons were all incomplete, but more complete

Bone	Man	Horse	Ox	Sheep	Deer	Pig	Small mammals	Fish	Birds	Un-identified	Total
Cranium	8 8		7	4			3				30
Face	2		1	6		2					11
Mandible	2 4		22	17 2		3 3	1				54
Horn and antler			7	2	8						17
Teeth			15 2	15		3					35
Vertebrae	32 57		17	4		3	5 1				119
Scapula	9 5		11	6							31
Clavicle	3 1										4
Humerus	5 9		5	15 41		1 2	6				84
Radius	2 3	4	8 4	15 39			1 1				77
Ulna	2 2		4	3			1				12
Carpals and tarsals	3	3	19	7			2				34
Metacarpals, -tarsals	11 1		23 5	34 21	2	2 2					101
Pelvis	6		3	3							12
Femur	5 11	1	1 1	3			5				27
Tibia	2 8		8	13	1		3				35
Phalanges	9		17	13		6					45
Shell								4			4
Long bones									37	323	
Burnt bones	Large number of small fragments										
Species totals	239	8	180	263	11	27	29	4	37		
Species (%)	30	1	22	33	1	3	4	½	5		
Immature bones	48	0	6	39	0	25					

than those of the adults and the bones were better preserved. They were healthy in appearance and gave no indication of the cause of death. The six infant skeletons are perhaps indicative of a high infant mortality.

Note

Mr. Hall's remarks on the adult human bones are added to the separate grave descriptions on pp. 90–3. Where two numbers occur in one column in the table on p. 178 the first number represents the number of mature bones, the second the number of immature bones.

12. THE CUT HUMAN BONES FROM THE SHRINE

by E. W. Richardson (pl. XLIII) (see pp. 84–5)

The human bones were found scattered throughout the temple building, mixed indiscriminately with the debris of the fallen walls and roof. There was no evidence of burial. All the bones were in a fragmented state, none was found in articulation, and no complete long bones or skulls were found. Apart from this damage the bones were, organically, in a good state of preservation.

A count of the identifiable fragments showed that at least 14 individuals were represented, and a few sufficiently large fragments of pelvis survived to show that both sexes were present. An assessment of the age distribution of the group was attempted by examining the teeth in the ten fragments of lower jaw which were sufficiently intact for this purpose. In one the second molar had erupted, but showed no signs of wear, and there was no sign of the third molar, indicating early teens; in three the third molar had erupted, but showed no signs of wear, indicating late teens to early twenties; in six there was full dentition with varying degrees of wear, but in no case was this extensive, indicating early twenties to possibly early middle age. No dental caries were seen, and there was no evidence of loss of teeth before death. The bones were also examined for any pathological changes, e.g. evidence of rickets, suggesting a poor diet, osteo-arthritic changes, as seen in the elderly, and united fractures, with negative results.

Of the many fragments of skull, ten showed penetrating cuts consistent with having been struck during life by heavy blows with a sharp instrument. These fragments originated, certainly, from more than one skull. There were also seven atlas and axis vertebrae showing a cut surface consistent with decapitation by a single blow with a very sharp weapon (pl. XLIII). Cuts were also found on a few other bones including ribs, arm, and leg bones. No ornaments or other identifying objects were found, although a few bones showed bronze and iron staining: one fragment of first rib at about the position for a cloak or dress fastening, two lower ends of humerus just above the elbow where a bangle would be worn, a lumbar vertebra from about waist level, which suggests a belt fastening, and a finger bone showing staining from a ring.

It could be inferred from this evidence that the bodies were left lying where they fell. It was not until after the soft tissues had disappeared and the bronze had stained the bones that the skeletons were disturbed, dismembered and scattered among the building rubble where they were found (see p. 85).

Table of Human Remains Found in the Temple

	Central shrine area	Sector 1	Sector 2	Sector 3	Sector 4	Sector 5	Sector 6	Sector 7	Sector 8	Ambu-latory	From building debris	Total
Skull	1		1	1		1	1	1			4	10 fragments
Tibia	2	2	2	1	2	3	2	1			13	28
Femur		1	1		2	2				1	9	16
Patella		2			2	1					3	8
Vertebrae	13	3	4	1	3	7	6				22	59
Foot and toe bones		1	1		1	2					1	6
Finger bones	1	1	1		1	1	1					6
Clavicle	2				2		1				6	11
Mandible	1						1				4	6
Arm bones	3		2	1	3	2	2		1		4	18
Pelvis		1	1	1	1	1		1	1		3	10
Ribs	1	1	1	1	1	1		1			2	9

13. THE SKELETAL REMAINS OF A GOOSE

by A. Hollowell, M.A.

The skeleton of a bird was found in the corner of sector III on the 'squatter' level of the former octagonal temple which had been converted into a stable and from the remains of the upper bill and the size of the hinder part of the skull can be identified as a goose. One tarso-metatarsal bone is 90 mm. long. In live birds and carcases the so-called tarsal measurement is a good approximation to the length of the tarso-metatarsal bone.

The ranges of tarsal measurements given for the species of British wild geese in Witherby's *Handbook of British Birds* are all well below the value of 90 mm. except those for three species which are unlikely to be represented by the bones found at Nettleton, for the reasons given.

Snow goose (*Anser hyperboreus* Pall) is only a rare vagrant to this country (tarsal measurement 78–91 mm.).

Greater snow goose (*Anser hyperboreus atlanticus* Kennard) is also only a rare vagrant to this country (tarsal measurement 86–97 mm.).

Canada goose (*Branto canadensis* (L)) is an introduced species known in domestication since 1678 (tarsal measurement 82–99 mm.).

From the above information one can deduce that the Nettleton bird bones represent a relatively large goose.

The Bristol City Museum has a few limb bones (though not a tarsal-metatarsal bone) of one specimen of a modern domestic goose. These limb bones are the same size (to within 2–3 mm.) as the corresponding bones from the Nettleton skeleton. Therefore, as far as I can judge from the information available to me, I consider that the Nettleton bones most nearly resemble those of a modern domestic goose (see also p. 83).

14. NOTES ON TWO STONE AXE-HEADS

by Dr. Isobel F. Smith, F.S.A. (fig. 74) (see p. 7)

Two stone axe-heads were recovered from the settlement. One (No. 1452) was found associated with material of first- and second-century date in the small cemetery. The other (No. 1453) came from the filling of the first-century A.D. enclosure ditch.

The Implement Petrology Survey of the South-West reports as follows:

No. 1452
(a) Macroscopic: greenish rock, showing felspar and a ferromagnesian mineral. Greenstone.

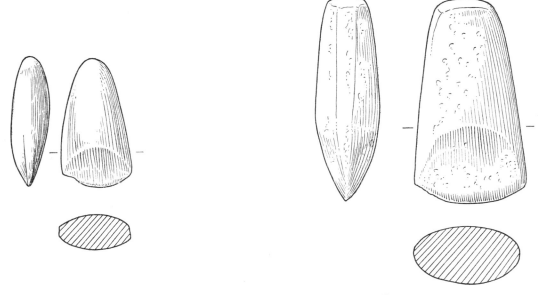

Fig. 74.   Neolithic stone axes (scale ½)

(b) Microscopic: a few medium sized plates of augite together with many smaller sub-angular pieces are imbedded in turbid felspar. There are grains of a very dissected ilmenite changing to bencosere and some short narrow streaks. Sometimes large grains of the rock appear to be separated from the bulk by an outline, but are not of different composition. This is specially noticeable towards the end of the section. A few quartz grains present. Greenstone.

No. 1453
(a) Macroscopic: dark green rock, showing felspar and ferromagnesian mineral. Greenstone.
(b) Microscopic: Group III. Marazion, Cornwall.

15. THE PAINTED PLASTER FROM THE OCTAGONAL SHRINE

by Eric W. Richardson (pls. XLI, XLII, figs. 75, 76)

The majority of the painted fragments were well preserved. Thickness varied from 0.4 to 2.35 in. (1–6 cm.) with up to four coats of plaster being used in the thicker fragments. The application followed the traditional method of applying a coarse mixture first, followed by a finer mixture, finishing with a final skimming coat. Crushed pottery, including Samian ware, was used as a filler for the coarse mixture. The finish varied from very smooth to quite rough, showing trowel and other tool marks. A few fragments showed evidence of redecoration, the original painted surface having been covered by further coats and then painted with a different decorative scheme.

Treatment

The plaster was washed with warm water and dried in an oven. After drying, the painted surface in many cases was found to be partially obscured by a thin layer of a calcareous deposit. Experiments were conducted to find a way of removing this deposit without affecting the underlying pigments. The method adopted consisted of carefully applying a 5% aqueous hydrochloric acid solution using a cotton wool swab or soft brush. This treatment almost instantly dissolved the deposit without damage to the painting. The plaster was well rinsed in water and dried in an oven.

Some means of protecting the plaster seemed desirable, and many small pieces were impregnated with a polyvinyl acetate solution in toluene under negative pressure. On drying, this method produced a rock-hard specimen, and the appearance of the painted surface was considerably enhanced. However, the main bulk of the plaster had to be treated with the PVA lacquer either by dipping or brushing in order to consolidate and protect the exposed surface. This produced a specimen of similar appearance to the first method, but rather friable.

Sorting

The plaster fragments were divided into four main groups:

1. Plain white and decorations on a white ground.
2. Plain buff and decorations on a buff ground.
3. Plain red.
4. All decorated plaster not covered by groups 1, 2, and 3.

Site Distribution of Groups

Group	Sector in temple								Building debris	Ambulatory	Central area
	1	*2*	*3*	*4*	*5*	*6*	*7*	*8*			
1					1	1		1	1	1	1
2		1	1	1		1		1	1	1	1
3				1		1		1		1	1
4			1			1		1	1		1

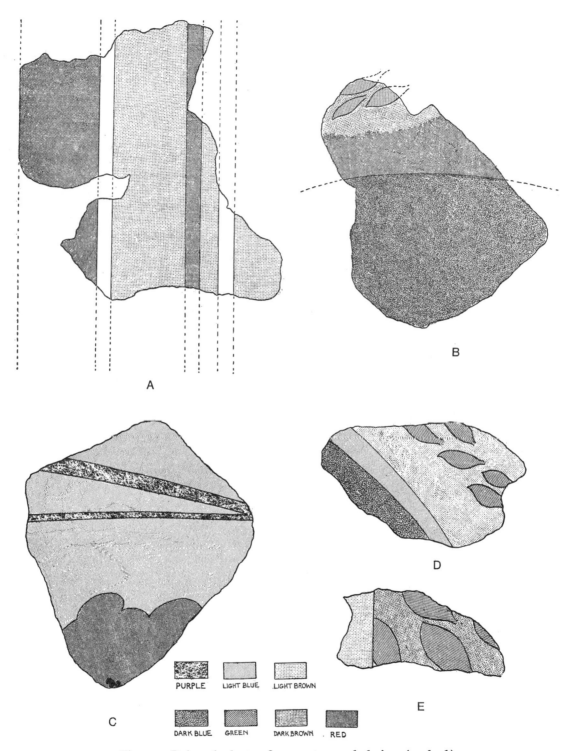

Fig. 75. Painted plaster from octagonal shrine (scale ¼)

Group 1

Appearance

The surface finish of this group varied. The thickness varied from 1.25 to 5 cm. and the thinner plaster tended to have the better finish. Most fragments possessed a flat surface, though some were concave, presumably from the vaulting, and a few had a slightly convex surface. Some pieces showed a grey-black superficial smoke stain, and a few had a brownish stain, possibly from contact with an iron object.

Decoration

The most common decoration in this group consisted of straight red bands from 0.8 to 6.2 cm. wide. These would appear to be borders from panels, since some showed corner angles of 30°, 65°, and 90°, and one fragment showed a part of a cross, or tee junction. One small piece showed a 0.6 cm. red band with a 1.2 cm. red circle, which was probably repeated along the band (fig. 76G). Two other instances of this detail were found, both on a white ground, one in dark brown with the ends between two bands of 0.6 cm. width (fig. 76M), the circle being repeated at 3 cm. intervals. A similar one in pale brown, with a 3.75 cm. interval, showed a red area separated from the brown band by 2 cm. (fig. 76H). Brownish-purple bands were present on a few fragments, in widths of 0.6–1.5 cm., among which were four pieces showing 90° corners. One was a simple turn, the other three had the corner extended in the form of a roundel up to 2 cm. in diameter with a radiating single line of smaller drops of diminishing size at 0.5 cm. intervals (fig. 76L). Some half a dozen small pieces of blue on white, showing portions of curvilinear bands, from 0.5 to 1 cm. in width, gave the impression of a ribbon-garlanded decoration (fig. 76K); one piece was concave. A few fragments showed straight, grey-black bands on a white ground, varying in width from 0.6 to 2.5 cm. A few fragments had indeterminate pale green markings on white, some associated with curvilinear red bands (fig. 76J) similar to the blue bands mentioned above. There were also several pieces of a complex interlacing trellis pattern of multi-coloured bands in shades of yellow, brown, green, red and purple (fig. 76F).

Site Distribution of Group 1 Plaster

Colour	1	2	3	4	5	6	7	8	Building debris	Ambulatory	Central area
Plain white						I			I	I	I
Red band on white					I	I		I	I	I	I
Purple band on white					I	I		I	I		
Blue band on white						I					
Trellis pattern					I	I				I	
Grey-black band on white									I	I	

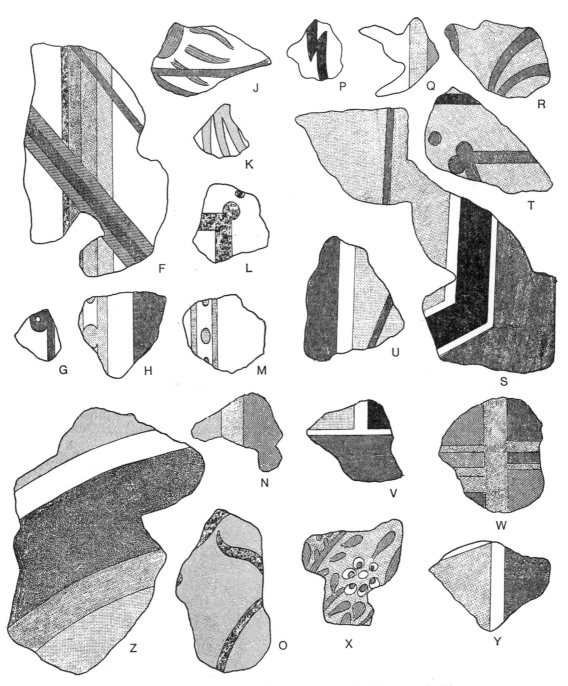

Fig. 76. Painted plaster from octagonal shrine (scale ¼)

Group 2

Appearance

The general remarks on the plaster in Group 1 also apply to this group.

Decoration

The evidence suggests a decoration of geometric panels, the buff ground varying from a light brown to a medium brown, bordered by coloured bands in white, red, and grey/black from 0.5 to 2 cm. wide, sometimes adjacent and sometimes separated from each other by a space of up to 6 cm. (fig. 76S). Several fragments of this brown plaster were overpainted by a random grey/black mottling, possibly to simulate marble.

Site Distribution of Group 2

	Sector in temple								Building debris	Ambulatory	Central area
1	*2*	*3*	*4*	*5*	*6*	*7*	*8*			
	I	I	I		I		I	I	I	I

Group 3

Appearance

The same remarks apply as for groups 1 and 2.

Decoration

About 50% of these fragments were painted a bright medium red, the shade varying slightly, and among this sub-group were found pieces from the architectural angles of the building. Some pieces displayed angles of 110°, 140°, and 160°, several pieces of each being present. The 110° angle could be a slightly rounded right angle, the 140° turn could have come from a sloped window embrasure, but the 160° turn is difficult to place. It is noteworthy that with the exception of one corner fragment in brown, all those found from the corners of the building were painted red, and it seems safe to assume that many of the architectural lines of the building were outlined in red. The remaining fragments were divided between a plain brownish red and a darker red overpainted with random black marks, possibly an attempt at marbling.

Site Distribution of Group 3

	Sector in temple								Building debris	Ambulatory	Central area
1	*2*	*3*	*4*	*5*	*6*	*7*	*8*			
			I		I		I		I	I

Group 4

Appearance

As for previous groups.

Decoration

The most interesting, and the most frustrating group. There were many small fragments from panel designs showing bands in all the major colours with black and white on grounds of purple, pink green and blue, while marbled and mottled effects were represented on similar ground colours.

Several fragments showed sprays of leaves on a grey-brown background (pl. XLI*a*) similar to a fragment in the Museum of London, from the Roman basilica site under Leadenhall Market. Two fragments showed a simple flower shape of 3 cm. diameter with petals in red and white and leaves (fig. 76X). One large fragment, 20 × 17 cm., had a leaf pattern at one edge merging into a red band 3–4 cm. wide and possibly slightly curved, the remainder being painted blue (fig. 75B). This fragment is concave along its greater axis suggesting vaulting. Two other fragments, concave along one axis, have a similar blue background with flowing purple bands up to 1 cm. wide, possibly denoting a ribbon or garland decoration for panels with a blue background in some parts of the temple (figs. 75C, 76O).

A few fragments had concentric, curved, multicoloured bands up to 10 cm. wide. The dominant colour was blue, in two shades, with two shades of brown, red, white and black. The fragments were too small for precise measurement of the diameter but calculation gave a result of approximately 2.5 m. Assuming the curve followed an architectural feature there would appear to be three possibilities: (i) the interior aspect of the exterior wall of a sector, on the curve following the vaulting line; (ii) on the central area walls above the arched openings into the chambers; (iii) above the lunette windows in the vaulting of the central area (fig. 76Z). Several small fragments with swirling brush strokes, in shades of brown, green, red, blue and white, might be from elaborate marbling effects or, perhaps, from something more ambitious.

From several fragments of a male figure dressed in purple it has been possible to reconstruct most of the face, which measures 10 × 8 cm. (pl. XLI*b*). The features, in a three-quarter view, are swarthy, represented in a very free, almost impressionistic style, with the head inclined slightly to the left. The hair is a dark reddish purple, and purple has been used in the shading of the face. The background was a plain yellow-brown. The right hand for this figure appeared on a separate plaster fragment and measured 8 × 3 cm., showing a dorsal view (pl. XLI*c*); the fingers are lossely extended and slightly crooked, the thumb is not shown, and the background is plain yellow-brown. It has not been possible to form an opinion as to the mode of dress on the figure, other than the colour, which seems to have been purple. The figure was painted on concave-faced plaster, and it most likely came from the vaulting of the central shrine or one of the sectors. Since it was approximately half life size it would have been rather lost in the high vaulting of the central area, and perhaps one of the sectors would be more appropriate. Since this was the only human figure found portrayed among the many plaster fragments recovered, it is very tempting to assume that it is a portrayal of the god Apollo to whom the temple was probably dedicated. The purple clothing certainly suggests that it was someone of considerable importance. The most likely position for this painting would be in a position facing the visitor in the entrance vestibule.

Site Distribution of Group 4

								Building debris	Ambulatory	Central area
		Sector in temple								
1	*2*	*3*	*4*	*5*	*6*	*7*	*8*			
	1	1		1		1		1	1	1

16. CATALOGUE OF ARCHITECTURAL FEATURES (figs. 77–81)

The architectural features found during the course of the excavation have as far as possible been arranged to indicate the building in which each feature was probably incorporated. But items found in Buildings VII, IX, X and XVIII may quite likely have been re-used features taken from the nearby octagonal shrine or the precinct gateway.

The Circular Shrine (Building V) Nos. 26, 47, 47A, 75.
The Octagonal Shrine (Building VI) Nos. 1–8, 16–27, 32, 36–9, 43, 45–7, 47A, 49, 52, 55–7, 60–1, 68–70, 78, 83–6.
The Rectangular Hall (Building VII) Nos. 28–31, 41, 48, 53, 58, 62–3, 76, 77, 79.
The Priest's or Custodian's House (Building IX) Nos. 9–14, 33–5, 42, 44, 50–1, 59, 64–6, 73.
The Precinct Shop (Building X) Nos. 40, 54, 67.
The House of the Strong-Room (Building XIII) No. 15.
The West Lodge (Building XVI) No. 71.
The later West Lodge (Building XVIII) No. 72.
Building XXVII. No. 81.

Columns

1 (fig. 78). Column from the ambulatory surrounding the octagonal shrine. Two of these columns were placed on the wall-bench, between the angle pilasters of the podium octagonal wall, to support the lean-to roof of the ambulatory. The columns have a double torus base with moulding, and a Tuscan type of capital. Height 117.5 cm., diameter of shaft 26–28 cm. Found with Nos. 2 and 37, lying at the foot of the podium wall of the octagonal shrine (see p. 43 and pl. XXIV*a*). Mr. Blagg cites the Bognor and Westcotes villas for close parallel, and Cunliffe, 1969, pl. LXXIV, nos. 7–10 (Bath).

2 (fig. 78). As No. 1. Height 121 cm., diameter of shaft 29–31.5 cm.

3 (fig. 77). As Nos. 1 and 2. Column capital. The broken column shaft has been roughly hollowed to form a cup-like receptacle and in reversed order was used in this way. A bronze coin of Valentinian (A.D. 364–78) was found lying in the cup-like hollow. Found in the north part of the central area of the octagonal shrine, in association with Nos. 4, 5 and 6. The mouldings are less steep than those of 1 and 2. Height 62 cm., diameter of shaft (which is broken) 30 cm. (pl. XXIV*a*).

4 (fig. 77). Column base, lathe-turned with double torus moulding. The plinth is 44.5 × 46 cm.,

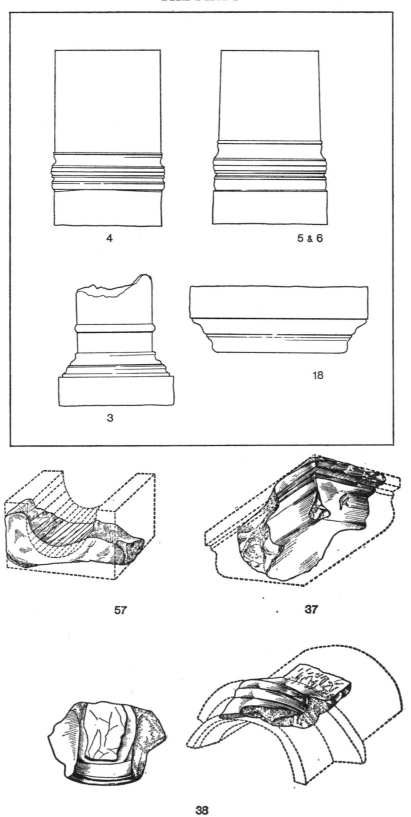

4   5 & 6

3   18

57   37

38

Fig. 77. Architectural features (scale ⅛)

height 73.5 cm., diameter of shaft 40–42 cm. This column with Nos. 5 and 6 probably formed part of the east inner entrance, from the vestibule, into the octagonal shrine. The corresponding column is missing, but the base for one of these columns was found *in situ*. Nos. 5 and 6 probably flanked the outer entrance into the vestibule. Found with Nos. 3, 5 and 6.

5 (fig. 77). Column base, lathe-turned of the same overall height as No. 4, but the mouldings are taller though their profile is of the same type. Diameter of shaft 40.5–41 cm. It has two rectangular grooves cut through the upper torus on opposite sides (see No. 6). Found with Nos. 3, 4 and 6.

6 (fig. 77). As No. 5. The mouldings appear to be identically carved to those of No. 5. Height 74.5 cm., diameter of shaft 40.7–42 cm. It also, like No. 5, has two rectangular cavities cut in the shaft just above the torus, measuring 4.5 cm. high and 23–25 cm. wide and 6.5 cm. deep respectively. Similar secondary slotting is shown on a column from Bath (Cunliffe, 1969, pl. XXX*a*). It is likely that Nos. 5 and 6 formerly stood on either side of the outer (east) side of the eastern vestibule into the octagonal shrine. The secondary slots were evidently made to receive, or secure, a rail which formed part of a balustrade around the ambulatory of the shrine. Found with Nos. 3, 4 and 5.

7 (fig. 81). Base of a rectangular pillar with chamfered base mould, possibly an altar or hypocaust pillar. From the north-west sector of the octagonal shrine (see pl. XXXVI*a*).

8 Part of a column capital of the same type as Nos. 1 and 2. Height 24 cm. (broken), diameter of upper moulding *c*. 40 cm. Found in the north-east corner of the temple in the late squatter level.

9 Column found in Building IX, with mouldings differently proportioned to those of Nos. 1 and 2. Height 89.5 cm., diameter of shaft 19.8–22.5 cm.

10 (fig. 78). Part of a column shaft with astragalus moulding. Height 20 cm., diameter 24 cm. From Building IX.

11 (fig. 78). Column base similar to No. 9. Height 24 cm., diameter of shaft 19.5 cm. Found near Building IX.

12 Middle part of a column shaft, same type as No. 9. Found in Building IX. This was stolen from the site.

13 Fragment of a small column, same as Nos. 9 and 12. Found in Building XII.

14 Part of a column shaft, same type as Nos. 9, 12 and 13. Found in Building IX.

15 (fig. 78). Stone column of small dwarf type, probably from a portico or colonnade. Found in the cellar filling in Building XIII (see Cunliffe, 1969, pl. LXXVIII, 7.40, p. 205).

16 Small piece of a column base. From the octagonal shrine (Building VI).

17 Column base with two torus mouldings. From the octagonal shrine (Building VI).

18 (fig. 77). Large capital of Tuscan type, with abacus, 62.2 cm. diameter, to cap a column 51 cm. in diameter. It is in good order and has been turned on the lathe. Height 27 cm., diameter of upper moulding 71 cm. The shaft is broken. Found blocking the late doorway into the central octagonal shrine (Building VI) on its north side (pl. XX*b*) (Cunliffe, 1969, pl. XLIX, 1.80, pp. 192–3, for similar moulding).

19 (figs. 78 and 79). Capital with flattened cavetto moulding for a column, *c*. 45 cm. in diameter, height 27 cm. The capital is fashioned with two projections to fit against two walls at right angles to each other. The projections are each 61 cm. wide. This was probably the capital from the eastern inner entrance of the vestibule, leading into the shrine. If so, the two projections would join the inner ambulatory wall which crossed the ambulatory to form the side wall of the eastern vestibule. Mr. Blagg suggests that the corner of the abacus has been cut out later and the projections could thus be secondary work. This capital is much more crudely made than other features attributed to the eastern entrance of the octagonal temple and it could well have been re-used and adapted for the octagonal temple entrance. It was probably made to form part of the portal of the circular

Fig. 78. Architectural features (scale ½)

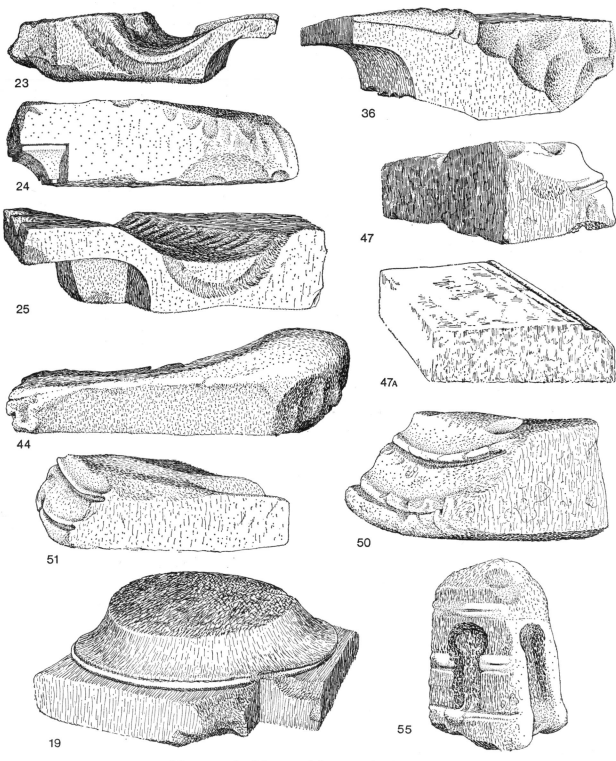

Fig. 79. Architectural features (scale ⅛)

temple on the same site. It was found just outside the eastern entrance of the octagonal temple (pl. XX*a*). Cf. Cunliffe, 1969, pl. LXXIV, 7.6, p. 204, bracket similar moulding and pl. LIX, 2.15, p. 196.

Cornices

20 (fig. 80). Large cornice with a cavetto moulding (Nos. 22, 23, 25, 32 and 36 are similar). This elaborate cornice, height 18 cm., width *c.* 60 cm., depth 69 cm., evidently came from a monumental type of octagonal building. A number of pieces of the same cornice were found, all from the immediate area of the shrine and mostly lying at the foot of the podium wall. The pilaster angle piece (No. 25) was found lying at the foot of the north-west angle of the podium. The overhanging flange of the cornice, on its upper face, was fashioned to accommodate a shallow rain-water gutter, 35.5 cm. wide. The cornice also provided an effective coping, at floor level, to the podium wall. On the east and west sides of the shrine the cornice merged into the hillside. The bench wall above the cornice was built on the inner lip of the rain-water channel. Each cornice joint was sealed to prevent water leakage by lead sheeting which was laid in a shallow recess on each block, and this covered the joint. Each block also had a small semi-circular hollow on the face of each stone joint to ensure a well-wedded joint. The water-gutter (fig. 79, Nos. 23–5) conformed to the angle pilasters of the podium. The gutter was no doubt the principal means of conveying the rain water from the shrine. No. 20 was found on the ambulatory floor on the west side of the shrine (see pl. XIV*a-c*).

21 (fig. 80). Pilaster with *cyma recta* moulding, probably used to form the wall-plate which capped the central octagonal wall above the central shrine at roof level. Height 28 cm., width 51 cm., depth 5.8 cm. From the north outer face of the podium.

22 (fig. 80). As No. 20. From the west side of the shrine. Height 19 cm., width 29 cm., depth 34 cm.

23 (fig. 79). Cornice with cavetto moulding, with lead jointing recess as in Nos. 20 and 25. Height 16 cm., width 69 cm., depth 43 cm. Found in the cobbled floor of Building VII.

24 (fig. 79). Cornice with a short return on the right hand side. It has a cavetto moulding, but one of shallower profile than that of No. 20 and its companions. It is likely that this lighter type cornice was used on the internal terminals of the eight radial walls in the octagon of the shrine and also possibly in the large window in the west angle of the octagonal wall. Height 19 cm., width 52 cm., depth 69 cm. Found near the south-west entrance into the octagonal shrine (pl. XXX*b*).

25 (fig. 79). Cornice of cavetto type, the same moulding as Nos. 20, 22, 23, 32 and 36. This is an important angle piece which was clearly used at the junction of the angle-pilasters on the podium wall. It indicates the correct projection of the angle pilaster and it is clear that the water-gutter on the upper surface conformed to the shape of the angle-pilaster. Height 20 cm., width 57 cm. (front), 39 cm. (rear), depth 72 cm. Found lying at the foot of the podium wall, from which it had no doubt, fallen (pl. XIV*b*, *c*).

26 Carved stone, probably from the circular temple, re-used later as an engaged column base with a double torus moulding in the octagonal temple. Found near the north-west entrance in the ambulatory. Height 32 cm., diameter of upper torus *c.* 34 cm., lower torus 35.5 cm.

27 (fig. 81). Cornice corner piece. Height 10.5 cm., width 31 cm., depth 21 cm. Found on the outside of the octagonal temple west wall in the building debris.

28 (fig. 81). Moulding with dentils. Four pieces. Height 5.8–6.4 cm., width 14–23.5 cm., depth 11–18 cm. From the south-east corner of the rectangular building (pl. IV*b*).

29 (pl. IV*b*). Moulding with dentils of similar type to No. 28. Two pieces, height 5.9 and 6.3 cm., width 14 and 25 cm., depth 16 and 19 cm. respectively. Found on the south-east corner of the rectangular Building VII.

30   (pl IV*c*). Fragment of cornice with cavetto profiled modillion. Height 10.5 cm. (bottom broken), width 18 cm., depth 24 cm. From the north wall of the rectangular building.

31   (fig. 81). Cornice with cavetto moulding. Found in the rectangular Building VII alongside the river wall.

32   Cornice, damaged, similar to Nos. 20, 23, 25 and 36. Found lying in the black layer outside the north-west corner of the rectangular building.

33   (fig. 81). Cornice piece with the same decorative features as No. 35. Found in the make-up of the late floor in Building IX. Height 8.5 cm., width 30 cm., depth 30 cm.

34   Cornice with *cyma recta* moulding on two adjacent sides. Height 9 cm., width 48 cm., depth 26 cm. Found in Building IX.

35   (fig. 81). Cornice with square modillion which has a V-shaped incision in the top, presumably a rain-water drip. Height 8.5 cm., width 51 cm., depth 25 cm. Found in the make-up of the late floor in Building IX (see pl. XVIII*c*).

36   (fig. 79). Cornice-mould of cavetto type similar to Nos. 20, 22, 23, 25 and 32. Height 18 cm., width 58 cm., depth 64 cm. Re-used to form part of the late floor in Building IX.

37   (fig. 77). Corner moulding. Found at the foot of the podium wall of the temple with columns Nos. 1 and 2. Height 22 cm., width 54 cm., depth 59 cm.

38   (fig. 77). Column casing with a moulding consisting of a torus, bordered by fillets and with pink mortar on its inner surface. Height 19 cm., width 23 cm. From the octagonal shrine.

39   (fig. 81). Part of a column shaft with a base moulding. Probably from the shrine, but re-used as a drain cover in Building IX.

40   (fig. 80). Column capital, broken through the mouldings, and with the top hollowed out. Height 10.5 cm., diameter of upper moulding 24 cm. Found near Building X.

41   (fig. 78). Probably part of an engaged column, and possibly from the circular temple re-used as a capital with abacus and necking. Height 45 cm., shaft diameter 27 cm. Mr. Blagg suggests that the cutting on the back is very similar to that on the column base No. 26. The dimensions are also comparable. He suspects that they are both parts of an engaged column perhaps fitting into or projecting from (depending on whether inside or outside) a corner. It could quite well be a feature of Building VII, where it was found.

42   (fig. 80). Fragment of the upper torus of a column base. Height 12 cm., diameter of torus *c.* 45 cm. Re-used as a drain cover stone in Building IX.

String Moulds

43   String mould. From the octagonal shrine.

44   (fig. 79). String mould. Re-used as a door threshold in Building IX.

45   String mould. From Building VI.

Voussoirs

46   A number of voussoirs from the arches which spanned the terminals of the eight radial walls to form the central octagon of the octagonal shrine. The arches were of lighter construction than those used in the circular shrine. Three were found cemented together and from these it was possible to re-construct an arch which was 6 ft. (1.83 m.) in diameter (pl. XXVIII*b*). Found in and around the central area of the octagonal shrine.

47   (fig. 79). Voussoir fashioned from a disused column cap. Re-used from the circular shrine. Found in Building VI.

47A   (fig. 79). Voussoir made from a moulding from the circular shrine. Found and re-used in the octagonal shrine.

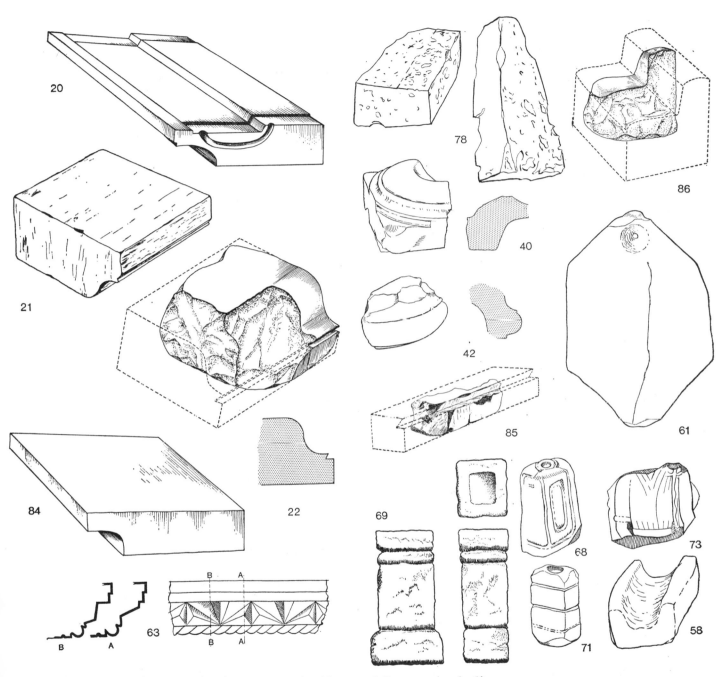

Fig. 80. Architectural features (scale ⅛)

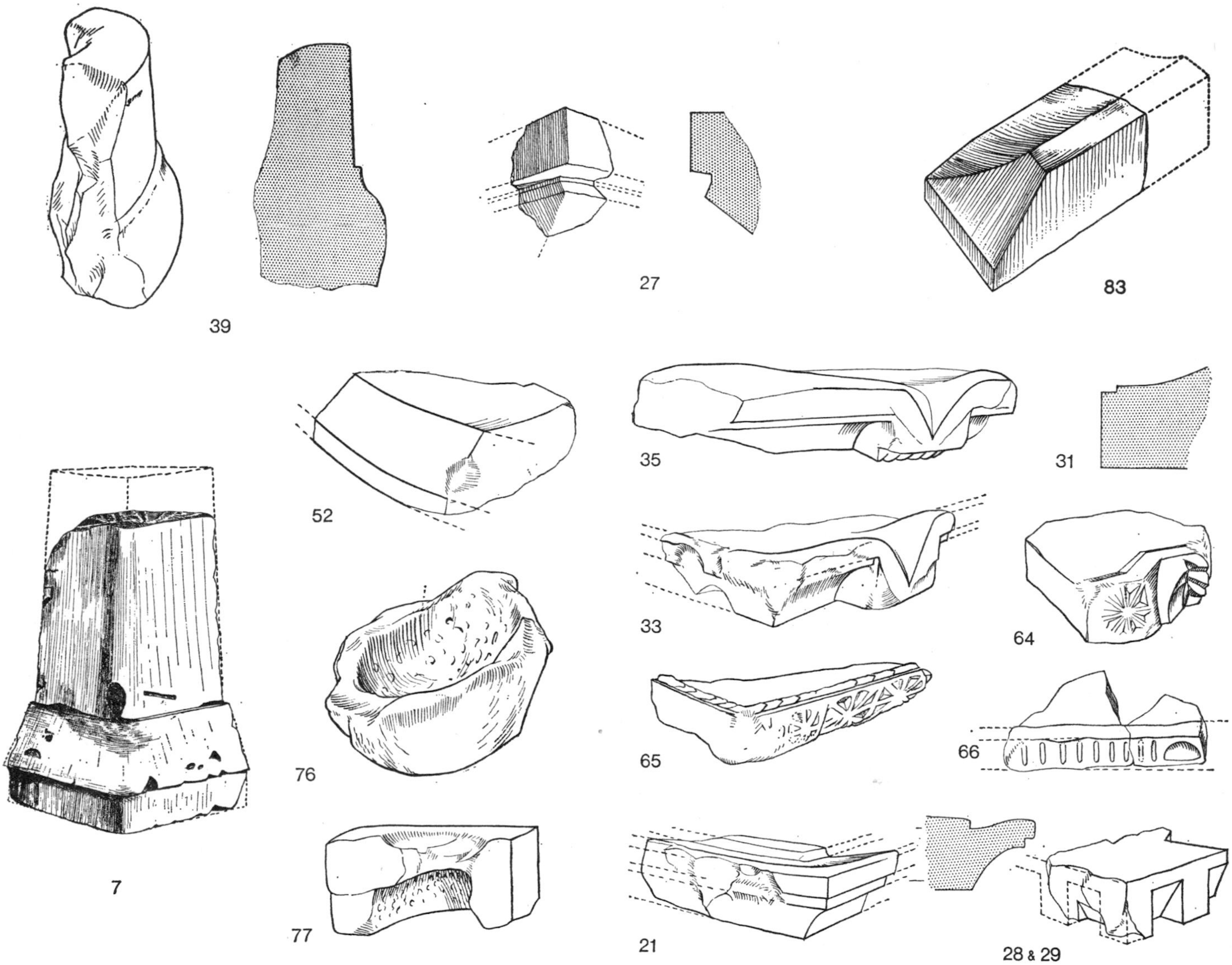

Fig. 81.   Architectural features (scale ⅛)

48 Voussoirs from the north wall of the rectangular Building VII. The arches in this building had voussoirs of a much heavier and sturdier type than those used in the octagonal shrine.

Hood Moulds

49 Hood mould from the octagonal shrine.
50 (fig. 79). Hood mould from an arch of the same type as No. 51. It was re-used to form part of the stone platform in the south-east part of Building IX (see pl. XVIII*b*).
51 (fig. 79). Hood mould from an arch which possibly spanned the eastern entrance to the octagonal shrine or the precinct gateway. Found in the stone platform in the south-east part of Building IX (see pl. XVIII*a*).

Archivolt

52 (fig. 81). Archivolt, the bevelled part of outer part of the arch. Found in the ambulatory of the octagonal temple on its west side.

Finials

53 (fig. 78). Roof finial of 'tower type' in the form of a miniature temple. Found on the cobbled floor at the west end of the rectangular temple. Height 54 cm. Cf. Blagg, 1977, Lowther, 1976, 40, and Cunliffe, 1969, pl. LXXIX, 8.1–13, p. 205.
54 (fig. 78). Roof finial. Height 48 cm. Incomplete but of unusual design. Found in the stony layer west of Building X. There are traces of red colour on the pine-cone terminal. A roof-finial found in the Roman villa at Rockbourne, Fordingbridge, Hants, is similar to this finial in that the upper part of the finial has a pine-cone termination, supported by four smaller fir-cones below (Hewitt, 1971, pl. VIIB and C). For pine-cone see *Brit* iv (1973), pl. XXXIIIA (Dewlish).
55 (fig. 79). Stone finial. Height 30 cm. (top broken). Badly damaged, but the same style as the Wellow Roman villa example (Skinner). From Building VII, east side.

Stone Guttering or Coping Stones

56 Stone guttering. From the octagonal shrine.
57 (fig. 77). Stone channel. Similar to Nos. 56 and 58. Re-buried on site. From the building rubble within the central area of the octagonal shrine.
58 (fig. 80). Stone guttering or coping. Found north of the north wall of Building VII.
59 Stone guttering. Found in Building IX.
60 Piece of coping, probably used on the roof of the side chambers of the octagonal temple. Found alongside its wall.

Stone Tiles

61 (fig. 80). Pennant stone tiles as used on the roof of the octagonal temple where they were found, in some quantity, lying alongside the west wall of the ambulatory, from which they had fallen. They were also found associated with other contemporary buildings in the settlement, especially Building XIII. The red brick Roman tiles were only found in the first- and second-century levels at Nettleton and were scarce.

Bench-tables

62 (fig. 78). Fragment of a bench-table with chamfered chevroned and rope design. Found outside the south-east corner of the rectangular Building VII.
63 (fig. 80). Bench-table with chevron and rope design. Found lying on the cobbled floor west of the partition wall in the rectangular Building VII (see pl. XXVa). Similar to stone with chevron decoration found at the Rockbourne villa, Fordingbridge, Hants (Hewitt, 1971, pl. IVC).
64 (fig. 81). Bow-fronted bench-table with bevelled edge and star and chevron design. For the bow-front, cf. that from Caerwent (*Arch.* lii (1911), 436, fig. 16). Found in the make-up of the late floor in Building IX (pl. XXVIa).
65 (fig. 81). Bench-table fragment similar to No. 64. From the late floor in Building IX (pl. XXVI b, c).
66 (fig. 81). Bench-table with milled decoration along its front edge. Found as 65 (pl. XXVc).
66A (fig. 78). Bench-table with a series of incised crosses on the chamfer and two on the corner. Found in Building XVIII.
66B (pl. XXVb). Fragment of a bench-table with relief circle, cross, rope and chevron decoration. Found by W. C. Priestley on the north side of the river.

Door Jamb

67   Door jamb. Medieval. Found in the additions made in the medieval period in Building XIII. Contemporary with the latest cobbled floor.

68   (fig. 80). Small stone altar with billet decoration and small circular focus. Found lying in the squatter level in the east sector of the octagonal shrine (pl. XXXVI*c*).

69   (fig. 80). Stone altar, uninscribed. From the east side of the octagonal shrine in the squatter level. (pl. XXXV*a*, *b*).

70   (pl. XXXIV). Stone altar with dedication inscription to the god Apollo. Found lying, face downward, in the squatter level in the north-east sector of the octagonal shrine (for full description see p. 135).

71   (fig. 80). Small stone altar, uninscribed. Found in the building rubble of Building XVI (p. 34).

72   (pl. XXXV*c*). Stone altar with dedicatory inscription to the god Silvanus. This mutilated altar was re-used as part of a furnace in Building XVIII (for detailed description see p. 136).

Statuary

73   (fig. 80). Upper part of a stone statuette with its head missing. Found in the stony layer within Building IX (pl. II*a*) (for detailed description see p. 137).

74   (pl. II*b*). Small stone statuette. Found in Building XXVI (for detailed description see p. 138).

Note: for the statuary found by Mr. Priestley see pl. I, and pp. 136–7.

Miscellaneous Stone Features

75   Slab of local limestone with a polished upper surface. The lower part of the stone is quite rough. Found inserted in a central position in the cobbled floor of the circular temple (see pl. VII*b* and p. 10).

76   (fig. 81). Small stone basin made from the local limestone. Found in the burnt level below the second cobbled floor within Building VII.

77   (fig. 81). Apsidal shaped stone head of a small *aedicula* for a small shrine. From the late floor level in Building VII.

78   (fig. 80). Tufa blocks (Combe stone) sawn to shape for used in the vaulting of the octagonal shrine (pl. XXXII*c*; see also p. 48). A quantity of shaped tufa blocks were found, some still mortared together, in the central area of the octagonal shrine. Tufa occurs in the Cotswold and Mendip Hills.

79   (fig. 78). Plan and section of the doorstep in the partition wall in Building VII.

80   (fig. 78). Cornice recovered from the field boundary wall near the octagonal temple. This could possibly be medieval.

81   (fig. 78). Stone recovered from the apse-like wall at the east end of Building XXVII. Purpose unknown, but possibly part of a stone mould.

82   (fig. 78). Suggested reconstruction of the entablature on the south-east corner of Building VII. The following features are included: Nos. 28 and 29 (dentils) and 31 (cornice) found in the south-east corner of Building VII; the attractive features Nos. 33 and 35 (cornice with square modillion to form a V-shaped rainwater spout), although re-used as a stone platform in the adjoining Building IX, clearly did not belong to that building and they therefore most probably formed part of its neighbour, Building VII, and they are incorporated. But it is possible that No. 30 (cornice) which was also found in Building VII, may have replaced No. 31. It is also possible, as Mr. Blagg suggests, that either No. 30 or 31 may have been placed above Nos. 28 and 29 rather than below. It is merely a tentative reconstruction to provoke discussion.

83   (fig. 81). Large cavetto moulding, possibly part of the pedestal base for an altar or statue. Found in the squatter debris below the west window within the former octagonal shrine.

84 (fig. 80). Large cornice, plain; recovered from the central area of the octagonal shrine, but in the level contemporary with the circular temple and possibly used as an internal feature.

85 (fig. 80). Fragment of a large cornice, similar to No. 22. From the octagonal shrine.

86 (fig. 80). Large angle piece found otuside the north wall of the octagonal shrine.

Note

The late Sir Ian Richmond strongly advised the compilation of this architectural catalogue in order to assist with any future reconstruction or study of the temples and other ancillary buildings at Nettleton. The features described in the catalogue, with one or two exceptions, are in the care of the Bristol City Museum. I am most grateful to Mr. T. F. C. Blagg, M.A., for his kind and generous assistance with the arrangement and terminology of this catalogue.

17. BONE OBJECTS

(details of size are given only when the object is not illustrated)

(a) *Miscellaneous*

1. Bone handle. At each end it has a zone of decoration consisting of a number of incised criss-cross lines contained within a single circular cut border line. Found in a third-century A.D. level (fig. 82(1)).

2. Bone handle, turned on the lathe. It is split in half and has a perforation at each side for a securing pin to pass through. Found within Building XVI (fig. 82(2)).

3. Picce of an antler tine 3 in. (7.6 cm.) long and $3\frac{1}{2}$ in. (8.8 cm.) wide, with a number of cut marks.

4. Part of a sheep tibia decorated with 21 circles and dots. It is only part of a complete tibia that was apparently decorated throughout its length with similar circle and dot decoration. It seems likely that this bone was used to impress the circle and dot device on to pottery and the end of the bone was also uscd for this purpose. Found near the temple in a fourth-century level (fig. 82(3)).

5. Bone tooth of a comb. $1\frac{1}{4}$ in. (3.1 cm.) long.

6. Bone spoon with circular bowl. The handle is broken (fig. 82(4)).

7. Small flat panel of bone decorated on its surface with longitudinal lines and a notched device on its upper and lower edges. There is also a broken perforation. One corner remains intact otherwise it is badly broken. From Building XVIII (fig. 82(5)).

8. Small triangular shaped polished bone. The three sides are neatly cut and the bone has a grccn stain. The right angle is missing. From Building XVIII. See pp. 86–8 (fig. 82(6)). Cf. Wheeler and Wheeler, 1932, pl. XXXI, 147 and 155.

9. Small bone tool used for marking. The stamp has seven deeply incised cut lines. A small six-sided bone handle is set centrally in the plate at an angle to facilitate the stamping operation. From Building XVIII (fig. 82(7)).

10. Bone awl made from a sheep bone. The pointed end is much worn through use (fig. 82(8)).

11. Antler tine $4\frac{1}{2}$ in. (11.4 cm.) long. From the first-century enclosure ditch.

12. Part of a plain bone handle, $3\frac{3}{4}$ in. (9.5 cm.) long and 1 in. (2.5 cm.) wide. Sharply cut at each end. From Building XVIII.

13. Bone tool made from a sheep tibia, $3\frac{1}{2}$ in. (8.8 cm.) long and 1 in. (2.5 cm.) wide. Sharply cut at both ends and hollowed. The sides are polished through use. From the ditch filling south of Building XVII.

14. Bone tool made from the tibia of a sheep $4\frac{3}{8}$ in. (11 cm.) long. The two ridges at the foot end are polished through constant use, and it is stained green (see below). From the first-century ditch filling.

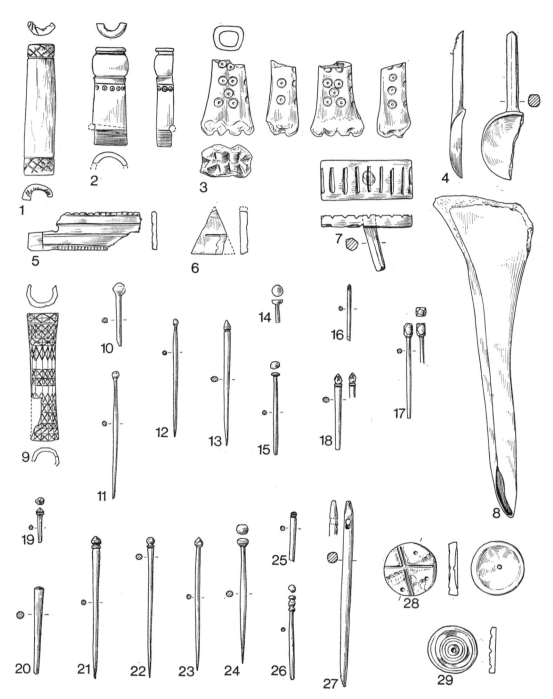

Fig. 82.   Bone objects (scale ⅓, except 3, 4, 6, 7, 8, 28 and 29, ⅔)

15. Octagonal bone handle in two pieces, heavily decorated with linear and criss-cross design. From the shrine (fig. 82(9)).
16. For ivory object see p. 145, pl. XXIIIb, and fig. 62.

(b) *Needles*

Three bone needles were found during the course of the excavation and in each case the bone was stained green. Two other fragments without head or tail, also stained green, were also likely to have been needles. Needles found at the Romano-British settlement at Camerton, Somerset (Wedlake, 1958, p. 264) also had this green stain, as did other bones found on both the Camerton and Nettleton settlements. This is generally taken to be evidence of close contact with bronze, but in a number of instances, when a green stained bone has been found during excavation, no bronze has been found in association despite careful search. In several instances tibia of sheep have also been found with this green staining, and these were often used for winding wool. It is suggested that the green stain found on some bones is not bronze-staining but the result of constant contact with dyed wool. This is particularly true with regard to the needles found on both the Camerton and Nettleton sites. The Nettleton needle was $2\frac{7}{8}$ in. (7.4 cm.) long but the point was missing. The circular eye was $\frac{1}{8}$ in. (3 mm.) diameter. The point end of a needle was $1\frac{3}{4}$ in. (4.4 cm.) long.

(c) *Pins* (fig. 82(10–27))

Seventy-five bone pins have been recovered during the course of the excavation. The greatest proportion (36) were found in association with the shrine, especially in the burnt material associated with the destruction of the circular shrine after A.D. 249. The majority of the pins had been broken, but 14 were complete. The pins themselves do not call for any special comment other than to state that 28 had simple round heads, three flat heads, three faceted lozenge-patterned heads, one each had acorn-, onion-shaped, and six-sided heads and eight others had various shaped heads.

18. THE SPOONS

by David Sherlock, F.S.A.

Remains of 28 spoons were recovered from the excavations, three with circular bowls, the remainder fragments of oval bowls or handles, apart from two complete spoons recovered from Building XVIII. All are of bronze except one circular bowl of bone (fig. 82(4)). They are mostly in poor and corroded condition but show no special signs of wear from use in antiquity. An additional spoon of tinned bronze now in the Devizes Museum was found in 1941.

(a) *Circular Bowls*

1. Diam. 2.2 cm. Thin bowl; handle broken off leaving wedge-shaped rat-tail soldered underneath. From north of temple in first- to second-century context (fig. 83(1)).
2. Diam. 2.4 cm. Bowl of thicker metal with rat-tail and specks of solder remaining. From a fourth-century level in Building XX.
3. Bone. Diam. 2.65 cm. Thick shallow bowl with part of handle. From a fourth-century level in Building XVI (fig. 82(4)).

The circular bowl is a very common type and there are many examples almost identical to these from Silchester, Cirencester and elsewhere. It is generally thought to belong mainly to the first and second centuries A.D. but few examples from dated contexts are actually

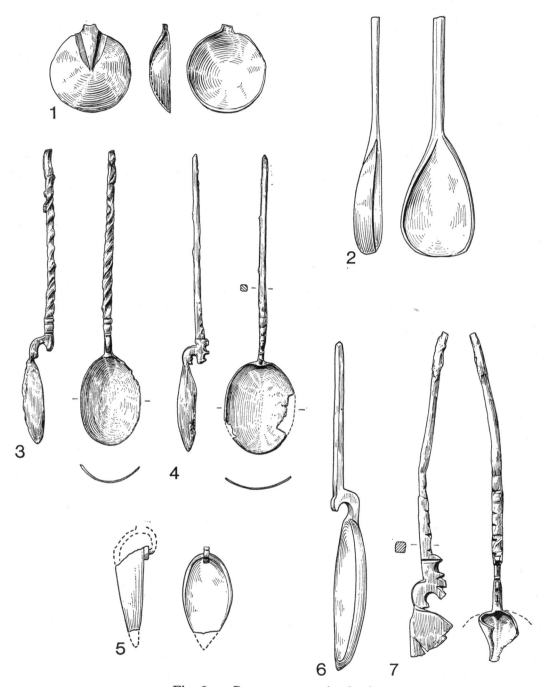

Fig. 83. Bronze spoons (scale ⅟₁)

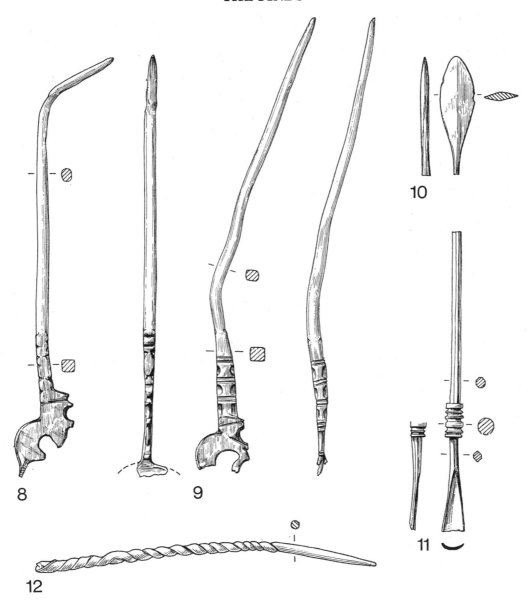

Fig. 84.   Bronze spoons (scale ¼)

recorded. One from the third-century temple at Jordan Hill, Dorset, is in the Pitt-Rivers Museum, Oxford, and another was found in a fourth-century level at Camerton.

(b) *Oval Bowls*

4. Width 2 cm. A common type on Romano-British sites from the second century onwards. From Building XII (fig. 83(6)).
5. Tinned bronze. Length 15.5 cm.; width 3.1 cm. This and no. 6, both heavily corroded, are the only complete spoons from the site. From Building XVIII. Late fourth-century (fig. 83(3)).

6. Length 15.5 cm.; width 4 cm. approx. From Building XVIII (fig. 83(4)).
7. Tinned bronze. Width 1.5 cm. Small boat-shaped bowl with remains of handle possibly in the form of a loop. Incised line around outside of rim. From a fourth-century level in Building IX. This type is hitherto unknown to the writer (fig. 83(5)).
8. Width 3.3 cm. From the late fourth-century improvised shrine (fig. 83(7)).
9. Fragment of a bowl. Late fourth-century. From Building XVIII.
10. Fragments of a large bowl. A late type. From Building XVIII.
11. Silvered bronze. Fragments of a bowl of similar shape to No. 10. Also from Building XVIII. Late fourth-century.
12. Tinned bronze. Fragments of a bowl of similar shape. From Building XVIII. Late fourth-century.
13. From Building XIII. Fourth-century.
14. From Building XXIV. Late fourth-century.
15. From Building XXVI. Late fourth-century.
16. From Building XVIII, lying on the floor. Late fourth-century.
17. From near Building XXIV. Late fourth-century.
18. From the west bank. Late fourth-century.

(c) *Handles*

19. Length 12 cm. Thickish, tapering to a point. Possibly from a circular bowl. First- to second-century. From pit under Building XXIV.
20. Square in section. From a second- to third-century level.
21. Twisted handle with twist reversed. 2 cm. from bowl end. From the road surface opposite Building XVIII. Third-century level.
22. From Building XIII. Third- to fourth-century level (fig. 84(9)).
23. Tinned bronze. From Building XVIII. Fourth-century (fig. 84(8)).
24. Tinned bronze. From Building XVIII. Late fourth-century.
25. Flat spear-shaped end not necessarily from a spoon. Good condition. From Building XV. Fourth-century. Spoon handles with spear-shaped ends are recorded from Holt, Denbighshire (silver) and Caerwent (bone) (fig. 84(10)).
26. From Building XIII. Fourth-century.
27. From Cemetery A. Fourth-century. Octagonal stem with decorative ridges at base (fig. 84(11)).

These bowls and handles are all of types familiar on town and country sides in south and west Roman Britain and do not call for special comment; nor indeed is closer comparison possible while so few others are recorded from archaeological contexts. The notches on both the handles and the sections between handles and bowls are especially characteristic of late Roman spoons. The twist in some handles was for additional strength as well as ornamentation. The tinning and silvering on the later spoons may be compared with the debasement of the coinage from the middle of the third century A.D.

19. BRONZE OBJECTS

(a) *Miscellaneous* (figs. 85–9)

Fig. 85

1. Small bronze hook with a perforation on its flattened end. Possibly an ear-ring. From a fourth-century level.
2. Hook similar to No. 1, with notched sides. From a fourth-century level.

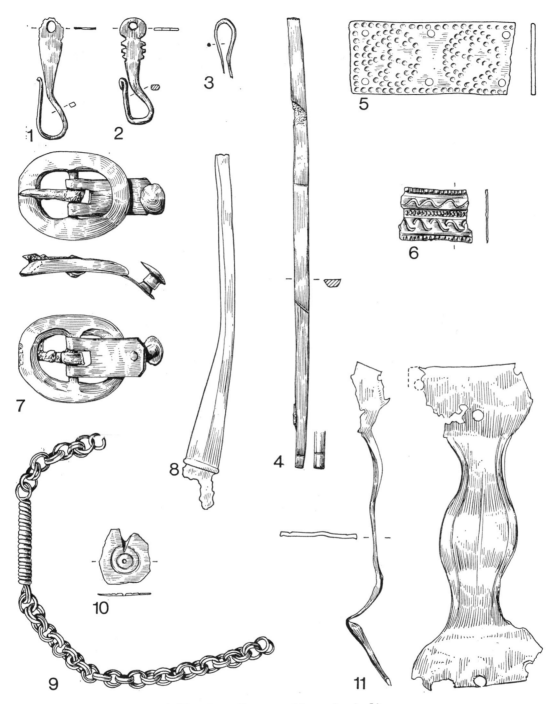

Fig. 85. Bronze objects (scale $\frac{1}{1}$)

15

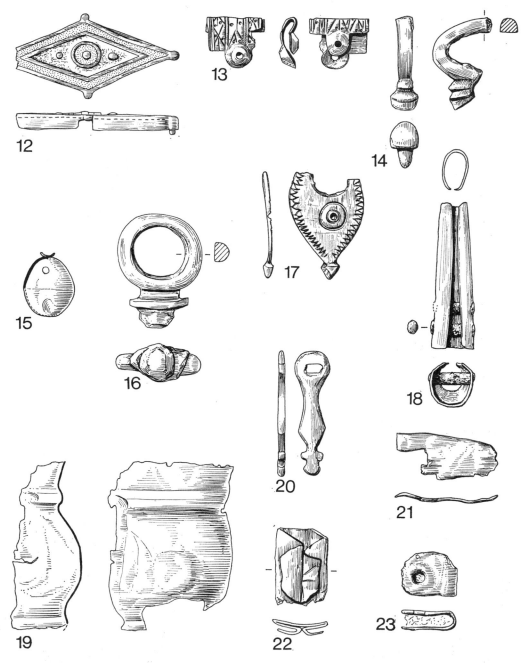

Fig. 86.   Bronze objects (scale ½)

3. Small bronze loop with pointed ends, the lower end being flattened. Late fourth-century level.
4. Bronze bar 4¾ in. (12 cm.) long. From a fourth-century level.
5. Bronze banding, decorated with a punched design consisting of circles enclosing crosses, with border punching and rivet holes at the end. From a third-century level.
6. Fragment of decorated banding, with notched and zigzag device. From a fourth-century level.
7. Bronze buckle, plain, with iron pin and loop for attachment of strap. Late fourth-century level.
8. Handle, with one broken end, and the other with part of an iron object attached to the socket. From a third-century level.
9. Double linked bronze chain, with a twisted wire fastening at the end. From a third-century level.
10. Small round disc, with two circles and a central dot. From a fourth-century level.
11. Bronze handle decorated with a linear device with splayed ends, and three rivet holes at each end for fixing to a box. From an early third-century level.

Fig. 86

12. Bronze seal box, lozenge-shaped with rounded ends. The face of the box is decorated with three bronze pin-head points centrally placed. The points are surrounded by green enamel set in a bronze circle, outside which there is a lozenge-shaped infill of green or yellow enamel. This is edged with a bronze band with a yellow zone of green enamel surrounding the edge of the seal box.
13. Small decorated band with one round eyelet at each end. Decorated with line and dot decoration. From a fourth-century level.
14. Bronze leg of a small candelabra in the form of a horse's hoof, no doubt one of three legs forming the stand. From a third-century level.
15. Small bronze bell or ball, made in two halves and joined in the centre. From a fourth-century level.
16. Heavy bronze ring, detached from a larger object, the riveted and torn end of which still adheres to the ring which probably served as a handle. From a fourth-century level.
17. Heart-shaped bronze object, with a pointed lobe. The face is decorated with three circles in the centre, and is rouletted around the edge. The top end appears to be broken. From a third-century level.
18. Bronze tube or ferrule, with two iron rivets at the wide end. From a fourth-century level.
19. Bronze object with a bulbous base, probably the casing from a wooden object.
20. Small decorated strap end. There is a loop for fastening to a strap at one end and a decorated shamrock leaf-shaped terminal. From an early third-century level.
21. Part of a bronze clasp. From a fourth-century level.
22. Small plain strap end with two bent flanges on its reverse side to secure a strap. From a fourth-century level.
23. Small strap end, with rivet holes to secure the strap. From a fourth-century level.

Fig. 87

24. Hinged clasp fastening probably for a wooden chest, with a hook at the end. The surface of the clasp is decorated with a number of small circles and dots. From a mid third-century level.
25. Small bronze cleat for fixing to leather. From a third-century level.
26. Small bronze object in the form of an axe. The stem is square, and pointed at the end, with a series of decorative notches about midway along one face. The stem curves at the end to form an axe-like end, but it has been bent back at its edge. See Wheeler and Wheeler, 1932, 83, fig. 18, 61.
27. Bronze banding, U-shaped and decorated on its face with two incised lines and three parallel ridges. From a late fourth-century level.

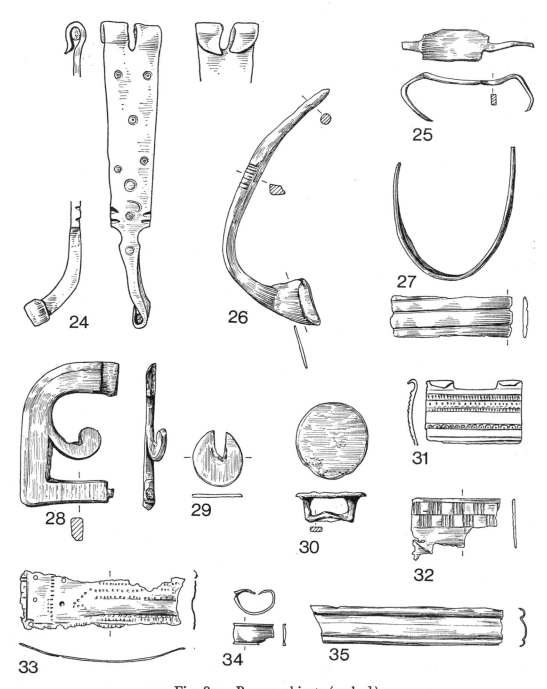

Fig. 87. Bronze objects (scale ¼)

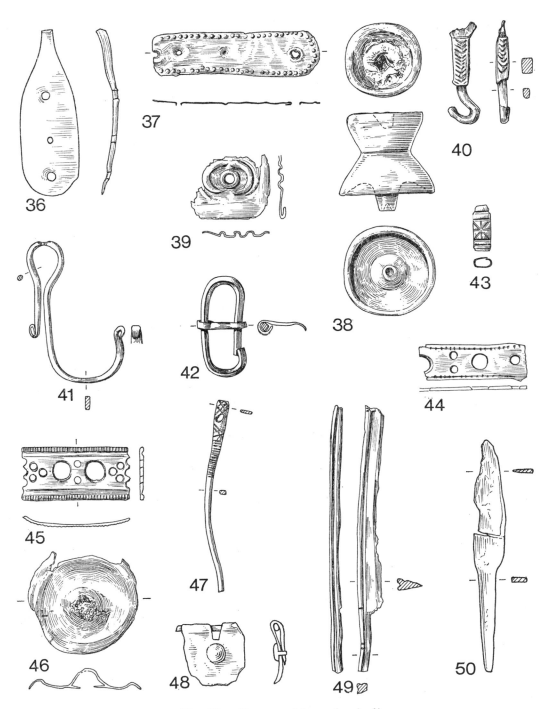

Fig. 88. Bronze objects (scale $\frac{1}{1}$)

28. Bronze ornament in the form of a letter E, with small tags at the two ends for fixing. The bottom arm is straight, and the centre and top arms curved. From a first- to second-century level.
29. Small washer. From a fourth-century level.
30. Small bronze button with loop for attachment. The face appears to have been decorated. From a first- to second-century level.
31. Small rectangular bronze plate with an open-ended clasp on each top corner. The plate is slightly curved and copiously decorated with zones of linear and stab devices. Probably a scale (*lorica*) from Roman armour. From a first- to second-century level.
32. Small bronze plate. Decorated with linear and notched devices. First- to second-century filling.
33. Terminal of bronze banding. The sides are decorated with a fine rouletted design and there are three small holes at the end and two others on the edge.
34. Small bronze band with a raised edge.
35. Bronze strip used as a border decoration on a larger object.

Fig. 88

36. Bronze tag end. The flattened end has three small perforations for attachment and the stem has been broken off.
37. Bronze strip decorated with a stamped spot device along its sides and rounded end. It has two perforations and a broken one at the end. An attempt has been made to stamp a central perforation.
38. Bronze finial or handle knob in the form of a reel. The upper surface is saucer-shaped with a raised central boss which is flat on the top with a circular depression. The lower part, also saucer-shaped, has been filled with lead, presumably to attach it to a larger object. From a second- to third-century level on the east bank.
39. Fragment of sheet bronze with *repoussé* decoration and a pleated edge, and an embossed circle enclosed within a crescent on either side. From the ditch filling of the first-century enclosure.
40. Bronze hook with a broken end. The square stem is decorated with a series of incised chevrons. From Building XVIII.
41. Bronze hook with both ends curled. From Building XVIII.
42. Small bronze buckle formed by bending a square sectioned length of bronze. From Building XVIII.
43. Small bronze strap-end. The terminal is wrapped around the end of a leather strap and is decorated with a series of cross links. From Building XVIII.
44. Decorated curved piece of bronze, broken at one end. There are a series of circular perforations between a striated line on either side with a number of small cross marks. The hole at the end was probably made to receive a hook. From Building XVIII.
45. Decorated piece of curved bronze similar to No. 58, but larger. It has large circular perforations and groups of two and four smaller perforations arranged alternately between the larger holes. It is broken at each end. From Building XVIII.
46 Saucer-shaped bronze object with raised central boss and round outer flange. On the under side there are indications that it has been attached to and probably formed the terminal of a larger object. From Building XVIII.
47. Piece of bronze, square section, but flattened out at the end and decorated with criss-cross lines. It has a small circular perforation at the end. From Building XVIII.
48. Part of a bronze clasp end. The end is bent back and riveted with one rivet forming a hinge to hold a wire pin. From Building XXVII.
49. Small bronze razor or strigil; the broken end indicates it was originally longer. The blade has a central groove along its back ridge. From the first-century ditch filling south of Building XXVII. This could well be a razor of Bronze Age date.

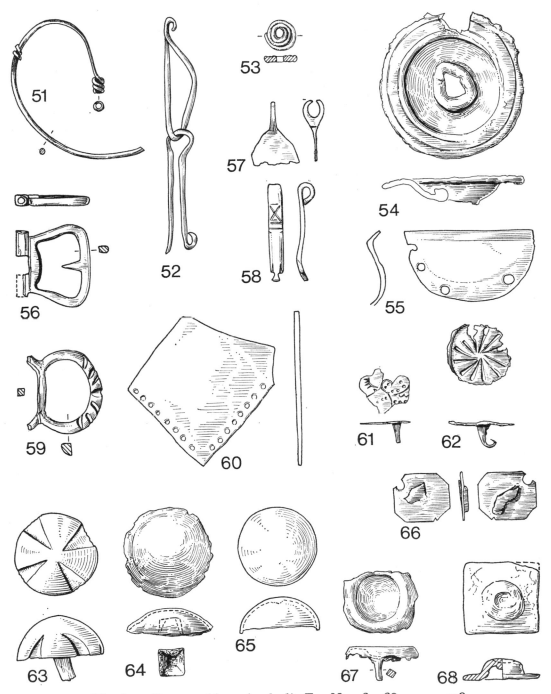

Fig. 89.   Bronze objects (scale ½). For Nos. 69–68, see p. 218

50. Small bronze object in the form of a small tanged knife, but it has no knife edge. Probably used for spreading paste, etc. From a fourth-century level.

Fig. 89

51. Curved piece of bronze wire with three spirals at one end and two other twists around the wire From Building XVIII.
52. Two links of bronze wire in the form of two linked safety pins, each with a point and hooked end for fastening. Probably used for securing cloth. From a first- to second-century level.
53. Spiral of bronze wire, incomplete, probably part of a brooch. From the first-century enclosure ditch.
54. Bronze boss with raised central part and centre hole. From the old river bed alongside Building VII.
55. Crescent-shaped piece of bronze. It has four, possibly five, perforations around its edge. From a first-century level.
56. Small bronze buckle. It has a point in the centre to secure a leather strap and there was a swivel hinge with a small securing pin. From a first-century level.
57. Part of a small pendant or ear-ring. The eyelet has been worn through by use. From a first-century level.
58. Bronze object with a loop at the end, probably part of a larger object. From a fourth-century level.
59. Loop of what appears to be a small bronze buckle. Unstratified.

Not illustrated

60. Small bronze key. The end is flattened with a circular hole for suspension. The end is bent at right angle to the stem and has two small teeth. From the south side of Building XXVII.
61. Fragment of bronze with punched decoration. Fourth-century level.
62. Small piece of bronze *repoussé* work. From a late fourth-century level.
63. Small bronze bar (incomplete), decorated with a notched device.
64. Bronze washer $\frac{3}{4}$ in. (19 mm.) diameter, with a perforation $\frac{1}{4}$ in. (6 mm.) diameter. Third-century level.
65. Small bronze ferrule $\frac{1}{8}$ in. (3 mm.) wide. From a fourth-century level.
66. Piece of bronze plating, probably part of a votive plaque $1\frac{3}{4}$ in. (4.4 cm.) long, with a rounded edge and a parallel ridge. From a second- to third-century level.
67. Bronze disc 1 in. (2.5 cm.) diameter, slightly concave. Possibly the back plate of a brooch.
68. Part of a circular disc $1\frac{1}{8}$ in. (2.8 cm.) diameter, with an incised circle near the rim. From a first- to second-century level.
69. Piece of bronze binding $2\frac{1}{4}$ in. (6.9 cm.) long, $\frac{3}{4}$ in. (1.9 cm.) wide, with a bronze rivet.
70. Miniature bronze-axe, with the head cast on a round stem. The well-fashioned blade has a fine edge. From the north side and contemporary with the circular shrine.
71. Part of an ear-ring $\frac{3}{4}$ in. (1.9 cm.) in diameter, decorated with incised lines on its outer edge. One end is pointed and the other missing.
72. Small bronze split pin $\frac{5}{8}$ in. (16 mm.) long. From the enclosure ditch filling.
73. Length of bronze wire $3\frac{1}{2}$ in. (8.9 cm.) long, pointed at each end.
74. Bronze ferrule with a trace of cement inside. From Building XVIII.
75. Bronze loop $\frac{3}{4}$ in. (19 mm.) diameter. Possibly a handle for a larger object.
76. Small piece of bronze chain. From the first-century enclosure level below Building XXVII.

For other bronze objects see pp. 258–9, pl. XXIIIa, and figs. 63, 113.

(b) *Bracelets* (figs. 90, 91)

A large number (55) of fragmentary bracelets were found and they carried a variety of designs which included: circle and dot; ribbed; ovolo; notched; castellated; zigzag; milled; billeted; stippled;

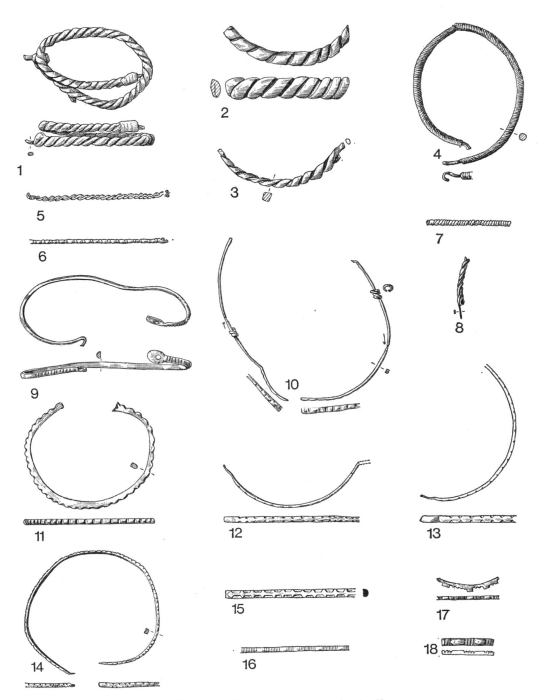

Fig. 90. Bronze bracelets (scale $\frac{2}{3}$)

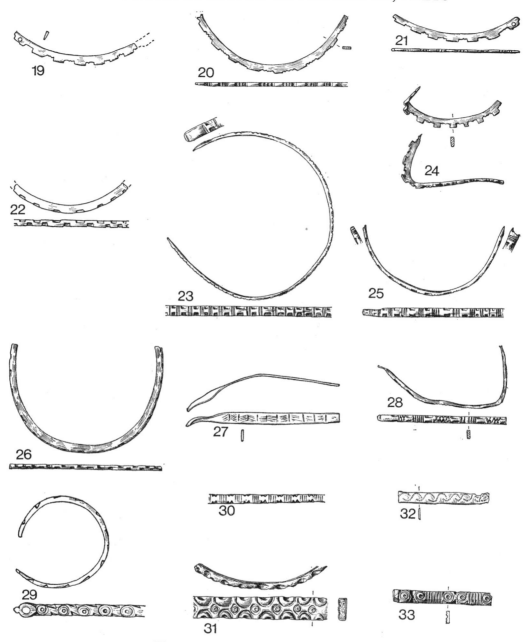

Fig. 91.   Bronze bracelets (scale ⅔)

twisted corded wires and plain. The diameters varied from 2 in. (5.1 cm.) to 4 in. (10.2 cm.). The greater number came from fourth-century levels and only one was found in the first-century enclosure ditch. See also figs. 63(8) and 113(3–4).

(c) *Dress and Signet Rings*

1. Bronze signet ring in perfect condition and little worn, with an internal diameter of ¾ in. (19 mm.) (fig. 92(7)). The bezel appears to be made of a light blue glass paste. The general shape of the ring with

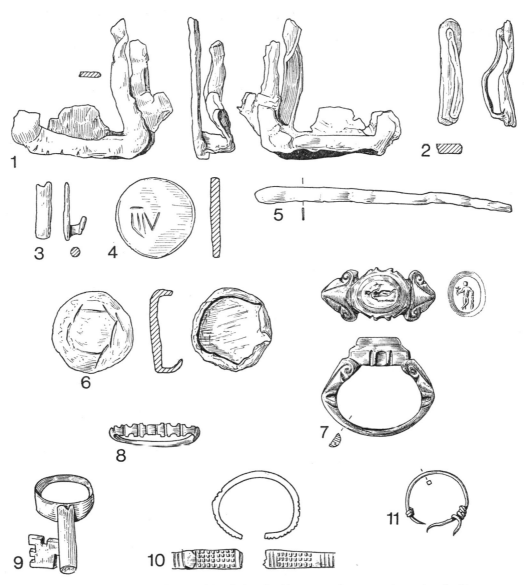

Fig. 92.   1–6, objects of lead (scale $\frac{1}{2}$); 7–11, bronze rings (scale $\frac{1}{1}$)

projecting, engraved 'wings' or 'shoulders' on either side of the group is similar to two in the British Museum (*BM Guide* (1), 68, fig. 82, right hand ring, and (2), fig. 13, no. 2). The spiral decoration on each of the 'wings' or 'shoulders' is well executed. The figure represented on the bezel, would certainly seem to be Apollo. The god stands naked, with legs crossed, leaning on a column on the top of which rests his lyre. He holds what appears to be a branch, the well-known symbol of his purifying and healing power. This is a well-known Greco-Roman type of Apollo, found in paintings, etc. (cf. Reinach, 1922, 23, fig. 1). No corresponding rendering of the god on a gem is known. This ring was found in association with No. 7 in the destruction material at the west end of Building XXI associated with Constantinian coins. See also Intaglios, p. 142.

Note. The writer has to thank Professor J. M. C. Toynbee for identifying the intaglio and for information concerning the ring.

2. Fragment of a bronze signet ring. The bezel is missing. Found in a fourth-century level.
3. Fragment of a signet ring with a bezel of bottle green coloured glass. Found in a second-century layer.
4. Part of a signet ring with a bezel of the same material as No. 3. Found in a fourth-century level.
5. Complete bronze ring with five decorated segments on the front of the ring and a central square bronze bezel in relief. Before A.D. 248 (fig. 92(8)).
6. Broken bronze ring. The front of the ring is decorated with an extension to the underside of the ring, with four circles merged together, each circle being pierced with a small hole. There is also a series of subsidiary circles with centred dot decoration. From a fourth-century level.
7. Bronze key-ring, plain and much worn. The hollow key extension is $\frac{5}{8}$ in. (16 mm.) long. Found in association with No. 1 in Building XXI (fig. 92(9)).
8. Plain bronze ring, from a third-century level.
9. Plain bronze wire ring, broken. From a third-century level.
10. Part of a plain bronze ring. Before A.D. 248.
11. Plain bronze ring. From a fourth-century level.
12. Plain flat sectioned ring with overlapping ends. From a fourth-century level.
13. Plain bronze ring.
14. Plain bronze ring, broken. From Building XVIII.
15. Part of a plain bronze ring. From Building XVIII.
16. Plain iron ring. From a late fourth-century level.
17. Bronze ring of signet type; part missing. Decorated with a chequered device. From Building XVIII (fig. 92(10)).
18. Small bronze ring broken in three pieces; plain.
19. Small bronze ring decorated with incised lines and a small central knob. From Building XVIII.
20. Small signet ring with an oval signet and signs of yellow enamel. From Building XVIII.
21. } Included in the list of Special Finds (see p. 148, pl. XXIIIa, and fig. 63(6) and (7)).
22. }
23. Small bronze ring. From the ditch filling, north-east corner of Building XXVII.
24. Small bronze ring of fine wire with the ends twisted in three twists around the wire. From the ditch filling on the north side of Building XXVII (fig. 92(11)).

(d) *Pins*

Sixty-three bronze pins were recovered from various levels, but many were incomplete. The principal pins are illustrated in fig. 93. Among those found in a first- to second-century context were Nos. 3, 7, 9, 16 and 26. Pins found in a third-century context were Nos. 1, 2, 4–6, 13 and 14, and those in a fourth-century context were Nos. 8, 10, 11, 14, 15 and 17–22.

(e) *Plate, Strip, etc.* (see p. 218)

1. Small pieces of plate about 1 in. (2.5 cm.) square with single incised line and a rivet in one corner. From fourth-century demolition level.
2. Piece of folded plate $1\frac{1}{4}$ in. (3.1 cm.) by 1 in. (2.5 cm.). From a first- to second-century level.
3. Two pieces of plate: (a) $1\frac{3}{4}$ in. (4.4 cm.) long, $1\frac{3}{8}$ in. (3.5 cm.) wide with four rivet holes; (b) $1\frac{1}{2}$ in. (3.8 cm.) wide with six rivet holes. From a fourth-century level.
4. Several fragments of a plaque or panel with a rounded bevelled edge.
5. Three pieces of sheet bronze: (a) $2\frac{1}{2}$ in. (6.3 cm.) long by $1\frac{1}{4}$ in. (3.1 cm.) wide, with three incised lines; (b) $2\frac{1}{4}$ in. (5.6 cm.) long with three rivet holes; (c) 1 in. (2.5 cm.) long with two rivet holes.

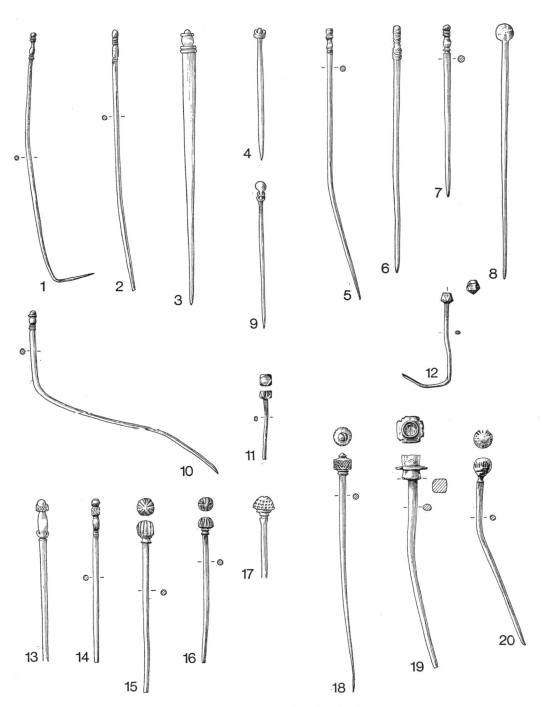

Fig. 93. Bronze pins (scale ⅔)

6. Bronze sheeting 2 in. (5.1 cm.) long, 1¾ in. (4.4 cm.) wide with five rivet holes. Three incised circles on surface drawn with a compass (central pin mark). From a fourth-century level.
7. Several fragments of thin sheet bronze. From a fourth-century level.
8. Bronze sheet folded several times. Associated with squatter level in shrine.
9. Bronze sheet. From a fourth-century level.
10. Several pieces of folded sheet bronze. From a fourth-century level.
11. Bronze strip 2½ in. (6.3 cm.) wide and folded several times. Associated with the octagonal shrine.
12. Piece of bronze strip 2½ in. (6.3 cm.) long, 1 in. (2.5 cm.) wide; at one end it is curved in a semi-circle to clasp a circular object by two rivets. From a fourth-century level.
13. Bronze wire folded several times, one end coiled. From a second-century level.
14. Small bronze point 1 in. (2.5 cm.) long and part of a larger object. From a fourth-century demolition level.
15. Curved bronze band with notched decoration, possibly part of a bracelet; one end is broken, the other flattened, with a small bronze rivet inserted. From Building XVIII.
16. (a) Bronze band with castellated decoration and a small hole in one end. (b) Bronze rivet with octagonal head. From Building XVIII.
17. Piece of bronze with pointed end and a series of small perforations along each edge. Probably part of a small plaque. From Building XVIII (fig. 89(60)).

Note

During the course of the excavation a number of pieces of scrap bronze were found, chiefly in the late levels within the settlement. Many of the pieces have been folded and hammered flat to form small parcels: they appear to be parts of votive plaques and other sheet bronze. Several bronze bracelets have also been found folded in this way. There is no doubt that this has been purposely done: it could not be accidental. The settlement was on at least two occasions the scene of violent raids, when it was plundered and burnt. It is chiefly in the levels associated with these raids that the small hammered parcels of bronze were found.

In the National Museum of Denmark at Copenhagen there are several hoards of looted material from Roman Britain, consisting of smashed up plates, fibulae, etc.[116] Similar packets of bronze and silver were also found in the well-known cache at Traprain Law, Scotland.[117]

(f) *Needles*

1. Bronze needle with plain stem, slightly curved (fig. 94(1)).
2. Bronze needle 3⅞ in. (9.8 cm.) long. Broken at the eye. From Building XVIII.
3. Bronze needle 4½ in. (11.3 cm.) long. Broken at the eye. From Building XVIII.

(g) *Spatula Probes*

Two plain probes came from the first-century ditch filling (fig. 94(16) and (17)). The remaining nine were found in third- and fourth-century levels and do not call for special comment.

(h) *Studs*

The principal bronze studs of the 45 found are illustrated in fig. 89(61)–(68). Nos. 61, 64, 65 and 67 came from first- to second-century levels, No. 62 from a third-century context and No. 63 from a fourth-century level. Nos. 61 and 62 are probably of military origin:

61. A small stud but in bad condition. The flat face of the stud is decorated with a four-petalled flower and there are traces of niello and tinning. Similar examples from Hofheim have niello and are tinned. Cf. *Ritterling*, 1913, Taf. XII, Nos. 35, 36, 41 and 42. Possibly military equipment.

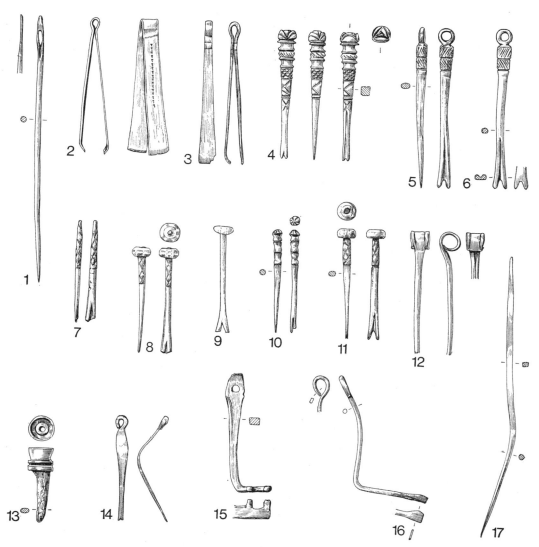

Fig. 94. Bronze objects (scale $\frac{2}{3}$)

62. Stud head decorated with star or flower pattern. The stripes are in red niello. This is a common
pattern but in military specimens it is not in the form of a stud but a thin rosette for decorating
loricae and helmets. From a third-century level.

(i) *Tweezers*

Nine pairs of tweezers were found but do not warrant any special comment. Two examples, both
from third-century levels (Nos. 30 and 31) are illustrated in fig. 94(2) and (3).

(j) *Bronze Toilet Accessories*

Eight of the ten found are illustrated in fig. 94(4)–(11). Nos. 8, 9 and 11 had bone heads. The
remainder do not call for special comment. All were found in third- to fourth-century levels.

20. BRICK AND TILE

Brick and tile fragments occurred primarily in levels earlier than A.D. 248. Of the 92 instances recorded, no less than 57 came from levels associated with the circular temple. Two fragments of hypocaust tile and 25 of red brick tile were noted; the remaining fragments were Roman brick. The use of brick ceased after the destruction of the circular shrine in A.D. 248. After this date the local Cotswold limestone was utilized for the walls and for roofing tiles.

A number of pieces of hypocaust tile and some of brick have also been found in the filling of the small ditches in the first-century enclosure. A piece of good quality red tile with incised lines was found in Building XVIII. This was probably part of an hexagonal shaped votive lamp. See p. 140.

21. COAL

The use of coal at Roman Nettleton was proved beyond doubt. It was found in at least seven different cuttings in stratified layers, in association with Buildings XI, XII, XIII and XXVI. The late occupation layers associated with these buildings were unusually black with an admixture of coal-fire ash. It also occurred in connection with the iron industry in Building XVI and bronze smelting in Building XIII. Further evidence of its use was found in and around the furnace used for casting pewter in Building XXI.

Coal was likewise used in the pewter-casting industry at Camerton, Somerset, in the late fourth century A.D. (Wedlake, 1958, pp. 94–5).

22. COUNTERS

Bone. Five bone counters, three $\frac{13}{16}$ in. (21 mm.) diameter and $\frac{1}{8}$ in. (3 mm.) thick; one $\frac{5}{8}$ in. (16 mm.) diameter and $\frac{1}{8}$ in. (3 mm.) thick, and the fifth $\frac{3}{4}$ in. (19 mm.) diameter and $\frac{1}{12}$ in. (2 mm.) thick. Four are concave on their upper face with a central pin-point hole, and three are flat on their underside, but the fourth has a rough cross with the intervening spaces polished, and in each space there is a single dot. Superimposed over this there are two scribed lines crossing each other (fig. 82(28)). The fifth is decorated with a series of concentric circles and is plain on its reverse (fig. 82(29)).

Glass. One counter of glass $\frac{9}{16}$ in. (14 mm.) in diameter and $\frac{1}{4}$ in. (6 mm.) thick, with a polished convex face and a flat, rough underside.

Bronze. A roughly cut circle, plain on each face; $\frac{1}{2}$ in. (13 mm.) diameter and $\frac{1}{32}$ in. (1 mm.) thick.

Silver. One $\frac{5}{8}$ in. (16 mm.) diameter and $\frac{1}{32}$ in. (1 mm.) thick, with fine scratch marks on its surface; the second $\frac{3}{4}$ in. (19 mm.) diameter, wafer thin and plain.

Pottery. Two, roughly made from coarse grey ware from the first-century enclosure ditch: one $1\frac{1}{4}$ in. (3.1 cm.) diameter, the other $\frac{3}{4}$ in. (19 mm.) diameter.

23. FLINTS

Three flint scrapers were found in association with the second- and third-century Roman material. A number of flint flakes were also recovered in the gravel layer which forms part of the sloping river-valley bank on which the shrine was built. Four flint scrapers and a small leaf-shaped arrowhead were also found on the site of the first-century enclosure. The small

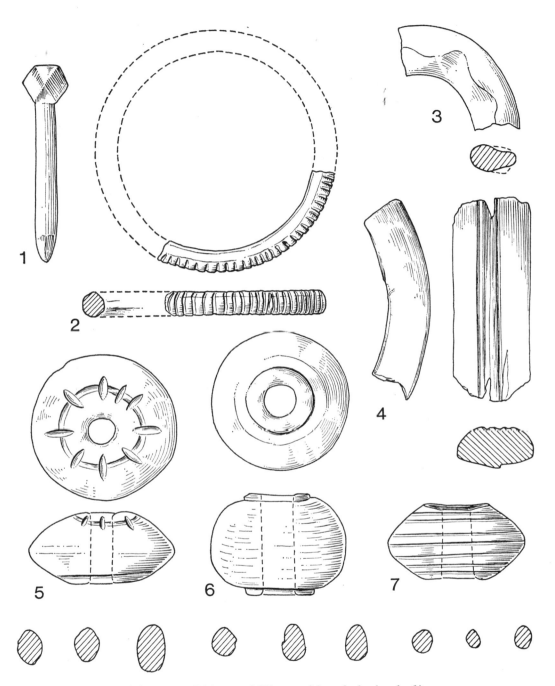

Fig. 95.   Objects of Kimmeridge shale (scale $\frac{1}{1}$)

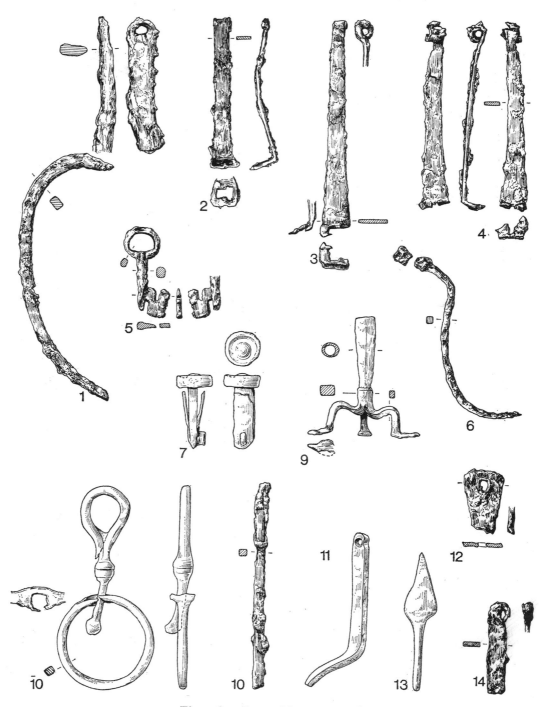

Fig. 96.   Iron objects (scale ⅛)

axe-head described on p. 181, also found on this site, suggests a possible prehistoric settlement. Two conjoining flints were found on the site of the late fourth-century cemetery; one
part in a grave filling and the other part, still stratified in the grave side, proved to be a flint
scraper broken when the grave was dug.

24. KIMMERIDGE SHALE AND JET (fig. 95)

(a) *Kimmeridge Shale Objects*

1. Four fragments of a shallow lathe-turned bowl. The bowl would be 1 ft. (0.3 m.) in diameter and
   about 1¾ in. (4.4 cm.) in depth with a slightly raised foot on its base, which is 5 in. (12.7 cm.) in
   diameter. The rim is curved with a flat top. The walls of the bowl are ¼ in. (6 mm.) thick at the
   top but increase to ⅜ in. (10 mm.) at the base of the bowl. Found in a layer contemporary with the
   octagonal shrine on its north side.
2. Small peg or pin, 2 in. (5.1 cm.) long. The stem has a blunt point and is ¼ in (6 mm.) in diameter;
   the square faceted head is ⅜ in. (10 mm.) square. From a third-century level near the temple
   (fig. 95(1)).

(b) *Kimmeridge Shale Bracelets*

Parts of 11 bracelets were found, all cut on the lathe. Five, round in section, were plain and 2⅝ in.
(6.6 cm.) in diameter; two of the same diameter had incised corded decoration (fig. 95(2)); two more
were 2⅞ in. (7.2 cm.) and 2⅛ in. (5.3 cm.) diameter. A heavier type was 3¾ in. (9.5 cm.) in diameter
and decorated with incised lines around its outer edge (fig. 95(4)). Another bracelet, from a third-century
level, had a series of scallops around its outer edge (fig. 95(3)).

(c) *Jet Ring*

Half of a jet ring with a very deep ribbed decoration. A similar ring was found at Camerton (Wedlake,
1958, fig. 57–9).

25. IRON OBJECTS (figs. 96–102)

(a) *Miscellaneous Iron Objects*

1. Small iron candelabra stand. The socket is set on a square base, supported by three legs with
   pointed feet. From a late fourth-century level on the east side of the temple (fig. 96(9)) (see
   Wheeler and Wheeler, 1932, fig. 23, 191 and 192).
2. Iron swivel or part of a horse-bit. At one end there is a loop formed by twisting the iron around its
   stem, which terminates at the other end in a round knob holding a large circular iron ring. The
   ring is attached to the stem by a hole made through a flattened part of the ring which acts as
   a swivel. From a third-century level (fig. 96(10)).
3. Iron rod 6 in. (15.2 cm.) long, and ¼ in. (6 mm.) square, with a flattened end ½ in. (13 mm.) wide.
   Possibly an iron dart.
4. Square iron plate with central circular boss raised ¼ in. (6 mm.) above the plate, and perforated
   at the top. Probably a decorative plate for a door. From a fourth-century level.
5. Iron object of unknown use, composed of a flat piece of iron with a circular hole at one end and
   bent upwards at the other. From a first- to second-century level (fig. 96(11)).
6. Broken end of a larger object, fan-shaped and pierced by a central hole. From Building XVIII
   (fig. 96(12)).
7. Arrowhead or small spear. The stem is round. From a mid fourth-century level (fig. 96(13)).
8. Flat iron pin terminating with an eyelet. From a third- to fourth-century level (fig. 96(14)).

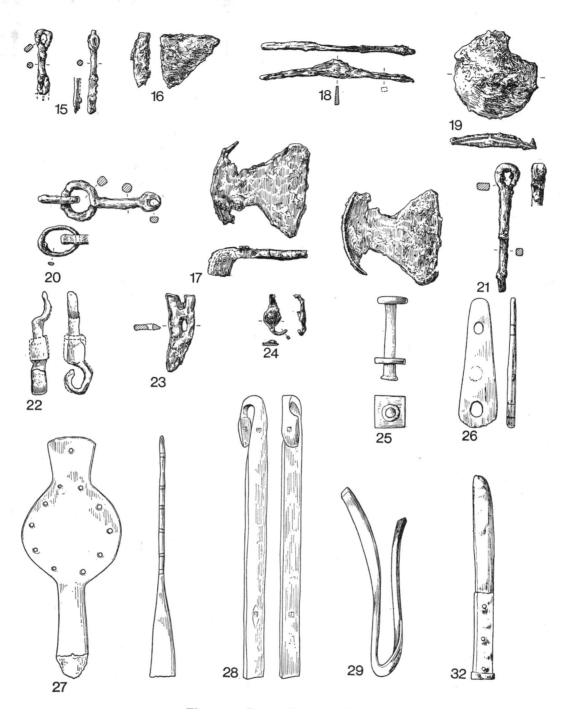

Fig. 97. Iron objects (scale ⅓)

9. Small iron pin with a loop at the end. From Building XVIII (fig. 97(15)).

10. Iron triangle. From the first-century enclosure ditch (fig. 97(16)).

11. Triangular-shaped object. It is broken at its top end, but it appears to have been a socket for the back end of an iron hand-axe. From Building XVIII (fig. 97(17)).

12. Part of an iron ox-shoe 4 in. (10.1 cm.) long with a maximum width of 2 in. (5.1 cm.). It has five oblong-shaped nail holes. From a fourth-century level.

13. Small nail or tool with pyramid-shaped head, 1 in. (2.5 cm.) long, the head being $\frac{1}{4}$ in. (6 mm.) long. From Building XVIII.

14. Flat iron plate 4 in. (10.1 cm.) long, $1\frac{3}{8}$ in. (3.5 cm.) wide at its broad rounded end and $\frac{1}{2}$ in. (13 mm.) at its narrow end, which is also rounded. There are two egg-shaped holes in the plate, one at each end, the larger $\frac{5}{8}$ in. (16 mm.) in diameter and the smaller $\frac{3}{8}$ in. (10 mm.). The plate has a thickness of $\frac{1}{8}$ in. (3 mm.) at the narrow end, but thickens to $\frac{1}{4}$ in. (6 mm.) at its wide end. From a fourth-century level.

15. Iron plate $3\frac{3}{4}$ in. (9.5 cm.) long by $1\frac{1}{4}$ in. (3.1 cm.) wide; it is $\frac{1}{4}$ in. (6 mm.) thick with three nails equally spaced 1 in. (2.5 cm.) apart for securing to wood. From Building XVIII.

16. Iron object, pointed at one end. From a level later than A.D. 285 (fig. 97(18)).

17. Concave iron disc, with a small central hole. From Building XXVII (fig. 97(19)).

18. One side of an iron horse-bit. The mouth end has been worn through and there are two rings at the rein end. From a third- to fourth-century level (fig. 97(20)).

19. Iron pin with a loop at one end and pointed. From a fourth-century level (fig. 97(21)).

20. Iron object. From a round central part an open-ended hook projects to each side. The hooks are square in section but the end of one hook is missing. Unstratified (fig. 97(22)).

21. Part of a horseshoe with two countersunk egg-shaped nail-holes. From a fourth-century level (fig. 97(23)).

22. Small iron hook, broken at one end and with a flat upper part. From a fourth-century level (fig. 97(24)).

23. Iron bolt found in association with No. 22 (fig. 97(25)).

24. Iron plate with an oval hole at each end and a slightly raised boss in the centre. From a late level east of the modern road (fig. 97(26)).

25. Iron plate. The centre part is a roughly circular plate 3 in. (7.6 cm.) wide with a series of circular holes around its edge. There is a central top projection $1\frac{1}{2}$ in. (3.8 cm.) long with rounded ends and a central hole, presumably for hanging purposes. Found near Building XXV in a late level (fig. 97(27)). Dr. Graham Webster suggests that this could be a kind of rattle (*sistrum*) used in temple ritual to scare away evil spirits and there would have been links in the holes attached to pieces of metal to jangle against the flat base when shaken. The flat tang fitted into a wooden handle. Alternatively it could have been a kind of religious standard but if it had been attached to a long shaft it would have been hammered into a socket.

26. Two identical iron bars 1 ft. 6 in. (0.46 m.) long and 1 in. (2.5 cm.) wide. There is a square hole recessed on one side for clamping. At the opposite end the bar narrows and is rounded on the outside. It turns to form an open-ended loop which widens at the end. There are square holes in the stem and the loop, opposite each other, presumably to take small iron bolts which secured it to wood. It is difficult to suggest a use for these well-made bars which were found together with Nos. 27 and 28 lying on the floor of Building XVI (fig. 97(28)).

27. A long bent piece of iron about 1 ft. 10 in. (0.56 m.) long. Found in association with Nos. 26 and 28 on the floor of Building XVI (fig. 97(29)).

28 Bar of wrought iron, 7 lb. in weight. It is $1\frac{1}{2}$ in. (3.8 cm.) thick, 6 in. (15.3 cm.) long, and 3 in. (7.6 cm.) wide, with one pointed end. Found with 26 and 27 on the floor of Building XVI.

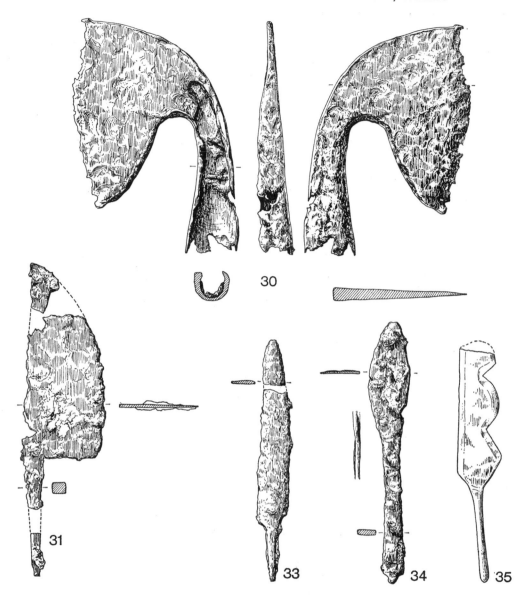

Fig. 98.   Iron objects (scale ⅓)

(b) *Door Bolts and Keys*

1. Door latch with flat handle; the loop is 7 in. (17.8 cm.) long. From a fourth-century level (fig. 96(1)).
2. Iron bolt. From a fourth-century level east of the octagonal temple.
3. Iron key. From a fourth-century level east of the octagonal temple (fig. 96(2)).
4. Iron key similar to No. 3, but with loop at the end. The key release end is similar to No. 3, but it is damaged. From a third-century level near the temple (fig. 96(3)).

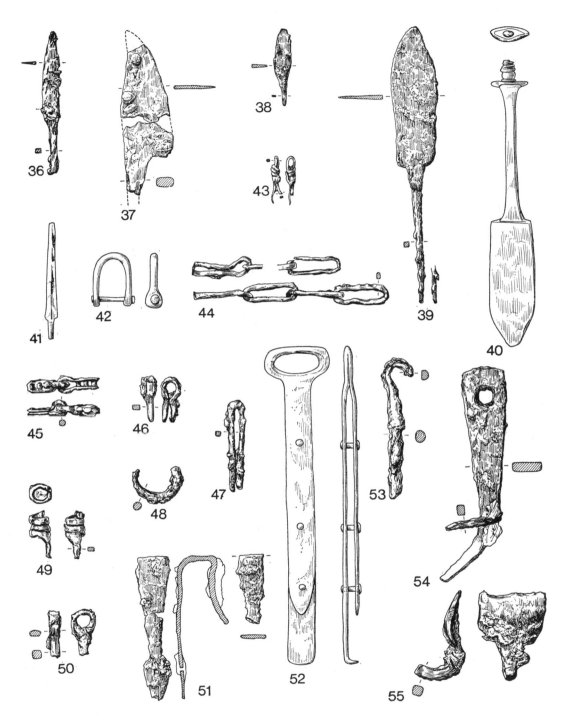

Fig. 99. Iron objects (scale ⅓)

5. Iron key with loop at end. The key release is an open end with two prongs. From a late fourth-century level (fig. 96(4)).
6. Iron key similar to No. 5, with loop at end. Length 5 in. (12.7 cm.) with bar ½ in. (13 mm.) wide. The key release is an open square end with two prongs ⅜ in. (10 mm.) long. From a fourth-century level.
7. Iron door-key. The key release is ¾ in. (19 mm.) square with two alternate notches. From a late fourth-century level (fig. 96(5)).
8. Door latch with knob at the end. The latch is straight for 1 in. (2.5 cm.) below the knob, but the remainder is a gentle curve. Square section. From Building XVIII (fig. 96(6)).
9. Iron lock bolt with thick circular end and two springs, similar to No. 2. There is an additional projection at the pointed end. From Priestley excavation (fig. 96(7)). For a similar bolt, see Wheeler, 1943, fig. 95, 2–3.

(c) Iron Hatchets and Choppers

Three choppers are illustrated in figs. 98(30) and (31) and 99(37). No. 31 came from a third-century level and Nos. 30 and 37 from late fourth-century levels. Two other examples were broken.

(d) Iron Knives

1. Table-knife shape with two rivets at haft end for handle. From a second-century level (fig. 97(32)).
2. Long-bladed knife with short tang. From a third-century level (fig. 98(33)).
3. Putty-knife shape with small tang at end of the round handle. From a fourth-century level (fig. 98(34)).
4. Knife of unusual type with serrated cutting edge and two large notches. From a fourth-century level (fig. 98(35)).
5. Knife with long thin pointed blade. From a second- to third-century level (fig. 99(36)).
6. Putty-knife type, haft missing; the blade is 2¾ in. (6.9 cm.) long. From a fourth-century level.
7. Blade of small thin knife 3½ in. (8.9 cm.) long. Late fourth-century level.
8. Knife with blade 1¾ in. (4.11 cm.) long and haft 1¼ in. (3.1 cm.). Late fourth-century level.
9. Putty-knife type, haft missing. From a fourth-century level.
10. Blade only, with curved back. From a fourth-century level.
11. Miniature knife with a fish-shaped blade. From a third-century level (fig. 99(38)).
12. Blade only, 4 in. (10.16 cm.) long. From a third-century level.
13. Broad-bladed knife, with long handle which is square in section (fig. 99(39)).
14. Complete knife with dagger-like blade. The haft is decorated with a bronze plate and band. Found on the late fourth-century floor in Building XIX (fig. 99(40)).
15. Complete knife, 4⅜ in. (11 cm.) long overall; the tang is 1½ in. (3.8 cm.) long. Found in association with the circular shrine.
16. Small knife with long thin blade. From a late level (fig. 99(41)).

For a bronze knife see p. 146 (pl. XXIIIa and fig. 63(2)).

(e) Iron Chain

Four instances of iron chain came from a third-century level and one (fig. 99(44)) came from a fourth-century level.

(f) Iron Split Pins

Of the eight split pins found, one came from a first-century level (fig. 99(46)) one from a second-century level, one from a third-century level (fig. 99(47)), and three from fourth-century levels; the others were unstratified.

(g) *Iron Rings*

Eight iron rings with an average diameter of 2 in. (5.1 cm.) were found. Apart from one in a second-century context the remainder were found in fourth-century levels. One example from Building XVIII is shown in fig. 99(48).

(h) *Iron Coils or Ox-goads* (fig. 99(49))

Five coils were found, all in fourth-century levels. Three had three coils each; one had only two coils, and one with a central pin through the coil is similar to one found at Lydney (see Wheeler and Wheeler, 1932, fig. 23, 189).

(i) *Iron Hinges*

Four hinges, all from third- to fourth-century levels, were found, one in Building XVIII (fig. 99(50)). Two others are figured (fig. 99(51) and (52)). The other hinge was similar to No. 51.

(j) *Iron Hooks*

Thirteen iron hooks came from third- and fourth-century levels. Seven are figured in figs. 99 and 100. Nos. 53–55 came from third-century levels and Nos. 56 and 57 from fourth-century levels. Nos. 58 and 59 came from Building XXVII. Nos. 55 and 57 are similar to the hooks attached to the sides of waggons for the straining ropes which makes loads of hay or straw secure. The remaining hooks do not call for any special comment.

(k) *Iron Slag*

Twenty-seven lumps of iron slag were recorded in the settlement but the greater number of these were found in and around Buildings XI, XII, XIII and XXVI in late fourth-century levels. This is the same area in which evidence for the use of coal was found. The iron slag, together with the nearby furnaces, suggests a small smelting industry possibly run in conjunction with the bronze-smelting and pewter-casting activities in the settlement (see p. 68). Several pieces of slag and a large lump of wrought iron were also found in association with these buildings (see p. 225). The iron slag was confined chiefly to the late domestic area of the settlement, but it was also found in association with the first-century enclosure on the higher level above the valley on the east side of the settlement, where a small furnace was also found (see p. 7).

(l) *Iron Tools* (figs. 100–102)

1. Iron tool with inner cutting edge and a ferruled end. Similar to a modern long handled pruning hook and probably used for a similar purpose. The iron rivets through the ferrule end suggest a wooden handle. Found in a second-century level (fig. 100(60)).
2. Iron file with a handle 2 in. (5.1 cm.) long. The deeply incised filing is present on both faces and edges. From a third-century level (fig. 100(61)).
3. Iron tool with a round handle end and a long flat blade. From a fourth-century level (fig. 100(62)).
4. Iron chisel with a 1 in. (2.5 cm.) cutting edge. The head is mushroom-shaped through use. From a fourth-century level (fig. 100(63)).
5. Small iron tool, probably a punch, with a fan-tail shaped end, $1\frac{3}{4}$ in. (4.4 cm.) long and $\frac{3}{4}$ in. 19 mm.) wide. From a fourth-century level.
6. Iron chisel $3\frac{1}{2}$ in. (8.9 cm.) long, with a blade $\frac{5}{8}$ in. (16 mm.) wide. From a fourth-century level.
7. Iron bit for boring with rounded stem and square end for securing in a brace. From a third-century level (fig. 100(64)).
8. Iron wrench with flattened, squared end with slot for wrenching or twisting operations. From a fourth-century level (fig. 100(65)).

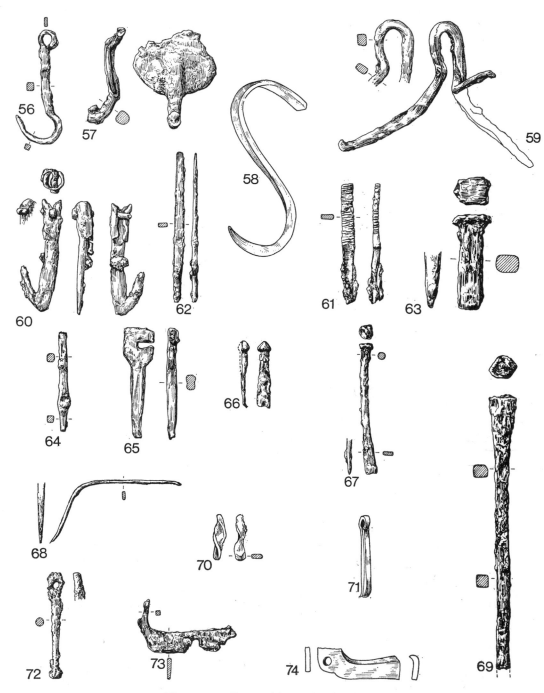

Fig. 100.   Iron objects (scale ⅓)

9. Small tool with a flat blade and a pyramid-shaped head. From a fourth-century level (fig. 100(66)).

10. Chisel with a round stem and small cutting edge; the head is rounded. From a third-century level (fig. 100(67)).

11. Iron leatherworker's tool for piercing holes. There are signs that it had a looped end. From a fourth-century level (fig. 100(68)).

12. Iron bar with square hollowed end. Possibly a spanner for tightening a square nut. From a fourth-century level (fig. 100(69)).

13. Fragment of a corkscrew-type bit. From a fourth-century level (fig. 100(70)).

14. Small tool with looped end. From a fourth-century level (fig. 100(71)).

15. Small tool with flattened pierced end and small knob on the top. From a fourth-century level (fig. 100(72)).

16. Tool broken at end, with tang for handle; notched on side with signs of a second notch at break. From a late fourth-century level (fig. 100(73)).

17. Part of an iron tool with pierced end. Use unknown. From a fourth-century level (fig. 100(74)).

18. Small iron scraper with rounded ends and a cutting edge. There is a central hole for the insertion of a handle. From a fourth-century level (fig. 101(75)).

19. Iron bar with a loop at the end. The bar is curved and was probably part of an horse-bit. From a third-century level (fig. 101(76)).

20. Iron cap probably from the end of a wooden pole; $1\frac{1}{2}$ in. (3.8 cm.) square at the base, with back plate and two prongs for clasping to wood. From a fourth-century level.

21. Chisel or punch 3 in. (7.6 cm.) long and $\frac{5}{8}$ in. (16 cm.) diameter at head with tapering point. From a fourth-century level.

22. Small iron punch 2 in. (5.1 cm.) long and $\frac{3}{8}$ in. (10 mm.) diameter at head with tapering point. From a fourth-century level.

23. Iron probe 6 in. (15.2 cm.) long, $\frac{1}{4}$ in. (6 mm.) wide at one end and pointed at the other. From a fourth-century level.

24. Small tool with flat blade. There are traces of a wooden handle on the shank (fig. 101(77)).

25. Small iron gouge with a circular stem. From a second-century level.

26. Iron punch $3\frac{1}{2}$ in. (8.9 cm.) long, round in section. From Building XVIII.

27. Iron tool with square haft terminating in a point. Traces of a wooden handle. From Building XVIII (fig. 101(78)).

28. Small chisel or punch terminating in a point. From a second-century level (fig. 101(79)).

29. Large flat iron tool probably used as a scraper. Its top end is broken, but it is curved over and was probably part of the socket which held the wooden handle. Similar to one from Lydney (cf. Wheeler and Wheeler, 1932, fig. 23, 184). From Building XVIII (fig. 101(80)).

30. Iron tool broken at one end; length $2\frac{3}{4}$ in. (6.9 cm.). It has two right-angle bends which terminate in a point and is square in section. From Building XVIII.

31. Iron punch 3 in. (7.6 cm.) long with pointed end. From a fourth-century level.

32. Small iron tool. The stem is square in section and it has a triangular-shaped head (fig. 101(81)).

33. Part of a thick iron loop, broken at the ends. From Building XVIII (fig. 101(82)).

34. Iron ring, circular in section. From the west bank fourth-century filling (fig. 101(83)).

35. Iron ring, probably the head of a larger object. Interior diameter 1 in. (2.5 cm.) and $\frac{1}{4}$ in. (6 mm.) thick. From Building XVIII.

36. Large staple; the legs are round and pointed and 1 in. (2.5 cm.) in length. The cross bar is flat. From a late Roman level (fig. 101(84)).

37. Oblong iron panel with a small border and plain back (fig. 101(85)).

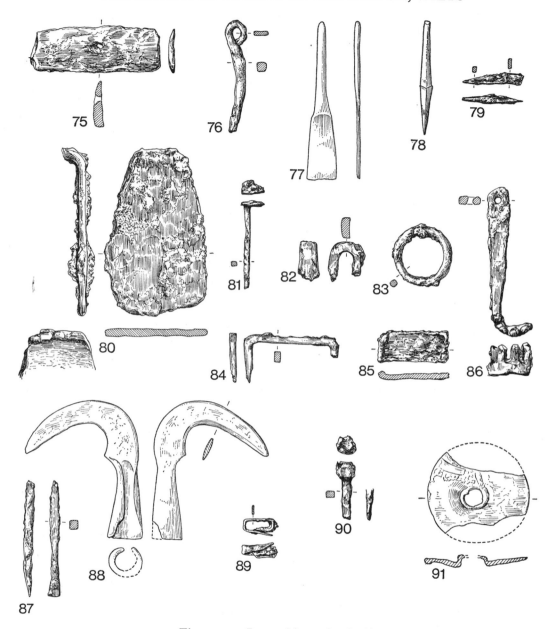

Fig. 101.   Iron objects (scale ⅓)

38. Iron pin ¾ in. (19 mm.) long, square in section and bent at one end. It appears to be part of a larger object. From Building XVIII.

39. Small iron pin with looped end 1½ in. (3.8 cm.) long. The stem is square in section. From Building XVIII.

40. Iron tool possibly used as a key. The handle is flat with a circular hole at the end. The operational end of the tool is curved and has four iron teeth about ¼ in. (6 mm.) square and ⅜ in. (10 mm.) long. The spaces between the teeth are also ¼ in. (6 mm.). Found in the north annexe to Building

XXVII in a fourth-century A.D. level (fig. 101(86)). A similar key has been found at the Paulton
Roman villa, Somerset.

41. Small iron chisel, square in section with a pointed end, which probably had a wooden handle.
From Building XXVII (fig. 101(87)).

42. Small iron sickle with socketed end for a wooden handle. The blade is 2½ in. (6.3 cm.) long with a
pointed end, and there is a small hole in the haft end for a nail. The tool is well made. From the
first-century enclosure ditch, upper filling (fig. 101(88)).

43. Small ferrule, probably from a wooden handle, with a rectangular end (fig. 101(89)).

44. Round-headed bolt with a square pin and a chisel finish at the end. From a fourth-century A.D.
level (fig. 101(90)).

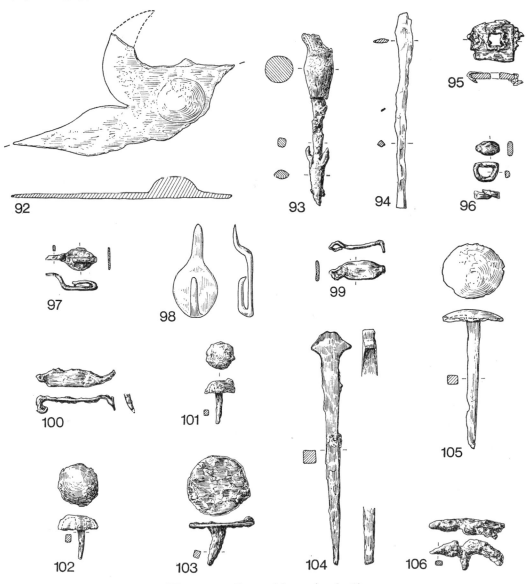

Fig. 102.   Iron objects (scale ⅓)

45. (a) Part of a circular iron disc; its outer edge is slightly raised to form a rim. The central hole is $\frac{3}{8}$ in. (10 mm.) in diameter and is surrounded by a raised ridge which appears, at one point, to extend across the disc to its outer rim, but it is broken at this point (fig. 101(91)).

46. (b) A curious shaped iron object, terminating at each end in a fine point. Just behind the forward point on the plate there is a large circular boss in relief, about $1\frac{1}{2}$ in. (3.8 cm.) in diameter. The rear wing is $3\frac{1}{2}$ in. (8.9 cm.) long to its pointed tip. At the centre, top part, there is an extension $2\frac{1}{2}$ in. (6.3 cm.) long, but this has a blunt end (fig. 102(92)). A large part of the edge is raised to form a rim in a similar manner to (a) above. Unfortunately, this object is in a very bad condition. Recovered with No. 45 from the Roman river bed alongside the river-side wall of Building VII, together with a number of other small finds; they were probably parts of a larger object (possibly decorative features from a wooden shield?). See p. 236.

47. A *plumbata* (*martiobarbulus*): an iron harpoon or javelin-head. It is $5\frac{3}{8}$ in. (13.6 cm.) long with side tangs $\frac{1}{4}$ in. (6 mm.) long. The arrow stem is round in section and 2 in. (5.1 cm.) long (fig. 102(93)). The stem is encased in lead, which forms the socket in which the stem of the javelin was held, and the leaded end was evidently added to provide additional impetus when thrown. Building XVIII, in which the javelin was found, was destroyed by fire, and there was no evidence of a stone or tiled roof. It does seem possible that this weapon was thrown from the higher ground to the west into the thatched roof as an incendiary device. See p. 88.

48. Small iron rod with an arrow-like end. From a level associated with the circular shrine (fig. 102(94)).

(m) *Iron Washers*

Two iron washers were found in fourth-century levels, and one (fig. 102(95)) in a third-century level.

26. NAILS AND CLEATS (figs. 89 and 102)

(a) *Sandal Cleats*

Thirteen sandal cleats were recovered, mostly from road surfaces. The smallest was $\frac{1}{2}$ in. (13 mm.) long, and the largest was $2\frac{1}{4}$ in. (6.3 cm.), but the average length was $\frac{3}{4}$ in. (19 mm.).

(b) *Sandal Nails*

Numerous sandal nails were found, often embedded in the road surface, but groups of sandal nails found together are evidently survivals from discarded footwear. Sixty-three were found in one group $\frac{1}{2}$ in. (13 mm.) long with five others $1\frac{1}{4}$ in. (3.1 cm.) long, and one small bronze-headed nail, in the fourth-century floor in Building XVIII. Another group of 30 nails, $\frac{3}{8}$ in. (10 mm.) long, came from the fourth-century floor in the cellar of Building XIII, and another group of 77 nails, $\frac{1}{2}$ in. (13 mm.) long, was found in a layer contemporary with the circular temple.

There were also five other groups of 8, 9, 10, 14 and 23 nails.

(c) *Large Nail Heads with Short Pins*

Eight nails with dome-shaped heads, evidently used for decorative purposes were found in various levels. The heads varied in diameter from $\frac{3}{4}$ in. (19 mm.) to 2 in. (5.1 cm.), and the pins were about 1 in. (2.5 cm.) long. One from Building XII had a bronze cap (fig. 89(63)).

(d) *Large Nails*

Nails found in association with the octagonal temple varied in length from $5\frac{1}{2}$ in. (14 cm.) to $7\frac{1}{4}$ in. (18.5 cm.). They were square in section, with diamond-shaped heads (fig. 102(104)). Four large nails found at the foot of the large west window of the shrine probably came from the window-frame.

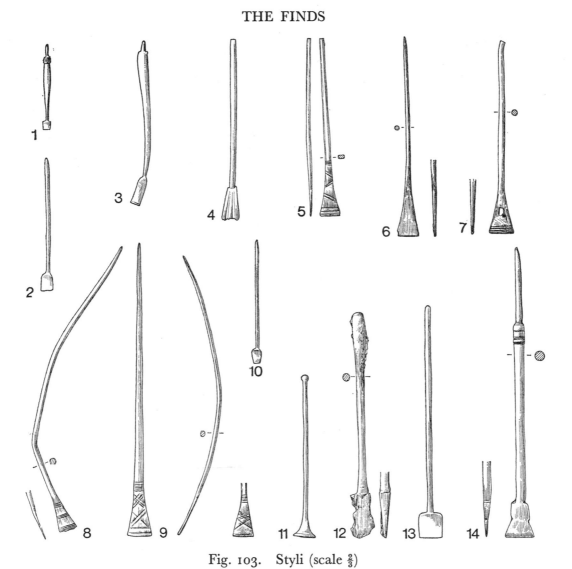

Fig. 103. Styli (scale $\frac{2}{3}$)

A nail with an unusually wide head of $2\frac{1}{4}$ in. (5.6 cm.) diameter came from the Roman river bed alongside Building VII (fig. 102(105)).

27. LEAD OBJECTS

1. Lead binding which appears to form three sides of a frame to enclose a wooden plaque. From a third-century level in Building X (fig. 92(1)).
2. Small lead handle. From a second-century level near the shrine (fig. 92(2)).
3. Lead rivet to secure a lead strip. From a fourth-century level (fig. 92(3)).
4. Inscribed lead roundel or counter (for description see p. 177). Found near Building IX in a third-century level (fig. 92(4)).
5. Lead strip broken at one end; it broadens at the other like a snake's head. From a third-century level near Building X (fig. 92(5)).

6. Roundel of lead with sides bent inwards to secure or clamp to a wooden stave. A rough hexagon is scratched on its base. From a fourth-century level (fig. 92(6)).

There were also 11 lumps of nondescript lead, and a lead pellet $\frac{1}{2}$ in. (13 mm.) in diameter from a late post-Roman level.

28. PEWTER

1. Small pewter plate 5 in. (12.7 cm.) in diameter. Ring base $2\frac{1}{4}$ in. (5.6 cm.) in diameter, with simple rounded rim. The plate has been folded into a roll suggesting it was intended as plunder by raiders. Found alongside the south wall of the octagonal temple (see p. 106).
2. Small fragment of a round rim of a pewter plate. From Building XXI in association with the moulds used for pewter-making (see pp. 68–74).
3. Four fragments of the round rim of a pewter plate with a rounded rim, of the same size as No. 1. From a fourth-century level near Building XVIII.
4. Fragment of the base of a pewter plate or dish.
5. A piece of alloy, possibly pewter. It weighs 3 lb. $6\frac{1}{2}$ oz., is $6\frac{1}{2}$ in. (16.5 cm.) long and 5 in. (12.7 cm.) wide, and has a maximum thickness of $\frac{1}{2}$ in. (12 mm.). The metal has a distinct ring when suspended. The back, which seems to be original, is quite flat apart from a small ridge $\frac{1}{8}$ in. (3 mm.) wide, which seems to follow what might have been its original outline before it was subjected to fire action. Much of its original face has been lost through fire action which caused the metal to run, but several of its original features have survived. They include two cross bars in relief across its top part: the top bar is $\frac{1}{4}$ in. (6 mm.) wide and the lower one is $\frac{5}{8}$ in. (1.6 cm.) in breadth, above which the face rises to a point. It was recovered from the old river bed alongside the piered wall of Building VII. A number of other finds were found here in association with burnt material and it was probably thrown in the river when the circular temple was destroyed about A.D. 249.

29. STYLI

Thirty-three styli were found, ten of bronze and the remainder in iron. Six of the bronze styli are figured (fig. 103(5–9 and 14)) and eight of those in iron (fig. 103(1–4 and 10–13)). Apart from Nos. 5 and 10 from first-century levels, the remainder from third- to fourth-century levels do not call for any special comment.

30. LEATHER

Only one instance of leather was found during the excavations. This occurred in material conducive to its preservation in the Roman river-bed alongside one of the river piers opposite Building VII. A number of small finds were recovered from this source, including a small tree stump with axe cut marks. The leather appeared to be part of a sandal with lace holes $\frac{1}{4}$ in (6 mm.) in diameter.

31. QUERNS

Eleven quern-stones are figured in fig. 104; No. 3 came from a third-century level, and Nos. 1, 2 and 4–11 came from the floors of the fourth-century buildings.

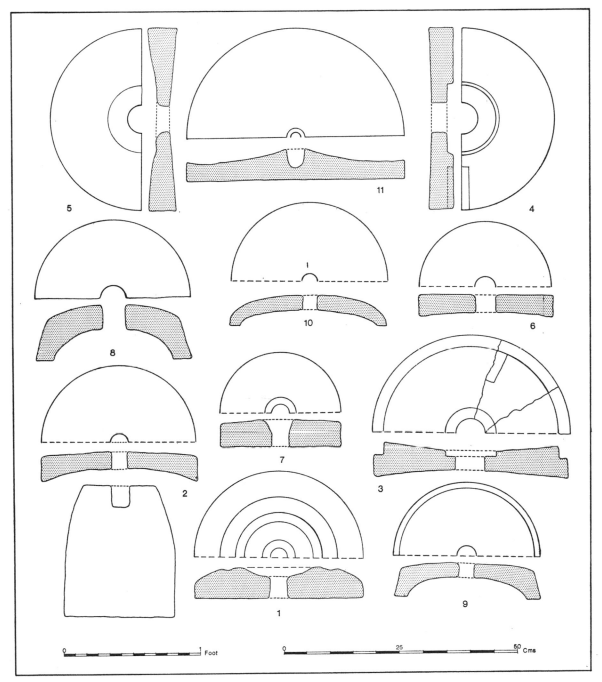

Fig. 104.   Querns and (bottom left) door pivot (scale ⅛)

32. SPINDLE-WHORLS (fig. 95)

Twenty-five spindle-whorls were found: 15 made from pottery sherds, four from stone, one from baked clay, and five from Kimmeridge Shale. Two (fig. 95(5 and 7)) are decorated and three Kimmeridge Shale whorls were found together in Building XVIII. One pottery whorl had the letters x y v scratched on its underside. Apart from two from first- to second-century levels, most of the others came from the fourth-century buildings.

33. STONE OBJECTS

1. Stone door pivot, found in Building XVIII. The sides taper towards the top. The pivot hole is square (fig. 104, bottom left).
2. Part of a stone oval dish or mortar with square lugs on the flat rim. The dish is $1\frac{1}{2}$ in. (3.8 cm.) deep and the sides vary in thickness. For a similar dish see Wheeler, 1943, fig. 80, 57 and 58.
3. Probably a loom-weight. On each side there is a hole, and a slot runs over the top of the stone presumably to house a rope. From Building XVIII.
4. Polished flat stone with rounded edge, evidently part of a larger object.
4. Polished flat stone with rounded edge, partially polished on one side. Evidently part of a larger object. The stone is green and full of minute fossils. From the squatter level on the north-west of the shrine.
5. Rough circular piece of limestone $5\frac{1}{2}$ in. (14 cm.) in diameter and 1 in. (2.5 cm.) thick with a well-cut central hole. Probably used as a weight for a loom or for roof protection. From the Wick valley in a late level.

34. WHETSTONES

A number of whetstones, all showing evidence of much use, are an indication of the practice of rural husbandry within the settlement.

35. POST-ROMAN FINDS

1. Brass shoe or belt buckle. Georgian. Found in debris west of the temple.
2. Shoe buckle; decorated. Georgian. Found in debris near the temple.
3. Brass shield; plain, $2\frac{1}{4}$ in. (5.6 cm.) wide, and the same in height.

The Georgian shoe buckles found on the temple site lend support to the theory that substantial remains of the temple were standing at that time, and the remains were of sufficient interest to encourage visits by the local dilettanti.

36. COARSE AND OTHER POTTERY

During the course of the excavation a large amount of coarse Roman pottery was found and most of the usual common types were represented. The Romano-British settlement at Camerton, Somerset, excavated by the writer, 1926–56, was placed, like Nettleton, alongside the Fosse Way and was the first known posting station south of Bath (*Aquae Sulis*), as Nettleton is similarly placed north of that city. A comparable area of the Camerton settlement (Wedlake, 1958) was excavated over a similar period of time and it therefore lends itself admirably for a fair comparison to be made of its pottery, and other finds, with those found at Nettleton.

The pottery from Camerton has been fully published (Wedlake, 1958) and, for reasons of economy, it is not necessary to repeat in detail pottery that is common to both settlements, and a comparative table is given below. In this table the number given in the Camerton Report for the pottery type has been quoted. Consequently examples which are not common to both sites are published in this report.

The most striking result of this comparison is the scarcity at Nettleton of the fine series of cordoned and other native pottery of the first to second century A.D. which was found in abundance at Camerton. At Nettleton a large quantity of coarse grey ware, including Savernake ware, was found, including several complete large urns. This pottery was re-covered from the ditches of the first-century A.D. enclosure in association with other wares, which included an unusual amount of Claudio-Neronian Samian (see p. 155), St. Remy ware, terra nigra, amphorae, and other imported cream-coloured and painted wares.

Nettleton and Camerton Comparative Pottery Table

Camerton group no.	Type of pottery	Nettleton no. of sherds recorded	Camerton no. of sherds recorded
15	Amphorae	93	140
16 and 17	Mugs or beakers with handles	Conspicuously absent	18
19	Flagons	Four in first- and second-century levels	28
20	Mortaria: vertical rim type	3	16
21	Mortaria: flanged type	88	25
28	New Forest ware	216	54
31	Heavy rim with thumb impressions	2	4
18	Jars	26	2
23	Cavetto rims and heavy rims	439	41
	Colour-coated ware	150	3
	Castor ware	6	3
	Rhenish ware	12	7
	St. Remy ware	18	9
	Strainers	3	3
	Coarse grey ware	220 (several complete pots in first-century ditches)	85
	Stamped decoration	20	—

The prevalence of cordoned and other native pottery at Camerton, together with the associated brooches, was probably, in some measure, due to a strong native tradition, and the fact that Camerton had a long pre-Roman occupation on the same site. The Camerton pottery shows a much more developed native tradition than that found at Nettleton. The pottery from the first- and second-century levels at Nettleton does not exhibit these charac-teristics in such detail, since the pottery is predominantly imported Samian, amphorae, and

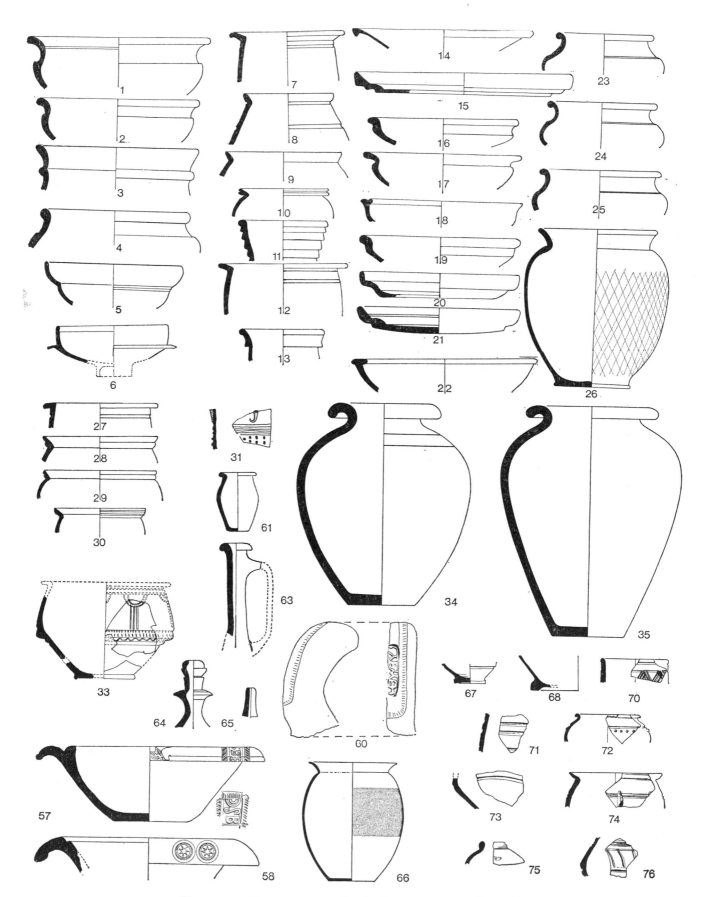

Fig. 105.   Coarse pottery (scale ¼, except 34 and 35, ⅛)

other well-established Roman wares. The large amount of Savernake and other coarse grey ware compares with a similar prevalence of this ware at Bagendon (Clifford, 1961, figs. 56, 68 and 69, and pl. LVII). Oxfordshire, New Forest, colour-coated, stamped wares, and other third- and fourth-century A.D. pottery types were also much more prevalent at Nettleton, and this accords with the flush of coins of this period on the site. These later wares are dealt with separately in this report.

The writer thanks Mrs. V. G. Swan for the identification of Savernake ware at Nettleton in the first-century A.D. ditches, and also Dr. Michael Fulford for valued help with the identification of Oxfordshire and New Forest wares.

(a) *Pottery: First- and Second-century A.D. Wares* (figs. 105–6)

Unless otherwise stated Nos. 1–84 came from the first-century enclosure ditch.

1. Bowl with pronounced shoulder and rolled rim, in red ware with a grey core (Wedlake, 1958, fig. 35, 141).
2. Bowl with overlapping rim in coarse black ware (Wedlake, 1958, fig. 37, 233).
3. Bowl with bold cordon in hard dark ware with good surface (Wedlake, 1958, fig. 34, 62).
4. Bowl in similar material to No. 3, with beaded rim (Wedlake, 1958, fig. 34, 67).
5. Small bowl, copy of Samian form 27, in soft orange ware.
6. Small bowl of terra nigra, copy of Samian form 24, in very soft black ware with white core.
7. Beaker with flat rim in coarse brown ware.
8. Butt beaker in soft grey ware (Wedlake, 1958, fig. 48, 585).
9. Butt beaker in brown ware (Wedlake, 1958, fig. 48, 585).
10. Small beaker with ridged rim in orange ware (Wedlake, 1958, fig. 48, 603).
11. Neck of a flagon with a series of overhanging ridges, soft orange ware (Wedlake, 1958, fig. 41, 342).
12. Beaker similar to No. 7 in dark grey ware with orange slip.
13. Neck of a flagon with a pronounced neck ring in orange ware.
14. Shallow plate with overhanging rim and thin sides in yellow ware with red specks.
15. A shallow plate with thick ridged side and heavy rim in dark grey ware (Wedlake, 1958, fig. 35, 113, is similar).
16. Plate with overhanging rim in hard dark grey ware (Wedlake, 1958, fig. 35, 109, is similar).
17. Shallow bowl with pronounced shoulder in black ware (Wedlake, 1958, fig. 36, 190).
18. Plate or dish with reeded rim in black ware with traces of mica.
19. Plate similar to No. 16 in hard black ware.
20. Plate similar to No. 15 in hard dark grey ware.
21. Plate similar to No. 15 in hard dark grey ware.
22. Plate with wide flat-topped rim in hard grey ware.
23. Bowl with beaded rim and pronounced shoulder in grey ware (Wedlake, 1958, fig. 35, 141–8).
24. Bowl similar to No. 23 in dark grey ware.
25. Bowl similar to No. 23 in black ware.
26. Pot with cavetto rim and lattice decoration around the body in dark grey ware. This pot containing cremated human bones was found on the slope in the field on the east side of the modern road. See p. 93.
27. A beaker similar to No. 7 in light grey ware.
28. Beaker with ridge below the rim in orange ware.
29. Butt beaker with ridged rim in red ware with speckled surface (Wedlake, 1958, fig. 48, 598, is similar).

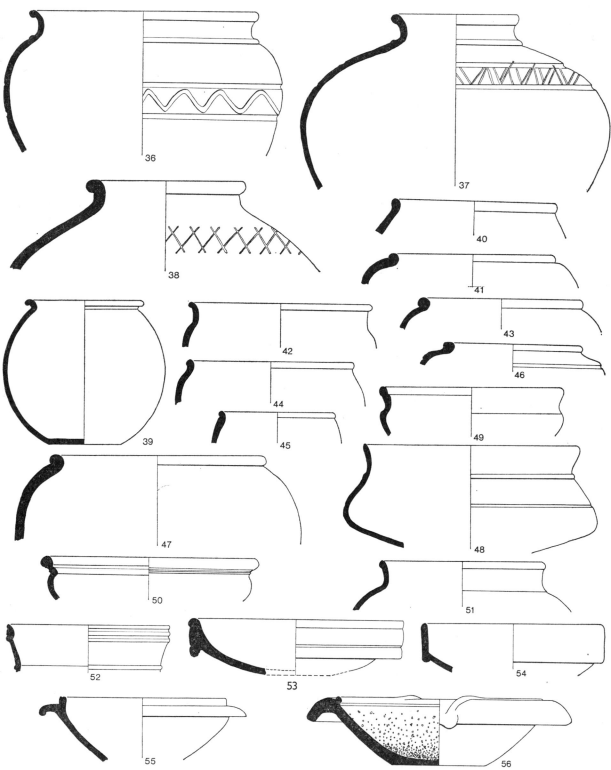

Fig. 106.   Coarse pottery (scale ¼, except 39, 1/16)

30. Butt beaker with ridged rim in rust-red ware.
31. A sherd of light grey ware with applied dot and ridge decoration. Found in association with crackled ware of similar composition.
32. Two small sherds of a similar bowl to No. 33, but from a different pot.
33. A small shouldered bowl decorated with a festoon of semi-circles below the rim and incised lines below in black ware. Similar pots were found at Jordans Hill, Weymouth; cf. also Wedlake, 1958, fig. 49, 701.
34. Large jar in coarse grey ware. A series of similar jars was found along the side of the east slope below the ditches of the first-century enclosure. They were probably used for cremations and in most instances the rim of the jar had been knocked off. Similar jars laid on their side were found at Camerton, and they were also common at Bagendon, Gloucestershire (pl. LVII).
35. Similar jar to No. 34 in coarse grey ware. Found on the east slope.
36. A large globular jar in dark grey ware. It has a beaded rim with a cordon below and there is a wide band of incised zigzag decoration around the body of the pot (Wedlake, 1958, fig. 34, 70–8).
37. A large globular jar in hard brittle dark brown ware. It has a small beaded rim and is decorated with a cordon and incised lines around the body of the pot. Found in the pre-Roman ditch below Building XXII.
38. A very large jar in coarse grey ware with walls one inch thick, a rolled rim and a band of lattice decoration around the flat slope below the rim.
39. A very large jar with walls 1 in. (2.5 cm.) thick and a heavy rolled rim. The height is estimated at 2 ft. (61 cm.) and maximum diameter at 1 ft. 8 in. (53 cm.). The surface is dark grey and the fabric is tempered with crushed quartzite and other grits.
40. A coarse grey ware pot.
41. A globular jar with a simple rounded rim.
42. A large jar with a straight neck and rounded rim.
43. A globular storage jar in coarse grey ware. From the pre-Roman ditch below Building XXII.
44. A storage jar in coarse grey ware.
45. A small bead-rimmed jar in dark hard ware. From the pre-Roman ditch below Building XXII.
46. A globular jar in coarse grey ware.
47. A large plain jar in coarse grey ware.
48. An unusual bowl in a light red soft ware. A bowl found at Maiden Castle, Dorset (Wheeler, 1943, fig. 47, 213) in a Belgic level is similar and is placed at about the time of the Roman conquest.
49. A bowl with a small ridge inside the rim, presumably to take a cover.
50. A bowl in dark ware with a thick angular rim.
51. A large jar with beaded rim in black ware.
52. A jar with a series of ridges below the round rim and a cordon below.
53. A mortarium with a straight heavy side. The external surface is light brown with traces of white slip, but the body of the dish is a hard dark grey. The internal surface is studded with fragments of red and white quartzite.
54. A mortarium with straight sides and round rim in pink ware with traces of a dark red slip and red and white quartzite grit internally.
55. A mortarium with wide flared rim in cream ware studded with red and white quartzite grit internally.
56. A large mortarium with thick flared rim in cream ware studded with quartzite grit internally.
57. A large mortarium with thick flared rim and spout, and a potter's mark on the rim that appears to read SBB. It is in red ware with a reddish brown slip studded with white quartzite internally.

58. A mortarium with a wide rolled rim and a stamped circular potter's mark on the rim in light red ware.

59. Sherd of light blue pottery encrusted with a series of irregular blotches.

60. Handle of a large amphora in stone-coloured ware with a potter's mark on the outer edge of the handle, which is difficult to decipher because the mark is broken lengthwise.

61. A miniature pot in dark grey ware. From an early level on the south bank.

62. Hollow tube of pottery with an irregular central hole. The tube is $\frac{1}{2}$ in. (13 mm.) in diameter and the two conjoining pieces are curved. The two pieces are $5\frac{1}{4}$ in. (13.3 cm.) long, but one end is broken and it was originally longer. On its upper side there is a small circular hole $\frac{1}{4}$ in. (6 mm.) in diameter. On either side of this hole the hollow tube is partially blocked and only a small vent hole is left at the top. The finished end is much worn and smooth, which suggests that it was probably used as a whistle or tubular musical instrument held in the mouth. The object is in a light sandy ware with a burnished black surface, similar in texture to the cordoned native wares found on Belgic sites. It was found in association with a quantity of first- to second-century A.D. Samian and brooches alongside the north wall of Building XXVII, in a level contemporary with the filling of the first-century enclosure ditch.

63. The long elegant neck of a single-handled flagon in grey ware with a red burnished surface. From an early Roman level near the river.

64. Decorated neck of a flagon with a rounded spout in red ware with a light brown slip. From a second- to third-century level north of Building VII.

65. The neck of a small bottle, possibly a feeding bottle, in red ware. From a level near the hostel.

66. A cavetto rim globular pot, with a zone of stippled decoration around the body. This pot contained a human cremation (see report, p. 177). It was found alongside the wall near Building XV.

67. See St. Remy ware (below).

68. Base in cream ware with thin walls, probably from a butt beaker. From a level contemporary with the first-century enclosure.

69. Sherd of cream ware with an applied rust-coloured decoration forming circles.

70. See St. Remy ware (below).

(b) *St. Remy Ware* (fig. 105(67–76))

This comparatively rare ware appeared to be more abundant at Nettleton than at Camerton (see table, p. 239). Most of the Nettleton sherds were recovered from the first-century enclosure ditches or associated with the enclosure.

67. Base of a small glazed olive-green pot with linear decoration. The pot was glazed both internally and externally.

70. Sherd with a patchy dark green glaze and linear and chevron decoration below a rounded rim in hard slaty ware.

71. Sherd glazed yellow-brown on both sides and decorated with two parallel ridges.

72. Part of a small globular bowl, glazed on both sides. Linear and raised dot decoration.

73. A shouldered and ridged yellow-glazed sherd in brown ware.

74. Rim of a butt beaker with linear decoration below and light green glaze on both sides.

75. Small glazed sherd, with a rounded rim.

76. Sherd of a shouldered olive-green glazed pot, decorated with incised lines. From a level contemporary with the first-century enclosure.

77. Base of a small olive-green bowl, glazed on both sides.

78. Sherd with olive-green glaze on both sides. From the south-west corner of the first-century enclosure.

79. Sherd of a hard metallic yellow and green glazed ware. Contemporary with the first-century enclosure.
80. Sherd with greenish yellow glaze decorated with two dark coloured spots and two small ridges below the rim. From an early level.
81. Sherd with yellowish brown glaze on both sides and a series of slight ridges below the rim.
82. Sherd of a globular pot with olive-green glaze on both faces and striated ribbed decoration. From a first-century level.
83. Small sherd in yellow-brown glazed ware. From a level earlier than the circular shrine.
84. Sherd with bead rim glazed dark olive-green on both sides. First-century enclosure.

(c) *Rhenish Ware*

Most of the sherds of this fine hard black metallic ware were recovered from material contemporary with the fire which destroyed the circular shrine about A.D. 250 and they had the appearance of breakage at the time of the fire.

85. Sherds comprising the rim, neck and part of the body of a beaker in very thin metallic ware. Found in the shrine in disturbed material below the *opus signinum* floor.
86. Sherds of rim and neck of a beaker. From a layer before the destruction of the circular shrine on its east side.
87. Two sherds of a thin metallic vessel with fluted sides and rouletting. From a level contemporary with the circular shrine.

(d) *Pottery with Stamped Decoration* (figs. 107–9 and 111)

The pottery with stamped decoration from the Nettleton settlement was found in association with colour-coated ware in late fourth-century levels. The stamped decoration was found on two distinct pottery types.

(a) A number of sherds recovered from Building XVIII, and its immediate surroundings had a chocolate-coloured coating with a hard core. This has been identified as Oxfordshire ware (see Nos. 3–6).

(b) The second type was a softer sandy ware which in several instances, Nos. 31 and 33, both Oxfordshire ware, had been colour-coated and decorated with a series of dimples encircling the pot. The space between the dimples was stamped with rosettes and festoons. The potter's mark freely used as a decorative feature on No. 32 closely resembles other potters' marks found on the colour-coated ware, Nos. 24, 25 and 32, which were imitations of Samian forms 31 and 38, and are all Oxfordshire ware. This similarity of potters' stamps used by illiterate potters suggests that the pots came from the same pottery.

The colour coating on the softer wares was not very durable and it is possible that a larger proportion of this ware was originally colour-coated. One or two instances of this late pottery also had a painted motive. The paint overlay bands of rouletting which encircled the body of the pot. The stamped pottery and the colour-coated ware should be studied together with other pottery types found in Building XVIII with a large number of late fourth-century coins (see pp. 250–4 and figs. 107–111).

1 (fig. 107(375)). Part of the upper part of a dark brown decorated flagon of Oxfordshire ware, with a globular shaped body. It has several bands of rouletting around the neck and body and a wide

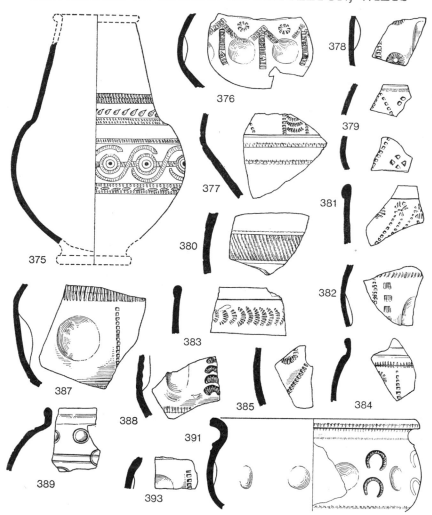

Fig. 107.   Coarse pottery (scale ⅓)

band of large S marks with circles and dots imposed on a straight line around the body of the pot. From the late floor level in Building XVI.

2 (fig. 107(376)). Part of the body of a globular pot in rusty brown Oxfordshire ware, with a dark brown slip. Arranged around the body are a series of saucer-shaped dimples and immediately above each dimple there is a stamped rosette. Between the depressions is a repeated stamped device: IXIXIII ↑ II. This potter's stamp is repeated twice above each depression and forms a zigzag decoration around the pot. The stamp is an imitation name stamp used by fourth-century potters but normally on the base of their vessels, obviously imitating Samian name stamps. It is not surprising that these illiterate potters should mix up number symbols with letters. The stamps are fairly common, but the use of a stamp as a purely decorative motive on the body is a little more unusual. From the late floor level in Building XVI.

3 (fig. 107(378)). Pot in light brown Oxfordshire ware with a dark brown slip with rosette and linear decoration. From the squatter dump in the south-west ambulatory of the shrine.

4 (fig. 107(377)). Light brown Oxfordshire ware with dark chocolate-coloured slip, and rosette and rouletted decoration. From a late level in Building XVI.

5 (fig. 107(379)). Hard dark brown Oxfordshire ware with chocolate-coloured slip, with stamped rosette and pendant decoration. From the squatter level within the shrine.

6 (fig. 107(380)). A thick dark brown Oxfordshire ware with an inch-wide band of rouletting running around the body of the pot. From the squatter level near the shrine.

7 (fig. 107(381)). Soft light red Oxfordshire ware with stamped pendant and rosette star decoration. From a late fourth-century level west of the shrine.

8 (fig. 107(382)). Fluted pot in biscuit-coloured Oxfordshire ware with stamped decoration. From a squatter level outside the north-west corner of the shrine.

9 (fig. 107(383)). Light brown Oxfordshire ware with rounded rim and a series of fan-like decorations below the rim. From a fourth-century level.

10 (fig. 107(384)). Light red Oxfordshire ware with dark brown slip stamped with star and linear decoration. From the squatter level east of the shrine.

11 (fig. 107(385)). Sandy, light brown Oxfordshire ware with stamped rosette and linear decoration. From a squatter level east of the shrine.

12 (fig. 107(389)). Soft sandy Oxfordshire ware, decorated with circular raised blobs and incised lines. From a late fourth-century level near Building XII.

13 Dark grey ware with black slip and dimple decoration with a series of horse-shoe shaped stamps. From the squatter level in the Wick valley.

14 (fig. 107(391)). Dark brown Oxfordshire ware with slaty blue core. Beneath the rolled rim is a shoulder with three bands of rouletting. The body has a series of horse-shoe shaped stamps with a ribbed pattern; between the stamps there are a series of circular depressions or dimples and below them two further bands of rouletting. From the debris in Building XVIII.

15 (fig. 107(393)). Two sherds of Oxfordshire ware, similar to No. 381 and with similar decoration, but with two circular dimples. From the squatter level east of the shrine.

16 See No. 33 (colour-coated ware, pp. 248–50).

17 Hard chocolate-coloured Oxfordshire ware. There is a pronounced cordon around the pot, above and below which there is a series of maggot-like stamps placed closely together. Below the rim there is a sharp cordon and a series of pointed impressions. From the debris in Building XVIII.

18 (fig. 107(388)). Soft grey Oxfordshire ware with a dark brown coating. The decoration is the same as that on No. 14 above. From Building XVIII.

19 (fig. 107(387)). Two sherds of light brown Oxfordshire ware with a red slip. There is an incised line running around the shoulder with a series of large circular depressions, between which there are a line of small stamp marks and below a wide band of rouletting. From the debris in Building XVIII.

20 Sherd from a large pot of similar texture to No. 17, but the depressions are elongated with a series of shell-like stamps between them. From Building XVIII.

21 Sherd of dark chocolate-coloured ware with a wide band of rouletting below the shouldered rim. From Building XVIII.

22 (fig. 111(448)). Three sherds of chocolate-coloured Oxfordshire ware. There is a wide band of rouletting below the shoulder, beneath this four rows of semi-circular raised ridges resembling scales, and finally a series of incised lines encircle the pot. From Building XVIII.

23 Similar to No. 20, but there is no rouletting and the raised ridges are pronounced. From Building XVIII.

23A (fig. 108(399)). Chocolate-coloured Oxfordshire ware with stamped decoration and rounded rim, similar to 43. From Building XVIII.

(e) *Colour-coated Ware* (figs. 107–9)

During the course of the excavation over 150 instances of this ware were recorded, consistently in late occupation levels throughout the settlement, especially in the squatter level within the former shrine and also in association with the pewter- and iron-smelting development in Buildings XVI, XVIII, XXI and XXVI. In Building XVIII, where it was most abundant, it was associated with the large number of late fourth-century coins and a series of pots with stamped rosettes, rouletting and other features. In some instances (Nos. 31 and 33) the stamped features were also colour-coated. In the squatter occupation within the shrine it was mixed with a hard brown ware which had a series of olive-green burnished streaks that extended from the rolled rim down the lower part of the globular body (cf. fig. 109(413)).

Any comment concerning the centres of production for colour-coated imitation Samian ware must be very tentative and it is only recently that these pottery industries have become the subject of a more comprehensive study, other than that by Sumner for New Forest ware. The presence of colour-coated vessels (forms 38 and 31) with stamped rosettes and rouletted patterns suggests that this pottery came from the Oxford region rather than the New Forest. Imitation vessels of form 31 were being produced from about A.D. 275 at Dorchester, Oxon., and continued to the end of the Roman occupation (see No. 24). The New Forest potters made relatively little use of rouletted decoration immediately under the rim but it was common in the Oxford region, and it also occurs at Hartshill, Warwickshire, and possibly Horningsea, near Cambridge. The metallic purple beaker which was peculiar to the New Forest occurred at Nettleton frequently in late levels with other New Forest ware, but both the Oxfordshire and New Forest potteries were equally accessible to Nettleton, and it is not surprising to find both well represented. It should be stated that there were two distinct types of colour-coating found at Nettleton: one which closely resembles the colour of the true Samian ware, found mostly on copies of form 31 and 38, and the other a bright cherry-red, occurring mostly in the sherds with dimpled, rouletted and stamped decoration from Building XVIII.

24S (fig. 108(395)). Imitation of form 31 in dark red colour-coated ware of the kind made at Dorchester (*Oxon* i (1936), 83ff.), Sandford (*Arch* lxxii (1922), 232ff.) and no doubt other kilns. This kind of ware was introduced about A.D. 275 and then continued to the end of the Roman period. The illiterate stamp is typical of the Oxfordshire centres. From a late level east of the shrine.

25S (fig. 108(396)). Imitation Samian with fragmentary potter's mark. Oxfordshire ware with good colour-coating and yellow-brown fabric. From the squatter level in the shrine.

26S Imitation Samian. Dr.31, with illegible name or cipher stamp. Soft orange colour.

27S (fig. 108(403)). Imitation Samian. Dr.31. Oxfordshire ware with a lead rivet. Fourth-century. From the squatter level in the shrine.

28S Imitation Samian. Dr.31, with illegible cipher stamp. Fourth century. From a late level east of the shrine.

29S Imitation Samian. Dr.31. Rouletted ring; fabric speckled with fine mica. Fourth century. From the late floor in Building XII.

30 Sherd in sandy reddish ware with traces of colour-coating, decorated with a relief of a stag with horns. From a late level within Building XII.

31 (fig. 108(398)). Sherd of soft red colour-coated Dorchester ware, with a stamp of circular decoration made on the circular dimples on the pot. From a late level west of the shrine.

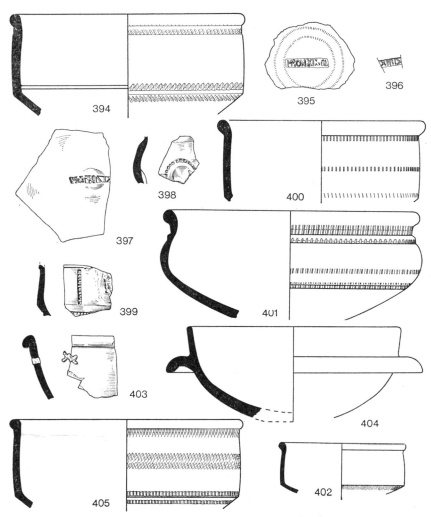

Fig. 108. Coarse pottery (scale ⅓)

32 Imitation Samian base with potter's stamp similar to the stamp on the small globular bowl (fig. 107(376)). It is evidently an attempt to imitate a Samian potter's stamp where numerals are mixed with letters; Nos. 24 and 25 are of the same type. From a late level near the podium.

33 Soft red colour-coated ware, with stamped decoration and dimples similar to No. 31. From the squatter level on the east side of the shrine.

34 (fig. 109(407)). Biscuit-coloured Oxfordshire ware with red colour-coating. Round trim with a cordoned shoulder and what appears to be a flared decoration below.

35 Colour-coated ware with potter's mark. From a late level in Building XII.

36 Base only of a colour-coated pot. From the squatter level within the shrine.

37, 38 Colour-coated ware. From a squatter level on the north side of the shrine.

39 (fig. 108(404)). Bowl with wide flange in colour-coated Oxfordshire ware imitating form Dr.38. From Building XVIII.

40 (fig. 108(394)). Imitation Samian form in Oxfordshire ware with a blue core. The colour-coating

on this pot is a rich red, especially on the inside. There is a band of rouletting below the rim and two at the bottom. From the debris over Building XVIII.

41 (fig. 108(400)). Imitation Samian form R.9 in soft red colour-coated Oxfordshire ware, similar to No. 40 but with three bands of rouletting round the body of the pot. From the debris over Building XVIII.

42 (fig. 108(405)). Colour-coated Oxfordshire ware imitating Samian form R.9. Similar to Nos. 40 and 41. The body of the pot is copiously decorated with five bands of rouletting of three different patterns. From the debris over Building XVIII.

43 (fig. 108(402)). Light red colour-coated Oxfordshire ware imitating Samian form R.9; a smaller version but the same type as Nos. 40–42, with a zone of rouletting below the body of the pot. From debris over Building XVIII.

44 (fig. 108(401)). Colour-coated Oxfordshire ware imitating Samian form Dr.44. Decorated with four bands of rouletting. From the debris over Building XVIII.

(f) *A Fourth- to Fifth-century Pottery Group from Building XVIII* (figs. 109–12)

Building XVIII was built during the first half of the fourth century A.D. but it was destroyed, apparently by fire, towards the close of that century or in the fifth century A.D. After the destruction of the building there seems to have been considerable looting on the site, in the course of which at least two coin hoards were dispersed. The coins, which range from A.D. 364 to 402, were found in debris which covered the dismantled walls of the building. Equally distributed with the coins in this debris was a quantity of potsherds. Some of this pottery has been described in the colour-coated and stamped-ware sections of this report (see pp. 245–50). The coins associated with this varied collection of pottery are of interest for dating purposes. Some of the pottery types in this collection are described below, but must be considered in conjunction with the colour-coated and stamped wares and the other varied finds from this debris. In addition to the wares already described, there were also a few sherds of the hard metallic-lustre fluted New Forest beakers. But there were also a number of sherds that included bases of a hard well-made reddish-brown ware, probably products of kilns in the Oxfordshire region (fig. 109(414)). There was also some coarse black ware with low thick walls. In one instance this was decorated with an impressed band below the rim (fig. 112(475)), reminiscent of the decoration on some Saxon pottery.

There were also a number of sherds, including rims and bases, of a coarse dark grey ware with broken shell and small fossil gritting from the oolitic limestone (fig. 110(438)). The rolled rims of this pottery were large and angular and the pots had globular bodies. Below the shoulder the body had a combed appearance evidently made when the pot was revolving on the wheel. This combing varied in its intensity on different pots (fig. 110, 422–34). In some cases, generally the larger pots, each small ridge was $\frac{1}{4}$ in. (6 mm.) in width, while in the smaller pots the combing was very fine. A number of the sherds exhibited this feature. In several instances the ware was quite thin and brittle (fig. 110(436)) and in one instance part of a graffito was found on a sherd (fig. 110(435)). Similar pottery has been found by Dr. Peter Fowler at Overton Down, Wilts., and it also occurs in a Saxon context at North Elham, Suffolk. There were also a number of sherds, including rims, of large fluted beakers in a coarse soft grey ware (fig. 112(477–8)). These are copies of the smaller New Forest fluted beakers. The same type has been found by Mr. Christopher Green in association with the late fourth- to fifth-century Christian cemetery at Poundbury, Dorset, and it has also been found

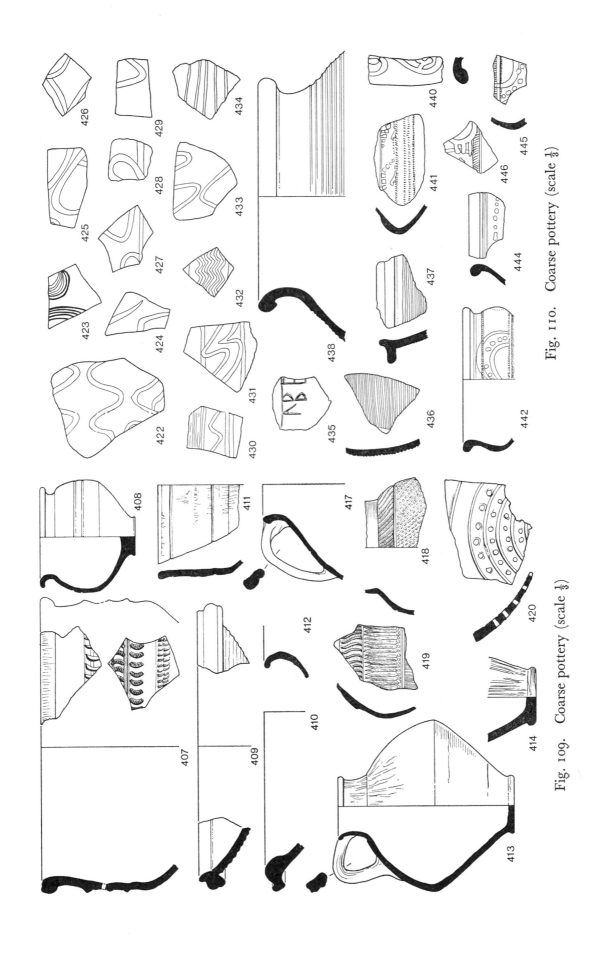

Fig. 110. Coarse pottery (scale ⅓)

Fig. 109. Coarse pottery (scale ⅓)

on a site on the North Somerset section of the M.5 motorway. This coarse soft dark grey ware was also used for the production of large straight-sided flat-bottomed pots which had flat rims (fig. 112(473)). The pots were decorated with a series of incised combed zigzags which encircled the body of the vessel. Another type was a large bowl with a cavetto rim and a wide band of rouletting around its girth.

There was also a sherd of a small red Oxfordshire ware bowl with bands of rouletted decoration at the shoulder below the rim and on the lower part of the body (fig. 110 (442)). Superimposed over the rouletting was a painted design executed in red on a dark background. The bowl was bright red on the inside, but most of the outside was a dark brown. The same form and ware is repeated on other sherds from the same group, also probably Oxfordshire ware.

A number of sherds in smooth pink ware from flanged bowls were in some instances used as mortaria (fig. 112(479–81)). Yet another type is represented by two bases in a hard brown ware with distinctive longitudinal incised lines extending upwards from the base of the vessels (fig. 109(414)). These belong to the same group as the two reconstructed pots from the squatter level within the former shrine. The upper part of these small handled flagons is covered with a series of green burnished longitudinal streaks and the ware is the same (fig. 109(408–13)).

Professor Charles Thomas, who has seen some of this pottery, writes that he thinks a great deal of pottery of the general period A.D. 375–425 has been compressed back for dating purposes before the latest coinage date on a site. But the latest coin evidence is not necessarily the date of the pottery found with the coins. He suggests that Nettleton may be just too far inland to get examples of the late imported Mediterranean wares, and he has the impression that some of the pottery is fifth-century, but probably not later than the third quarter of that century. But at Nettleton we have late copies of Samian, New Forest, and other wares, presumably produced locally, and also the coarse dark ware with small fossil and broken shell tempering, which has been found on other sites associated with Saxon pottery (see (v) to (vii) below).

Other pottery from the late infilling of Building XVIII includes:

(i) Mortaria in light cream Oxfordshire ware, with red and white quartzite (fig. 109(409–10)).

(ii) Rims in hard light red pottery (fig. 109(411–12)) which belong to the same group as pots found in the squatter debris within the shrine. The latter fall into two groups: (1) a slightly overhanging rim (fig. 112(484–6)), and (2) a flat rim similar to a butt beaker (fig. 112(487–90)). The same ware was also used for making an irregular greenish burnishing around the neck and body, while the small flagons had single handles (fig. 109(413 and 417)).

(iii) A series of small bowls of soft light red and light brown Oxfordshire ware, colour-coated, some rouletted and overpainted with white designs (fig. 110(440–6)).

(iv) Colanders in dark grey ware with holes arranged in rows between two incised lines (fig. 109 (420)).

(v) Pots with wide wavy lines (fig. 110(422–34)). The sherds indicate a number of different pots but unfortunately there are no rims or bases. The distinctive feature is the broad waved lines on the body of the pot. The sherds in most cases have traces of mica in the sandy brown fabric which is similar to amphorae, though some sherds are reddish brown. The lines in some cases are combed and vary in depth.

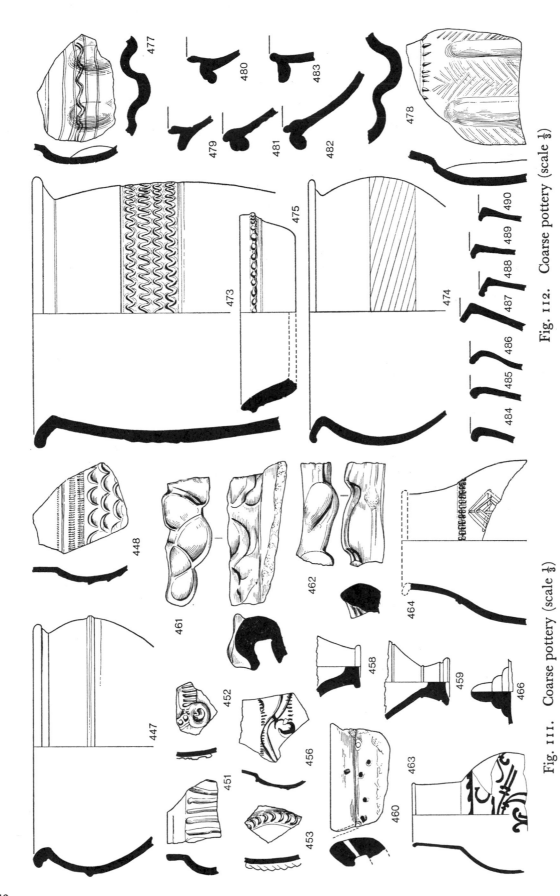

Fig. 112. Coarse pottery (scale ⅓)

Fig. 111. Coarse pottery (scale ⅓)

(vi) Small globular flagons in hard light red ware with greenish burnished stripes (fig. 109(417)) with a single handle. A similar pot is shown in fig. 109(413).

(vii) A small group of fluted and dimpled sherds in a coarse thick dark ware (fig. 112(477–8)). They are an imitation of the hard purple-lustre metallic fluted New Forest beakers but larger and more crudely made. A complete example has been found by Mr. Green in the late fourth- to fifth-century cemetery at Poundbury, Dorset. No. 477 is burnished and has a series of oval dimples around the pot. The body is decorated with a series of incised lines and a band of combed lines. The rim is missing but it has the same type of shoulder as its prototype. No. 478 has elongated fluting around its body, and the raised space between the flutes is decorated with a series of lightly burnished lines which cross each other. Below the rim there is a series of irregular stabbed marks around the shoulder of the pot. It is a clumsy imitation of its New Forest prototype.

(viii) Fragments of bowls with zones of rouletting and incised lines (fig. 109(418–19)).

(ix) Other various sherds. Fig. 110(437), coarse grey ware similar to 438. Fig. 112(473), large straight-sided grey ware jar, with a heavy sloping rim and a band of zigzag decoration around the body of the pot similar to those on the series 422–33. Fig. 112(474), large globular bowl with a heavy sloping rim and a band of incised lines around the bowl.

(g) *Other Late Roman Pottery with Thumb or Finger Prints on the Rim* (figs. 109, 111)

1 Heavy rim in grey ware with light brown interior. The wide overhanging rim has a series of thumb impressions made alternately along the top of the rim in a rather haphazard fashion. From a late level near the hostel (fig. 111(461)).

2 Dark grey ware with thumb impressions at intervals along the top ridge of the rim. From a late Roman level near the temple (fig. 111(462)).

3 Rim in thick coarse blueish-grey ware. It has eight holes about $\frac{1}{4}$ in. (6 mm.) in diameter, made on the outer face of the rim and side. Three of the holes are pierced through the sherd, but the others are only partially pierced. From a late level near the hostel (fig. 111(460)).

4 Soft cinnamon-coloured Oxfordshire ware with scale and rouletted decoration. From the destruction level of Building VII (fig. 111(448)).

5 Soft light-coloured Oxfordshire ware with scale decoration. From a late level near the hostel.

6 Large bowl in dark brittle ware with a thick rolled rim. It has a prominent cordon around the body of the bowl. From the late floor of Building XVI.

7 The globular body of this Oxfordshire ware pot has a series of longitudinal ridges and grooves. From the south bank (fig. 111(451)).

8 Sherd of dark brown Oxfordshire ware with an applied design in relief similar to that on No. 446. Unstratified (fig. 111(452)).

9 Sherd of soft sandy Oxfordshire ware, with an applied band design of a series of crescents which overlie each other around the pot. From a late layer near the shrine (fig. 111(453)).

10 Sherd of Oxfordshire ware, with a series of notches painted with white lines. From the squatter level near the shrine.

11 Soft brown Oxfordshire ware, with rouletted decoration surmounted by applied decoration in relief. From a late level near the shrine (fig. 111(456)).

12 Hard brittle New Forest ware beaker. From a late level near the shrine.

13 Base of a small hard lustrous New Forest beaker. From a late level near the shrine (fig. 111(458)).

14 As 458, but a large beaker (fig. 111(459)).

15 Small reconstructed pot in hand metallic brown ware. The globular body is encircled by two incised lines and the rim is rolled. Found in the squatter level within the former shrine (fig. 109(408)).

16 Small reconstructed flagon $5\frac{1}{2}$ in. (14 cm.) high. It has a single handle and is made of the same

material as 406. It has a series of greenish-coloured burnished streaks running down the side of the flagon. From the squatter level in the former shrine (fig. 109(413)).

17 Pot base. The pottery has the same distinctive colour and hardness as 408 and 413. It has a series of incised lines around its base. From the north-west corner of the shrine in the squatter level (fig. 109(414)).

18 Sharply curved rim in very hard dark brown ware. From sector 4 of the former shrine in the squatter level (fig. 109(412)).

19 Rim and side in a very hard metallic ware, reddish brown on both faces with a blue core. The exterior has a washed appearance with reddish streaks. From the squatter level in the shrine (fig. 109(411)).

20 The upper part of a Castor beaker ware with thin sides, decorated with white barbotine. Below the shoulder there seems to be one surviving letter C of a name between two bands of decoration. From the shrine (fig. 111(463)).

21 The upper part of a New Forest beaker in hard lustrous ware. There is a band of indentations around the neck, and below this a white painted linear decoration. In a level associated with Building XVIII (fig. 111(464)).

22 Sherd of stone-coloured pottery with a bright red slip on the inside and a dark brown slip on the outside, covered with bands of small diamond-shaped impressions. From material associated with Building XX.

23 The small knob of a dish cover in light red ware. From the hypocaust in Building XXVII (fig. 111(466)).

37. W. C. PRIESTLEY'S EXCAVATIONS 1938–54

The late Mr. W. C. Priestley conducted excavations at Nettleton on the north side of the Broadmead Brook during the years 1938–54. The work was done at weekends with voluntary labour and included the period of the second world war. Apart from occasional notices in the local Bath press, no report on this work has been published. The notes which follow, recovered from several sources, are an attempt to make good this omission. Information concerning the site is also given in a letter written by Priestley to the late Mr. Bushe-Fox, reproduced on pp. 55–7 of this report.

Following the death of Priestley in 1956 the two wooden huts used by him on the site were purchased by the writer for the Bath and Camerton Archaeological Society. The huts, securely locked, contained all the finds made by him during his excavation: the chief finds were in a show case, and were exhibited to visitors to the site, but the other finds were contained in paper bags and small tin boxes with little or no information to indicate the cutting or layer in which the find was made. Most of the pottery and some bronze finds were taken by Dr. Ilid Anthony to the Roman Baths Museum at Bath, where she was at that time curator. All the finds made by Priestley were later placed in the Museum at Devizes where they still are (see pp. 257–60).

In *WAM* lxv (1970), 195–7, a small bronze loop and plate from Priestley's excavation are described by Mrs. Vivian G. Swan. It was after reading this report that Mr. D. B. Corbyn, who had assisted Priestley for several years, supplied additional information in a letter to Mr. K. Annable, curator at the Devizes Museum, and he in turn passed this information to the writer. Mr. Corbyn has since given me much additional evidence of Priestley's excavation gathered from others who assisted with the work. The writer thanks Mr. Annable, Mr. and

Mrs. Corbyn, Mr. A. W. Rawlings, Miss M. Hicks and Mr. H. M. Hoather for their kind help with the information which has been incorporated in this report. Mr. Hoather also supplied a number of snapshot photographs of the Priestley excavation (pls. III, XII and XLVIII).

Human Skeleton Found on the North-west Corner of Building I in 1945 (pl. XLVIIIa)

The skeleton was found in a prone position, not in a grave, but presumably in the position where the person had died. The level in which the skeleton was found was above the latest Roman level on the site and contemporary with the squatter occupation. The impression of the excavator 'was that of a person lying flat on her face with her hands pressed on the upper abdomen and the elbow consequently sticking up'. The skull was damaged by a pick-axe 'as no one was expecting to find a skeleton so high up'. Half a bronze bracelet and some small jet beads on a necklace, in position, were found with the skeleton. There was also a piece of coarse woven woollen material found caught up in the humerus shoulder joint socket, presumably carried in as the body decayed, but this has been lost. The prone position of the skeleton and its position on the corner of Building I suggests that the person was seeking a hiding place in the small cave in the rock face behind Building I, but she was struck down just short of this place of refuge. The high level in which the skeleton was found suggests that it was contemporary with the human bones bearing evidence of sword cuts found in the latest level in the former shrine of Apollo on the south side of the river.

There is some doubt concerning the bracelet found with the skeleton. The late Mrs. Swanson, a friend of Mr. Priestley, showed the writer a plain bronze bracelet, which she had often worn, and she said it was found with a human skeleton near Mr. Priestley's 'temple' at Nettleton.

Report on the Skeleton by Hedley Hall, F.R.C.S. (1972)

The bones were only incompletely preserved. There was for instance no complete long bone. Both femora were missing and neither innominate bone was represented. There were a few disintegrating specimens of vertebrae from each region. From the slender nature of the bones they are almost certainly female and the age can be fairly accurately gauged at between 18 and 19 years. There was no evidence on the bones of injury or disease. This skeleton is in the possession of Mr. A. W. Rawlings of Bradford on Avon. The skull was not available at the time this report was made in 1972.

A second human skeleton was also found by Priestley 'quite near the west wall of the temple' (Building I). This appears to have been a normal extended burial. The skeleton was left *in situ* (pl. XLVIIIb).

Mr. Corbyn states that the bronze cockerel, reported by Professor J. C. M. Toynbee on p. 143, was discovered 'in the inner temple, containing the gully'. The bronze loop described by Vivian Swan was found in this small drain which was covered with re-used stone tiles and appears to have been a late fourth-century construction.

Mr. Corbyn writes that 'even in Mr. Priestley's time there were some doubts about the "temple" and its meaning. The ashlar blocks are so big' (the earlier back wall) 'that I would expect to find some still in the bank . . . at least towards the east (quarry) end of the footpath'

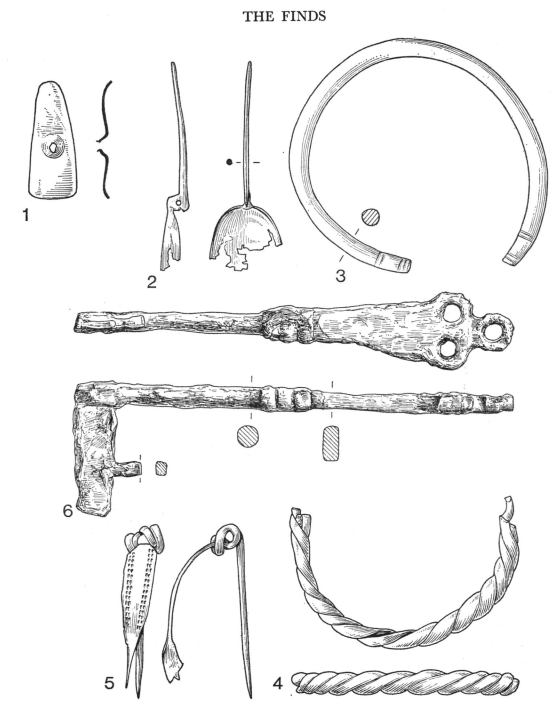

Fig. 113. Bronze and iron objects from W. C. Priestley's excavations 1938–54 (scale ¼ except 6, ½)

to the road. Mr. Corbyn did not see a site notebook in use during his association with the excavation, but a surveyor assisted with site measurements. The plan, reproduced as fig. 34, was found among papers given to the writer by the late Mrs. Swanson, and was drawn by Mr. I. G. Moore for Priestley in 1947.

There is no trace of a silver Elizabethan coin found by Mrs. Corbyn on a cobbled area near the building of medieval date (Building IV). Some medieval pottery was also found by Priestley.

(a) *Coins*

One hundred and ninety-six coins were found wrapped in paper and in small tin boxes in the excavation hut. Only 16 coins had identity of location with them. This is particularly to be regretted, since when the coins were submitted to Miss Dorothy Bushell, then curator of the Bath Roman Baths Museum, for identification, the collection was found to include two Greek coins; one third-century B.C. Republican coin; two Byzantine coins; and a seventeenth-century token from Tetbury, Gloucestershire. The coins had not been cleaned and the patination and general condition was similar to other coins in the collection. The writer has since made enquiries from Mr. Priestley's assistants and they are not aware of any other coins being brought to the site from outside sources during the course of the excavation. The writer thanks Miss Bushell for identifying the coins.

Coins numbered 1–14 came from the 'Temple Area B' from below the fallen tile layer and all fall within the period A.D. 330–40. Coin No. 15 (probably Constantine I) was labelled 'Sept. 1939 from the Rectangular wall area'. Coin No. 1 (Gallienus A.D. 259–68) came from 'the rear of the temple'. The remainder of the coins had no information concerning their location. Coins 17–41 were found wrapped in paper and are all fourth-century coins. Coins 42–53 were in a tin box; two are third-century and the remainder fourth century. Coins 54–157 were also in a tin box and are mostly fourth century, but include one Greek coin (AE coin of Sicyon in Greece, c. 251–146 B.C.), one sextans of the Roman Republic (probably late third-century B.C.), one Byzantine coin, a 20 nummia piece, probably Justinian I (struck c. A.D. 546–7), but possibly of Maurice Tiberius (c. A.D. 601–2), and one token OBADIAH ARROWSMITH (The Haberdashers Arms); IN TEDBURY BAYLEF—O A A. Coins 158–196 were also in a tin box and are mostly fourth-century, with four first- to second-century, one AE Greek coin, and one Byzantine coin, a 12 nummia piece struck at Alexandria c. A.D. 540–640.

(b) *Bronze and Iron Finds from the Priestley Excavation* (fig. 113)

The following finds were all found on the north side of the Broadmead Brook, and came from the vicinity of the 'temple' found by Priestley. Unfortunately the exact location of most of the finds was not recorded, but where it is known it is stated. The writer thanks Mr. K. Annable, Curator of the Devizes Museum, for kindly providing access to the Priestley Collection.

Bronze Objects

1. A small turn-button with a countersunk centre perforation. Found near the human burial on the west side of the 'temple' (fig. 113(1)).
2. Bronze spoon, with a round section stem, terminating in a point. The bowl is incomplete. Found with Samian pot base, form 37, 'alongside the stream' (fig. 113(2)).

3. Two bronze bracelets found with the human burial on the west side of the 'temple'. (a) Plain, round in section and with four incised lines at each end (fig. 113(3)). (b) Broken, made with three strands of twisted wire (fig. 113(4)).

4. Bronze brooch, made from one piece of bronze. The pin has four coils at the head and the bow is flattened with two lines of pin-point stamped decoration on either side. The catch-plate is broken. Found under the foundation course of the east wall of the 'temple' (fig. 113(5)).

The bronze cockerel found by Priestley (pl. XXXIa) is separately reported by Professor Toynbee on p. 143 of this report. A small bronze loop and plate have been described by Mrs. V. G. Swan in *WAM* lxv (1970), 195–7.

Iron Objects

1. Iron key 9 in. (22.9 cm.) long. The lower part is round in section and has a projection, with one surviving tooth. The upper part of the stem is flat and widens at the top with three perforations (fig. 113(6)).
2. Iron key $5\frac{1}{2}$ in. (14 cm.) long, with a looped end.
3. Iron key $5\frac{1}{2}$ in. (14 cm.) long. The lower part of the stem is round in section, but it is flat at the top. The key projection is $1\frac{1}{4}$ in. (3.1 cm.) long.
4. Iron bolt for a lock $4\frac{1}{2}$ in. (11.4 cm.) long. The end for securing the bolt is 1 in. (2.5 cm.) long and terminates in a circular loop.
5. Iron sickle with upper part of the blade missing. Haft 2 in. (5.1 cm.) long.
6. Iron bar 6 in. (15.2 cm.) long. The stem is $\frac{1}{2}$ in. (13 mm.) in diameter and square. The end flattens and has an hooked end.
7. Flat iron pin $\frac{3}{8}$ in. (10 mm.) wide terminating in a flange at right angle to the stem.
8. Iron knife 4 in. (10.16 cm.) long with a square tang 2 in. (5.1 cm.) long.
9. Iron gate hook $5\frac{3}{4}$ in. (14.6 cm.) long with a square stem.
10. Iron tool, probably a punch, $4\frac{1}{2}$ in. (11.4 cm.) long, square in section.
11. Iron bar, round in section, 6 in. (15.2 cm.) long. At the centre it is square in section and pierced by a small hole.
12. Two iron nails with unusually large and slightly convex circular heads.
13. Strap end, semi-circular, $1\frac{1}{2}$ in. (3.8 cm.) wide with straight bar for holding the leather strap.
14. Iron bolt (see p. 228 and fig. 96(7)).

(c) Pottery

The pottery from Priestley's excavation had been sorted into types, but there was no indication of the building or layer in which it had been found. The following points were noted.

1. There was a surprising amount of the first- to second-century coarse grey ware, which was found in abundance on the first-century enclosure site.
2. There were a number of colour-coated ware and late fourth-century imitation Samian ware forms including a number of the shallow globular bowls in pink ware (see fig. 110 (441–2)).
3. The pottery from the site consisted predominantly of the common black cavetto-rim jars and low-sided dishes. There was also some Samian ware (see fig. 72).

4. Medieval wares were more plentiful on the north side of the river and presumably came from the medieval Building IV.

(d) *Iron Slag*

A number of large lumps of iron slag with red fire ash adhering to them found by Priestley suggests that there was some form of metal working carried out on the north side of the river, but there was no indication of which period this could be assigned to.

NOTES

(for abbreviations, see *Abbreviations and Bibliography*, p. xvi)

1. The C.B.A. scheme for volunteers, through the medium of its *Calendar of Excavations*, proved useful, and a number of volunteers assisted.

2. During the excavation paid labour was used for the removal of alluvium and reconditioning the site. Several hundred tons of building debris were removed by volunteers. The excavation began in 1956 and was completed in 1972. The writer thanks all who assisted with the hope that this report of their labours will in some measure signify their valued contribution, without which this account could not have been written. Thanks are especially due to Mr. and Mrs. A. L. Webb, who kindly provided camping facilities and especially for the enjoyable end of season parties given at their home, Manor Farm; to Mr. Richard Dumbreck for his unfailing support and for arranging parties of diggers from his school, Boarzel, Sussex; to Mrs. D. M. Brackenbury, who acted as recorder, and to her assistant, the late Mrs. Marlyn Willcox; to Mr. Rex Willcox, Mr. Oswald Lloyd, Cdr. E. H. D. Williams, R.N., and Lt. Cdr. D. Andrews, R.N., for sustained co-operation, and also to Miss J. Cooper, Miss Sarah Haslett, Miss Sally Ledbury, Miss Hannah Williams, Miss Barbara Harvey, Miss Joyce Medcalfe, Mrs. Andrews and Roger, Tom Atthill, Col. Botting, Dennis Brown, Bob Dunning, Andrew Kneen, Michael Owen, Derek Painter, Phillip Twentymen, Ron Wilcox, John Lewis, John Macdonald, John Maddacott, Robert Scott, Dennis Nicol, and John Lyddieth; also to the boys of Clifton College; Colston School, Bristol; King Edward's School, Bath; and students from Bristol and other universities; also to the Commanding Officer, R.A.F. Station, Hullavington, for arranging assistance by a number of R.A.F. trainee pilots; to those who responded to appeals in the C.B.A. *Calendar of Excavations* and finally to the members of the Bath and Camerton Archaeological Society for their painstaking work at the Society's headquarters at Gay Street, Bath.

3. *WAM* lvii (1958), 104.

4. The bridge over the Broadmead Brook carries the road from the Shoe Inn, on the Marshfield–Chippenham road, to the Salutation Inn at Castle Combe. The bridge forms the boundary of four parishes: north-west, Castle Combe; south-east, North Wraxall; south-west, West Kington; and north-west, Nettleton. In the Anglo-Saxon charter, *c*. A.D. 940, the brook was known as the 'Alderbrook' and the river crossing at or near the site of the present bridge was called 'Ford of the Street'. This suggests that the river had no bridge crossing in Saxon times.

5. The manor of Nettleton was granted by King Edmund to Wulfric, Abbot of Glastonbury, in 944 (Watkin, 1947, 1952, 1956).

6. Confirmation of this has been obtained by the finding of medieval walls with rounded corners and pottery, etc., on the south side of the river. Other notes on the site: *WAM* xxxviii (1913–14), 113–14, 295; xlv (1930–2), 198; *JRS* xxix (1938), 220; and Haverfield, 1914, 49.

7. Two British coins have been identified as Dobunnic (p. 112), and the Nettleton site was clearly in Dobunnic territory (cf. Clifford, 1961, 129, and Stevens, 1940).

8. The field now known as 'Truckle Hill' is shown on the tithe award map for 1840 as 'Foss Bridge Field'.

9. Kempe, 1829, pl. XXXI; Collingwood and Richmond, 1969, 171–2, and fig. 57a.

10. Koethe, 1933, 47–53, Taf. I, Abb. 10.

11. Steer, 1958; Skinner.

12. *SxAC* xi (1859), 140–4; Collingwood and Richmond, 1969, 170, and fig. 56c.

13. Meates, 1979, 119–22, and fig. 29.

14. Swift, 1951, 37.

15. *Ibid.*, 36.

16. Rivoira, 1925, 5–12, fig. 3.

17. Boehringer, 1959.

18. Talbot Rice, 1954, 61.

19. Ward-Perkins, 1947.

20. Wheeler and Wheeler, 1932, 35.

21. La Croix, 1883.

22. Wheeler and Wheeler, 1932, 51–4.

23. 'The sanctuaries of the gods, so rich in their variety, played a big part in the special life . . . . The elaborate precincts found round so many of them are a clear indication of the large crowds of worshippers which they expected at any rate for the special festivals.' Brogan, 1953, 202.

24. This material was contemporary with the circular temple, and the first phase of the rectangular building.

25. Parker, 1850, pl. 110.
26. Koethe, 1933, 71–2, Abb. 20.
27. The dimensions of the voussoirs associated with the circular temple were 1 ft. 8 in. (0.51 m.) long, 6 in. (15.2 cm.) wide at the base and 8 in. (20.3 cm.) wide at the top. Those associated with the octagonal temple were 1 ft. 1 in. (0.33 m.) long, 3 in. (7.6 cm.) wide at the base and 4 in. (10.16 cm.) wide at the top, and those associated with the rectangular building were 1 ft. 2½ in. (0.37 m.) long, 5 in. (12.7 cm.) wide at the base and 7 in. (17.8 cm.) at the top.
28. Koethe, 1933, Taf. VIII, 1 and 2.
29. Rivoira, 1925, 10, fig. 9 (tomb of the Servilii, annular passage).
30. *Ibid.*, 14 (tomb of Severus Alexander at Monte del Grano).
31. Koethe, 1933, 66–7, Abb. 18.
32. *Ibid.*, 66, Abb. 17.
33. Wilkes, 1969, 350, pls. 48 and 49.
34. Wheeler and Wheeler, 1932, 62.
35. Chadwick, 1963, 24.
36. Clapham, 1922.
37. Rahtz, 1951 and 1956/7.
38. Meates, 1979, 33.
39. Blair, 1963, 141.
40. Tufa is a porous stone deposited by calcareous waters. It was used freely both in Roman and medieval buildings for vaulting, arches and other purposes. Deposits of tufa are made by streams in the limestone districts of Gloucestershire and the Mendip hills of Somerset. In Gloucestershire it is known as 'Puff Stone' and deposits may be seen exposed at Ferney Hill, Dursley, Bristol. Tufa was used extensively in the monastic buildings of Glastonbury Abbey, Somerset, where it is known as 'Combe Stone'. Cf. *TBGAS* lv (1933), 330, and *PCNFC* xxii (1924–6), 267ff.
41. Blair, 1963, 143, and Koethe, 1933, 33–43.
42. The stone tiles were made of Pennant sandstone of Upper Carboniferous age. This stone was used extensively in Roman buildings in Somerset and Gloucestershire. Its fairly fissile nature suggests it was originally quarried in the Brislington, Hanham or Winterbourne districts near Bristol.
43. *JRS* lii (1962), 191, no. 4.
44. Larousse, 1968, 113–16.
45. Blair, 1963, 138.
46. *Ibid.*, 141, and Wedlake, 1958, 245.
47. Powell, 1959, 138ff.
48. Wheeler and Wheeler, 1932, 33–43.
49. La Croix, 1883, pl. III.
50. The possible use of the later building as a Christian church was first suggested by Sir Mortimer Wheeler during a discussion concerning the purpose of the sealed chambers in the temple.
51. Wedlake, 1958, 82–93, pl. XX.
52. *AJ* xxii (1942), 33–8.
53. Wedlake, 1958, pl. XVII*b*, fig. 27, no. 1.
54. For the custom of placing offerings of food and drink on pagan and Christian graves see Dyggve, 1951; O'Connor, 1969; St. Augustine's *Confessions*, VI, ii.
55. The writer is grateful to the excavator, Mr. Christopher Green, for this information. Cf. *PDNHAS* xci (1969), 184.
56. Wedlake, 1958, 66, and 214, pl. XV.
57. Wheeler, 1943, 135.
58. *JRS* li (1961), 187 and pl. XX.
59. Rahtz, 1956/7, 31.
60. Lewis, 1966, 143–4.
61. Apart from the cemeteries described on pp. 90–3 there was one human burial found outside the shrine on its north side. The burial must have been made before the destruction of the circular temple and also before the construction of the podium wall before A.D. 230. There were also two instances of human foetus disposal in the domestic buildings and a human cremation in a cavetto-rim type vessel (see p. 93).
62. The human bones from the shrine have been carefully examined by Mr. E. W. Richardson and his report is included on pp. 179–80. The writer is most grateful to Mr. Richardson for his patient research on the human remains.
63. Scrope, 1862, 7.
64. Hawkes, 1961, 25.
65. Frere, 1967, 248–57.

66. Boon and Williams, 1966.
67. Wheeler and Wheeler, 1932.
68. Rahtz, 1951.
69. La Croix, 1883.
70. Clapham, 1922.
71. Hudd, 1913.
72. Rahtz, 1951.
73. Neville, 1849; *VCH Berks.* i (1906), p. 216.
74. Koethe, 1933, 55–7, Abb. 12.
75. *Ibid.*, 62, Abb. 14.
76. *Ibid.*, 59–62, Abb. 13.
77. Meates, 1979, 97.
78. Hayward, 1952.
79. Richmond, 1969, 118.
80. Painter, 1967–8, 15–19, pls. VI–VIII; Toynbee, 1964c.
81. Smith, 1965, 99–116.
82. Toynbee, 1953.
83. Blair, 1963, 148.
84. Wedlake, 1958, 82–93.
85. *AntJ* xxii (1942), 33–8.
86. Palmer and Ashworth, 1956/7; Elkington, 1976.
87. Haverfield, 1906, 338–9.
88. Curle, 1923.
89. Cox, 1895.
90. Gough, 1967, 25; *IO*, xxii (1867), 234.
91. 'The western coasts of Britain from the southern shores of the Bristol Channel northwards . . . were exposed to attack from at least the fourth century, and in some instances such attacks were followed by enduring settlements. Archaeological discoveries at Lydney in Gloucestershire have revealed the existence there of a prosperous community in the late fourth century which worshipped a god with close Irish affinities' (Blair, 1977, 5).
92. Toynbee, 1964, 441–2.
93. Wedlake, 1958, 96–9.
94. *CA* 25 (March 1971), 48–9 (Wroxeter).
95. Wheeler and Wheeler, 1932, 64–5.
96. Fowler, 1971, 211–12. The writer is grateful to Mr. Peter Fowler for a sight of this pottery.
97. Noticed at a Burlington House C.B.A. Conference exhibition.
98. Rivet, 1969, 214.
99. *Ibid.*, 220.
100. Scrope, 1862, 7; Hawkes, 1961, 25.
101. Porter, 1966, 9–21.
102. I owe this interpretation to Mr. R. P. Wright (*JRS* lix (1969), 235).
103. *RIB*, 181.
104. Fishwick, 1969.
105. Haverfield, 1923, 73, fig. 26; Toynbee, 1964a, 161–2, p. 45a.
106. Toynbee, 1964b, 140–1, and pl. 41, 2.
107. Unpublished.
108. Toynbee, 1964a, 157–8.
109. *Ibid.*, pl. 92.
110. *JRS* xlviii (1958), pl. XXI, 1.
111. Budge, 1907, 66, 67, 70, 161–2.
112. Lowther, 1976.
113. Toynbee, 1964, 128, pl. 35a.
114. Dorset County Museum, Dorchester (unpublished).
115. Cunliffe, 1969, 68, fig. 25, 13, and pp. 70–1.
116. Voss, 1954; Munksgaard, 1955.
117. Curle, 1923.

INDEX

PLATE I

a. Air view of Nettleton site, looking east. The position of the temple is indicated by the arrows.

b. The Nettleton site from the east, with the Fosse Way in the foreground.

Photographs: James Hancock

PLATE II

a. Sculptured figures, probably of Diana and hound, found in 1911 on site of rectangular building excavated by W. C. Priestley in 1939

c. Part of a stone statuette of a male figure, probably Mercury. Found in Building IX

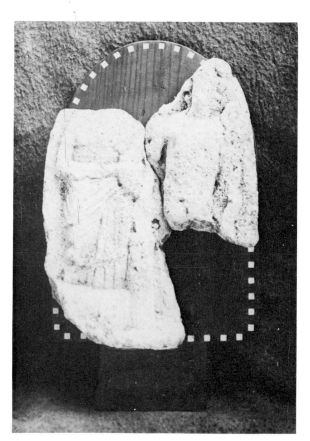

b. Stone plaque with relief representation of Mercury and Rosmerta. Found in Building I by W. C. Priestley

d. Stone statuette of unknown identity. From a late fourth-century level in Building XXVI

Photographs: James Hancock

PLATE III

a. General view looking north of Building I, excavated by W. C. Priestley in 1939

b. Rusticated north wall of Building I, as excavated by Priestley, showing the position (right) in which the sculpture of Diana and hound was found

PLATE IV

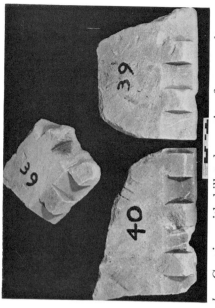

b. Cornice with billet decoration from south-east corner of Building VII

c. Stone cornice from Building VII

a. Building VII. North riverside wall, looking west, with large stone pier at north-west corner of building

PLATE V

b. Western sector of third-phase octagonal temple. The white mortared wall of the first-phase circular temple crosses the sector. The ambulatory window sill is in the foreground and the squatter hearth is on the right

a. Section of pre-Roman ditch (foreground) underlying first-century A.D. Roman enclosure ditch filling covered by the store debris of Building XXII

PLATE VI

b

a

a. Stone floor of second-phase octagonal podium beneath south-east angle of phase-**III** octagonal temple wall

b. South ambulatory of third-phase octagonal temple, looking east, showing south angle buttress and south side of south-west entrance in foreground

PLATE VII

a. Central shrine area of octagonal temple. The figure kneels on the cobbled floor of the first-phase circular temple and her hand rests on the later squatter floor. The pennant limestone floor of the fourth-phase octagonal shrine is to the right

b. Cobbled floor of first-phase circular temple with polished circular limestone block inserted in the centre

PLATE VIII

b. Foundation of second-phase podium wall, against survey pole, built on offset of rectangular Building VII

a. Paved eastern entrance to first-phase circular temple with its door-step worn on either side to denote a double door

PLATE IX

a. Building XIII. Cellar or strong-room looking west, with window splay in its west wall

b. Building XIII. Cellar or strong-room looking east

PLATE X

a. North face of rusticated second-phase octagonal podium wall of temple, looking east

b. North face of rusticated second-phase octagonal podium wall of temple, looking west. The dry-stone walling has been inserted to protect the upper floor levels of the temple

PLATE XI

a. Panoramic view of temple of Apollo in Wick Wood, looking east. The two pillars are not in position

b. Reconstruction, looking south, of temple area. The rectangular riverside Building VII is in the foreground and the hostelry is to the left

c. Third-phase octagonal shrine. Reconstruction of interior looking towards the eastern entrance

PLATE XII

c. Building I. The fourth- or fifth-century A.D. drain running from the north wall to the river

d. Section against wall of Building I showing the wall built on late fourth-century stratified material

a. The wall on the right is in alignment with the wall on the north side of the Roman river, opposite Building VII (see fig. 2). Walls marked H are later additions

b. Building I. The north rusticated wall, with later east wall of Building I adjoining

Excavations by W. C. Priestley, 1938–40

PLATE XIII

a. North radial wall of the third-phase octagonal temple resting on inner sleeper wall (left) and outer second-phase podium wall foundation (right). The white mortared wall of the first-phase circular temple lies between the two foundations. Looking west

b. First-phase circular temple wall, looking east, lying between the inner third-phase sleeper wall (right) and the outer second-phase podium wall foundation (left) against survey pole

PLATE XIV

a. Octagonal second-phase podium wall (below survey pole) with cavetto cornice replaced at its approximate floor level position in the wall

b. Cavetto angle cornice (reversed) from the north-west angle buttress of the second-phase podium wall, showing water-gutter and recess made for lead water-proofing joint

c. Rusticated second-phase podium wall as first exposed, showing north-west angle buttress cornice lying as it was found

PLATE XV

a. Inner circular face of second-phase octagonal podium wall, looking south-west, with third-phase octagonal wall and ambulatory floor level to left of survey pole

b. Third-phase octagonal wall of later temple and ambulatory floor level (right), looking north-east. The projecting radial wall foundation is shown below the floor level continuing as a sleeper wall across the ambulatory to tie in with the earlier podium wall foundation

PLATE XVI

b. Building IX. South-west corner with east doorway in fore-ground. The square platform is superimposed over the stone drain which crosses the floor and the squatter hearth is in the top right-hand corner

a. Building IX. South-east corner and east doorway (opposite survey pole). The later square platform composed of re-used architectural features, probably from the former temple, lies on the floor of the building

Plate XVII

b. Building IX. Partition wall with stone blocking removed, revealing iron door socket and stop. The stone drain passes under the well worn doorstep

a. Building IX. Blocked doorway in partition wall

20

PLATE XVIII

b

c

b. Limestone block with mouldings, probably a hood mould from an arch. Recovered from the fourth- or fifth-century stone platform in Building IX

c. Building IX. Cornice with square modillion to form a rainwater spout recovered from the late fourth-century floor. Probably originally from Building VII

a. Large limestone block, probably a hood mould from a monumental gateway recovered from the fourth- or fifth-century stone platform in Building IX

PLATE XIX

a. West sector of the third-phase octagonal temple, looking south, showing painted plaster sealing the wall junction between the radial wall and the fourth-phase partition wall. Wall of underlying first-phase circular temple and later doorway cut through the radial wall by squatters (left)

b. South sector of third-phase octagonal temple, looking south from central area of shrine. The footings of the fourth-phase partition wall are just beyond the blue pennant stone floor

PLATE XX

b. Stone capital, probably from outer portal of east entrance. It was later re-used in the late fourth-century improvised shrine

a. Doric (Tuscan) capital, after excavation, showing angle cut to incorporate it into the third-phase octagonal temple

PLATE XXI

a. Paved cast entrance of fourth-phase temple, looking east. The base of the south pier is on the right

b. Northern area of central shrine showing west part of later improvised shrine, formed partly by re-used columns

PLATE XXII

a. Entrance to improvised shrine, looking south. The wall is built with voussoirs from the derelict temple and the capital (pl. XX*b*) has been removed to show the entrance

b. Iron rods, probably from a wooden shield, and a bronze sacrificial knife as found with the bronze plaque and other objects in the fourth-century improvised shrine

PLATE XXIII

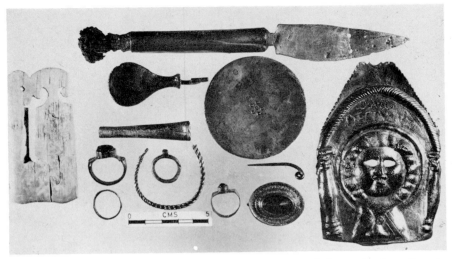

a. Bronze plaque and other bronze finds recovered from the late fourth-century floor of the improvised shrine

b. Part of an ivory object, possibly of a waist girdle. Found with the bronze plaque and other objects in the improvised shrine

PLATE XXIV

a. Two columns as found alongside the second-phase octagonal podium wall of the temple. They lie on the squatter debris where they have fallen from the higher level octagonal ambulatory after A.D. 392

b. West walk of third-phase octagonal temple ambulatory looking south-east with window (left) and south-west entrance pier (foreground)

PLATE XXV

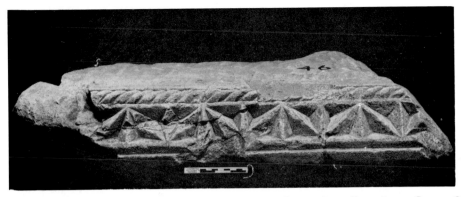

a. Limestone block with cable and chevron decoration. Found on floor of west portico in Building VII, next to the shrine

b. Limestone block with cable, circle and cross decoration. Found by Priestley on the north side of the Broadmead Brook

c. Fragment of a bench-table with milled and crescent decoration. Recovered from the late fourth-century floor in Building IX

PLATE XXVI

a. Fragment of a bow-fronted bench table with star and chevron decoration. Recovered from late fourth-century floor in Building IX

b, c. Two views of fragment of bench-table with star and lozenge decoration, and raised ridge with incised arrow decoration on upper face. Recovered from the late fourth-century floor in Building IX

PLATE XXVII

a. Eastern entrance sector of third-phase octagonal temple, showing junction of later radial wall and octagonal wall with entrance pier base

b. General view, looking north-east, across octagonal temple. In foreground is the window in the south-west sector, showing the slots for the timber window frame (the timber sill was inserted to prevent the collapse of the wall after excavation). The voussoirs on the window sill were inserted by the squatter occupants. The eight radial walls of the third-phase octagonal temple are shown converging on the central area of the shrine

PLATE XXVIII

a. View of north-east side of central shrine showing entrance to north-east sectors. The fourth-phase pennant floor overlies the earlier floors. The late squatter wall overlies the remains of the central radial wall

b. Stone arch reconstructed from voussoirs recovered within the central shrine area of the third-phase temple. Some of the voussoirs were still joined with their original mortar

PLATE XXIX

a. The fourth-phase blue pennant stone floor of the central shrine, looking south. The square oolite base of the central altar lies beneath the survey pole

b. The floor levels within the central shrine: lowest cobble floor of the first-phase circular temple, third-phase *opus signinum* floor and fourth-phase pennant stone floor of the octagonal temple

PLATE XXX

b. Cavetto cornice found in west walk of ambulatory, probably used to cap the terminals of the third-phase radial walls

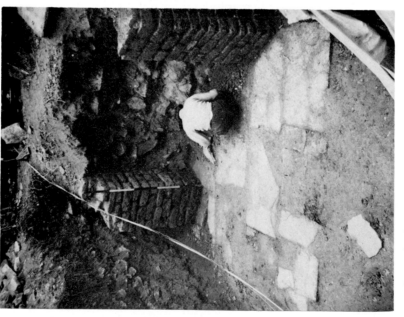

a. Central shrine area of temple with pennant flooring, looking south-west to show the filling between the radial walls before excavation

PLATE XXXI

a.   Bronze cockerel found by Priestley on the north side of
the Broadmead Brook in 1938

b.   Terracotta representation of a cockerel's
head. Found on the latest floor level in
Building X

PLATE XXXIV

Limestone votive altar, dedicated to Apollo Cunomaglos (Apollo the Hound-prince) found on squatter floor where it had served as a fireside seat. The original base was not found

Plate XXXV

a, b. Miniature stone altar, uninscribed. Found lying on the squatter floor on the east side of the temple

c. Mutilated limestone altar dedicated to Silvanus. It was found in Building XVIII incorporated in a stone furnace

PLATE XXXVIII

a, b. Two limestone blocks (two views) used as moulds to cast ribbed
strips of pewter

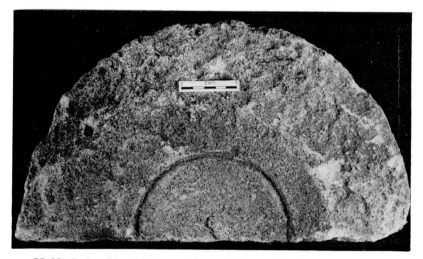

c. Half of circular stone mould used for casting large pewter dishes

Building XXI

PLATE XXXIX

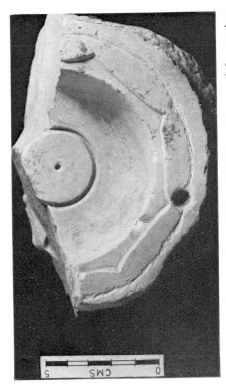

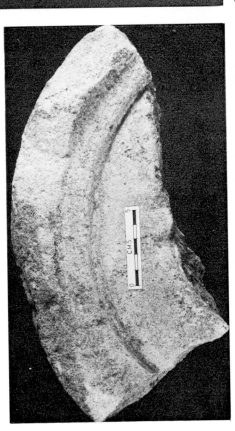

c. Part of a decorated mould in white lias stone used for casting small circular bowls or skillets

d. Side view of *c* showing stain of an iron band placed around the top of the mould to prevent its cracking

a. Half of circular stone mould used for casting pewter dishes

b. Part of stone mould used for casting large pewter dishes

Building XXI

PLATE XL

a. South-west sector of third-phase octagonal temple, looking south-west. The white mortar footings of the first-phase circular temple cross the foreground and the splayed west window with its squatter blocking is in the background

b. Squatter hearth on east side of central shrine area

c. Squatter hearth built against south radial wall in south-west sector of third-phase octagonal temple

PLATE XLI

b. Plaster with painting of a male human head, possibly a representation of the god Apollo. From painted plaster vault of central shrine

a. Painted plaster with foliage and floral decoration from central area of shrine

c. Plaster with painting of a human hand. From painted plaster vault of central shrine

Octagonal temple: third phase

PLATE XLII

a. Central area of third-phase octagonal temple looking north, showing fourth-phase blocking wall to the north sector with its painted plaster face

b. Central shrine of third-phase octagonal temple looking west, showing fourth-phase blocking wall with its painted plaster design

PLATE XLIII

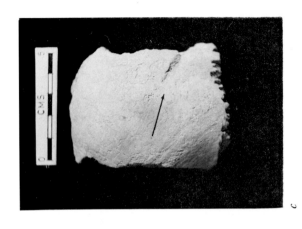

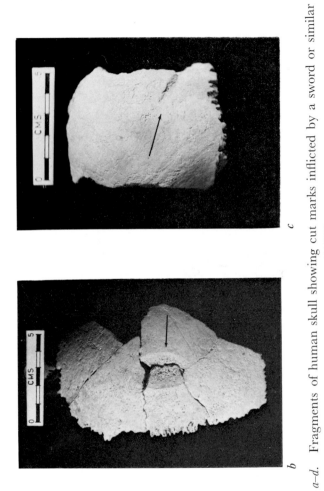

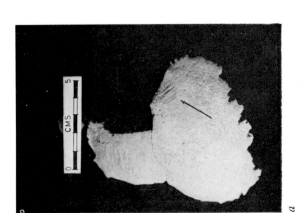

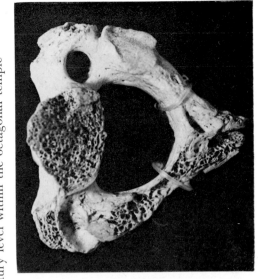

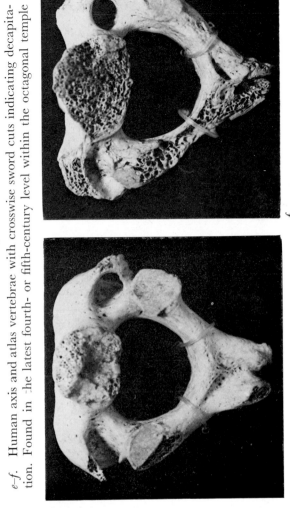

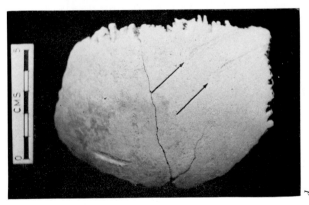

a–d. Fragments of human skull showing cut marks inflicted by a sword or similar weapon

e–f. Human axis and atlas vertebrae with crosswise sword cuts indicating decapitation. Found in the latest fourth- or fifth-century level within the octagonal temple

PLATE XLIV

a. Cemetery burial partially excavated to show side stones covering the skeleton (looking towards head)

b. Cemetery burial fully excavated (looking towards feet)

c. Building XVIII. Late fourth-century central hearth

PLATE XLV

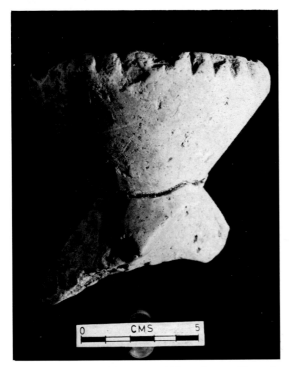

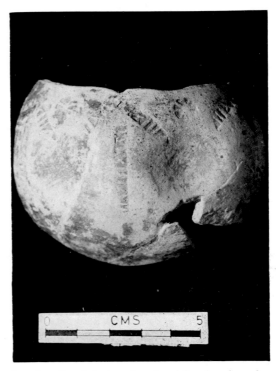

a. Terracotta object, possibly a lamp. Found in a late level near the hostelry

b. Small globular bowl with circular depressions, stamped with rosettes and a stamp in Roman numerals: IXIXIII↑II

c. Fragments of late fourth-century pottery with stamped circle and linear motif

d. Late fourth-century pottery sherds with rosette and other stamped motifs. From the squatter level

PLATE XLVI

a. Building **XXVII**. Small rectangular annexe on the north-west side of the building

b. Building **XXVII**. The apsidal west end of the building, looking north, showing the elaborate double hypocaust with blocking channel

PLATE XLVII

a.   The water-wheel housing at the east (downstream) end of the Nettleton settlement
looking east

b.   Detail of water-wheel housing, looking east. The slot for the sluice which controlled the water supply to the water-wheel may be seen on the side stone blocks
(the left-hand block has fallen from its original position)

PLATE XLVIII

a. Human skeleton, as found, lying in a prone position near the north-west corner of Building I in the squatter level

b. Human skeleton found near the west wall of Building I

Priestley excavation